atlanta-fulton
public library
foundation

PRESENTED TO

FULTON COUNTY
PUBLIC LIBRARY

2022 ONE BOOK, ONE READ

By Isabel Wilkerson

THE WARMTH OF OTHER SUNS: THE EPIC STORY OF
AMERICA'S GREAT MIGRATION

CASTE: THE ORIGINS OF OUR DISCONTENTS

Caste
The Origins of Our Discontents

CASTE

THE ORIGINS OF OUR DISCONTENTS

◇

ISABEL WILKERSON

Random House | New York

Published in the United States by Random House,
an imprint and division of Penguin Random House LLC, New York.

RANDOM HOUSE and the HOUSE colophon are registered trademarks of
Penguin Random House LLC.

LIBRARY OF CONGRESS CATALOGING-IN-PUBLICATION DATA

Names: Wilkerson, Isabel, author.
Title: Caste : the origins of our discontents / Isabel Wilkerson.
Description: New York : Random House, [2020] |
Includes bibliographical references and index.
Identifiers: LCCN 2020012794 (print) | LCCN 2020012795 (ebook) |
ISBN 9780593230251 (hardcover) | ISBN 9780593230268 (ebook)
Subjects: LCSH: Caste—United States. | Social stratification—
United States. | Ethnicity—United States. | Power (Social sciences)—
United States. | United States—Race relations.
Classification: LCC HT725.U6 W55 2020 (print) |
LCC HT725.U6 (ebook) | DDC 305.5/122—dc23
LC record available at https://lccn.loc.gov/2020012794
LC ebook record available at https://lccn.loc.gov/2020012795

Printed in the United States of America on acid-free paper

randomhousebooks.com

14 16 18 19 17 15 13

Title-page art by Bruce Davidson/Magnum Photos

*To the memory of my parents
who survived the caste system
and to the memory of Brett
who defied it*

Because even if I should speak,
no one would believe me.
And they would not believe me precisely because
they would know that what I said was true.
— JAMES BALDWIN

If the majority knew of the root of this evil,
then the road to its cure would not be long.
— ALBERT EINSTEIN

CONTENTS

The Man in the Crowd   xv

Part One: Toxins in the Permafrost
and Heat Rising All Around

Chapter One: The Afterlife of Pathogens   3

The Vitals of History   13

Chapter Two: An Old House and an Infrared Light   15

Chapter Three: An American Untouchable   21

An Invisible Program   33

Part Two: The Arbitrary Construction
of Human Divisions

Chapter Four: A Long-Running Play and the Emergence
of Caste in America   39

Chapter Five: "The Container We Have Built for You"   54

Chapter Six: The Measure of Humanity   62

Chapter Seven: Through the Fog of Delhi to the Parallels
in India and America   73

Chapter Eight: The Nazis and the Acceleration of Caste   78

Chapter Nine: *The Evil of Silence*   89

Part Three: THE EIGHT PILLARS OF CASTE

The Foundations of Caste: *The Origins of Our Discontents*   99

Pillar Number One: Divine Will and the Laws of Nature   101

Pillar Number Two: Heritability   105

Pillar Number Three: Endogamy and the Control of
Marriage and Mating   109

Pillar Number Four: Purity versus Pollution   115

Pillar Number Five: Occupational Hierarchy:
The Jatis and the Mudsill   131

Pillar Number Six: Dehumanization and Stigma   141

Pillar Number Seven: Terror as Enforcement, Cruelty
as a Means of Control   151

Pillar Number Eight: Inherent Superiority versus
Inherent Inferiority   159

Part Four: THE TENTACLES OF CASTE

Brown Eyes verus Blue Eyes   167

Chapter Ten: Central Miscasting   171

Chapter Eleven: Dominant Group Status Threat and the Precarity
of the Highest Rung   178

Chapter Twelve: A Scapegoat to Bear the Sins of the World   190

Chapter Thirteen: The Insecure Alpha and the Purpose
of an Underdog   202

Chapter Fourteen: The Intrusion of Caste in Everyday Life   208

Chapter Fifteen: The Urgent Necessity of a Bottom Rung   224

Chapter Sixteen: Last Place Anxiety: Packed in a
Flooding Basement   238

Chapter Seventeen: On the Early Front Lines of Caste   245

Chapter Eighteen: Satchel Paige and the Illogic of Caste   257

Part Five: The Consequences of Caste

Chapter Nineteen: *The Euphoria of Hate* 263

Chapter Twenty: The Inevitable Narcissism of Caste 268

Chapter Twenty-One: The German Girl with the Dark, Wavy Hair 279

Chapter Twenty-Two: The Stockholm Syndrome and the Survival of the Subordinate Caste 282

Chapter Twenty-Three: Shock Troops on the Borders of Hierarchy 292

Chapter Twenty-Four: Cortisol, Telomeres, and the Lethality of Caste 302

Part Six: Backlash

Chapter Twenty-Five: A Change in the Script 311

Chapter Twenty-Six: Turning Point and the Resurgence of Caste 322

Chapter Twenty-Seven: The Symbols of Caste 333

Chapter Twenty-Eight: Democracy on the Ballot 350

Chapter Twenty-Nine: The Price We Pay for a Caste System 353

Part Seven: Awakening

Chapter Thirty: Shedding the Sacred Thread 361

The Radicalization of the Dominant Caste 365

Chapter Thirty-One: The Heart Is the Last Frontier 370

Epilogue: A World Without Caste 377

Acknowledgments 389

Notes 397

Bibliography 443

Index 455

The Man in the Crowd

There is a famous black-and-white photograph from the era of the Third Reich. It is a picture taken in Hamburg, Germany, in 1936, of shipyard workers, a hundred or more, facing the same direction in the light of the sun. They are heiling in unison, their right arms rigid in outstretched allegiance to the Führer.

If you look closely, you can see a man in the upper right who is different from the others. His face is gentle but unyielding. Modern-day displays of the photograph will often add a helpful red circle around the man or an arrow pointing to him. He is surrounded by fellow citizens caught under the spell of the Nazis. He keeps his arms folded to his chest, as the stiff palms of the others hover just inches from him. He alone is refusing to salute. He is the one man standing against the tide.

Looking back from our vantage point, he is the only person in the entire scene who is on the right side of history.

Everyone around him is tragically, fatefully, categorically wrong. In that moment, only he could see it.

His name is believed to have been August Landmesser. At the time, he could not have known the murderous path the hysteria around him would lead to. But he had already seen enough to reject it.

He had joined the Nazi Party himself years before. By now though, he knew firsthand that the Nazis were feeding Germans lies about Jews, the outcastes of his era, that, even this early in the Reich, the Nazis had caused terror, heartache, and disruption. He knew that Jews were anything but Untermenschen, *that they were German citizens, human as anyone else. He was an Aryan in love with a Jewish woman, but the recently enacted Nuremberg Laws had made their relationship illegal. They were forbidden to marry or to have sexual relations, either of which amounted to what the Nazis called "racial infamy."*

His personal experience and close connection to the scapegoated caste allowed him to see past the lies and stereotypes so readily embraced by susceptible members—the majority, sadly—of the dominant caste. Though Aryan himself, his openness to the humanity of the people who had been deemed beneath him gave him a stake in their well-being, their fates tied to his. He could see what his countrymen chose not to see.

In a totalitarian regime such as that of the Third Reich, it was an act of bravery to stand firm against an ocean. We would all want to believe that we would have been him. We might feel certain that, were we Aryan citizens under the Third Reich, we surely would have seen through it, would have risen above it like him, been that person resisting authoritarianism and brutality in the face of mass hysteria.

We would like to believe that we would have taken the more difficult path of standing up against injustice in defense of the outcaste. But unless people are willing to transcend their fears, endure discomfort and derision, suffer the scorn of loved ones and neighbors and co-workers and friends, fall into disfavor of perhaps everyone they know, face exclusion and even banishment, it would be numerically impossible, humanly impossible, for everyone to be that man. What would it take to be him in any era? What would it take to be him now?

Part One

Toxins in the
Permafrost and
Heat Rising All Around

CHAPTER ONE

The Afterlife of Pathogens

In the haunted summer of 2016, an unaccustomed heat wave struck the Siberian tundra on the edge of what the ancients once called the End of the Land. Above the Arctic Circle and far from the tectonic plates colliding in American politics, the heat rose beneath the earth's surface and also bore down from above, the air reaching an inconceivable 95 degrees on the Russian peninsula of Yamal. Wildfires flared, and pockets of methane gurgled beneath the normally frozen soil in the polar region.

Soon, the children of the indigenous herdsmen fell sick from a mysterious illness that many people alive had never seen and did not recognize. A twelve-year-old boy developed a high fever and acute stomach pangs, and passed away. Russian authorities declared a state of emergency and began airlifting hundreds of the sickened herding people, the Nenets, to the nearest hospital in Salekhard.

Scientists then identified what had afflicted the Siberian settlements. The aberrant heat had chiseled far deeper into the Russian permafrost than was normal and had exposed a toxin that had been encased since 1941, when the world was last at war. It was the pathogen anthrax, which had killed herds of reindeer all those decades ago and lain hidden in the animal carcasses long since buried in the permafrost. A thawed and tainted carcass rose to the surface that summer, the pathogen awakened, intact and as powerful as it had ever been. The pathogen spores seeped into the grazing land and infected the reindeer and spread to the herders who raised and relied upon them. The anthrax, like the reactivation of the human pathogens of hatred and tribalism in this evolving century, had never died. It lay in wait, sleeping, until extreme circumstances brought it to the surface and back to life.

On the other side of the planet, the world's oldest and most powerful democracy was in spasms over an election that would transfix the Western world and become a psychic break in American history, one that will likely be studied and dissected for generations. That summer and into the fall and in the ensuing years to come, amid talk of Muslim bans, nasty women, border walls, and shithole nations, it was common to hear in certain circles the disbelieving cries, "This is not America," or "I don't recognize my country," or "This is not who we are." Except that this was and is our country and this was and is who we are, whether we have known or recognized it or not.

The heat rose in the Arctic and in random encounters in America. Late that summer, in New York City, an indigo harbor in a safely blue state, a white man in Brooklyn, an artist, was helping a middle-aged white woman carry her groceries to a southbound subway in the direction of Coney Island.

By then, it was impossible to avoid talk of the campaign. It had been a political season unlike any other. For the first time in history, a woman was running as a major party candidate for president of the United States. A household name, the candidate was a no-nonsense national figure overqualified by some estimates, conventional and measured if uninspiring to her detractors, with a firm grasp of any policy or crisis that she might be called upon to address. Her opponent was an impetuous billionaire, a reality television star prone to insulting most anyone unlike himself, who had never held public office and who pundits believed had no chance of winning his party's primaries much less the presidency.

Before the campaign was over, the male candidate would stalk the female candidate from behind during a debate seen all over the world. He would boast of grabbing women by their genitals, mock the disabled, encourage violence against the press and against those who disagreed with him. His followers jeered the female candidate, chanting "Lock her up!" at mass rallies over which the billionaire presided. His comments and activities were deemed so coarse that some news reports were preceded by parental advisories.

Here was a candidate "so transparently unqualified for the job," wrote *The Guardian* in 2016, "that his candidacy seemed more like a prank than a serious bid for the White House."

On the face of it, what is commonly termed race in America was not at issue. Both candidates were white, born to the country's historic dominant majority. But the woman candidate represented the more liberal party made up of a patchwork of coalitions of, roughly speaking, the humanitarian-minded and the marginalized. The male candidate represented the conservative party that in recent decades had come to be seen as protecting an old social order benefitting and appealing largely to white voters.

The candidates were polar opposites, equally loathed by the fans of their respective adversary. The extremes of that season forced Americans to take sides and declare their allegiances or find a way to dance around them. So, on an otherwise ordinary day, as the Brooklyn artist was helping the older woman with her groceries, she turned to him, unbidden, and wanted to know who he was voting for. The artist, being a progressive, said he was planning to vote for the Democrat, the more experienced candidate. The older woman with the groceries must have suspected as much and was displeased with his answer. She, like millions of other Americans in the historic majority, had brightened to the blunt-spoken appeals of the nativist billionaire.

Only weeks before, the billionaire had said that he could shoot someone on Fifth Avenue and his followers would still vote for him, devoted as they were. The woman overladen with groceries was one of them. In the bluest of sanctuaries, she had heard his call and decoded his messages. She took it upon herself to instruct the artist on the error of his thinking and why it was urgent that he vote the right way.

"Yes, I know he mouths off at times," she conceded, drawing closer to her potential convert. "But, he will restore our sovereignty."

It was then, before the debates and cascading revelations to come, that the Brooklyn man realized that, despite the odds and all historic precedent, a reality star with the least formal experience of perhaps anyone who had ever run for president could become the leader of the free world.

The campaign had become more than a political rivalry—it was an existential fight for primacy in a country whose demographics had been shifting beneath us all. People who looked like the Brooklyn artist and the woman headed toward Coney Island, those whose ancestry traced back to Europe, had been in the historic ruling majority, the dominant racial caste in an unspoken hierarchy, since before the founding of the republic. But in the years leading to this moment, it had begun to spread on talk radio and cable television that the white share of the population was shrinking. In the summer of 2008, the U.S. Census Bureau announced its projection that, by 2042, for the first time in American history, whites would no longer be the majority in a country that had known of no other configuration, no other way to be.

Then, that fall, in the midst of what seemed a cataclysmic financial crisis and as if to announce a potential slide from preeminence for the caste that had long been dominant, an African-American, a man from what was historically the lowest caste, was elected president of the United States. His ascension incited both premature declarations of a post-racial world and an entire movement whose sole purpose was to prove that he had not been born in the United States, a campaign led by the billionaire who was now in 2016 running for president himself.

A low rumble had been churning beneath the surface, neurons excited by the prospect of a cocksure champion for the dominant caste, a mouthpiece for their anxieties. Some people grew bolder because of it. A police commander in southern New Jersey talked about mowing down African-Americans and complained that the woman candidate, the Democrat, would "give in to all the minorities." That September, he beat a handcuffed black teenager who had been arrested for swimming in a pool without authorization. The commander grabbed the teenager's head and, witnesses said, rammed it "like a basketball" into a metal doorjamb. As the election drew near, the commander told his officers that the reality television star "is the last hope for white people."

Observers the world over recognized the significance of the election. Onlookers in Berlin and Johannesburg, Delhi and Moscow, Beijing and Tokyo, stayed up late into the night or the next morning to watch the returns that first Tuesday in November 2016. Inexplicably to many outside the United States, the outcome would turn not on the popular vote, but on the Electoral College, an American invention from the founding era of slavery by which each state has a say in declaring the winner based on the electoral votes assigned them and the outcome of the popular ballot in their jurisdiction.

By then, there had been only five elections in the country's history in which the Electoral College or a similar mechanism had overruled the popular vote, two such cases occurring in the twenty-first century alone. One of those two was the election of 2016, a collision of unusual circumstance.

The election would set the United States on a course toward isolationism, tribalism, the walling in and protecting of one's own, the worship of wealth and acquisition at the expense of others, even of the planet itself. After the votes had been counted and the billionaire declared the winner, to the shock of the world and of those perhaps less steeped in the country's racial and political history, a man on a golf course in Georgia could feel freer to express himself. He was a son of the Confederacy, which had gone to war against the United States for the right to enslave other humans.

The election was a victory for him and for the social order he had been born to. He said to those around him, "I remember a time when everybody knew their place. Time we got back to that."

The sentiment of returning to an old order of things, the closed hierarchy of the ancestors, soon spread across the land in a headline-grabbing wave of hate crime and mass violence. Shortly after Inauguration Day, a white man in Kansas shot and killed an Indian engineer, telling the immigrant and his Indian co-worker to "get out of my country" as he fired upon them. The next month, a clean-cut white army veteran caught a bus from Baltimore to New York on a mission to kill black people. He stalked a sixty-six-year-old black man in Times Square and stabbed him to death with a sword. The attacker would become the first white suprema-cist convicted on terrorism charges in the state of New York.

On a packed commuter train in Portland, Oregon, a white man hurling racial and anti-Muslim epithets, attacked two teenaged girls, one of whom was wearing a hijab. "Get the fuck out," he ranted. "We need Americans here." When three white men rose to the girls' defense, the attacker stabbed the men for doing so. "I'm a patriot," the attacker told the police en route to jail, "and I hope everyone I stabbed died." Tragically two of the men did not sur-vive their wounds. Then in that summer of 2017, a white suprem-acist drove into a crowd of anti-hate protesters in Charlottesville, Virginia, killing a young white woman, Heather Heyer, in a stand-off over monuments to the Confederacy that drew the eyes of the world.

The year 2017 would become the deadliest to date for mass shootings in modern American history. In Las Vegas, there oc-curred the country's largest such massacre, followed by one mass shooting after another in public schools, parking lots, city streets, and superstores across the nation. In the fall of 2018, eleven wor-shippers were slain at a Jewish synagogue in Pittsburgh in the worst anti-Semitic attack on U.S. soil. Outside Louisville, Ken-tucky, a man attempted a similar assault on a black church, yank-ing the locked doors to try to break in and shoot parishioners at their Bible study. Unable to pry the doors open, the man went to a nearby supermarket and killed the first black people he saw—a black woman in the parking lot headed in for groceries and a black man buying poster board with his grandson. An armed by-stander happened to see the shooter in the parking lot, which got the shooter's attention. "Don't shoot me," the shooter told the on-looker, "and I won't shoot you," according to news reports. "Whites don't kill whites."

In the ensuing months, as the new president pulled out of trea-ties and entreated dictators, many observers despaired of the end of democracy and feared for the republic. On his own, the new leader withdrew the world's oldest democracy from the 2016 Paris Agreement, in which the nations of the world had come together to battle climate change, leaving many to anguish over an already losing race to protect the planet.

Soon, a group of leading psychiatrists, whose profession per-mits them to speak of their diagnoses only in the event of a per-son's danger to oneself or to others, took the extraordinary step of forewarning the American public that the newly installed leader of the free world was a malignant narcissist, a danger to the pub-lic. By the second year of the administration, brown children were behind bars at the southern border, separated from their parents as they sought asylum. The decades-old protections of air and water and endangered species were summarily rolled back. Multiple campaign advisors faced prison terms in widening investigations into corruption, and a sitting president was being described as an agent of a foreign power.

The opposition party had lost all three branches of government and fretted over what to do. It managed to win back the House of Representatives in 2018, but this left the party with only one-sixth of the government—meaning one-half of the legislative branch—and thus hesitant at first to begin impeachment proceedings that were its purview. Many feared a backlash, feared riling up the bil-lionaire's base, in part because, though it represented a minority of the electorate, his base was made up overwhelmingly of people in the dominant caste. The single-mindedness of the president's followers and the anguish of the opposition seemed to compromise the system of checks and balances thought to be built into the foundation and meant that, for a time, the United States was not, in the words of a Democratic Party chair in South Carolina, a "fully functional democracy."

At the start of the third year, the president was impeached by opponents in the lower chamber and acquitted by loyalists in the Senate, their votes falling along party lines that reflected the fractures in the country as a whole. It was only the third such impeachment trial in American history. By now, more than three hundred days had passed without a White House press briefing, a Washington ritual of accountability. It had fallen away so quietly that few seemed to notice this additional breach of normalcy.

Then the worst pandemic in more than a century brought humanity to a standstill. The president dismissed it as a Chinese virus that would disappear like a miracle, called the growing uproar a hoax, disparaged those who disagreed or sought to forewarn him. Within weeks, the United States would be afflicted with the largest outbreak in the world, governors pleading for test kits and ventilators, nurses seen wrapping themselves in trash bags to shield against contagion as they aided the sick. The country was losing the capacity to be shocked; the unfathomable became just another part of one's day.

What had happened to America? What could account for tens of millions of voters choosing to veer from all custom and to put the country and thus the world in the hands of an untested celebrity, one who had never served in either war or public office, unlike every man before him, and one whose rhetoric seemed a homing device for extremists? Were the coal miners and auto workers restless in a stagnating economy? Were the people in the heartland lashing back at the coastal elites? Was it that a portion of the electorate was just ready for a change? Was it really true that the woman in the race, the first to make it this close to the nation's highest office, had run an "unholy mess" of a campaign, as two veteran political journalists put it? Was it that urban (meaning black) voters did not turn out, and the evangelical (meaning white) voters did? How could so many people, ordinary working folks, who needed healthcare and education for their children, protection of the water they drink and the wages they depended upon, "vote against their own interests," as many progressives were heard to say in the fog of that turning point in political history? These were all popular theories in the aftermath, and there may have been some element of truth in a few of them.

The earth had shifted overnight, or so it appeared. We have long defined earthquakes as arising from the collision of tectonic plates that force one wedge of earth beneath the other, believed that the internal shoving match under the surface is all too easily recognizable. In classic earthquakes, we can feel the ground shudder and crack beneath us, we can see the devastation of the landscape or the tsunamis that follow.

What scientists have only recently discovered is that the more familiar earthquakes, those that are easily measured while in progress and instantaneous in their destruction, are often preceded by longer, slow-moving, catastrophic disruptions rumbling twenty miles or more beneath us, too deep to be felt and too quiet to be measured for most of human history. They are as potent as those we can see and feel, but they have long gone undetected because they work in silence, unrecognized until a major quake announces itself on the surface. Only recently have geophysicists had technology sensitive enough to detect the unseen stirrings deeper in the earth's core. They are called silent earthquakes. And only recently have circumstances forced us, in this current era of human rupture, to search for the unseen stirrings of the human heart, to discover the origins of our discontents.

By the time of the American election that fateful year, back on the northernmost edge of the world, the Siberians were trying to recover from the heat that had stricken them months before. Dozens of the indigenous herding people had been relocated, some quarantined and their tents disinfected. The authorities embarked on mass vaccinations of the surviving reindeer and their herders. They had gone for years without vaccinations because it had been decades since the last outbreak, and they felt the problem was in the past. "An apparent mistake," a Russian biologist told a Russian news site. The military had to weigh how best to dispose of the two thousand dead reindeer to keep the spores from spreading again. It was not safe merely to bury the carcasses to rid themselves of the pathogen. They would have to incinerate them in combustion fields at up to five hundred degrees Celsius, then douse the cinders and surrounding land with bleach to kill the spores to protect the people going forward.

Above all, and more vexing for humanity at large, was the sobering message of 2016 and the waning second decade of a still-new millennium: that rising heat in the earth's oceans and in the human heart could revive long-buried threats, that some pathogens could never be killed, only contained, perhaps at best managed with ever-improving vaccines against their expected mutations.

What humanity learned, one would hope, was that an ancient and hardy virus required perhaps more than anything, knowledge of its ever-present danger, caution to protect against exposure, and alertness to the power of its longevity, its ability to mutate, survive and hibernate until reawakened. It seemed these contagions could not be destroyed, not yet anyway, only managed and anticipated, as with any virus, and that foresight and vigilance, the wisdom of never taking them for granted, never underestimating their persistence, was perhaps the most effective antidote, for now.

The Vitals of History

When we go to the doctor, he or she will not begin to treat us without taking our history—and not just our history but that of our parents and grandparents before us. The doctor will not see us until we have filled out many pages on a clipboard that is handed to us upon arrival. The doctor will not hazard a diagnosis until he or she knows the history going back generations.

As we fill out the pages of our medical past and our current complaints, what our bodies have been exposed to and what they have survived, it does us no good to pretend that certain ailments have not beset us, to deny the full truths of what brought us to this moment. Few problems have ever been solved by ignoring them.

Looking beneath the history of one's country is like learning that alcoholism or depression runs in one's family or that suicide has occurred more often than might be usual or, with the advances in medical genetics, discovering that one has inherited the markers of a BRCA mutation for breast cancer. You don't ball up in a corner with guilt or shame at these discoveries. You don't, if you are wise, forbid any mention of them. In fact, you do the opposite. You educate yourself. You talk to people who have been through it and to specialists who have researched it. You learn the consequences and obstacles, the options and treatment. You may pray over it and meditate over it. Then you take precautions to protect yourself and succeeding generations and work to ensure that these things, whatever they are, don't happen again.

CHAPTER TWO

An Old House and an Infrared Light

The inspector trained his infrared lens onto a misshapen bow in the ceiling, an invisible beam of light searching the layers of lath to test what the eye could not see. This house had been built generations ago, and I had noticed the slightest welt in a corner of plaster in a spare bedroom and had chalked it up to idiosyncrasy. Over time, the welt in the ceiling became a wave that widened and bulged despite the new roof. It had been building beyond perception for years. An old house is its own kind of devotional, a dowager aunt with a story to be coaxed out of her, a mystery, a series of interlocking puzzles awaiting solution. Why is this soffit tucked into the southeast corner of an eave? What is behind this discolored patch of brick? With an old house, the work is never done, and you don't expect it to be.

America is an old house. We can never declare the work over. Wind, flood, drought, and human upheavals batter a structure that is already fighting whatever flaws were left unattended in the original foundation. When you live in an old house, you may not want to go into the basement after a storm to see what the rains have wrought. Choose not to look, however, at your own peril. The owner of an old house knows that whatever you are ignoring will never go away. Whatever is lurking will fester whether you choose to look or not. Ignorance is no protection from the consequences of inaction. Whatever you are wishing away will gnaw at you until you gather the courage to face what you would rather not see.

We in the developed world are like homeowners who inherited a house on a piece of land that is beautiful on the outside, but whose soil is unstable loam and rock, heaving and contracting over generations, cracks patched but the deeper ruptures waved away for decades, centuries even. Many people may rightly say, *"I had nothing to do with how this all started. I have nothing to do with the sins of the past. My ancestors never attacked indigenous people, never owned slaves."* And, yes. Not one of us was here when this house was built. Our immediate ancestors may have had nothing to do with it, but here we are, the current occupants of a property with stress cracks and bowed walls and fissures built into the foundation. We are the heirs to whatever is right or wrong with it. We did not erect the uneven pillars or joists, but they are ours to deal with now.

And any further deterioration is, in fact, on our hands.

Unaddressed, the ruptures and diagonal cracks will not fix themselves. The toxins will not go away but, rather, will spread, leach, and mutate, as they already have. When people live in an old house, they come to adjust to the idiosyncrasies and outright dangers skulking in an old structure. They put buckets under a wet ceiling, prop up groaning floors, learn to step over that rotting wood tread in the staircase. The awkward becomes acceptable, and the unacceptable becomes merely inconvenient. Live with it long enough, and the unthinkable becomes normal. Exposed over the generations, we learn to believe that the incomprehensible is the way that life is supposed to be.

––––

The inspector was facing the mystery of the misshapen ceiling, and so he first held a sensor to the surface to detect if it was damp. The reading inconclusive, he then pulled out the infrared camera to take a kind of X-ray of whatever was going on, the idea being that you cannot fix a problem until and unless you can see it. He could now see past the plaster, beyond what had been wallpapered or painted over, as we now are called upon to do in the house we all live in, to examine a structure built long ago.

Like other old houses, America has an unseen skeleton, a caste system that is as central to its operation as are the studs and joists that we cannot see in the physical buildings we call home. Caste is the infrastructure of our divisions. It is the architecture of human hierarchy, the subconscious code of instructions for maintaining, in our case, a four-hundred-year-old social order. Looking at caste is like holding the country's X-ray up to the light.

A caste system is an artificial construction, a fixed and embedded ranking of human value that sets the presumed supremacy of one group against the presumed inferiority of other groups on the basis of ancestry and often immutable traits, traits that would be neutral in the abstract but are ascribed life-and-death meaning in a hierarchy favoring the dominant caste whose forebears designed it. A caste system uses rigid, often arbitrary boundaries to keep the ranked groupings apart, distinct from one another and in their assigned places.

Throughout human history, three caste systems have stood out. The tragically accelerated, chilling, and officially vanquished caste system of Nazi Germany. The lingering, millennia-long caste system of India. And the shape-shifting, unspoken, race-based caste pyramid in the United States. Each version relied on stigmatizing those deemed inferior to justify the dehumanization necessary to keep the lowest-ranked people at the bottom and to rationalize the protocols of enforcement. A caste system endures because it is often justified as divine will, originating from sacred text or the presumed laws of nature, reinforced throughout the culture and passed down through the generations.

As we go about our daily lives, caste is the wordless usher in a darkened theater, flashlight cast down in the aisles, guiding us to our assigned seats for a performance. The hierarchy of caste is not about feelings or morality. It is about power—which groups have it and which do not. It is about resources—which caste is seen as worthy of them and which are not, who gets to acquire and control them and who does not. It is about respect, authority, and assumptions of competence—who is accorded these and who is not.

As a means of assigning value to entire swaths of humankind, caste guides each of us often beyond the reaches of our awareness. It embeds into our bones an unconscious ranking of human characteristics and sets forth the rules, expectations, and stereotypes that have been used to justify brutalities against entire groups within our species. In the American caste system, the signal of rank is what we call race, the division of humans on the basis of their appearance. In America, race is the primary tool and the visible decoy, the front man, for caste.

Race does the heavy lifting for a caste system that demands a means of human division. If we have been trained to see humans in the language of race, then caste is the underlying grammar that we encode as children, as when learning our mother tongue. Caste, like grammar, becomes an invisible guide not only to how we speak, but to how we process information, the autonomic calculations that figure into a sentence without our having to think about it. Many of us have never taken a class in grammar, yet we know in our bones that a transitive verb takes an object, that a subject needs a predicate; we know without thinking the difference between third person singular and third person plural. We may mention "race," referring to people as black or white or Latino or Asian or indigenous, when what lies beneath each label is centuries of history and assigning of assumptions and values to physical features in a structure of human hierarchy.

What people look like, or, rather, the race they have been assigned or are perceived to belong to, is the visible cue to their caste. It is the historic flash card to the public of how they are to be treated, where they are expected to live, what kinds of positions they are expected to hold, whether they belong in this section of town or that seat in a boardroom, whether they should be expected to speak with authority on this or that subject, whether they will be administered pain relief in a hospital, whether their neighborhood is likely to adjoin a toxic waste site or to have contaminated water flowing from their taps, whether they are more or less likely to survive childbirth in the most advanced nation in the world, whether they may be shot by authorities with impunity.

We know that the letters of the alphabet are neutral and meaningless until they are combined to make a word which itself has no significance until it is inserted into a sentence and interpreted by those who speak it. In the same way that *black* and *white* were applied to people who were literally neither, but rather gradations of brown and beige and ivory, the caste system sets people at poles from one another and attaches meaning to the extremes, and to the gradations in between, and then reinforces those meanings, replicates them in the roles each caste was and is assigned and permitted or required to perform.

Caste and race are neither synonymous nor mutually exclusive. They can and do coexist in the same culture and serve to reinforce each other. Race, in the United States, is the visible agent of the unseen force of caste. Caste is the bones, race the skin. Race is what we can see, the physical traits that have been given arbitrary meaning and become shorthand for who a person is. Caste is the powerful infrastructure that holds each group in its place.

Caste is fixed and rigid. Race is fluid and superficial, subject to periodic redefinition to meet the needs of the dominant caste in what is now the United States. While the requirements to qualify as white have changed over the centuries, the fact of a dominant caste has remained constant from its inception—whoever fit the definition of white, at whatever point in history, was granted the legal rights and privileges of the dominant caste. Perhaps more critically and tragically, at the other end of the ladder, the subordinated caste, too, has been fixed from the beginning as the psychological floor beneath which all other castes cannot fall.

Thus we are all born into a silent war-game, centuries old, enlisted in teams not of our own choosing. The side to which we are assigned in the American system of categorizing people is proclaimed by the team uniform that each caste wears, signaling our presumed worth and potential. That any of us manages to create abiding connections across these manufactured divisions is a testament to the beauty of the human spirit.

The use of inherited physical characteristics to differentiate inner abilities and group value may be the cleverest way that a culture has ever devised to manage and maintain a caste system.

"As a social and human division," wrote the political scientist Andrew Hacker of the use of physical traits to form human categories, "it surpasses all others—even gender—in intensity and subordination."

CHAPTER THREE

An American Untouchable

In the winter of 1959, after leading the Montgomery bus boycott that arose from the arrest of Rosa Parks and before the trials and triumphs to come, Martin Luther King, Jr., and his wife, Coretta, landed in India, in the city then known as Bombay, to visit the land of Mohandas Gandhi, the father of nonviolent protest. They were covered in garlands upon arrival, and King told reporters, "To other countries, I may go as a tourist, but to India I come as a pilgrim."

He had long dreamed of going to India, and they stayed an entire month, at the invitation of Prime Minister Jawaharlal Nehru. King wanted to see for himself the place whose fight for freedom from British rule had inspired his fight for justice in America. He wanted to see the so-called Untouchables, the lowest caste in the ancient Indian caste system, whom he had read of and had sympathy for, but who had still been left behind after India gained its independence the decade before.

He discovered that people in India had been following the trials of his own oppressed people in America, knew of the bus boycott he had led. Wherever he went, the people on the streets of Bombay and Delhi crowded around him for an autograph.

One afternoon, King and his wife journeyed to the southern tip of the country, to the city of Trivandrum in the state of Kerala, and visited with high school students whose families had been Untouchables. The principal made the introduction.

"Young people," he said, "I would like to present to you a fellow untouchable from the United States of America."

King was floored. He had not expected that term to be applied to him. He was, in fact, put off by it at first. He had flown in from another continent, had dined with the prime minister. He did not see the connection, did not see what the Indian caste system had to do directly with him, did not immediately see why the lowest-caste people in India would view him, an American Negro and a distinguished visitor, as low-caste like themselves, see him as one of them. "For a moment," he wrote, "I was a bit shocked and peeved that I would be referred to as an untouchable."

Then he began to think about the reality of the lives of the people he was fighting for—20 million people, consigned to the lowest rank in America for centuries, "still smothering in an airtight cage of poverty," quarantined in isolated ghettoes, exiled in their own country.

And he said to himself, "Yes, I am an untouchable, and every Negro in the United States of America is an untouchable."

In that moment, he realized that the Land of the Free had imposed a caste system not unlike the caste system of India and that he had lived under that system all of his life. It was what lay beneath the forces he was fighting in America.

———

What Martin Luther King, Jr., recognized about his country that day had begun long before the ancestors of our ancestors had taken their first breaths. More than a century and a half before the American Revolution, a human hierarchy had evolved on the contested soil of what would become the United States, a concept of birthright, the temptation of entitled expansion that would set in motion the world's first democracy and, with it, a ranking of human value and usage.

It would twist the minds of men as greed and self-reverence eclipsed human conscience to take land and human bodies that the conquering men convinced themselves they had a right to. If they were to convert this wilderness and civilize it to their liking, they decided they would need to conquer, enslave, or remove the people already on it and transport those they deemed lesser beings to tame and work the land to extract the wealth that lay in the rich soil and shorelines.

To justify their plans, they took preexisting notions of their own centrality, reinforced by their self-interested interpretation of the Bible, and created a hierarchy of who could do what, who could own what, who was on top and who was on the bottom and who was in between. There emerged a ladder of humanity, global in nature, as the upper-rung people would descend from Europe with rungs inside that designation, the English Protestants at the very top as their guns and resources would ultimately prevail in the bloody fight over North America. Everyone else would rank in descending order on the basis of their proximity to those deemed most superior. The ranking would continue downward until one arrived at the very bottom—African captives transported to build the New World and to serve the victors for all their days, one generation after the next, for twelve generations.

There developed a caste system, based upon what people looked like, an internalized ranking, unspoken, unnamed, unacknowledged by everyday citizens even as they go about their lives adhering to it and acting upon it subconsciously to this day. Just as the studs and joists and beams that form the infrastructure of a building are not visible to those who live in it, so it is with caste. Its very invisibility is what gives it power and longevity. And though it may move in and out of consciousness, though it may flare and reassert itself in times of upheaval and recede in times of relative calm, it is an ever-present through line in the country's operation.

Caste is not a term often applied to the United States. It is considered the language of India or feudal Europe. But some anthropologists and scholars of race in America have made use of the term for decades. Before the modern era, one of the earliest Americans to take up the idea of caste was the antebellum abolitionist and U.S. senator Charles Sumner as he fought against segregation in the North. "The separation of children in the Public Schools of Boston, on account of color or race," he wrote, "is in the nature of Caste, and on this account is a violation of Equality." He quoted a fellow humanitarian: "Caste makes distinctions where God has made none."

We cannot fully understand the current upheavals or most any turning point in American history, without accounting for the human pyramid encrypted into us all. The caste system, and the attempts to defend, uphold, or abolish the hierarchy, underlay the American Civil War and the civil rights movement a century later and pervade the politics of twenty-first-century America. Just as DNA is the code of instructions for cell development, caste is the operating system for economic, political, and social interaction in the United States from the time of its gestation.

In 1944, the Swedish social economist Gunnar Myrdal and a team of the most talented researchers in the country produced a 2,800-page, two-volume work that is still considered perhaps the most comprehensive study of race in America, *An American Dilemma*. Myrdal's investigation into race led him to the realization that the most accurate term to describe the workings of American society was not *race*, but *caste*, that perhaps it was the only term that addresses what seemed a stubbornly fixed ranking of human value. He came to the conclusion that America had created a caste system and that the effort "to maintain the color line has, to the ordinary white man, the 'function' of upholding that caste system itself, of keeping the 'Negro in his place.'"

The anthropologist Ashley Montagu was among the first to argue that race is a human invention, a social construct, not a biological one, and that in seeking to understand the divisions and disparities in the United States, we have typically fallen into the quicksand and mythology of race. "When we speak of the race problem in America," he wrote in 1942, "what we really mean is the caste system and the problems which that caste system creates in America."

———

There was little confusion among some of the leading white supremacists of the previous century as to the connections between India's caste system and that of the American South, where the purest legal caste system existed in the United States. "A record of the desperate efforts of the conquering upper classes in India to preserve the purity of their blood persists until this very day in their carefully regulated system of castes," wrote Madison Grant, a popular eugenicist, in his 1916 bestseller, *The Passing of the Great Race.* "In our Southern States, Jim Crow cars and social discriminations have exactly the same purpose."

A caste system has a way of filtering down to every inhabitant, its codes absorbed like mineral springs, setting the expectations of where one fits on the ladder. "The mill worker with nobody else to 'look down on,' regards himself as eminently superior to the Negro," observed the Yale scholar Liston Pope in 1942. "The colored man represents his last outpost against social oblivion."

It was in 1913 that a prominent southern educator, Thomas Pearce Bailey, took it upon himself to assemble what he called the racial creed of the South. It amounted to the central tenets of the caste system. One of the tenets was "Let the lowest white man count for more than the highest negro."

That same year, a man born to the bottom of India's caste system, born an Untouchable in the central provinces, arrived in New York City from Bombay. That fall, Bhimrao Ambedkar came to the United States to study economics as a graduate student at Columbia, focused on the differences between race, caste, and class. Living just blocks from Harlem, he would see firsthand the condition of his counterparts in America. He completed his thesis just as the film *Birth of a Nation,* the incendiary homage to the Confederate

South, premiered in New York City in 1915. He would study further in London and return to India to become the foremost leader of the Untouchables and a preeminent intellectual who would help draft a new Indian constitution. He would work to dispense with the demeaning term *Untouchable*. He rejected the term *Harijans* applied to them by Gandhi, patronizingly so to their minds. He spoke of his people as *Dalits*, meaning "broken people," which, due to the caste system, they were.

It is hard to know what effect his exposure to the social order in America had on him personally. But over the years, he paid close attention, as did many Dalits, to the subordinate caste in America. Indians had long been aware of the plight of enslaved Africans and of their descendants in the pre–Civil War United States. Back in the 1870s, after the end of slavery and during the brief window of black advancement known as Reconstruction, an Indian social reformer named Jotiba Phule found inspiration in the abolitionists. He expressed hope "that my countrymen may take their noble example as their guide."

Many decades later, in the summer of 1946, acting on news that black Americans were petitioning the United Nations for protection as minorities, Ambedkar reached out to the best known African-American intellectual of the day, W.E.B. Du Bois. He told Du Bois that he had been a "student of the Negro problem" from across the oceans and recognized their common fates.

"There is so much similarity between the position of the Untouchables in India and of the position of the Negroes in America," Ambedkar wrote to Du Bois, "that the study of the latter is not only natural but necessary."

Du Bois wrote back to Ambedkar to say that he was, indeed, familiar with him, and that he had "every sympathy with the Untouchables of India." It had been Du Bois who seemed to have spoken for the marginalized in both countries as he identified the double-consciousness of their existence. And it was Du Bois who, decades before, had invoked an Indian concept in channeling the bitter cry of his people in America: "Why did God make me an outcast and a stranger in mine own house?"

―――

I embarked upon this book with a similar desire to reach out across the oceans to better understand how all of this began in the United States: the assigning of meaning to unchangeable physical characteristics, the pyramid passed down through the centuries that defines and directs politics and policies and personal interactions. What are the origins and workings of the hierarchy that intrudes upon the daily life and life chances of every American? That had intruded upon my own life with disturbing regularity and consequences?

I began investigating the American caste system after nearly two decades of examining the history of the Jim Crow South, the legal caste system that grew out of enslavement and lasted into the early 1970s, within the life spans of many current-day Americans. I discovered, while working on *The Warmth of Other Suns*, that I was not writing about geography and relocation, but about the American caste system, an artificial hierarchy in which most everything that you could and could not do was based upon what you looked like and that manifested itself north and south. I had been writing about a stigmatized people, six million of them, who were seeking freedom from the caste system in the South, only to discover that the hierarchy followed them wherever they went, much in the way that the shadow of caste, I would soon discover, follows Indians in their own global diaspora.

For this book, I wanted to understand the origins and evolution of classifying and elevating one group of people over another and the consequences of doing so to the presumed beneficiaries and to those targeted as beneath them. Moving about the world as a living, breathing caste experiment myself, I wanted to understand the hierarchies that I and many millions of others have had to navigate to pursue our work and dreams.

To do so meant, for one, looking into the world's most recognized caste system, India's, and examining the parallels, overlaps, and contrasts between the one that prevailed in my own country and the original. I also sought to comprehend the molecular, concentrated evil that had produced the caste system imposed in Nazi Germany and found startling, unsettling connections between the United States and Germany in the decades leading to the Third Reich. Searching the histories of all three hierarchies and poring over a wealth of studies on caste across many disciplines, I began to compile the parallels in a more systematic way and identified the essential shared characteristics of these hierarchies, what I call the eight pillars of caste, traits disturbingly present in all of them.

Scholars have devoted tremendous energy to studying the Jim Crow caste system, under whose shadow the United States still labors, while others have intensely studied the millennia-old caste system of India. Scholars have tended to regard them in isolation, specializing in one or the other. Few have held them side by side, and those who have done so have often been met with resistance. Undeterred by what, for me, became a mission, I sought to dig up the taproots of hierarchy and the distortions and injustice it yields. Beyond the United States, my research took me to London, Berlin, Delhi, and Edinburgh, following the historic threads of inherited human rank. To further document this phenomenon, I chose to describe scenes of caste throughout this work—some drawn reluctantly from my own encounters with caste and others told to me by the people who experienced them or who had intimate knowledge of them.

While this book seeks to consider the effects on everyone caught in the hierarchy, it devotes significant attention to the poles of the American caste system, those at the top, European Americans, who have been its primary beneficiaries, and those at the bottom, African-Americans, against whom the caste system has directed its full powers of dehumanization.

―――

The American caste system began in the years after the arrival of the first Africans to Virginia colony in the summer of 1619, as the colony sought to refine the distinctions of who could be enslaved for life and who could not. Over time, colonial laws granted English and Irish indentured servants greater privileges than the Africans who worked alongside them, and the Europeans were fused into a new identity, that of being categorized as white, the polar opposite of black. The historian Kenneth M. Stampp called this assigning of race a "caste system, which divided those whose appearance enabled them to claim pure Caucasian ancestry from those whose appearance indicated that some or all of their forebears were Negroes." Members of the Caucasian caste, as he called it, "believed in 'white supremacy,' and maintained a high degree of caste solidarity to secure it."

Thus, throughout this book you will see many references to the American South, the birthplace of this caste system. The South is where the majority of the subordinate caste was consigned to live for most of the country's history and for that reason is where the caste system was formalized and most brutally enforced. It was there that the tenets of intercaste relations first took hold before spreading to the rest of the country, leading the writer Alexis de Tocqueville to observe in 1831: "The prejudice of race appears to be stronger in the states that have abolished slavery than in those where it still exists; and nowhere is it so intolerant as in those states where servitude has never been known."

To recalibrate how we see ourselves, I use language that may be more commonly associated with people in other cultures, to suggest a new way of understanding our hierarchy: *Dominant caste, ruling majority, favored caste,* or *upper caste,* instead of, or in addition to, *white. Middle castes* instead of, or in addition to, *Asian* or *Latino. Subordinate caste, lowest caste, bottom caste, disfavored caste, historically stigmatized* instead of *African-American. Original, conquered,* or *indigenous peoples* instead of, or in addition to, *Native American. Marginalized people* in addition to, or instead of, women of any race, or minorities of any kind.

Some of this may sound like a foreign language. In some ways it is and is meant to be. Because, to truly understand America, we must open our eyes to the hidden work of a caste system that has gone unnamed but prevails among us to our collective detriment, to see that we have more in common with each other and with cultures that we might otherwise dismiss, and to summon the courage to consider that therein may lie the answers.

In embarking upon this work, I devoured books about caste in India and in the United States. Anything with the word *caste* in it lit up my neurons. I discovered kindred spirits from the past— sociologists, anthropologists, ethnographers, writers—whose work carried me through time and across generations. Many had labored against the tide, and I felt that I was carrying on a tradition and was not walking alone.

In the midst of the research, word of my inquiries spread to some Indian scholars of caste, based here in America. They invited me to speak at an inaugural conference on caste and race at the University of Massachusetts in Amherst, the town where W.E.B. Du Bois's papers are kept.

There, I told the audience that I had written a six-hundred-page book about the Jim Crow era in the American South, the time of naked white supremacy, but that the word *racism* did not appear anywhere in the narrative. I told them that, after spending fifteen years studying the topic and hearing the testimony of the survivors of the era, I realized that the term was insufficient. *Caste* was the more accurate term, and I set out to them the reasons why. They were both stunned and heartened. The plates of Indian food kindly set before me at the reception thereafter sat cold due to the press of questions and the sharing that went into the night.

At a closing ceremony that I had not been made aware of ahead of time, the hosts presented to me a bronze-colored bust of the patron saint of the low-born of India, Bhimrao Ambedkar, the Dalit leader who had written to Du Bois all those decades before.

It felt like an initiation into a caste to which I had somehow always belonged. Over and over, they shared scenarios of what they had endured, and I responded in personal recognition, as if even to anticipate some particular turn or outcome. To their astonishment, I began to be able to tell who was high-born and who was low-born among the Indian people among us, not from what they looked like, as one might in the United States, but on the basis of the universal human response to hierarchy—in the case of an upper-caste person, an inescapable certitude in bearing, demeanor, behavior, a visible expectation of centrality.

After one session, I went up to a woman presenter whose caste I had ascertained from observing her interactions. I noticed that she had reflexively stood over the Dalit speaker and had taken it upon herself to explain what the Dalit woman had just said or meant, to take a position of authority as if by second nature, perhaps without realizing it.

We chatted a bit, and then I said to her, "I believe you must be upper caste, are you not?" She looked crestfallen. "How did you know?" she said, "I try so hard." We talked for what seemed an hour more, and I could see the effort it took to manage the unconscious signals of encoded superiority, the presence of mind necessary to counteract the programming of caste. I could see how hard it was even for someone committed to healing the caste divide, who was, as it turned out, married to a man from the subordinate caste and who was deeply invested in egalitarian ideals.

On the way home, I was snapped back to my own world when airport security flagged my suitcase for inspection. The TSA worker happened to be an African-American who looked to be in his early twenties. He strapped on latex gloves to begin his work. He dug through my suitcase and excavated a small box, unwrapped the folds of paper and held in his palm the bust of Ambedkar that I had been given.

"This is what came up in the X-ray," he said. It was heavy like a paperweight. He turned it upside down and inspected it from all sides, his gaze lingering at the bottom of it. He seemed concerned that something might be inside.

"I'll have to swipe it," he warned me. He came back after some time and declared it okay, and I could continue with it on my journey. He looked at the bespectacled face with the receding hairline and steadfast expression, and seemed to wonder why I would be carrying what looked like a totem from another culture.

"So who is this?" he asked. The name Ambedkar alone would not have registered; I had learned of him myself only the year before, and there was no time to explain the parallel caste system. So I blurted out what seemed to make the most sense.

"Oh," I said, "this is the Martin Luther King of India."

"Pretty cool," he said, satisfied now, and seeming a little proud. He then wrapped Ambedkar back up as if he were King himself and set him back gently into the suitcase.

An Invisible Program

In the imagination of two late-twentieth-century filmmakers, an unseen force of artificial intelligence has overtaken the human species, has managed to control humans in an alternate reality in which everything one sees, feels, hears, tastes, smells, touches is in actuality a program. There are programs within programs, and humans become not just programmed but are in danger of and, in fact, well on their way to becoming nothing more than programs. What is reality and what is a program morph into one. The interlocking program passes for life itself.

The great quest in the film series The Matrix *involves those humans who awaken to this realization as they search for a way to escape their entrapment. Those who accept their programming get to lead deadened, surface lives enslaved to a semblance of reality. They are captives, safe on the surface, as long as they are unaware of their captivity. Perhaps it is the unthinking acquiescence, the blindness to one's imprisonment, that is the most effective way for human beings to*

remain captive. People who do not know that they are captive will not resist their bondage.

But those who awaken to their captivity threaten the hum
of the matrix. Any attempt to escape their imprisonment risks
detection, signals a breach in the order, exposes the artifice
of unreality that has been imposed upon human beings.
The Matrix, the unseen master program fed by the survival
instinct of an automated collective, does not react well to
threats to its existence.

In a crucial moment, a man who has only recently awakened to the program in which he and his species are en-
snared consults a wise woman, the Oracle, who, it appears,
could guide him. He is uncertain and wary, as he takes a
seat next to her on a park bench that may or may not be real.
She speaks in code and metaphor. A flock of birds alights on
the pavement beyond them.

"See those birds," the Oracle says to him. "At some point a
program was written to govern them."

She looks up and scans the horizon. "A program was written to watch over the trees and the wind, the sunrise and
sunset. There are programs running all over the place."

Some of these programs go without notice, so perfectly attuned they are to their task, so deeply embedded in the drone
of existence. "The ones doing their job," she tells him, "doing
what they were meant to do are invisible. You'd never even
know they were here."

So, too, with the caste system as it goes about its work in

silence, the string of a puppet master unseen by those whose subconscious it directs, its instructions an intravenous drip to the mind, caste in the guise of normalcy, injustice looking just, atrocities looking unavoidable to keep the machinery humming, the matrix of caste as a facsimile for life itself and whose purpose is maintaining the primacy of those hoarding and holding tight to power.

Part Two

—

The Arbitrary
Construction of
Human Divisions

CHAPTER FOUR

A Long-Running Play and the Emergence of Caste in America

D ay after day, the curtain rises on a stage of epic proportions, one that has been running for centuries. The actors wear the costumes of their predecessors and inhabit the roles assigned to them. The people in these roles are not the characters they play, but they have played the roles long enough to incorporate the roles into their very being, to merge the assignment with their inner selves and how they are seen in the world.

The costumes were handed out at birth and can never be removed. The costumes cue everyone in the cast to the roles each character is to play and to each character's place on the stage.

Over the run of the show, the cast has grown accustomed to who plays which part. For generations, everyone has known who is center stage in the lead. Everyone knows who the hero is, who the supporting characters are, who is the sidekick good for laughs, and who is in shadow, the undifferentiated chorus with no lines to speak, no voice to sing, but necessary for the production to work.

The roles become sufficiently embedded into the identity of the players that the leading man or woman would not be expected so much as to know the names or take notice of the people in the back, and there would be no need for them to do so. Stay in the roles long enough, and everyone begins to believe that the roles are preordained, that each cast member is best suited by talent and temperament for their assigned role, and maybe for only that role, that they belong there and were meant to be cast as they are currently seen.

The cast members become associated with their characters, typecast, locked into either inflated or disfavored assumptions. They become their characters. As an actor, you are to move the way you are directed to move, speak the way your character is expected to speak. You are not yourself. You are not to be yourself. Stick to the script and to the part you are cast to play, and you will be rewarded. Veer from the script, and you will face the consequences. Veer from the script, and other cast members will step in to remind you where you went off-script. Do it often enough or at a critical moment and you may be fired, demoted, cast out, your character conveniently killed off in the plot.

The social pyramid known as a caste system is not identical to the cast in a play, though the similarity in the two words hints at a tantalizing intersection. When we are cast into roles, we are not ourselves. We are not supposed to be ourselves. We are performing based on our place in the production, not necessarily on who we are inside. We are all players on a stage that was built long before our ancestors arrived in this land. We are the latest cast in a long-running drama that premiered on this soil in the early seventeenth century.

It was in late August 1619, a year before the Pilgrims landed at Plymouth Rock, that a Dutch man-of-war set anchor at the mouth of the James River, at Point Comfort, in the wilderness of what is now known as Virginia. We know this only because of a haphazard line in a letter written by the early settler John Rolfe. This is the oldest surviving reference to Africans in the English colonies in America, people who looked different from the colonists and who would ultimately be assigned by law to the bottom of an emerging caste system. Rolfe mentions them as merchandise and not necessarily the merchandise the English settlers had been expecting. The ship "brought not anything but 20 and odd Negroes," Rolfe wrote, "which the Governor and Cape Marchant bought for victualles."

These Africans had been captured from a slave ship bound for the Spanish colonies but were sold farther north to the British. Historians do not agree on what their status was, if they were bound in the short term for indentured servitude or relegated immediately to the status of lifetime enslavement, the condition that would befall most every human who looked like them arriving on these shores or born here for the next quarter millennium.

The few surviving records from the time of their arrival show they "held at the outset a singularly debased status in the eyes of white Virginians," wrote the historian Alden T. Vaughan. If not yet consigned formally to permanent enslavement, "black Virginians were at least well on their way to such a condition."

In the decades to follow, colonial laws herded European workers and African workers into separate and unequal queues and set in motion the caste system that would become the cornerstone of the social, political, and economic system in America. This caste system would trigger the deadliest war on U.S. soil, lead to the ritual killings of thousands of subordinate-caste people in lynchings, and become the source of inequalities that becloud and destabilize the country to this day.

With the first rough attempts at a colonial census, conducted in Virginia in 1630, a hierarchy began to form. Few Africans were seen as significant enough to be listed in the census by name, as would be the case for the generations to follow, in contrast to the majority of European inhabitants, indentured or not. The Africans were not cited by age or arrival date as were the Europeans, information vital to setting the terms and time frame of indenture for Europeans, or for Africans, had they been in the same category, been seen as equal, or seen as needing to be accurately accounted for.

Thus, before there was a United States of America, there was the caste system, born in colonial Virginia. At first, religion, not race as we now know it, defined the status of people in the colonies. Christianity, as a proxy for Europeans, generally exempted European workers from lifetime enslavement. This initial distinction is what condemned, first, indigenous people, and, then, Africans, most of whom were not Christian upon arrival, to the lowest rung of an emerging hierarchy before the concept of race had congealed to justify their eventual and total debasement.

The creation of a caste system was a process of testing the bounds of human categories and not the result of a single edict. It was a decades-long sharpening of lines whenever the colonists had a decision to make. When Africans began converting to Christianity, they posed a challenge to a religion-based hierarchy. Their efforts to claim full participation in the colonies was in direct opposition to the European hunger for the cheapest, most pliant labor to extract the most wealth from the New World.

The strengths of African workers became their undoing. British colonists in the West Indies, for example, saw Africans as "a civilized and relatively docile population," who were "accustomed to discipline," and who cooperated well on a given task. Africans demonstrated an immunity to European diseases, making them more viable to the colonists than were the indigenous people the Europeans had originally tried to enslave.

More pressingly, the colonies of the Chesapeake were faltering and needed manpower to cultivate tobacco. The colonies farther south were suited for sugarcane, rice, and cotton—crops with which the English had little experience, but that Africans had either cultivated in their native lands or were quick to master. "The colonists soon realized that without Africans and the skills that they brought, their enterprises would fail," wrote the anthropologists Audrey and Brian Smedley.

In the eyes of the European colonists and to the Africans' tragic disadvantage, they happened to bear an inadvertent birthmark over their entire bodies that should have been nothing more than a neutral variation in human appearance, but which made them stand out from the English and Irish indentured servants. The Europeans could and did escape from their masters and blend into the general white population that was hardening into a single caste. "The Gaelic insurrections caused the English to seek to replace this source of servile labor entirely with another source, African slaves," the Smedleys wrote.

The colonists had been unable to enslave the native population on its own turf and believed themselves to have solved the labor problem with the Africans they imported. With little further use for the original inhabitants, the colonists began to exile them from their ancestral lands and from the emerging caste system.

This left Africans firmly at the bottom, and, by the late 1600s, Africans were not merely slaves; they were hostages subjected to unspeakable tortures that their captors documented without remorse. And there was no one on the planet willing to pay a ransom for their rescue.

Americans are loath to talk about enslavement in part because what little we know about it goes against our perception of our country as a just and enlightened nation, a beacon of democracy for the world. Slavery is commonly dismissed as a "sad, dark chapter" in the country's history. It is as if the greater the distance we can create between slavery and ourselves, the better to stave off the guilt or shame it induces.

But in the same way that individuals cannot move forward, become whole and healthy, unless they examine the domestic violence they witnessed as children or the alcoholism that runs in their family, the country cannot become whole until it confronts what was not a chapter in its history, but the basis of its economic and social order. For a quarter millennium, slavery *was* the country.

Slavery was a part of everyday life, a spectacle that public officials and European visitors to the slaving provinces could not help but comment on with curiosity and revulsion.

In a speech in the House of Representatives, a nineteenth-century congressman from Ohio lamented that on "the beautiful avenue in front of the Capitol, members of Congress, during this session, have been compelled to turn aside from their path, to permit a coffle of slaves, *males and females chained to each other by their necks* to pass on their way to this *national slave market.*"

The secretary of the U.S. Navy expressed horror at the sight of barefoot men and women locked together with the weight of an ox-chain in the beating sun, forced to walk the distance to damnation in a state farther south, and riding behind them, "a white man on horse back, carrying pistols in his belt, and who, as we passed him, had the impudence to look us in the face without blushing."

The Navy official, James K. Paulding, said: "When they [the slaveholders] permit such flagrant and indecent outrages upon humanity as that I have described; when they sanction a villain, in thus marching half naked women and men, loaded with chains, without being charged with a crime but that of being *black*, from one section of the United States to another, hundreds of miles in the face of day, they disgrace themselves, and the country to which they belong."

———

Slavery in this land was not merely an unfortunate thing that happened to black people. It was an American innovation, an American institution created by and for the benefit of the elites of the dominant caste and enforced by poorer members of the dominant caste who tied their lot to the caste system rather than to their consciences. It made lords of everyone in the dominant caste, as law and custom stated that "submission is required of the Slave, not to the will of the Master only, but to the will of all other White Persons." It was not merely a torn thread in "an otherwise perfect cloth," wrote the sociologist Stephen Steinberg. "It would be closer to say that slavery provided the fabric out of which the cloth was made."

American slavery, which lasted from 1619 to 1865, was not the slavery of ancient Greece or the illicit sex slavery of today. The abhorrent slavery of today is unreservedly illegal, and any current-day victim who escapes, escapes to a world that recognizes her freedom and will work to punish her enslaver. American slavery, by contrast, was legal and sanctioned by the state and a web of enforcers. Any victim who managed to escape, escaped to a world that not only did not recognize her freedom but would return her to her captors for further unspeakable horrors as retribution. In American slavery, the victims, not the enslavers, were punished, subject to whatever atrocities the enslaver could devise as a lesson to others.

What the colonists created was "an extreme form of slavery that had existed nowhere in the world," wrote the legal historian Ariela J. Gross. "For the first time in history, one category of humanity was ruled out of the 'human race' and into a separate subgroup that was to remain enslaved for generations in perpetuity."

The institution of slavery was, for a quarter millennium, the conversion of human beings into currency, into machines who existed solely for the profit of their owners, to be worked as long as the owners desired, who had no rights over their bodies or loved ones, who could be mortgaged, bred, won in a bet, given as wedding presents, bequeathed to heirs, sold away from spouses or children to cover an owner's debt or to spite a rival or to settle an estate. They were regularly whipped, raped, and branded, subjected to any whim or distemper of the people who owned them. Some were castrated or endured other tortures too grisly for these pages, tortures that the Geneva Conventions would have banned as war crimes had the conventions applied to people of African descent on this soil.

Before there was a United States of America, there was enslavement. Theirs was a living death passed down for twelve generations.

"The slave is doomed to toil, that others may reap the fruits" is how a letter writer identifying himself as Judge Ruffin testified to what he saw in the Deep South.

"The slave is entirely subject to the will of his master," wrote William Goodell, a minister who chronicled the institution of slavery in the 1830s. "What he chooses to inflict upon him, he must suffer. He must never lift a hand in self-defense. He must utter no word of remonstrance. He has no protection and no redress," fewer than the animals of the field. They were seen as "not capable of being injured,"Goodell wrote. "They may be punished at the discretion of their lord, or even put to death by his authority."

As a window into their exploitation, consider that in 1740, South Carolina, like other slaveholding states, finally decided to limit the workday of enslaved African-Americans to fifteen hours from March to September and to fourteen hours from September to March, double the normal workday for humans who actually get paid for their labor. In that same era, prisoners found guilty of actual crimes were kept to a maximum of ten hours per workday. Let no one say that African-Americans as a group have not worked for our country.

For the ceaseless exertions of their waking hours, many subsisted on a peck of corn a week, which they had to mill by hand at night after their labors in the field. Some owners denied them even that as punishment and allowed meat for protein only once a year. "They were scarcely permitted to pick up crumbs that fell from their masters' tables," George Whitefield wrote. Stealing food was "a crime, punished by flogging."

"Your slaves, I believe, work as hard, if not harder, than the horses whereon you ride," Whitefield wrote in an open letter to the colonies of the Chesapeake in 1739. "These, after their work is done, are fed and taken proper care of."

Enslavers bore down on their hostages to extract the most profit, whipping those who fell short of impossible targets, and whipping all the harder those who exceeded them to wring more from their exhausted bodies.

"Whipping was a gateway form of violence that led to bizarrely creative levels of sadism," wrote the historian Edward Baptist. Enslavers used "every modern method of torture," he observed, from mutilation to waterboarding.

Slavery made the enslavers among the richest people in the world, granting them "the ability to turn a person into cash at the shortest possible notice." But from the time of enslavement, southerners minimized the horrors they inflicted and to which they had grown accustomed. "No one was willing," Baptist wrote, "to admit that they lived in an economy whose bottom gear was torture."

———

The vast majority of African-Americans who lived in this land in the first 246 years of what is now the United States lived under the terror of people who had absolute power over their bodies and their very breath, subject to people who faced no sanction for any atrocity they could conjure.

"This fact is of great significance for the understanding of racial conflict," wrote the sociologist Guy B. Johnson, "for it means that white people during the long period of slavery became accustomed to the idea of 'regulating' Negro insolence and insubordination by force with the consent and approval of the law."

Slavery so perverted the balance of power that it made the degradation of the subordinate caste seem normal and righteous. "In the gentlest houses drifted now and then the sound of dragging chains and shackles, the bay of the hounds, the report of pistols on the trail of the runaway," wrote the southern writer Wilbur J. Cash. "And as the advertisements of the time incontestably prove, mutilation and the mark of the branding iron."

The most respected and beneficent of society people oversaw forced labor camps that were politely called plantations, concentrated with hundreds of unprotected prisoners whose crime was that they were born with dark skin. Good and loving mothers and fathers, pillars of their communities, personally inflicted gruesome tortures upon their fellow human beings.

"For the horrors of the American Negro's life," wrote James Baldwin, "there has been almost no language."

This was what the United States was for longer than it was not. It is a measure of how long enslavement lasted in the United States that the year 2022 marks the first year that the United States will have been an independent nation for as long as slavery lasted on its soil. No current-day adult will be alive in the year in which

African-Americans as a group will have been free for as long as they had been enslaved. That will not come until the year 2111.

———

It would take a civil war, the deaths of three-quarters of a million soldiers and civilians, the assassination of a president, Abraham Lincoln, and the passage of the Thirteenth Amendment to bring the institution of enslavement in the United States of America to an end. For a brief window of time, the twelve years known as Reconstruction, the North sought to rebuild the South and help the 4 million people who had been newly liberated. But the federal government withdrew for political expediency in 1877, and left those in the subordinate caste in the hands of the very people who had enslaved them.

Now, nursing resentments from defeat in the war, people in the dominant caste took out their hostilities on the subordinate caste with fresh tortures and violence to restore their sovereignty in a reconstituted caste system.

The dominant caste devised a labyrinth of laws to hold the newly freed people on the bottom rung ever more tightly, while a popular new pseudoscience called eugenics worked to justify the renewed debasement. People on the bottom rung could be beaten or killed with impunity for any breach of the caste system, like not stepping off the sidewalk fast enough or trying to vote.

The colonists made decisions that created the caste system long before the arrival of the ancestors of the majority of people who now identify as Americans. The dominant caste controlled all resources, controlled whether, when, and if a black person would eat, sleep, reproduce, or live. The colonists created a caste of people who would by definition be seen as dumb because it was illegal to teach them to read or write, as lazy to justify the bullwhip, as immoral to justify rape and forced breeding, as criminal because the colonists made the natural response to kidnap, floggings, and torture—the human impulse to defend oneself or break free—a crime if one were black.

Thus, each new immigrant—the ancestors of most current-day Americans—walked into a preexisting hierarchy, bipolar in construction, arising from slavery and pitting the extremes in human pigmentation at opposite ends. Each new immigrant had to figure out how and where to position themselves in the hierarchy of their adopted new land. Oppressed people from around the world, particularly from Europe, passed through Ellis Island, shed their old selves, and often their old names to gain admittance to the powerful dominant majority.

Somewhere in the journey, Europeans became something they had never been or needed to be before. They went from being Czech or Hungarian or Polish to white, a political designation that only has meaning when set against something not white. They would join a new creation, an umbrella category for anyone who entered the New World from Europe. Germans gained acceptance as part of the dominant caste in the 1840s, according to immigration and legal scholar Ian Haney López, the Irish in the 1850s to 1880s, and the eastern and southern Europeans in the early twentieth century. It was in becoming American that they became white.

"In Ireland or Italy," López wrote, "whatever social or racial identities these people might have possessed, being White wasn't one of them."

Serbs and Albanians, Swedes and Russians, Turks and Bulgarians who might have been at war with one another back in their mother countries were fused together, on the basis not of a shared ethnic culture or language or faith or national origin but solely on the basis of what they looked like in order to strengthen the dominant caste in the hierarchy.

"No one was white before he/she came to America," James Baldwin once said.

Their geographic origin was their passport to the dominant caste. "The European immigrants' experience was decisively shaped by their entering an arena where Europeanness—that is to say, whiteness—was among the most important possessions one could lay claim to," wrote the Yale historian Matthew Frye Jacobson. "It was their whiteness, not any kind of New World magnanimity that opened the Golden Door."

To gain acceptance, each fresh infusion of immigrants had to enter into a silent, unspoken pact of separating and distancing themselves from the established lowest caste. Becoming white meant defining themselves as furthest from its opposite—black. They could establish their new status by observing how the lowest caste was regarded and imitating or one-upping the disdain and contempt, learning the epithets, joining in on violence against them to prove themselves worthy of admittance to the dominant caste.

They might have arrived as neutral innocents but would have been forced to choose sides if they were to survive in their adopted land. Here they had to learn how to be white. Thus Irish immigrants, who would not have had anything against any one group upon arrival and were escaping famine and persecution of their own under the British, were pitted against black residents when they were drafted to fight a war over slavery from which they did not benefit and that they did not cause.

Unable to attack the white elites who were sending them to war and who had prohibited black men from enlisting, Irish immigrants turned their frustration and rage against the scapegoats who they by now knew were beneath them in the American hierarchy. They hung black men from lamp poles and burned to the ground anything associated with black people—homes, businesses, churches, a black orphanage—in the Draft Riots of 1863, considered the largest race riot in American history. A century later and in living memory, some four thousand Italian and Polish immigrants went on a rampage when a black veteran tried to move his family into the all-white suburb of Cicero, Illinois, in 1951. Hostility toward the lowest caste became part of the initiation rite into citizenship in America.

Thus, people who had descended from Africans became the unifying foil in solidifying the caste system, the bar against which all others could measure themselves approvingly. "It was not just that various white immigrant groups' economic successes came at the expense of nonwhites," Jacobson wrote, "but that they owe their now stabilized and broadly recognized whiteness itself in part to those nonwhite groups."

————

The institution of slavery created a crippling distortion of human relationships where people on one side were made to perform the role of subservience and to sublimate whatever innate talents or intelligence they might have had. They had to suppress their grief over the loss of children or spouses whose bodies had not died but in a way had died because they had been torn from them never to be seen again and at the hands of the very people they were forced to depend upon for their very breath—the reward for all this being that they might not be whipped that day or their remaining son or daughter might not be taken from them this time.

On the other side, the dominant caste lived under the illusion of an innate superiority over all other groups of humans, told themselves that the people they forced to work for up to eighteen hours, without the pay that anyone had a right to expect, were not, in fact, people, but beasts of the field, childlike creatures, not men, not women, that the performance of servility that had been flogged out of them arose from genuine respect and admiration for their innate glory.

These disfigured relationships were handed down through the generations. The people whose ancestors had put them atop the hierarchy grew accustomed to the unearned deference from the subjugated group and came to expect it. They told themselves that the people beneath them did not feel pain or heartache, were debased machines that only looked human and upon whom one could inflict any atrocity. The people who told themselves these things were telling lies to themselves. Their lives were to some degree a lie and in dehumanizing these people whom they regarded as beasts of the field, they dehumanized themselves.

Americans of today have inherited these distorted rules of engagement whether or not their families had enslaved people or had even been in the United States. Slavery built the man-made chasm between blacks and whites that forces the middle castes of Asians, Latinos, indigenous people, and new immigrants of African descent to navigate within what began as a bipolar hierarchy.

Newcomers learn to vie for the good favor of the dominant caste and to distance themselves from the bottom-dwellers, as if everyone were in the grip of an invisible playwright. They learn to conform to the dictates of the ruling caste if they are to prosper in their new land, a shortcut being to contrast themselves with the degraded lowest caste, to use them as the historic foil against which to rise in a harsh, every-man-for-himself economy.

By the late 1930s, as war and authoritarianism were brewing in Europe, the caste system in America was fully in force and into its third century. Its operating principles were evident all over the country, but caste was enforced without quarter in the authoritarian Jim Crow regime of the former Confederacy.

"Caste in the South," wrote the anthropologists W. Lloyd Warner and Allison Davis, "is a system for arbitrarily defining the status of all Negroes and of all whites with regard to the most fundamental privileges and opportunities of human society." It would become the social, economic, and psychological template at work in one degree or another for generations.

———

A few years ago, a Nigerian-born playwright came to a talk that I gave at the British Library in London. She was intrigued by the lecture, the idea that 6 million African-Americans had had to seek political asylum within the borders of their own country during the Great Migration, a history that she had not known of. She talked with me afterward and said something that I have never forgotten, that startled me in its simplicity.

"You know that there are no black people in Africa," she said.

Most Americans, weaned on the myth of drawable lines between human beings, have to sit with that statement. It sounds nonsensical to our ears. Of course there are black people in Africa. There is a whole continent of black people in Africa. How could anyone not see that?

"Africans are not black," she said. "They are Igbo and Yoruba, Ewe, Akan, Ndebele. They are not black. They are just themselves. They are humans on the land. That is how they see themselves, and that is who they are."

What we take as gospel in American culture is alien to them, she said.

"They don't become black until they go to America or come to the U.K.," she said. "It is then that they become black."

It was in the making of the New World that Europeans became white, Africans black, and everyone else yellow, red, or brown. It was in the making of the New World that humans were set apart on the basis of what they looked like, identified solely in contrast to one another, and ranked to form a caste system based on a new concept called race. It was in the process of ranking that we were all cast into assigned roles to meet the needs of the larger production.

None of us are ourselves.

CHAPTER FIVE

"The Container We Have Built for You"

Her name is Miss. It is only Miss. It is Miss for a reason. She was born in Texas in the 1970s to parents who came of age under Jim Crow, the authoritarian regime that laid the ground rules for the rest of a willing country. The overarching rule was that the lowest caste was to remain low in every way at all times, at any cost. Every reference was intended to reinforce their inferiority. In describing a train wreck, for instance, newspapers would report, "two men and two women were killed, and four Negroes." Black men were never to be addressed as "Mister," and black women were never to be addressed as "Miss" or "Mrs.," but rather by their first name or "auntie" or "gal," regardless of their age or marital status.

These rules were as basic as the change in the seasons, and a mayoral campaign in Birmingham, Alabama, turned almost entirely on a breach of a sacrosanct protocol. The supremacist police chief, Bull Connor, had a favorite in that 1961 race. He decided to secure the election of the man he wanted to win by framing the man he wanted to lose: he paid a black man to shake the opposing candidate's hand in public as a photographer lay in wait. The story took up a full page in a local newspaper, and the opponent lost the election as Bull Connor knew he would. For white southerners, it was a "cardinal sin," it was "harrowing," wrote the historian Jason Sokol, "to call a black man 'Mister' or to shake hands with him."

A young boy growing up ninety miles south, in Selma, watched white people, complete strangers, children even, call his mother and grandmother by their first names, have the nerve to call out "Pearlie!" to his mother instead of "Mrs. Hale," despite their upright bearing and church gloves and finery. Harold Hale came to hate this presumption of overfamiliarity, their putting his high-minded Mama and Big Mama in their place, and, worse still, knowing that there was nothing he could do about it.

In early 1965, Dr. Martin Luther King, Jr., came to town. It had been one hundred years since the end of the Civil War, and the subordinate caste was still not permitted to vote, despite the Fifteenth Amendment granting that right. Harold Hale signed up for the march Dr. King was planning from Selma to Montgomery.

The Edmund Pettus Bridge that they would have to cross to begin the journey was a few blocks from Hale's house. When he and the six hundred other marchers arrived at the foot of the bridge, a column of state troopers in helmets and on horseback blocked their path. The troopers stormed the protesters. They gassed, beat, and trampled them, "charging horses, their hoofs flashing over the fallen," in the words of the writer George B. Leonard, who watched in horror from his black-and-white television set. ABC News had cut into the middle of *Judgment at Nuremberg*, a movie about Nazi war crimes, to broadcast the grainy footage from Selma, one nightmare fusing into another.

Hale, a teenager far from the leaders up front, was unharmed physically. But he worried now about how long it might take for change to come. He decided then and there that if there was one thing he would do, he would make the dominant caste respect the next generation in his line. He decided he would stand up to the caste system by naming his firstborn daughter, whenever he might be so blessed, "Miss." He would give no one in the dominant caste the option but to call her by the title they had denied his foremothers. Miss would be her name. When his firstborn daughter arrived, his wife, Linda, went along with the plan.

Miss was now seated across from me at her lace-covered dinner table one summer evening. The homemade lasagna and strawberry cake had been put away. The kids and her husband were otherwise occupied, and she was recounting her life, north and south, how her father's dreams have brushed up against caste as she moves about the world.

A white porcelain sugar bowl sat between us on the table. She swept her hand over the top of the bowl. "I find that white people are fine with me," she said, "as long as I stay in my place. As long as I stay in 'the container we have built for you.'"

She tapped the side of the sugar bowl, gentle, insistent taps.

"As soon as I get out of the container," she said, lifting the lid from its bowl, "it's a problem."

She held the lid up to the light and then closed it back in its place.

When she was a little girl, her family moved to a small town in East Texas. They were the only black family on their block. Her father took delight in keeping the front yard pristine and tended to it in his off hours. He would change out the annuals in the flower beds overnight so that people would awaken to the surprise of a practically new yard. One day, a white man who lived in the neighborhood saw her father out front mowing the lawn. The man told her father he was doing a mighty fine job and asked what he was charging for yard work.

"Oh, I don't charge anything," Harold Hale said. "I get to sleep with the lady of the house."

He smiled at the man. "I live here."

Once word got out, people took baseball bats and knocked down the mailbox in front of the Hales' carefully tended garden. So Harold Hale set the next mailbox in concrete. One day, someone rolled by and tried to knock it down again from the car window, and when they did, the family heard a yell from outside.

"The person had hurt their arm trying to hurl the bat at the new mailbox," Miss said. "But it was in concrete, and the bat kicked back at them." People left the mailbox alone after that.

The local high schools began permitting the two castes to go to school together in the early 1970s, before the family had arrived. When she was in tenth grade, she and her friends attracted unexpected attention for the walkie-talkies they used during their breaks between classes. This was before cellphones, and it allowed her to keep in touch with her friends, who'd gather at her locker at break time. The principal called her into his office one day, suspicious of the activity and wanting to know why these people were gathered around her locker. She showed him the device.

He asked her name.

"Miss Hale," she said.

"What's your first name?"

"It's Miss."

"I said, what is your first name?"

"My name is Miss."

"I don't have time for this foolishness. What's your real name?"

She repeated the name her father had given her. The principal was agitated now, and told an assistant to get her records. The records confirmed her name.

"Hale. Hale," he repeated to himself, trying to figure out the origins of this breach in protocol. In small southern towns, the white people knew or expected to know all the black people, the majority of whom would be dependent on the dominant caste for their income or survival one way or the other. He was trying to figure out what black family had had the nerve to name their daughter Miss, knowing the fix it would put the white people in.

"Hale. I don't know any Hales," he finally said. "You're not from around here. Where is your father from?"

"He's from Alabama."

"Who does he work for?"

She told him the name of the company, which was based outside of Texas. She told him it was a Fortune 500 company. Her parents had taught her to say this in hopes of giving her some extra protection.

"I knew you weren't from around here," he said. "Know how I know?"

She shook her head, waiting to be excused.

"You looked me in the eye when I was talking," he said of this breach in caste. "Colored folks from around here know better than to do that."

She was finally excused, and when she got home that day, she told her father what happened. He had waited twenty years for this moment.

"What did he say? And then what did you say? And what did he say after that?"

He could barely contain himself. The plan was working.

He told her over and over that she must live up to the name she was given. "They don't have the corner on humanity," he told her. "They don't have the corner on femininity. They don't have the corner on everything it means to be a whole, admirable, noble, honorable female member of the species. They haven't cornered that."

Years later, Miss had a chance to see life in another part of America. In college, she was invited to spend the summer with the family of a fellow student on Long Island in New York. The family welcomed her and got a kick out of her name and how her family had stuck it to those bigots down South.

She was attentive to the grandmother in the family, so the grandmother grew especially fond of her. Miss had a graceful, easygoing manner, and was respectful toward the elders in the long tradition of black southern life. When the summer came to a close, and it was time to return to school, the grandmother was despondent at her leaving, so attached had she grown to her.

"I wish you would stay," the matriarch said, looking forlorn and hoping to convince her still.

Miss reminded her that she would need to be leaving.

"There was a time," the matriarch said, in warning and regret, "when I could have made you stay." She adjusted herself, her voice trailing off at her impotence. . . .

———

Each of us is in a container of some kind. The label signals to the world what is presumed to be inside and what is to be done with it. The label tells you which shelf your container supposedly belongs on. In a caste system, the label is frequently out of sync with the contents, mistakenly put on the wrong shelf and this hurts people and institutions in ways we may not always know.

Back before Amazon and iPhones, I was a national correspondent at *The New York Times*, based in Chicago. I had decided to do a lighthearted piece about Chicago's Magnificent Mile, a prime stretch of Michigan Avenue that had always been the city's showcase, but now some big names from New York and elsewhere were about to take up residence. I figured New York retailers would be delighted to talk. As I planned the story, I reached out to them for interviews. Everyone I called was thrilled to describe their foray into Chicago and to sit down with the *Times*.

The interviews went as expected until the last one. I had arrived a few minutes early to make sure we could start on time, given the deadline I was facing.

The boutique was empty at this quiet hour of the late afternoon. The manager's assistant told me the manager would be arriving soon from another appointment. I told her I didn't mind the wait. I was happy to get another big name in the piece. She went to a back corner as I stood alone in a wide-open showroom. A man in a business suit and overcoat walked in, harried and breathless. From the far corner she nodded that this was him, so I went up to introduce myself and get started. He was out of breath, had been rushing, coat still on, checking his watch.

"Oh, I can't talk with you now," he said, brushing past me. "I'm very, very busy. I'm running late for an appointment."

I was confused at first. Might he have made another appointment for the exact same time? Why would he schedule two appointments at once? There was no one else in the boutique but the two of us and his assistant in back.

"I think I'm your appointment," I said.

"No, this is a very important appointment with *The New York Times*," he said, pulling off his coat. "I can't talk with you now. I'll have to talk with you some other time."

"But I am with *The New York Times*," I told him, pen and notebook in hand. "I talked with you on the phone. I'm the one who made the appointment with you for four-thirty."

"What's the name?"

"Isabel Wilkerson with *The New York Times*."

"How do I know that?" he shot back, growing impatient. "Look, I said I don't have time to talk with you right now. She'll be here any minute."

He looked to the front entrance and again at his watch.

"But I am Isabel. We should be having the interview right now."

He let out a sigh. "What kind of identification do you have? Do you have a business card?"

This was the last interview for the piece, and I had handed them all out by the time I got to him.

"I've been interviewing all day," I told him. "I happen to be out of them now."

"What about ID? You have a license on you?"

"I shouldn't have to show you my license, but here it is."

He gave it a cursory look.

"You don't have anything that has *The New York Times* on it?"

"Why would I be here if I weren't here to interview you? All of this time has passed. We've been standing here, and no one else has shown up."

"She must be running late. I'm going to have to ask you to leave so I can get ready for my appointment."

I left and walked back to the *Times* bureau, dazed and incensed, trying to figure out what had just happened. This was the first time I had ever been accused of impersonating myself. His caste notions of who should be doing what in society had so blinded him that he dismissed the idea that the reporter he was anxiously awaiting, excited to talk to, was standing right in front him. It seemed not to occur to him that a *New York Times* national correspondent could come in a container such as mine, despite every indication that I was she.

The story ran that Sunday. Because I had not been able to interview him, he didn't get a mention. It would have amounted to a nice bit of publicity for him, but the other interviews made it unnecessary in the end. I sent him a clip of the piece along with the business card that he had asked for. To this day, I won't step inside that retailer. I will not mention the name, not because of censorship or a desire to protect any company's reputation, but because of our cultural tendency to believe that if we just identify the presumed-to-be-rare offending outlier, we will have rooted out the problem. The problem could have happened anyplace, because the problem is, in fact, at the root.

CHAPTER SIX

The Measure of Humanity

In a parallel universe with laws of nature similar to our own, a conquering people with powerful weaponry journeyed across the oceans and discovered people who looked different from themselves. They were startled to chance upon humans who towered above them, were taller than any humans they had ever seen before. They did not know what to make of this discovery. They had thought of, and measured themselves as, the standard for human existence. But the indigenous people they saw were at the outer limits of a particular human trait: their height. Even the women averaged over six feet, some of the men approached seven. The well-armed explorers were the opposite. Their weapons were deadly, and their bodies were closer to the ground.

At this moment in human history, as the world was being claimed by competing tribes of the well-armed, two peoples who were at the extremes of a highly visible yet arbitrary human characteristic—being tall or short—were confronting each other for the first time. A tribe of the shortest humans were now face-to-face with the tallest. Those with the most advanced weapons prevailed and found use for the tallest people. They decided to transport them to the New World they were creating.

They joined forces with other Shorts around the world, with whom they made common cause. With their superior guns and stratagems, they conquered the Talls, captured and enslaved them for a quarter millennium, and built a great democracy. They told themselves the Talls deserved no better, that they were uncultured, backward, inferior, had not made use of their strengths and resources. They were an altogether different species, born to serve the conquerors, deserving of their debasement. They were a separate and subordinate race.

This story of conquest sounds preposterous to our ears, not because it did not happen, but because of the seeming absurdity of height as a means of categorizing humanity and determining race.

We could have been divided up by any number of other traits. And yet height, like skin pigment, is overwhelmingly an inherited trait, controlled by as much as 80 percent of one's genes and fairly consistent in family and tribal groupings. As with the pigment of skin, height falls within a wide range among adults in the species, with most people in the middle and with extremes at the poles, from a maximum of seven feet for adults to a minimum of under four feet. Were height the measure for determining race, as arbitrary a measure as any and less arbitrary than some, the Dutch people of the Netherlands would be the same "race" as the Nilote people of South Sudan or the Tutsis of Rwanda, as they are all among the tallest in our species, even the women averaging well over six feet. On the other end, the Pygmies and Sardinians would be their own separate "race," as they have historically been among the shortest humans.

If current caste behavior were any guide, everyone else would be in the middle, perhaps playing up to whichever height was in power, wearing platform heels if the Tall people ruled, bragging that height ran in their families, choosing the tallest people to date and to marry to gain the advantages of the ruling caste. Stereotypes would calcify, as they already do for extremes in height, but magnify to justify the lowly or elevated position of whichever group was in power.

In a caste system dominated by Short people, anyone in the subordinate race of Tall people would be dismissed merely as brawn, consigned to menial, servile positions, seen as good only for entertainment or servitude. Short people would be seen as born to leadership due to their presumed innate intellect and culture, admired for the longevity said to attend people smaller in stature, regarded as the standard of beauty, the default setting for human.

Tall people would be made to feel insecure and self-conscious, gangly and unappealing, having been born at the opposite end of the ideal. Society would assume that any Tall person was good at sports and physical labor, whether or not he or she had interest or aptitude. Scientists might devise tests to measure the difference between Talls and Shorts beyond height alone, tests that would largely track the results of generations of either advantage or exclusion and likely affirm widely held assumptions about the Shorts' inherent supremacy and the Talls' misfortune of deficits. There would be few Tall people in the boardrooms and corridors of power, and a disproportionate number of them in prisons and on the streets. Being tall would become shorthand for inferior in a caste system ruled by Short people, and vice versa.

Ludicrous though it may sound to us now, had height been the means of categorizing humans for centuries as it has been for skin color and facial features, people would have accepted it as the received wisdom of the laws of nature. It would have seemed ridiculous that, in an alternate universe, people would ever be divided by color, given that, clearly, it would have been obvious that height was the determining factor in beauty, intelligence, leadership, and supremacy. The idea of linking disparate groups together on the basis of an arbitrary shared characteristic of being extremely tall or short sounds farcical to us, but only because this characteristic is not the one that has been used to divide humans into seemingly immutable "races."

The idea of race is a recent phenomenon in human history. It dates to the start of the transatlantic slave trade and thus to the subsequent caste system that arose from slavery. The word *race* likely derived from the Spanish word *raza* and was originally used to refer to the "'caste or quality of authentic horses,' which are branded with an iron so as to be recognized," wrote the anthropologists Audrey and Brian Smedley. As Europeans explored the world, they began using the word to refer to the new people they encountered. Ultimately, "the English in North America developed the most rigid and exclusionist form of race ideology," the Smedleys wrote. "Race in the American mind was and is a statement about profound and unbridgeable differences. . . . It conveys the meaning of social distance that cannot be transcended."

Geneticists and anthropologists have long seen race as a man-made invention with no basis in science or biology. The nineteenth-century anthropologist Paul Broca tried to use thirty-four shades of skin color to delineate the races, but could come to no conclusion. If all the humans on the planet were lined up by a single physical trait, say, height or color, in ascending or descending order, tallest to shortest, darkest to lightest, it would confound us to choose the line between these arbitrary divisions. One human would blend into the next and it would be nearly impossible to make the cutoff between, say, the San people of South Africa and the indigenous people along the Marañón River in Peru, who are scientifically measured to be the same color, even though they live thousands of miles apart and do not share the same immediate ancestry.

As a window into the random nature of these categories, the use of the term *Caucasian* to label people descended from Europe is a relatively new and arbitrary practice in human history. The word was not passed down from the ancients but rather sprang from the mind of a German professor of medicine, Johann Friedrich Blumenbach, in 1795. Blumenbach spent decades studying and measuring human skulls—the foreheads, the jawbones, the eye sockets—in an attempt to classify the varieties of humankind.

He coined the term *Caucasian* on the basis of a favorite skull of his that had come into his possession from the Caucasus Mountains of Russia. To him, the skull was the most beautiful of all that he owned. So he gave the group to which he belonged, the Europeans, the same name as the region that had produced it. That is how people now identified as white got the scientific-sounding yet random name Caucasian. More than a century later, in 1914, a citizenship trial was under way in America over whether a Syrian could be a Caucasian (and thus white), which led an expert witness in the case to say of Blumenbach's confusing and fateful discovery: "Never has a single head done more harm to science."

The epic mapping of the human genome and the quieter, long-dreamt-of results of DNA kits ordered in time for a family reunion have shown us that race as we have come to know it is not real. It is a fiction told by modern humans for so long that it has come to be seen as a sacred truth.

Two decades ago, analysis of the human genome established that all human beings are 99.9 percent the same. "Race is a social concept, not a scientific one," said J. Craig Venter, the geneticist who ran Celera Genomics when the mapping was completed in 2000. "We all evolved in the last 100,000 years from the small number of tribes that migrated out of Africa and colonized the world." Which means that an entire racial caste system, the catalyst of hatreds and civil war, was built on what the anthropologist Ashley Montagu called "an arbitrary and superficial selection of traits," derived from a few of the thousands of genes that make up a human being. "The idea of race," Montagu wrote, "was, in fact, the deliberate creation of an exploiting class seeking to maintain and defend its privileges against what was profitably regarded as an inferior caste."

We accept the illogic of race because these are the things we have been told. We see a person with skin that is whiter than that of most "white" people, and we accept that they are not "white" (and thus of a different category) because of the minutest difference in the folds of their eyelids and because perhaps their great-grandparents were born in Japan. We see a person whose skin is espresso, darker than most "black" people in America, and accept that he is, in fact, not "black," absolutely not "black" (and is thus a completely separate category), because his hair has a looser curl and perhaps he was born in Madagascar. We have to be taught this illogic. Small children who have yet to learn the rules will describe people as they see them, not by the political designations of black, white, Asian, or Latino, until adults "correct" them to use the proper caste designations to make the irrational sound reasoned. Color is a fact. Race is a social construct.

"We think we 'see' race when we encounter certain physical differences among people such as skin color, eye shape, and hair texture," the Smedleys wrote. "What we actually 'see' . . . are the learned social meanings, the stereotypes, that have been linked to those physical features by the ideology of race and the historical legacy it has left us."

And yet, observed the historian Nell Irvin Painter, "Americans cling to race as the unschooled cling to superstition."

————

The word *caste*, which has become synonymous with India, did not, it turns out, originate in India. It comes from the Portuguese word *casta*, a Renaissance-era word for "race" or "breed." The Portuguese, who were among the earliest European traders in South Asia, applied the term to the people of India upon observing Hindu divisions. Thus, a word we now ascribe to India actually arose from Europeans' interpretations of what they saw; it sprang from the Western culture that created America.

The Indian concept of rankings, however, goes back millennia and is thousands of years older than the European concept of race. The rankings were originally known as *varnas*, the ancient term for the major categories in what Indians have in recent centuries called the caste system. The human impulse to create hierarchies runs across societies and cultures, predates the idea of race, and thus is farther reaching, deeper, and older than raw racism and the comparatively new division of humans by skin color.

Before Europeans expanded to the New World and collided with people who looked different from themselves, the concept of racism as we know it did not exist in Western culture. "Racism is a modern conception," wrote the historian Dante Puzzo, "for prior to the XVIth century there was virtually nothing in the life and thought of the West that can be described as racist."

The R Word

What we face in our current day is not the classical racism of our forefathers' era, but a mutation of the software that adjusts to the updated needs of the operating system. In the half century since civil rights protests forced the United States into making state-sanctioned discrimination illegal, what Americans consider to be racism has shifted, and now the word is one of the most contentious and misunderstood in American culture. For the dominant caste, the word is radioactive—resented, feared, denied, lobbed back toward anyone who dares to suggest it. Resistance to the word often derails any discussion of the underlying behavior it is meant to describe, thus eroding it of meaning.

Social scientists often define racism as the combination of racial bias and systemic power, seeing racism, like sexism, as primarily the action of people or systems with personal or group power over another person or group with less power, as men have power over women, whites over people of color, and the dominant over the subordinate.

But over time, racism has often been reduced to a feeling, a character flaw, conflated with prejudice, connected to whether one is a good person or not. It has come to mean overt and declared hatred of a person or group because of the race ascribed to them, a perspective few would ever own up to. While people will admit to or call out sexism or xenophobia and homophobia, people may immediately deflect accusations of racism, saying they don't have "a racist bone in their body," or are the "least racist person you could ever meet," that they "don't see color," that their "best friend is black," and they may have even convinced themselves on a conscious level of these things.

What does *racist* mean in an era when even extremists won't admit to it? What is the litmus test for racism? Who is racist in a society where someone can refuse to rent to people of color, arrest brown immigrants en masse, or display a Confederate flag, but not be "certified" as a racist unless he or she confesses to it or is caught using derogatory signage or slurs? The fixation with smoking out individual racists or sexists can seem a losing battle in which we fool ourselves into thinking we are rooting out injustice by forcing an admission that (a) is not likely to come, (b) keeps the focus on a single individual rather than the system that created that individual, and (c) gives cover for those who, by aiming at others, can present themselves as noble and bias-free for having pointed the finger first, all of which keeps the hierarchy intact.

Oddly enough, the instinctive desire to reject the very idea of current discrimination on the basis of a chemical compound in the skin is an unconscious admission of the absurdity of race as a concept.

This is not to say that the consequences of this social construct are not real or that abuses should not be prosecuted to the full extent of the law. It is to say that the word *racism* may not stand as the only term or the most useful term to describe the phenomena and tensions we experience in our era. Rather than deploying *racism* as an either/or accusation against an individual, it may be more constructive to focus on derogatory actions that harm a less powerful group rather than on what is commonly seen as an easily deniable, impossible-to-measure attribute.

With no universally agreed-upon definition, we might see racism as a continuum rather than an absolute. We might release ourselves of the purity test of whether someone is or is not racist and exchange that mindset for one that sees people as existing on a scale based on the toxins they have absorbed from the polluted and inescapable air of social instruction we receive from childhood.

Caste, on the other hand, predates the notion of race and has survived the era of formal, state-sponsored racism that had long been openly practiced in the mainstream. The modern-day version of easily deniable racism may be able to cloak the invisible structure that created and maintains hierarchy and inequality. But caste does not allow us to ignore structure. Caste *is* structure. Caste is ranking. Caste is the boundaries that reinforce the fixed assignments based upon what people look like. Caste is a living, breathing entity. It is like a corporation that seeks to sustain itself at all costs. To achieve a truly egalitarian world requires looking deeper than what we think we see. We cannot win against a hologram.

Caste is the granting or withholding of respect, status, honor, attention, privileges, resources, benefit of the doubt, and human kindness to someone on the basis of their perceived rank or standing in the hierarchy. Caste pushes back against an African-American woman who, without humor or apology, takes a seat at the head of the table speaking Russian. It prefers an Asian-American man to put his technological expertise at the service of the company but not aspire to CEO. Yet it sees as logical a sixteen-year-old white teenager serving as store manager over employees from the subordinate caste three times his age. Caste is insidious and therefore powerful because it is not hatred, it is not necessarily personal. It is the worn grooves of comforting routines and unthinking expectations, patterns of a social order that have been in place for so long that it looks like the natural order of things.

What is the difference between racism and casteism? Because caste and race are interwoven in America, it can be hard to separate the two. Any action or institution that mocks, harms, assumes, or attaches inferiority or stereotype on the basis of the social construct of race can be considered racism. Any action or structure that seeks to limit, hold back, or put someone in a defined ranking, seeks to keep someone in their place by elevating or denigrating that person on the basis of their perceived category, can be seen as casteism.

Casteism is the investment in keeping the hierarchy as it is in order to maintain your own ranking, advantage, privilege, or to elevate yourself above others or keep others beneath you. For those in the marginalized castes, casteism can mean seeking to keep those on your disfavored rung from gaining on you, to curry the favor and remain in the good graces of the dominant caste, all of which serve to keep the structure intact.

In the United States, racism and casteism frequently occur at the same time, or overlap or figure into the same scenario. Caste-ism is about positioning and restricting those positions, vis-à-vis others. What race and its precursor, racism, do extraordinarily well is to confuse and distract from the underlying structural and more powerful Sith Lord of caste. Like the cast on a broken arm, like the cast in a play, a caste system holds everyone in a fixed place.

For this reason, many people—including those we might see as good and kind people—could be casteist, meaning invested in keeping the hierarchy as it is or content to do nothing to change it, but not racist in the classical sense, not active and openly hateful of this or that group. Actual racists, actual haters, would by defini-tion be casteist, as their hatred demands that those they perceive as beneath them know and keep their place in the hierarchy.

In everyday terms, it is not racism that prompts a white shop-per in a clothing store to go up to a random black or brown person who is also shopping and to ask for a sweater in a different size, or for a white guest at a party to ask a black or brown person who is also a guest to fetch them a drink, as happened to Barack Obama as a state senator, or even perhaps a judge to sentence a subordinate-caste person for an offense for which a dominant-caste person might not even be charged. It is caste or rather the policing of and adherence to the caste system. It's the autonomic, unconscious, reflexive response to expectations from a thousand imaging inputs and neurological societal downloads that affix people to certain roles based upon what they look like and what they historically have been assigned to or the characteristics and stereotypes by which they have been categorized. No ethnic or racial category is immune to the messaging we all receive about the hierarchy, and thus no one escapes its consequences.

What some people call racism could be seen as merely one

manifestation of the degree to which we have internalized the larger American caste system, a measure of how much we ascribe to it and how deeply we uphold it, act upon it, and enforce it, often unconsciously, in our daily lives.

When we assume that the woman is not equipped to lead the meeting or the company or the country, or that a person of color or an immigrant could not be the one in authority, is not a resident of a certain community, could not have attended a particular school or deserved to have attended a particular school, when we feel a pang of shock and resentment, a personal wounding and sense of unfairness and perhaps even shame at our discomfort upon seeing someone from a marginalized group in a job or car or house or college or appointment more prestigious than we have been led to expect, when we assume that the senior citizen should be playing Parcheesi rather than developing software, we are reflecting the efficient encoding of caste, the subconscious recognition that the person has stepped out of his or her assumed place in our society. We are responding to our embedded instructions of who should be where and who should be doing what, the breaching of the structure and boundaries that are the hallmarks of caste.

Race and caste are not the cause and do not account for every poor outcome or unpleasant encounter. But caste becomes a factor, to whatever infinitesimal degree, in interactions and decisions across gender, ethnicity, race, immigrant status, sexual orientation, age, or religion that have consequences in our everyday lives and in policies that affect our country and beyond. It may not be as all-consuming as its targets may perceive it to be, but neither is it the ancient relic, the long-ago anachronism, that post-racialists, post-haters of everything, keep wishing away. Its invisibility is what gives it power and longevity. Caste, along with its faithful servant race, is an x-factor in most any American equation, and any answer one might ever come up with to address our current challenges is flawed without it.

CHAPTER SEVEN

Through the Fog of Delhi to the Parallels in India and America

The flight to India landed in a gray veil that hid the terminal and its tower at the international airport in Delhi. It was January 2018, my first moments on the subcontinent. The pilot searched for a jetway through the drapery of mist. It was two in the morning, and it was as if we had landed in a steam kettle, were still airborne in a cloud, the night air pressing against cabin windows, and we could see nothing of the ground. I had not heard of rain in the forecast and was fascinated by this supernatural fog in the middle of the night, until I realized that it was not fog at all, but smoke—from coal plants, cars, and burning stubble—trapped in stagnant wind. The pollution was a shroud at first to seeing India as it truly was.

At daybreak, the sun pushed through the haze, and, once I connected with my hosts, I raced along with them to cross an intersection, an open stretch of asphalt with cars hurtling in every direction with no lanes or speed limits. We made our way along the side streets to the conference we were attending. I saw the wayside altars and mushroom temples with their garlands and silk flowers to the Hindu deities at the base of the sacred fig trees. There, commuters can pause for reflection as they head to work or an exam or a doctor's visit. The sidewalk shrines seemed exotic to me until I thought of the American ritual of spontaneous altars of flowers and balloons at the site of something very different, at the site of an accident or tragedy, as for the young woman killed at the infamous rally in Charlottesville, Virginia, just months before. Both reflect a human desire to connect with and honor something or someone beyond ourselves.

The United States and India are profoundly different from each other—in culture, technology, economics, ethnic makeup. And yet, many generations ago, these two great lands paralleled each other, both protected by oceans and ruled for a time by the British, fertile and coveted. Both adopted social hierarchies and abide great chasms between the highest and the lowest in their respective lands. Both were conquered by people said to be Aryans arriving, in one case, from across the Atlantic Ocean, in the other, from the north. Those deemed lowest in each country would serve those deemed high. The younger country, the United States, would become the most powerful democracy on earth. The older country, India, the largest.

Their respective hierarchies are profoundly different. And yet, as if operating from the same instruction manual translated to fit their distinctive cultures, both countries adopted similar methods of maintaining rigid lines of demarcation and protocols. Both countries kept their dominant caste separate, apart and above those deemed lower. Both exiled their indigenous peoples—the Adivasi in India, the Native Americans in the United States—to remote lands and to the unseen margins of society. Both countries enacted a fretwork of laws to chain the lowliest group—Dalits in India and African-Americans in the United States—to the bottom, using terror and force to keep them there.

"Perhaps only the Jews have as long a history of suffering from discrimination as the Dalits," wrote the Dalit journalist V. T. Rajshekar. "However, when we consider the nature of the suffering endured by the Dalits, it is only the African American parallel of enslavement, apartheid and forced assimilation that comes to mind."

Both countries have since abolished the formal laws that defined their caste systems—the United States in a series of civil rights laws in the 1960s and India decades before, in the 1940s, but both caste systems live on in hearts and habits, institutions and infrastructures. Both countries still live with the residue of codes that prevailed for far longer than they have not.

This description of caste history from the 2017 Indian book *Ground Down by Growth* could be said of the American caste system with only a few word changes, as noted by parentheses: *"The colonial powers officially abolished slavery in India (the United States) in 1843 (1865), but this simply led to its transformation into bondage through relations of debt, what has been called 'debt peonage' by scholars."*

In both countries and at the same time, the lowest castes toiled for their masters—African-Americans in the tobacco fields along the Chesapeake or in the cotton fields of Mississippi, Dalits plucking tea in Kerala and cotton in Nandurbar. Both worked as enslaved people and later for the right to live on the land that they were farming, African-Americans in the system of sharecropping, Dalits in the Indian equivalent, known as *saldari*, both still confined to their fixed roles at the bottom of their respective worlds.

"Both occupy the lowest positions on the status hierarchies in their societies," wrote Harvard political scientist Sidney Verba and his colleagues in a study of Dalits and African-Americans. Both have been "particularly singled out from other groups" based on characteristics ascribed to them.

While doors have opened to the subordinated castes in India and in America in the decades since discrimination was officially prohibited, the same spasms of resistance have afflicted both countries. What is called "affirmative action" in the United States is called "reservations" in India, and they are equally unpopular with the upper castes in both countries, language tracking in lockstep, with complaints of reverse discrimination in one and reverse casteism in the other.

There are many overarching similarities but they are not the same in how they are structured or operate. The American system was founded as a primarily two-tiered hierarchy with its contours defined by the uppermost group, those identified as white, and by the subordinated group, those identified as black, with immigrants from outside of Europe forming blurred middle castes that sought to adjust themselves within a bipolar structure.

The Indian caste system, by contrast, is an elaborate fretwork of thousands of subcastes, or *jatis*, correlated to region and village, which fall under the four main *varnas*, Brahmin, Kshatriya, Vaishya, and Shudra, and the excluded fifth, known as Untouchables or Dalits. It is further complicated by non-Hindus—Muslims, Buddhists, and Christians—who are outside the caste system but have incorporated themselves into the workings of the country and, while eschewing rigid caste, may or may not have informal rankings among themselves and in relation to the *varnas*.

Unlike the United States, which primarily uses physical features to tell the castes apart, in India it is people's surnames that may most readily convey their caste. Dalit names are generally "contemptible" in meaning, referring to the humble or dirty work they were relegated to, while the Brahmins carry the names of the gods. Generally, you must know the significance of the name, learn the occupation of their forefathers, and perhaps know their village or their place in the village to ascertain their caste. But after centuries of forced submission and in-group marriage, they may also be identified by their bearing, accents, and clothing, all of which, over the centuries, were required to be lowly and menial, as well as a tendency to be darker than upper-caste people, though not always.

The Indian caste system is said to be stable and unquestioned by those within it, bound as it is by religion and in the Hindu belief in reincarnation, the belief that one lives out in this life the karma of the previous ones, suffers the punishment or reaps the rewards for one's deeds in a past life, and that the more keenly one follows the rules for the caste they were born to, the higher their station will be in the next life.

Some observers say that this is what distinguishes the Indian caste system from any other, that people in the lowest caste accept their lot, that it is fixed and unbending, that Dalits live out their karma decreed by the gods, and do their lowly work without complaint, knowing not to dream of anything more. In order to survive, some people in a subordinated caste may learn and believe that resistance is futile. But this condescending view disregards generations of resistance, as well as the work of Ambedkar and the reformer Jotiba Phule before him. It was also wrongly assumed of enslaved Africans, and it disregards a fundamental truth of the species, that all human beings want to be free.

The Dalits were no more contented with their lot than anyone would be. In a caste system, conflating compliance with approval can be dehumanizing in itself. Many Dalits looked out beyond their homeland, surveyed the oppressed people all over the world, and identified the people closest to their lamentations. They recognized a shared fate with African-Americans, few of whom would have known of the suffering of Dalits. Some Dalits felt so strong a kinship with one wing of the American civil rights movement and had followed it so closely that, in the 1970s, they created the Dalit Panthers, inspired by the Black Panther Party.

A few years ago, a group of African-American professors made a trip to a rural village in Uttar Pradesh, India. There, hundreds of villagers from the lowliest subcaste, the scavengers, came together for a ceremony to welcome the Americans. The villagers sang Dalit liberation songs for the occasion. Then they turned to their American guests and invited them to sing a liberation song of their own. A law professor from Indiana University, Kenneth Dau Schmidt, began a song that the civil rights marchers sang in Birmingham and Selma before they faced sheriffs' dogs and water hoses. As he reached the refrain, the Dalit hosts joined in and began to sing with their American counterparts. Across the oceans, they well knew the words to "We Shall Overcome."

CHAPTER EIGHT

The Nazis and the Acceleration of Caste

Berlin, June 1934

In the early stages of the Third Reich, before the world could imagine the horrors to come, a committee of Nazi bureaucrats met to weigh the options for imposing a rigid new hierarchy, one that would isolate Jewish people from Aryans now that the Nazis had taken control. The men summoned in the late spring of 1934 were not, at that time, planning, nor in a position to plan, extermination. That would come years later at a chillingly bloodless and cataclysmic meeting in Wannsee deeper into a world war that had not yet begun.

On this day, June 5, 1934, they were there to debate the legal framework for an Aryan nation, to turn ideology into law, and were now anxious to discuss the findings of their research into how other countries protected racial purity from the taint of the disfavored. They sat down for a closed-door session in the Reich capital that day, and considered it serious enough to bring a stenographer to record the proceedings and produce a transcript. As they settled into their chairs to hash out what would eventually become the Nuremberg Laws, the first topic on the agenda was the United States and what they could learn from it.

The man chairing the meeting, Franz Gürtner, the Reich minister of justice, introduced a memorandum in the opening minutes, detailing the ministry's investigation into how the United States managed its marginalized groups and guarded its ruling white citizenry. The seventeen legal scholars and functionaries went back and forth over American purity laws governing intermarriage and immigration. In debating "how to institutionalize racism in the Third Reich," wrote the Yale legal historian James Q. Whitman, "they began by asking how the Americans did it."

The Nazis needed no outsiders to plant the seeds of hatred within them. But in the early years of the regime, when they still had a stake in the appearance of legitimacy and the hope of foreign investment, they were seeking legal prototypes for the caste system they were building. They were looking to move quickly with their plans for racial separation and purity, and knew that the United States was centuries ahead of them with its anti-miscegenation statutes and race-based immigration bans. "For us Germans, it is especially important to know and see how one of the biggest states in the world with Nordic stock already has race legislation which is quite comparable to that of the German Reich," the German press agency Grossdeutscher Pressedienst wrote as the Nazis were solidifying their grip on the country.

Western Europeans had long been aware of the American paradox of proclaiming liberty for all men while holding subsets of its citizenry in near total subjugation. The French writer Alexis de Tocqueville toured antebellum America in the 1830s and observed that only the "surface of American society is covered with a layer of democratic paint." Germany well understood the U.S. fixation on race purity and eugenics, the pseudoscience of grading humans by presumed group superiority. Many leading Americans had joined the eugenics movement of the early twentieth century, including the inventor Alexander Graham Bell, the auto magnate Henry Ford, and Charles W. Eliot, the president of Harvard University. During the First World War, the German Society for Racial Hygiene applauded "the dedication with which Americans sponsor research in the field of racial hygiene and with which they translate theoretical knowledge into practice."

The Nazis had been especially taken with the militant race theories of two widely known American eugenicists, Lothrop Stoddard and Madison Grant. Both were men of privilege, born and raised in the North and educated in the Ivy League. Both built their now discredited reputations on hate ideology that devised a crude ranking of European "stock," declared eastern and southern Europeans inferior to "Nordics" and advocated for the exclusion and elimination of "races" they deemed threats to Nordic racial purity, foremost among them Jews and "Negroes."

A racial slur that the Nazis adopted in their campaign to dehumanize Jews and other non-Aryans—the word *Untermensch*, meaning "subhuman"—came to them from the New England–born eugenicist Lothrop Stoddard. A 1922 book he wrote carried the subtitle *The Menace of the Under-man*, which translated into *Untermenschen* in the German edition. The Nazis took the word as their own and would most become associated with it. They made Stoddard's book on white supremacy a standard text in the Reich's school curriculum and accorded him a private audience with the purposely remote Adolf Hitler at the Reich Chancellery in December 1939. Well into World War II, Stoddard sat in on Nazi sterilization trials and commended the Nazis for "weeding out the worst strains in the Germanic stock in a scientific and truly humanitarian way." He lamented, though, that, "if anything, their judgments were almost too conservative."

Madison Grant, a leading eugenicist from New York whose social circle included Presidents Theodore Roosevelt and Herbert Hoover, converted his zeal for Aryan supremacy into helping enact a series of American immigration and marriage restrictions in the 1920s, as the Nazi Party was forming across the Atlantic. Grant went far beyond southern segregationists in his contempt for marginalized people. He argued that "inferior stocks" should be sterilized and quarantined in "a rigid system of elimination of those who are weak or unfit" or "perhaps worthless race types." Grant published a rabid manifesto for cleansing the gene pool of undesirables, his 1916 book, *The Passing of the Great Race*, the German edition of which held a special place in the *Führer*'s library.

Hitler wrote Grant a personal note of gratitude and said, "The book is my Bible."

Hitler had studied America from afar, both envying and admiring it, and attributed its achievements to its Aryan stock. He praised the country's near genocide of Native Americans and the exiling to reservations of those who had survived. He was pleased that the United States had "shot down the millions of redskins to a few hundred thousand." He saw the U.S. Immigration Restriction Act of 1924 as "a model for his program of racial purification," historian Jonathan Spiro wrote. The Nazis were impressed by the American custom of lynching its subordinate caste of African-Americans, having become aware of the ritual torture and mutilations that typically accompanied them. Hitler especially marveled at the American "knack for maintaining an air of robust innocence in the wake of mass death."

By the time that Hitler rose to power, the United States "was not just a country with racism," Whitman, the Yale legal scholar, wrote. "It was *the* leading racist jurisdiction—so much so that even Nazi Germany looked to America for inspiration." The Nazis recognized the parallels even if many Americans did not.

Thus, on that day in June 1934, as seventeen Reich bureaucrats and legal scholars began to deliberate what would become unprecedented legislation for Germany, they were scrutinizing the United States, and they had done their homework. One of the men, Heinrich Krieger, had studied law in the American South, as an exchange student at the University of Arkansas. He had written extensively about foreign race regimes, having spent two years in South Africa, and was at that very moment completing a book that would be titled *Race Law in the United States* to be published in Germany two years hence. The Nazi lawyers had researched U.S. jurisprudence well enough to know that, from the fugitive slave cases to *Plessy v. Ferguson* and beyond, "the American Supreme Court entertained briefs from southern states whose arguments were indistinguishable from those of the Nazis," Whitman observed.

In their search for prototypes, the Nazis had looked into white-dominated countries such as Australia and South Africa, but "there were no other models for miscegenation law that the Nazis could find in the world," Whitman wrote. "Their overwhelming interest was in the 'classic example,' the United States of America."

———

These seventeen men were convening at a time of intrigue and upheaval in a country descending into dictatorship. The Nazis were in the final throes of consolidating their power after their takeover the year before. Hitler had been sworn in as chancellor but was not yet the *Führer*. That would not happen until later that summer, in August 1934, when the death of Germany's ailing president, Paul von Hindenburg, the last holdover of the Weimar regime, cleared the way for Hitler to seize total control.

Hitler had made it to the chancellery in a brokered deal that conservative elites agreed to only because they were convinced they could hold him in check and make use of him for their own political aims. They underestimated his cunning and overestimated his base of support, which had been the very reason they had felt they needed him in the first place. At the height of their power at the polls, the Nazis never pulled the majority they coveted and drew only 38 percent of the vote in the country's last free and fair elections at the onset of their twelve-year reign. The old guard did not foresee, or chose not to see, that his actual mission was "to exploit the methods of democracy to destroy democracy."

By the time they recognized their fatal miscalculation, it was too late. Hitler had risen as an outside agitator, a cult figure enamored of pageantry and rallies with parades of people carrying torches that an observer said looked like "rivers of fire." Hitler saw himself as the voice of the *Volk*, of their grievances and fears, especially those in the rural districts, as a god-chosen savior, running on instinct. He had never held elected office before.

As soon as he was sworn in as chancellor, the Nazis unfurled their swastikas, a Sanskrit symbol linking them to their Aryan "roots," and began to close in on the Jews. They stoked ancient resentments that dated back to the Middle Ages but that rose again when the Jews were made the scapegoats for Germany's loss and humiliation at the end of World War I. Seen as dominant in banking and finance, Jews were blamed for the insufficient financial support of the war effort, although historians now widely acknowledge that Germany lost on the battlefield and not solely for lack of funds.

Still, Nazi propaganda worked to turn Germans against Jewish citizens. Nazi thugs taunted and beat up Jews in the streets and any Aryans who were found to be in relationships with them. The regime began restricting Jews from working in government or in high-status professions like medicine or the law, fields that incited jealousy among ordinary Germans who could not afford the expensive cars and villas on the lake that many successful Jews had acquired. This was the middle of the Great Depression, and more than a third of Germans were out of work in 1933, the year the Nazis came to power. The Jews' prestige and wealth were seen as above the station of a group that Nazis decreed were beneath the Aryans.

Mindful of appearances beyond their borders, for the time being at least, the Nazis wondered how the United States had managed to turn its racial hierarchy into rigid law yet retain such a sterling reputation on the world stage. They noticed that in the United States, when it came to these racial prohibitions, "public opinion accepted them as natural," wrote the historian Claudia Koonz.

A young Nazi intellectual named Herbert Kier was tasked with compiling a table of U.S. race laws, and was confounded by the lengths to which America went to segregate its population. He made note that, by law in most southern states, "white children and colored children are sent to different schools" and that most states "further demand that race be given in birth certificates, licenses and death certificates." He discovered that "many American states even go so far as to require by statute segregated facilities for coloreds and whites in waiting rooms, train cars, sleeping cars, street cars, buses, steamboats and even in prisons and jails." In Arkansas, he noted, the tax rolls were segregated. He later remarked that, given the "fundamental proposition of the equality of everything that bears a human countenance, it is all the more astonishing how extensive race legislation is in the USA."

Kier was just one of several Nazi researchers "who thought American law went overboard," Whitman wrote.

With the results of their research laid out before them, the men at the June meeting began debating two main pathways to their version of a caste system: first, creating a legal definition for the categories of Jews and Aryans, and, second, prohibiting intermarriage between the two. Germany had looked at America's miscegenation laws decades before and tested its own intermarriage ban at the turn of the twentieth century, when it forbade its settlers to mix with indigenous people in its colonies in South West Africa. In so doing, Germany went further than most colonial powers, but it did not come close to the American model. Now Nazi extremists pushed for ways to prevent "any further penetration of Jewish blood into the body of the German *Volk*."

As the debate got under way, Krieger, the former University of Arkansas law student, reported that Americans had gone so far as to make interracial marriage a crime punishable by as much as ten years' imprisonment in many jurisdictions. He pointed out that the United States had divided its population in two with "artificial line-drawing" between white and colored people. He and other Nazis showed a fascination with the American habit of assigning humans to categories by fractions of perceived ancestry. "There is a growing tendency in judicial practice," Krieger said, "to assign a person to a group of coloreds whenever there is even a trace of visible Negro physical features."

The men who gathered for that meeting did not agree on how much to draw from American jurisprudence. The moderates at the table, among them the chair himself, Franz Gürtner, argued for

less onerous methods than the Americans were using. He suggested that "education and enlightenment" about "the perils of
race-mixing" might be enough to discourage Aryans from inter-
marrying with others. At one point, he sought to downplay the
U.S. prototype because he had a hard time believing that Americans actually enforced the laws the Nazis had uncovered. "Gürtner simply refused to concede that the Americans actually went so
far as to prosecute miscegenists," Whitman wrote.

One of the hard-liners at the table, the Nazi radical Roland
Freisler, was impatient with the pace of the proceedings. He had
joined the Nazi Party back in the 1920s and was pushing for a law
to punish Jews and Aryans for "racial treason" if they intermar-
ried. Time and again, he and the other extremists in the room
brought the discussion back to the American statutes, explained
and defended them and tried to convince the skeptics.

"How have they gone about doing this?" Freisler asked at one
point, breaking down his research into the United States and its
laws of human classification. The Americans, he explained, used a
range of motley parameters to separate white people from everyone else. One state, he said, classified as nonwhite any and all
"persons from Africa, Korea or Malaysia." In another example, he
said, "Nevada speaks of Ethiopians or of the black race, Malay-
sians or of the brown race, Mongols or of the yellow race." Freisler
argued that the overlapping contradictions could work to their
advantage. The tangle of American definitions lent a measure of
latitude and a useful inconsistency to the task of human division.
The Americans had come up with a definition of race apart from
logic or science, an approach that Freisler called the "political construction of race."

What the Nazis could not understand, however, was why, in
America, "the Jews, who are also of interest to us, are not reckoned
among the coloreds," when it was so obvious to the Nazis that
Jews were a separate "race" and when America had already shown
some aversion by imposing quotas on Jewish immigration. Aside
from what, to the Nazis, was a single vexing omission, "this juris-

prudence would suit us perfectly," said Freisler, who, unbeknownst to those at the table would one day be in a position to
make heartless use of it in his career as the hanging judge of the
Reich. "I am of the opinion that we need to proceed with the same
primitivity that is used by these American states," he said. "Such
a procedure would be crude but it would suffice."

The doubters continued to question the American statutes.
They went back and forth on exactly how a marriage ban would
work, parsed the proposed definitions of Jew and Aryan, tried to
make sense of the American fraction system. Moderates were disturbed by the idea that people who were half-Jewish and half-
Aryan would be cut off from their Aryan side and deprived of
caste privileges they would otherwise be accorded. Rather than
defining such people as half-Jewish, the skeptics wondered, would
they not also be half-Aryan? But one hard-liner, Achim Gercke,
referred back to the prototype they had been studying. He proposed a definition of one-sixteenth Jewish for classification of
Jews, Koonz wrote, "because he did not wish to be less rigorous
than the Americans."

The men debated for ten hours that day and ended without
agreement. "We have been talking past one another," Freisler,
frustrated by the lack of progress, said toward the end. The moderates had managed for now to contain the radicals who had
pushed for the American prototype. But fifteen months later, the
radicals would prevail.

In September 1935, Hitler summoned the Reichstag to the an-
nual Nazi rally in Nuremberg to announce new legislation that
had been incubating since the Nazi takeover. By then, Hitler had
either imprisoned or killed many of his political opponents, including the murders of twelve members of the Reichstag and of
his longtime friend Ernst Röhm, the head of a Nazi paramilitary
unit, the S.A. All of this rendered the Reichstag a puppet arm of
the government, having been intimidated into submission. At that
very moment, the Nazis were building concentration camps all

over the country. One was soon to open in Sachsenhausen, north of the Reich capital, and would become one of their "showcases."

The plan was to announce the legislation, ultimately known as the Blood Laws, on the final day of the rally. The night before, Hitler directed a small group of deputies to draft a version for him to deliver to the Reichstag to rubber-stamp. The Nazi researchers had come across a provision in some of the U.S. miscegenation laws that could help them define whether a person who was half-Jewish should count as a Jew or an Aryan. It turned out that Texas and North Carolina had an "association clause" in their marriage bans that helped those states decide if an ambiguous person was black or white, privileged or disfavored. Such a person would be counted in the disfavored group if they had been married to or had been known to associate with people in the disfavored group, thus defying caste purity.

This was what Hitler announced that September and expanded in the months to come: The Law for the Protection of German Blood and German Honor defined a Jew as a person with three Jewish grandparents. It also "counted" as Jewish anyone descended from two Jewish grandparents and who practiced Judaism or was accepted into the Jewish community or was married to a Jew, in line with the Americans' association clause.

Secondly, the law banned marriage and intercourse outside of marriage between Jews and Germans, and it forbade German women under forty-five to work in a Jewish household.

Thus began a campaign of ever-tightening restrictions. Jews were henceforth stripped of citizenship, prohibited from displaying the German flag, denied passports. With that announcement, "Germany became a full-fledged racist regime," the historian George M. Fredrickson wrote. "American laws were the main foreign precedents for such legislation."

But given the Nazis' own fixation on race, the American prototype had its limits. "The scholars who see parallels between the American and Nazi racial classification schemes are to that extent wrong," Whitman said, "but only because they understate the relative severity of American law."

As cataclysmic as the Nuremberg Laws were, the Nazis had not gone as far with the legislation as their research into America had taken them. What did not gain traction on the day of the closed-door session or in the final version of the Nuremberg Laws was one aspect of the American system. While the Nazis praised "the American commitment to legislating racial purity," they could not abide "the unforgiving hardness" under which "'an American man or woman who has even a drop of Negro blood in their veins' counted as blacks," Whitman wrote. "The one-drop rule was too harsh for the Nazis."

CHAPTER NINE

The Evil of Silence

The ash rose from the crematorium into the air, carried by karma and breeze, and settled onto the front steps and geranium beds of the townspeople living outside the gates of death at Sachsenhausen, north of Berlin. The ash coated the swing sets and paddling pools in the backyards of the townspeople.

There was no denying the slaughter and torment on the other side of the barbed wire. The fruit of evil fell upon villagers like snow dust. They were covered in evil, and some were good parents and capable spouses, and yet they did nothing to stop the evil, which had now grown too big for one person to stop, and thus no one person was complicit, and yet everyone was complicit. It had grown bigger than them because they had allowed it to grow bigger than them, and now it was raining down onto their gingerbread cottages and their lives of pristine conformity.

The dissident theologian Dietrich Bonhoeffer was one of the millions who suffered and perished behind the electrified walls of a Nazi concentration camp, tortured and kept in solitary confinement. Could the townspeople hear the prayers of the innocents? "Silence in the face of evil is itself evil," Bonhoeffer once said of bystanders. "God will not hold us guiltless. Not to speak is to speak. Not to act is to act."

The villagers were not all Nazis, in fact, many Germans were not Nazis. But they followed the Nazi leaders on the radio, waited to hear the latest from Hitler and Goebbels, the Nazis having seized the advantage of this new technology, the chance to reach Germans live and direct in their homes anytime they chose, an intravenous drip to the mind. The people had ingested the lies of an inherent Untermenschen, *that these prisoners—Jews, Sinti, homosexuals, opponents of the Reich—were not humans like themselves, and thus the townspeople swept the ash from their steps and carried on with their days. Mothers pulled their children inside when the wind kicked up, hurried them along, to keep them from being covered in the ash of fellow human beings.*

•

In the middle of Main Street in a southern American town, there stood a majestic old tree, an elm or an oak or a sycamore, that had been planted before modern roads were paved. It held a sacred place in the hearts of the townspeople, though it was an altogether inconvenient location for a shade tree. It blocked traffic, coming and going, and motorists were forced to curve around it to get through town. It was the potential cause of many accidents, given that motor-ists could not always see past it or know for sure who had the right of way.

And yet it could not be cut down. It was the local lynching tree, and it was performing its duty to "perpetually and eter-nally" remind the black townspeople of who among them had last been hanged from its limbs and who could be next. The tree was awaiting its appointed hour, and the white townspeople were willing to risk inconvenience, injury, and death, even to themselves, to keep the tree and the subordi-nate caste in their places. The tree bore silent witness to black citizens of their eternal lot, and in so doing, it whis-pered reassurances to the dominant caste of theirs.

•

The townspeople of the East Texas village of Leesburg ham-mered a buggy axle into the ground to serve as a stake. Then they chained nineteen-year-old Wylie McNeely to it. They collected the kindling they would use for the fire at the base of his feet, despite his protestations of innocence in connec-tion to the white girl they said he had assaulted. Five hun-dred people gathered that fall in 1921 to see Wylie McNeely burn to death in front of them. But first, the leaders of the lynching had to settle a matter of importance. The leaders drew lots to see who would get which piece of McNeely's body after they had burned him alive, figure out the body parts "which they regarded as the choicest souvenir." This they did in front of the young man facing his final seconds on this earth, there chained up and left to hear of the disposition of his fingers and ears to the men who had kidnapped him outside of the law. The leaders debated this in front of the five hundred people who had come to watch him die and who were impatient for the festivities to begin. After the men had decided and after all was settled, they lit the match.

•

The little girls appear to be in grade school, in light cotton dresses with a sailor's collar and their hair cut in precise pageboys just below their ears. In the picture the two younger girls seem to be fidgeting in shadow, close to the women in the group, who were perhaps their mothers or aunts. The girl you notice first, though, looks to be about ten years old, positioned at the front of the group of grown-ups and children, her eyes alert and riveted. A man is at her side, crisp in his tailored white pants, white shirt, and white Panama hat, as if headed to cocktail hour at a boating party, his arms folded, face at rest, unperturbed, vaguely bored.

It is July 19, 1935. They are all standing at the base of a tree in the pine woods of Fort Lauderdale, Florida. Above them hangs the limp body of Rubin Stacy, his overalls torn and bloodied, riddled with bullets, his hands cuffed in front of him, head snapped from the lynching rope, killed for frightening a white woman. The girl in the front is looking up at the dead black man with wonderment rather than hor-

ror, a smile of excitement on her face as if show ponies had just galloped past her at the circus. The fascination on her young face set against the gruesome nature of the gathering was captured by a photographer and is among the most widely circulated of all lynching photographs of twentieth-century America.

Lynchings were part carnival, part torture chamber, and attracted thousands of onlookers who collectively became accomplices to public sadism. Photographers were tipped off in advance and installed portable printing presses at the lynching sites to sell to lynchers and onlookers like photographers at a prom. They made postcards out of the gelatin prints for people to send to their loved ones. People mailed postcards of the severed, half-burned head of Will James atop a pole in Cairo, Illinois, in 1907. They sent postcards of burned torsos that looked like the petrified victims of Vesuvius, only these horrors had come at the hands of human beings in modern times. Some people framed the lynching photographs with locks of the victim's hair under glass if they had been able to secure any. One spectator wrote on the back of his postcard from Waco, Texas, in 1916: "This is the Barbecue we had last night my picture is to the left with the cross over it your son Joe."

This was singularly American. "Even the Nazis did not stoop to selling souvenirs of Auschwitz," wrote Time magazine many years later. Lynching postcards were so common a form of communication in turn-of-the-twentieth-century

America that lynching scenes "became a burgeoning sub-department of the postcard industry. By 1908, the trade had grown so large, and the practice of sending postcards featuring the victims of mob murderers had become so repugnant, that the U.S. postmaster general banned the cards from the mails." But the new edict did not stop Americans from sharing their lynching exploits. From then on, they merely put the postcards in an envelope.

•

In downtown Omaha, they started a bonfire and readied it for Will Brown. The newspapers had advertised the lynching in advance, and as many as fifteen thousand people gathered on the courthouse square that day in September 1919, so many people that one cannot make out the faces in the human sea in a wide shot taken from above. These thousands of dots on a gelatin print—fathers, grandfathers, uncles, nephews, brothers, teenagers—were of one mind, had fused into an organism unto itself, intent on a single mission, not only to kill but to humiliate, torture, and incinerate another human being, and, together, to breathe in the smoke of burning flesh.

Two days before, a white woman and her boyfriend had said that a black man had molested her when the couple were out on the town. No one alive knows what happened for sure, and there were questions even then. Resentment had been building against the influx of black southerners arriv-

ing north during the Great Migration, and Will Brown, a packinghouse worker, was the man the sheriffs arrested. There was no investigation, no due process. That day, the mob looted guns from local pawnshops and general stores and fired on the courthouse where Brown had been detained.

Before they could even get to him, the mob killed two of their own—a bystander and a fellow rioter—with their ragged gunshots. They set the courthouse on fire to force the sheriff to hand Brown over to them. They cut the water hoses to keep the firefighters from putting out the blaze. And when the mayor tried to appeal to the mob, the leaders put a rope around his neck, and inflicted injuries that put him in the hospital.

The leaders of the mob pulled Brown from the rooftop of the courthouse where the courthouse workers had escaped from the fire and where the prisoners had been taken. Then the people in the mob began the task for which they had gathered. First, they stripped Will Brown, and those up front fought each other to beat him. They hoisted him, half-conscious, onto a lamppost outside the courthouse. Then they fired bullets into his dangling body, cheering as they fired, and it was from these gunshots that the coroner said Brown died. They burned his body in the bonfire they had made on the courthouse square. Then they tied the body to a police car and dragged the corpse through the streets of Omaha.

They cut the pieces of rope they had used to hoist him,

and these they sold as keepsakes for people's display cabinets and fireplace mantels. The photographers on the scene captured the lynching from different angles and produced postcards of the men in business suits and teenagers in newsboy hats posing as if at a wedding reception, crowding into the frame above the charred torso, sparks of fire amid the ash, an image they would send to cousins and in-laws and former neighbors around the country.

A fourteen-year-old boy was helping his father at his printing plant across the street from the courthouse in the middle of the riot. The boy's name was Henry Fonda, and he would leave Omaha when he grew up and make a name for himself as a leading man in Hollywood.

That evening in 1919, against the hollers of the mob and the man hanging from a lamppost and the cinders of the bonfire, Fonda and his father locked the plant, and drove home in silence. "It was the most horrendous sight I've ever seen," he would say years later when he was an old man. The decades had not swept the ash from his memory.

It was perhaps no coincidence that he would appear in many movies in which he was the moral voice calling for a life to be spared. In the 1943 film The Ox-Bow Incident, *about vigilante violence, it is Fonda's character who warns a blood-lusting mob: "Man just naturally can't take the law into his own hands, and hang people, without hurting everybody in the world."*

Part Three

The Eight
Pillars of Caste

The Origins of Our Discontents

These are the historic origins, the pillars upholding a belief system, the piers beneath the surface of a caste hierarchy. As these tenets took root in the firmament, it did not matter so much whether the assumptions were true, as most were not. It mattered little that they were misperceptions or distortions of convenience, as long as people accepted them and gained a sense of order and means of justification for the cruelties to which they had grown accustomed, inequalities that they took to be the laws of nature.

These are the pillars of caste, the ancient principles that I researched and compiled as I examined the parallels, overlap, and commonalities of three major caste hierarchies. These are the principles upon which a caste system is constructed, whether in America, India, or Nazi Germany, beliefs that were at one time or another burrowed deep within the culture and collective subconscious of most every inhabitant, in order for a caste system to function.

Divine Will and the Laws of Nature

Before the age of human awareness, according to the ancient Hindu text of India, Manu, the all-knowing, was seated in contemplation, when the great men approached him and asked him, "Please, Lord, tell us precisely and in the proper order the Laws of all the social classes as well as of those born in between."

Manu proceeded to tell of a time when the universe as we know it was in a deep sleep, and the One "who is beyond the range of senses," brought forth the waters and took birth himself as Brahma, the "grandfather of all the worlds."

And then, to fill the land, he created the Brahmin, the highest caste, from his mouth, the Kshatriya from his arms, the Vaishya from his thighs, and, from his feet, the Shudra, the lowest of the four *varnas*, or divisions of man, millennia ago and into the fullness of time.

The fragment from which each caste was formed foretold the position that each would fill and their placement, in order, in the caste system. From lowest to highest, bottom to top: The Shudra, the feet, the servant, the bearer of burdens. The Vaishya, the thighs, the engine, the merchant, the trader. The Kshatriya, the arms, the warrior, the protector, the ruler. And above them all, the Brahmin, the head, the mouth, the philosopher, the sage, the priest, the one nearest to the gods.

"The Brahmin is by Law the lord of this whole creation," according to the Laws of Manu. "It is by the kindness of the Brahmin that other people eat."

Unmentioned among the original four *varnas* were those deemed so low that they were beneath even the feet of the Shudra. They were living out the afflicted karma of the past, they were not to be touched and some not even to be seen. Their very shadow was a pollutant. They were outside of the caste system and thus outcastes. These were the Untouchables who would later come to be known as Dalits, the subordinate caste of India.

———

In the words of the sacred text of the Western world, the Old Testament, there had been a Great Flood. The windows of heaven had opened, along with the fountains of the deep, and all of humankind was said to have descended from the three sons of the patriarch Noah. By divine instruction, they survived the floodwaters in an ark, for more than forty days and forty nights, and thereafter, Noah became a man of the soil. His sons were Shem, Ham, and Japheth, who would become the progenitors of all humanity.

One season, Noah planted a vineyard, and he later drank of the wine of the fruit of the vineyard. The wine overtook him, and he lay uncovered inside his tent. Ham, who would become the father of a son, Canaan, happened into the tent and saw his father's nakedness and told his two brothers outside. Shem and Japheth took a garment and laid it across their shoulders. They walked backward into the tent and covered their father's nakedness. Their faces were turned in the other direction so that they would not see their father unclothed. When Noah awoke from his wine and found out what Ham had done, he cursed Ham's son, Canaan, and the generations to follow, saying, "Cursed be Canaan! The lowest of slaves will he be to his brothers."

The story of Ham's discovery of Noah's nakedness would pass down through the millennia. The sons of Shem, Ham, and Japheth spread across the continents, Shem to the east, Ham to the south,

Japheth to the west, it was said. Those who decreed themselves the descendants of Japheth would hold fast to that story and translate it to their advantage. As the riches from the slave trade from Africa to the New World poured forth to the Spaniards, to the Portuguese, to the Dutch, and lastly to the English, the biblical passage would be summoned to condemn the children of Ham and to justify the kidnap and enslavement of millions of human beings, and the violence against them. From the time of the Middle Ages, some interpreters of the Old Testament described Ham as bearing black skin and translated Noah's curse against him as a curse against the descendants of Ham, against all humans with dark skin, the people who the Europeans told themselves had been condemned to enslavement by God's emissary, Noah himself.

They found further comfort in Leviticus, which exhorted them, "Both thy bondmen, and thy bondmaids, which thou shalt have, shall be of the heathen that are round about you; of them shall ye buy bondmen and bondmaids." This they took as further license to enslave those they considered religious heathens to build a new country out of wilderness.

And thus, a hierarchy evolved in the New World they created, one that set those with the lightest skin above those with the darkest. Those who were darkest, and those who descended from those who were darkest, would be assigned to the subordinate caste of America for centuries.

"The curse of Ham is now being executed upon his descendants," Thomas R. R. Cobb, a leading Confederate and defender of slavery, wrote, 240 years into the era of human bondage in America. "The great Architect had framed them both physically and mentally to fill the sphere in which they were thrown. His wisdom and mercy combined in constituting them thus suited to the degraded position they were destined to occupy."

Slavery officially ended in 1865, but the structure of caste remained intact, not only surviving but hardening. "Let the negro have the crumbs that fall from the white man's table," Thomas

Pearce Bailey, a twentieth-century author, recorded in his list of the caste codes of the American South, echoing the Indian Laws of Manu.

The United States and India would become, respectively, the oldest and the largest democracies in human history, both built on caste systems undergirded by their reading of the sacred texts of their respective cultures. In both countries, the subordinate castes were consigned to the bottom, seen as deserving of their debasement, owing to the sins of the past.

These tenets, as interpreted by those who put themselves on high, would become the divine and spiritual foundation for the belief in a human pyramid willed by God, a Great Chain of Being, that the founders would further sculpt in the centuries to follow, as circumstances required. And so we have what could be called the first pillar of caste, Divine Will and the Laws of Nature, the first of the organizing principles inherent in any caste system.

Heritability

To work, each caste society relied on clear lines of demarcation in which everyone was ascribed a rank at birth, and a role to perform, as if each person were a molecule in a self-perpetuating organism. You were born to a certain caste and remained in that caste, subject to the high status or low stigma it conferred, for the rest of your days and into the lives of your descendants. Thus, heritability became the second pillar of caste.

In India, it was generally the father who passed his rank to his children. In America, dating back to colonial Virginia, children inherited the caste of their mother both by law and by custom. And in disputes beyond these parameters, a child was generally to take the status of the lower-ranking parent.

The Virginia General Assembly declared the status of all people born in the colony. "Whereas some doubts have arisen whether children got by any Englishman upon a negro woman should be slave or free," the Assembly decreed in 1662, "be it therefore enacted and declared by this present Grand Assembly, that all children borne in this country shall be held bond or free only according to the condition of the mother."

With this decree, the colonists were breaking from English legal precedent, the only precepts they had ever known, the ancient order that gave children the status of the father. This new law allowed enslavers to claim the children of black women, the vast majority of whom were enslaved, as their property for life and for ensuing generations. It invited them to impregnate the women themselves if so inclined, the richer it would make them. It converted the black womb into a profit center and drew sharper lines around the subordinate caste, as neither mother nor child could make a claim against an upper-caste man, and no child springing from a black womb could escape condemnation to the lowest rung. It moved the colonies toward a bipolar hierarchy of whites and nonwhites, and specifically a conjoined caste of whites at one end of the ladder and, at the other end, those deemed black, due to any physical manifestation of African ancestry.

Tied conveniently as it was to what one looked like, membership in either the upper or the lowest caste was deemed immutable, primordial, fixed from birth to death, and thus regarded as inescapable. "He may neither earn nor wed his way out," wrote the scholars Allison Davis and Burleigh and Mary Gardner in *Deep South*, their seminal 1941 study of caste in America.

It is the fixed nature of *caste* that distinguishes it from *class*, a term to which it is often compared. Class is an altogether separate measure of one's standing in a society, marked by level of education, income, and occupation, as well as the attendant characteristics, such as accent, taste, and manners, that flow from socioeconomic status. These can be acquired through hard work and ingenuity or lost through poor decisions or calamity. If you can act your way out of it, then it is class, not caste. Through the years, wealth and class may have insulated some people born to the subordinate caste in America but not protected them from humiliating attempts to put them in their place or to remind them of their caste position.

Centuries after the American caste system took shape along the Chesapeake, the most accomplished of lower-caste people have often found ways to transcend caste, but rarely to fully escape it.

"Like the Hindu caste system, the black-white distinction in the United States has supplied a social hierarchy determined at birth, and arguably immutable, even by achievement," wrote the legal scholars Raymond T. Diamond and Robert J. Cottrol. "Blacks became like a group of American untouchables, ritually separated from the rest of the population."

In the winter of 2013, the Academy Award–winning actor Forest Whitaker, a distinguished, middle-aged, African-American man, walked into a gourmet delicatessen on the West Side of Manhattan for a bite to eat. Seeing it crowded or not finding what he wanted, he turned to leave without making a purchase, as many customers might. An employee thought it suspicious and blocked him at the door. That level of intervention was uncharacteristic at an establishment frequented by celebrities and college students. The employee frisked him up and down in front of other customers. Finding nothing, he allowed Whitaker, visibly shaken, to leave. The delicatessen owners later apologized for the incident and fired the employee. But the degradation of that moment stayed with the actor. "It's a humiliating thing for someone to come and do that," Whitaker said afterward. "It's attempted disempowerment."

Neither wealth nor celebrity has insulated those born to the subordinate caste from the police brutality that seems disproportionately trained on those at the bottom of the hierarchy. In 2015, New York City police officers broke an NBA player's leg outside of a nightclub in Manhattan. The injury left the player, a forward for the Atlanta Hawks, disabled for the rest of the season. It resulted in a $4 million settlement, the proceeds of which the player promptly said he would donate to a foundation for public defenders.

In 2018, police officers slammed a former NFL player to the ground after a disagreement he had with another motorist who had thrown coffee at his car, according to news reports. The video that surfaced that spring shows officers twisting Desmond Marrow's arms and legs and shoving him facedown onto the pavement. Then they turn him over and hold him down by the throat. He passes out under their weight. After the video went viral, an internal investigation was conducted and an officer was fired.

"No matter how great you become in life, no matter how wealthy you become, how people worship you, or what you do," NBA star LeBron James told reporters just the year before, "if you are an African-American man or African-American woman, you will always be that."

Endogamy and the Control
of Marriage and Mating

The framers of the American caste system took steps, early in its founding, to keep the castes separate and to seal off the bloodlines of those assigned to the upper rung. This desire led to the third pillar of caste—endogamy, which means restricting marriage to people within the same caste. This is an ironclad foundation of any caste system, from ancient India, to the early American colonies, to the Nazi regime in Germany. Endogamy was brutally enforced in the United States for the vast majority of its history and did the spade work for current ethnic divisions.

Endogamy enforces caste boundaries by forbidding marriage outside of one's group and going so far as to prohibit sexual relations, or even the appearance of romantic interest, across caste lines. It builds a firewall between castes and becomes the primary means of keeping resources and affinity within each tier of the caste system. Endogamy, by closing off legal family connection, blocks the chance for empathy or a sense of shared destiny between the castes. It makes it less likely that someone in the dominant caste will have a personal stake in the happiness, fulfillment, or well-being of anyone deemed beneath them or personally identify with them or their plight. Endogamy, in fact, makes it more likely that those in the dominant caste will see those deemed beneath them as not only less than human but as an enemy, as not of their kind, and as a threat that must be held in check at all costs.

"Caste," wrote Bhimrao Ambedkar, the father of the anti-caste movement in India, "means an artificial chopping off of the population into fixed and definite units, each one prevented from fusing into another through the custom of endogamy." Thus, "in showing how endogamy is maintained," he added, "we shall practically have proved the genesis and also the mechanism of Caste."

Before there was a United States of America, there was endogamy, said to be ordained by God. One of the earliest references to what would come to be known as race in America arose over the matter of sexual relations between a European and an African. In 1630, the Virginia General Assembly sentenced Hugh Davis to a public whipping for having "abused himself to the dishonor of God and the shame of Christians, by defiling his body in lying with a Negro." The assembly went to the trouble of specifying that Africans, who might not normally be permitted to observe the punishment of a dominant-caste man, had to attend and witness the whipping of Davis. This served a dual function in the emerging caste system. It further humiliated Davis before an audience of people deemed beneath him. And it signaled a warning to those being banished to the lowest caste in a country that did not yet even exist: *If this was the fate of a white man who did not adhere to caste boundaries, so much worse will it be for you.*

By the time of Davis's sentencing, European men had been having sex with African women, often without consent or consequence to themselves, throughout the era of the slave trade, and had grown accustomed to acting upon their presumed sovereignty over Africans. So, for the colonial fathers to condemn Hugh Davis to public humiliation for behavior that many took as a birthright meant that he had crossed a line they found threatening to the hierarchy, something about the way he related to his mate that got their attention and required their intervention. The emerging caste system permitted the exploitation of the lowest caste but not equality, or the appearance of equality, which is why endogamy, which confers an alliance between equals in the eyes of the law, was strictly policed and rape of lower-caste women ignored. The case of Hugh Davis was not only the first mention of race and hierarchy in America, but also the first attempt at setting the boundaries of publicly known relationships across caste lines.

Ten years later, another white man, Robert Sweet, was forced to do penance when it came to light that he had gotten an enslaved black woman, owned by another white man, pregnant. By then, the focus of caste enforcement had shifted. In that case, it was the pregnant woman who was whipped, a sign of her degraded caste status despite a medical condition that would have protected her in most civilized nations.

In 1691, Virginia became the first colony to outlaw marriage between blacks and whites, a ban that the majority of states would take up for the next three centuries. Some states forbade the marriage of whites to Asians or Native Americans in addition to African-Americans, who were uniformly excluded. While there was never a single nationwide ban on intermarriage, despite several attempts to enact one, forty-one of the fifty states passed laws making intermarriage a crime punishable by fines of up to $5,000 and up to ten years in prison. Some states went so far as to forbid the passage of any *future* law permitting intermarriage. Outside of the law, particularly in the South, African-Americans faced penalty of death for even the appearance of breaching this pillar of caste.

The Supreme Court did not overturn these prohibitions until 1967. Still, some states were slow to officially repeal their endogamy laws. Alabama, the last state to do so, did not throw out its law against intermarriage until the year 2000. Even then, 40 percent of the electorate in that referendum voted in favor of keeping the marriage ban on the books.

It was the caste system, through the practice of endogamy—essentially state regulation of people's romantic choices over the course of centuries—that created and reinforced "races," by permitting only those with similar physical traits to legally mate. Combined with bans on immigrants who were not from Europe for much of American history, endogamy laws had the effect of controlled breeding, of curating the population of the United States. This form of social engineering served to maintain the superficial differences upon which the hierarchy was based, "race" ultimately becoming the result of who was officially allowed to procreate with whom. Endogamy ensures the very difference that a caste system relies on to justify inequality.

"What we look like," wrote the legal scholar Ian Haney López, "the literal and 'racial' features we in this country exhibit, is to a large extent the product of legal rules and decisions."

This pillar of caste was well enough understood and accepted that, as late as 1958, a Gallup poll found that 94 percent of white Americans disapproved of marriage across racial lines. "You know the Negro race is inferior mentally," a southern physician told researchers back in 1940, expressing a commonly held view. "Everyone knows that, and I don't think God meant for a superior race like the whites to blend with an inferior race."

As this was the prevailing sentiment for most of the country's history, an unknowable number of lives were lost due to this defining pillar of caste, the presumed breach of which triggered the most publicized cases of lynchings in America. The protocol was strictly enforced against lower-caste men and upper-caste women, while upper-caste men, the people who wrote the laws, kept full and flagrant access to lower-caste women, whatever their age or marital status. In this way, the dominant gender of the dominant caste, in addition to controlling the livelihood and life chances of everyone beneath them, eliminated the competition for its own women and in fact for all women. For much of American history, dominant-caste men controlled who had access to whom for romantic liaisons and reproduction.

This inverted the natural expression of manhood—total freedom for one group and life-or-death policing of another—and served further to reinforce caste boundaries and the powerlessness of subordinated men who might dare try to protect their own daughters, wives, sisters, and mothers. At the same time, it reminded everyone in the hierarchy of the absolute power of dominant-caste men. This was a cloud that hung over the lives of everyone consigned to the lowest caste for most of the time that there has been a United States of America.

In the mid-1830s in Grand Gulf, Mississippi, white men burned a black man alive and stuck his head on a pole at the edge of town for all to see, as a lesson to men in the subordinate caste. The black man had been tortured and beheaded after he stood up and killed the dominant-caste man "who owned his wife and was in the habit of sleeping with her," according to a contemporaneous account. As he faced death for taking an extreme and assuredly suicidal step to protect his wife in that world, the doomed husband said that "he believed he should be rewarded in heaven for it."

More than a century later, in December 1943, an earnest fifteen-year-old boy named Willie James Howard was working during the holiday school break at a dime store in Live Oak, Florida. He was an only child and, having made it to the tenth grade, was expected to exceed what anyone else in the family had been able to accomplish. That December, he made a fateful gesture, unknowing or unmindful of a central pillar of caste. He was hopeful and excited about his new job and wanted so badly to do well that he sent Christmas cards to everyone at work. In one Christmas card, the one to a girl his age named Cynthia, who worked there and whom he had a crush on, he signed, "with L" (for love).

It would seem an ordinary gesture for that time of the year, sweet even, but this was the Jim Crow South; the boy was black, and the girl was white. She showed the card to her father. Word got back to Willie James that his card had somehow disturbed her. So, on New Year's Day 1944, he hand-delivered an apologetic note trying to explain himself: "I know you don't think much of our kind of people but we don't hate you, all we want [is] to be your friends but you [won't] let us please don't let anybody else see this I hope I haven't made you mad. . . ." He added a rhyme: "I love your name, I love your voice, for a S.H. (sweetheart) you are my choice."

The next day, the girl's father and two other white men dragged Willie James and his father to the banks of the Suwannee River. They hog-tied Willie James and held a gun to his head. They forced him to jump and forced his father at gunpoint to watch him drown. Held captive and outnumbered as the father was, he was helpless to save his only child.

The men admitted to authorities that they had abducted the boy and bound his hands and feet. They said he just jumped and drowned on his own. Within days, the boy's parents fled for their lives. A young Thurgood Marshall of the NAACP alerted the Florida governor, to no avail. The NAACP field secretary, Harry T. Moore, managed to convince the boy's parents to overcome their terror and to sign affidavits about what had happened the day their son was killed. A local grand jury refused to indict the boy's abductors, and federal prosecutors would not intervene.

No one was ever held to account or spent a day in jail for the death of Willie James. His abduction and death were seen as upholding the caste order. Thus the terrors of the southern caste system continued, carried forth without penalty. Sanctioned as it was by the U.S. government, the caste system had become not simply southern, but American.

Purity versus Pollution

The fourth pillar of caste rests upon the fundamental belief in the purity of the dominant caste and the fear of pollution from the castes deemed beneath it. Over the centuries, the dominant caste has taken extreme measures to protect its sanctity from the perceived taint of the lower castes. Both India and the United States at the zenith of their respective caste systems, and the short-lived but heinous regime of the Nazis, raised the obsession with purity to a high, if absurdist, art.

In some parts of India, the lowest-caste people were to remain a certain number of paces from any dominant-caste person while walking out in public—somewhere between twelve and ninety-six steps away, depending on the castes in question. They had to wear bells to alert those deemed above them so as not to pollute them with their presence. A person in the lowest subcastes in the Maratha region had to "drag a thorny branch with him to wipe out his footprints" and prostrate himself on the ground if a Brahmin passed, so that his "foul shadow might not defile the holy Brahmin."

Touching or drawing near to anything that had been touched by an Untouchable was considered polluting to the upper castes and required rituals of purification for the high-caste person following this misfortune. This they might do by bathing at once in flowing water or performing Pranayama breaths along with meditation to cleanse themselves of the pollutants.

In Germany, the Nazis banned Jewish residents from stepping onto the beaches at the Jews' own summer homes, as at Wannsee, a resort suburb of Berlin, and at public pools in the Reich. "They believed the entire pool would be polluted by immersion in it of a Jewish body," Jean-Paul Sartre once observed.

In the United States, the subordinate caste was quarantined in every sphere of life, made untouchable on American terms, for most of the country's history and well into the twentieth century. In the South, where most people in the subordinate caste were long consigned, black children and white children studied from separate sets of textbooks. In Florida, the books for black children and white children could not even be stored together. African-Americans were prohibited from using white water fountains and had to drink from horse troughs in the southern swelter before the era of separate fountains. In southern jails, the bedsheets for the black prisoners were kept separate from the bedsheets for the white prisoners. All private and public human activities were segregated from birth to death, from hospital wards to railroad platforms to ambulances, hearses, and cemeteries. In stores, black people were prohibited from trying on clothing, shoes, hats, or gloves, assuming they were permitted in the store at all. If a black person happened to die in a public hospital, "the body will be placed in a corner of the 'dead house' away from the white corpses," wrote the historian Bertram Doyle in 1937.

This pillar of caste was enshrined into law in the United States in 1896, after a New Orleans man challenged an 1890 Louisiana law that separated "the white and colored races" in railroad cars. Louisiana had passed the law after the collapse of Reconstruction and the return to power of the former Confederates. A committee of concerned citizens of color came together and raised money to fight the law in court. On the appointed day, June 7, 1892, Homer A. Plessy, a shoemaker who looked white but was categorized as black under the American definition of race, bought a first-class ticket from New Orleans to Covington on the East Louisiana Railroad and took his seat in the whites-only car. In that era, a person of ambiguous racial origin was presumed not to be white, so the conductor ordered him to the colored car. Plessy refused and was arrested, as the committee had anticipated. His case went to the Supreme Court, which ruled seven to one in favor of Louisiana's "separate but equal" law. It set in motion nearly seven decades of formal, state-sanctioned isolation and exclusion of one caste from the other in the United States.

In southern courtrooms, even the word of God was segregated. There were two separate Bibles—one for blacks and one for whites—to swear to tell the truth on. The same sacred object could not be touched by hands of different races.

This pillar of purity, as with the others, endangered the lives of the people in the subordinate caste. One day in the 1930s, a black railroad switchman was working in Memphis and slipped and fell beneath a switch engine. He lay bleeding to death, his right arm and leg severed. "Ambulances rushed to the man's aid," according to reports of the incident. "They took one look, saw that he was a Negro, and backed away."

The Sanctity of Water

The waters and shorelines of nature were forbidden to the subordinate castes if the dominant caste so desired. Well into the twentieth century, African-Americans were banned from white beaches and lakes and pools, both north and south, lest they pollute them, just as Dalits were forbidden from the waters of the Brahmins, and Jews from Aryan waters in the Third Reich.

This was a sacred principle in the United States well into the second half of the twentieth century, and the dominant caste went to great lengths to enforce it. In the early 1950s, when Cincinnati agreed under pressure to allow black swimmers into some of its public pools, whites threw nails and broken glass into the water to keep them out. In the 1960s, a black civil rights activist tried to integrate a public pool by swimming a lap and then emerging to towel off. "The response was to drain the pool entirely," wrote the legal historian Mark S. Weiner, "and refill it with fresh water."

Decades before, in 1919, a black boy paid with his life and set off a riot in Chicago for inadvertently breaching this pillar of caste. Seventeen-year-old Eugene Williams was swimming in Lake Michigan, at a public beach on the city's South Side, and happened to wade past the imaginary line that separated the races. He unknowingly passed into the white water, which flowed into and looked no different from the black water. He was stoned and drowned to death for doing so. The tensions over the breaching of boundaries that summer incited the dominant caste and set off one of the worst race riots in U.S. history.

In the decades after, in middle American places like Newton, Kansas, and Marion, Indiana, in Pittsburgh and St. Louis, people in the upper caste rose up in hysterics at the sight of a subordinate-caste person approaching their water. In August 1931, a new public park opened in Pittsburgh, with pools the size of a football field and big enough for ten thousand swimmers. But soon afterward, as the *Pittsburgh Post-Gazette* reported, "each Negro who entered the pool yesterday was immediately surrounded by whites and slugged or held beneath the water until he gave up his attempts to swim and left."

In the summer of 1949, the city of St. Louis had what was considered the largest city pool in the country, at its Fairground Park. When the city, under pressure from black citizens, took up the issue of allowing black people into the pool, the backlash was immediate. A man who happened to have the same name as the official in charge of integrating the pool required police protection due to the mistaken threats against him. Lifeguards considered quitting in protest.

The day the first African-Americans arrived to swim, a crowd gathered with knives, bricks, and bats. They set upon the black children who had come to swim, forcing them to walk a gauntlet, striking and taunting them. The mob grew to five thousand people, who chased after any black person they saw approaching the park—children on bicycles, a man stepping off a streetcar, a truck stalled in traffic, a black man on a porch at a house next to the park. They kicked him as he lay on the ground, limp and bleeding.

The town of Newton, Kansas, went to the state supreme court to keep black people out of the pool it built in 1935. The city and its contractor argued that black people could never be permitted in the pool, not on alternate days, not at separate hours, not ever, because of the type of pool it was. They told the court that it was "a circulatory type of pool," in which "the water is only changed once during the swimming season." White people, they argued, would not go into water that had touched black skin. "The only way white residents would swim in a pool after blacks," wrote the historian Jeff Wiltse, "was if the water was drained and the tank scrubbed." The operators couldn't do all that every time a black person went into the pool, so they banned black people altogether. The court sided with the city, and, for decades more, the town's only public pool remained for the exclusive use of the dominant caste.

A public pool outside Pittsburgh solved this problem by keeping black people out until after the season was over in September, which meant it was closed to black swimmers at the precise time that they or anyone else would have wanted to use it. The manager said this was the only way the maintenance crew could get "sufficient time to properly cleanse and disinfect it after the Negroes have used it."

A white woman in Marion, Indiana, seemed to be speaking for many in the dominant caste across America when she said that white people wouldn't swim with colored people because they "didn't want to be polluted by their blackness." Far from her, in Elizabeth, New Jersey, whites blocked African-Americans at the stairwells and entrances the week the city first allowed black swimmers to its public pool. There, and elsewhere, "every black swimmer that entered the water quite literally risked his or her life," Wiltse wrote.

It was in this atmosphere, in 1951, that a Little League baseball team in Youngstown, Ohio, won the city championship. The coaches, unthinkingly, decided to celebrate with a team picnic at a municipal pool. When the team arrived at the gate, a lifeguard stopped one of the Little Leaguers from entering. It was Al Bright, the only black player on the team. His parents had not been able to attend the picnic, and the coaches and some of the other parents tried to persuade the pool officials to let the little boy in, to no avail. The only thing the lifeguards were willing to do was to let them set a blanket for him outside the fence and to let people bring him food. He was given little choice and had to watch his team-mates splash in the water and chase each other on the pool deck while he sat alone on the outside.

"From time to time, one or another of the players or adults came out and sat with him before returning to join the others," his childhood friend, the author Mel Watkins, would write years later.

It took an hour or so for a team official to finally convince the lifeguards "that they should at least allow the child into the pool for a few minutes." The supervisor agreed to let the Little Leaguer in, but only if everyone else got out of the water, and only if Al followed the rules they set for him.

First, everyone—meaning his teammates, the parents, all the white people—had to get out of the water. Once everyone cleared out, "Al was led to the pool and placed in a small rubber raft," Watkins wrote. A lifeguard got into the water and pushed the raft with Al in it for a single turn around the pool, as a hundred or so teammates, coaches, parents, and onlookers watched from the sidelines.

After the "agonizing few minutes" that it took to complete the circle, Al was then "escorted to his assigned spot" on the other side of the fence. During his short time in the raft, as it glided on the surface, the lifeguard warned him over and over again of one important thing. "Just don't touch the water," the lifeguard said, as he pushed the rubber float. "Whatever you do, don't touch the water."

The lifeguard managed to keep the water pure that day, but a part of that little boy died that afternoon. When one of the coaches offered him a ride home, he declined. "With champion trophy in hand," Watkins wrote, Al walked the mile or so back home by himself. He was never the same after that.

The Hierarchy of Trace Amounts:

Griffes, Marabons, and Sangmelees

The American caste system was an accelerated one, compressed into a fraction of the time that India's caste system has been in existence. Its founders used the story of Noah and his sons to justify the bottom of the hierarchy but, without further biblical instruction, as in the Laws of Manu, they shaped the upper caste as they went along. This policing of purity in the United States began with the task of defining the dominant caste itself.

While all the countries in the New World created hierarchies with Europeans on top, the United States alone created a system based on racial absolutism, the idea that a single drop of African blood, or varying percentages of Asian or Native American blood, could taint the purity of someone who might otherwise be presumed to be European, a stain that would thus disqualify the person from admittance to the dominant caste. This was a punitive model of racial superiority as opposed to the South African model, which rewarded those with any proximity to whiteness and created an official mid-caste of colored people as a buffer between black and white. South Africa granted privileges on a graded scale based on how much European blood was thought to be coursing through one's veins, seeing "white" blood as a cleansing antiseptic to that of lowlier groups in the purity-pollution paradigm. Both were forms of white supremacy crafted to fit the demographics of each country. South Africa's white minority had an incentive to grow its power and numbers by granting honorary whiteness to those deemed close enough. The white majority in the United

States had no such incentive and, in fact, benefited by elevating itself and holding those fewer in number apart and beneath them to serve as their subordinates.

"Degradation, resulting from the taint of blood, adheres to the descendants of Ham in this country, like the poisoned tunic of Nessus," wrote Joseph Henry Lumpkin, the antebellum chief justice of the Georgia Supreme Court, managing to combine Greek mythology and two pillars of caste—divine will and pollution —into a single ruling. (The mythical tunic was the blood-soaked garment of the fallen centaur Nessus, which came to represent inescapable misfortune and ruin to those who wore it.)

The founders labored from the start over who should be allowed into the dominant caste. The vast majority of human beings, including many who are now considered white, would not have fit their definition. Twenty-five years before the American Revolution, Benjamin Franklin worried that, with its growing German population, Pennsylvania would "become a Colony of Aliens, who will shortly be so numerous as to Germanize us, instead of our Anglifying them, and will never adopt our Language or Customs any more than they can acquire our Complexion."

Ultimately, the dominant caste used immigration and marriage law to control who could join its ranks and who would be excluded. That took constant redefinition. "The law could not separate what it failed to categorize," wrote the legal scholars Raymond T. Diamond and Robert J. Cottrol. "A legally mandated caste system needed at a minimum to define caste membership."

At first, Congress, in 1790, restricted American citizenship to white immigrants, "free white persons," according to the statute. But "whiteness" had yet to be settled, and by the mid-nineteenth century, with millions of people immigrating from Germany and fleeing famine in Ireland, supremacists on both sides of the Atlantic fretted over what was to become of a country flooded by "the most degenerate races of olden day Europe," in the words of Arthur de Gobineau, a widely read nineteenth-century advocate of Aryan supremacy. "They are the human flotsam of all ages: Irish,

cross-bred Germans and French, and Italians of even more doubt-
ful stock."

For most of American history, anyone not Anglo-Saxon fell
somewhere on a descending scale of human "pollution." Like a
field marshal defending his flanks in multiple theaters, the dominant caste fought the "tainted" influx of new immigrants with two
of the most stringent immigration bans ever enacted, just before
and after the turn of the twentieth century.

The country tried to block the flow of Chinese immigrants into
the western states with the Chinese Exclusion Act of 1882. Then it
turned to the immigrants arriving from southern and eastern Europe, the "scum and offscouring," as a former Virginia governor
put it, newcomers who purportedly brought crime and disease
and polluted the bloodlines of America's original white stock.
Congress commissioned an analysis of the crisis, an influential
document known as the Dillingham Report, and the House Committee on Immigration and Naturalization called hearings as the
United States tried to further curate its population.

"The moral fiber of the nation has been weakened and its very
life-blood vitiated by the influx of this tide of oriental scum," Rev.
M. D. Lichliter, a minister from Harrisburg, Pennsylvania, said in
his testimony before the committee in 1910. "Our grand Anglo-
Saxon character must be preserved, and the pure unmixed blood
flowing down from our Aryan progenitors must not be mixed
with the Iberic race," a term applied to southern Italians in the era
of eugenics.

The findings set the stage for the 1924 Immigration Act, which
restricted immigration to quotas based on the demographics of
1890—that is, before Poles, Jews, Greeks, Italians, and others outside of western Europe had arrived in great numbers.

Their status contested, these groups were not always extended
the protections accorded to unassailably "white" people, not then
anyway. There was an attempt to exclude Italian voters from
"white" primaries in Louisiana in 1903. The decade before, in
1891, eleven Italian immigrants in New Orleans lost their lives in

one of the largest mass lynchings in American history, after the police chief was assassinated and the immigrants were seen as the prime suspects. After the lynching, hundreds more were rounded up and arrested. One of the organizers of the lynch mob, John M. Parker, later described Italians as "just a little worse than the Negro, being if anything filthier in [their] habits, lawless, and treacherous." He went on to be elected governor of Louisiana.

Later, in 1922, a black man in Alabama named Jim Rollins was convicted of miscegenation for living as the husband of a white woman named Edith Labue. But when the court learned that the woman was Sicilian and saw "no competent evidence" that she was white, the judge reversed the conviction. The uncertainty surrounding whether she was "conclusively" white led the court to take the extraordinary step of freeing a black man who in other circumstances might have faced a lynching had she been seen as a white woman.

By then, a majority of the states had devised, or were in the process of devising, ever more tortured definitions of *white* and *black*.

Arkansas first defined *Negro* as "one in whom there is a visible and distinct admixture of African blood." Then in 1911, the state changed it to anyone "who has . . . any negro blood whatever," as it made interracial sex a felony. The state of Alabama defined a black person as anyone with "a drop of negro blood," in its intermarriage ban. Oregon defined as nonwhite any person "with ¼ Negro, Chinese or any person having ¼ Negro, Chinese or Kanaka blood or more than ½ Indian blood." North Carolina forbade marriage between whites and any person "of Negro or Indian descent to 3rd generation inclusive." The state of Georgia defined *white* to mean "no ascertainable trace of Negro, African, West Indian, Asiatic blood."

Louisiana had a law on the books as recently as 1983 setting the boundary at "one-thirty-second Negro blood." Louisiana culture went to great specificity, not so unlike the Indian Laws of Manu, in delineating the various subcastes, based on the estimated percentage of African "blood." There was griffe (three-fourths black), marabon (five-eighths black), mulatto (one-half), quadroon (one-fourth), octaroon (one-eighth), sextaroon (one-sixteenth), demi-meamelouc (one-thirty-second), and sangmelee (one-sixty-fourth). The latter categories, as twenty-first-century genetic testing has now shown, would encompass millions of Americans now classified as Caucasian. All of these categories bear witness to a historic American, dominant-caste preoccupation with race and caste purity.

Virginia went all in and passed what it called the Racial Integrity Act of 1924, which besides prohibiting interracial marriage, defined a white person as one "who has no trace whatsoever of any blood other than Caucasian."

"The 'traceable amount' was meant to ensure that even blacks who did not look black were kept in their place," wrote Diamond and Cottrol. "Tracing black ancestry as far back as possible became a prerequisite to the smooth functioning of the caste system."

The Trials of the Middle Castes:

The Race to Get Under the White Tent

By extending the dream of dominion over the land and all others in it to anyone who could meet the definition of *white*, the American caste system became an all-or-nothing gambit for the top rung. Which is why, when Ybor City, Florida, began segregating its streetcars in 1905, Cubans, who had been uncertain as to how they would be classified, were relieved and overjoyed "to discover that they were allowed to sit in the white section."

Those permitted under the white tent could reap the rewards of full citizenship, rise to positions of high status, or as far as their talents could take them, get access to the best the country had to offer, or, at the very least, be accorded respect in everyday interactions from subordinate groups who risked assault for any misstep. A two-tiered caste system raised the stakes for whiteness, leading to court dockets filled with people on the borderline seeking admission to the upper caste.

A Japanese immigrant named Takao Ozawa had lived in the United States for more than twenty years. He tried to make the case that he was worthy of citizenship and should qualify as white because his skin was lighter than that of many "white people." He argued, what really was the difference? How could he not be white if his skin was white? What did it mean to be white if someone with actual white skin was not white?

His case went all the way to the U.S. Supreme Court. In 1922, the Court held unanimously that *white* meant not skin color but "Caucasian," and that Japanese were not Caucasian, notwithstanding the fact that few white Americans had origins in the Caucasus Mountains of Russia either and that those who did were at that very moment being kept out, too.

After the ruling, a newspaper that catered to Japanese immigrants mocked the decision: "Since this newspaper did not believe whites are the 'superior race,' it is 'delighted' the high tribunal 'did not find the Japanese to be free white persons.'"

A few months later, an immigrant from the dominant caste of India sought to make common cause with his upper-caste counterparts in America when his application for citizenship made it to the Supreme Court. Bhagat Singh Thind argued that he was Caucasian, Aryan in fact, descended from the same stock as Europeans, given that it was widely held that Aryans migrated south to India and formed that country's upper caste. It could be said that he had a more rightful claim to being Caucasian than the people judging him. After all, the Caucasus Mountains were next to Iran and closer to neighboring India than to western Europe.

The Court did not agree and rejected Thind's quest for citizenship in 1923. "It may be true that the blond Scandinavian and the brown Hindu have a common ancestor in the dim reaches of antiquity," wrote the Court, "but the average man knows perfectly well that there are unmistakable and profound differences between them today."

These decisions were a heartbreaking catastrophe for Asians seeking citizenship. With pro–western European sentiment running high, the government began rescinding the naturalized citizenship of people of Asian descent who were already here. This amounted to an abandonment of people who had lived legally in the United States for most of their adult lives, as would echo a century later with immigrants crossing the southern U.S. border with Mexico.

It could lead to tragic consequences. Vaishno Das Bagai, an Indian immigrant, had been in the United States for eight years by the time the Supreme Court ruled that Indians were not white and thus were ineligible for citizenship. He had a wife and three children and his own general store on Fillmore Street in San Francisco. He tended his store in three-piece suits and kept his hair cut short with a part on the side. Bagai lost his citizenship in the crackdown on nonwhite immigrants. He was then stripped of the business he had built, due to a California law restricting the economic rights of people who were not citizens. Shorn of a passport, he was then thwarted in his attempt to get back to India and was now a man without a country.

Far from his original home and rejected by his new one, he rented a room in San Jose, turned on the gas and took his life. He left a suicide note, in which he lamented the futility of all that he had sacrificed to come to America: "Obstacles this way, blockades that way, and bridges burnt behind."

No matter which route a borderline applicant took to gain acceptance, the caste system shape-shifted to keep the upper caste pure by its own terms. What a thin, frayed thread held the illusions together. A Japanese novelist once noted that, on paper anyway, it was a single apostrophe that stood between rejection and citizenship for a Japanese Ohara versus an Irish O'Hara. These cases laid bare not just the absurdity but the inaccuracy of these artificial labels and the perception of purity or pollution implied by them. At the same time, they exposed the unyielding rigidity of a caste system, defiant in the face of evidence contrary to its foundation, how it holds fast against the assault of logic.

Defining Purity and the Constancy of the Bottom Rung

As the middle castes pressed for admittance to the rungs above them, what was consistent was the absolute exclusion of the "polluting" lowest caste. African-Americans were not just *not* citizens, they were, like their Dalit counterparts in India, forced outside the social contract.

They and the Dalits bore the daily brunt of the taint ascribed to their very beings. The Dalits were not permitted to drink from the same cups as the dominant castes in India, live in the villages of the upper-caste people, walk through the front doors of upper-caste homes, and neither were African-Americans in much of the United States for most of its history. African-Americans in the South were required to walk through the side or back door of any white establishment they approached. Throughout the United States, sundown laws forbade them from being seen in white towns and neighborhoods after sunset, or risk assault or lynching. In bars and restaurants in the North, though they might be permitted to sit and eat, it was common for the bartender to make a show of smashing the glass that a black patron had just sipped from. Heads would turn as restaurant patrons looked to see where the crashing sound had come from and who had offended the sensibilities of caste pollution.

Untouchables were not allowed inside Hindu temples, and black Mormons in America, by way of example, were not allowed inside the temples of the religion they followed and could not become priests until 1978. Enslaved black people were prohibited from learning to read the Bible or any book for that matter, just as Untouchables were prohibited from learning Sanskrit and sacred texts. In churches in the South, black worshippers sat in the galleries or in the back rows, and, when such arrangements were inconvenient to the dominant caste, "the negroes must catch the gospel as it escapes through the windows and doors" from outside. To this day, Sunday morning has been called the most segregated hour in America.

Well into the civil rights era, the caste system excluded African-Americans from the daily activities of the general public in the South, the region where most of them lived. They knew to disregard any notice of a circus coming to town or of a political rally; those things were not intended for them. "They were driven from Independence Day parades," wrote the historian David Roediger, "as 'defilers' of the body politic."

What a British magistrate observed about the lowest castes in India could as well have been said of African-Americans. "They were not allowed to be present at the great national sacrifices, or at the feasts which followed them," wrote the colonial administrator and historian W. W. Hunter. "They could never rise out of their servile condition; and to them was assigned the severest toil in the fields."

Their exclusion was used to justify their exclusion. Their degraded station justified their degradation. They were consigned to the lowliest, dirtiest jobs and thus were seen as lowly and dirty, and everyone in the caste system absorbed the message of their degradation.

The burden fell on those in the lowest caste to adjust themselves for the convenience of the dominant caste whenever in contact with white people. An African-American man who managed to become an architect during the nineteenth century had to train himself "to read architectural blueprints upside down," wrote the scholar Charles W. Mills, "because he knew white clients would be made uncomfortable by having him on the same side of the desk as themselves."

Well into the twentieth century, a panic could afflict people in the dominant caste if ever a breach occurred. A frantic white mother in civil-rights-era Mississippi yanked her young daughter inside one day, held her over the kitchen sink and scrubbed her little hand with a Brillo pad as if both their lives depended on it. The girl had touched the hand of a little black girl who was working on the family's land. The mother told her never to touch that girl's hand again, though that was not the term she used.

"They have germs," the mother said. "They're nasty." The mother's fury frightened the little girl and brought her to tears as they stood there, bent over the sink. And the daughter's tears brought the mother to tears over the manufactured terror she had allowed to consume her and over the box that she realized in that moment had imprisoned her for all of her life.

This was a sacred prohibition, and it was said that, into the 1970s, the majority of whites in the South had not so much as shaken the hands of a black person.

A young dominant-caste man raised in the Depression-era South had been well taught the rules of the caste system and adhered to them as expected. When he went north in the mid-twentieth century and joined the military, he had to confront the mythologies of his upbringing.

"Strange things pop up at us like gargoyles when we are liberated from our delusions," the white southerner said.

Up north, on occasion, he found himself in situations where black people were permitted in the same work settings as whites. "I thought I was entirely prepared, emotionally and intellectually," the man, an editor at *Look* magazine, recalled years later.

But he discovered that he was a captive of his own conditioning, which he called a certain madness.

Every time he reached the point where he had to shake hands with a black person, he felt an automatic revulsion that had been trained into him. He recoiled even though it had been black women who had bathed him as a child, had mixed the dough for his biscuits, and whose touch had not repulsed him when extended in servitude. But with presumed equals, "each time I shook hands with a Negro," he said, "I felt an urge to wash my hands. Every rational impulse, all that I considered best in myself struggled against this urge. But the hand that had touched the dark skin had a will of its own and would not be dissuaded from signaling it was unclean. That is what I mean by madness."

Occupational Hierarchy:
The Jatis and the Mudsill

When a house is being built, the single most important piece of the framework is the first wood beam hammered into place to anchor the foundation. That piece is called the mudsill, the sill plate that runs along the base of a house and bears the weight of the entire structure above it. The studs and subfloors, the ceilings and windows, the doors and roofing, all the components that make it a house, are built on top of the mudsill. In a caste system, the mudsill is the bottom caste that everything else rests upon.

A southern politician declared this central doctrine from the floor of the U.S. Senate in March 1858. "In all social systems, there must be a class to do the menial duties, to perform the drudgery of life," Sen. James Henry Hammond of South Carolina told his fellow senators. "That is a class requiring but a low order of intellect and but little skill. Its requisites are vigor, docility, fidelity. Such a class you must have. . . . It constitutes the very mud-sill of society."

He exulted in the cunning of the South, which, he said, had "found a race adapted to that purpose to her hand. . . . Our slaves are black, of another and inferior race. The status in which we have placed them is an elevation. They are elevated from the condition in which God first created them, by being made our slaves."

Hammond owned several plantations and more than three

hundred souls, having acquired this fortune by marrying the plain and callow young daughter of a wealthy landowner in South Carolina. He rose to become governor of the state and a leading figure in the antebellum South. Well before making this speech, he had established himself as one of the more repugnant of men ever to rise to the Senate, one scholar calling him "nothing less than a monster." He is known to have repeatedly raped at least two of the women he enslaved, one of them believed to have been his daughter by another enslaved woman.

His political career was nearly derailed when it became public that he had sexually abused his four young nieces, their lives so ruined that none of them ever married after reaching adulthood. In his diary, he spoke blithely of the nieces, blaming them for the "intimacies." For these and other things, his wife left him, taking their children with her, only to later return. He rebounded from these malefactions to be elected to the U.S. Senate.

But he is best known for the speech that distilled the hierarchy of the South, which spread in spirit to the rest of the country, into a structure built on a mudsill. In so doing, he defined the fifth pillar of caste, the division of labor based on one's place in the hierarchy. Therein, he identified the economic purpose of a hierarchy to begin with, that is, to ensure that the tasks necessary for a society to function get handled whether or not people wish to do them, in this case, by being born to the disfavored sill plate.

In the Indian caste system, an infinitely more elaborate hierarchy, the subcaste, or *jati,* to which a person was born established the occupation their family fulfilled, from cleaners of latrines to priests in the temples. Those born to families who collected refuse or tanned the hides of animals or handled the dead were seen as the most polluted and lowest in the hierarchy, untouchable due to the dreaded and thankless though necessary task they were presumably born to fulfill.

Similarly, African-Americans, throughout most of their time in this land, were relegated to the dirtiest, most demeaning and least desirable jobs by definition. After enslavement and well into the twentieth century, they were primarily restricted to the role of sharecroppers and servants—domestics, lawn boys, chauffeurs, and janitors. The most that those who managed to get an education could hope for was to teach, minister to, attend to the health needs of, or bury other subordinate-caste people.

"There is severe occupational deprivation in each country," wrote the scholars Sidney Verba, Bashiruddin Ahmed, and Anil Bhatt in a 1971 comparative study of India and the United States. "A deprivation—at least in terms of level—of roughly similar magnitude."

The state of South Carolina, right after the Civil War, explicitly prohibited black people from performing any labor other than farm or domestic work, setting their place in the caste system. The legislature decreed that "no person of color shall pursue or practice the art, trade or business of an artisan, mechanic or shopkeeper, or any other trade, employment or business (besides that of husbandry, or that of a servant under contract for labor) on his own account and for his own benefit until he shall have obtained a license from the judge of the district court, which license shall be good for one year only." The license was set at an intentionally prohibitive cost of $100 a year, the equivalent of $1,500 in 2018. This was a fee not required of the dominant caste, whose members, having not been enslaved for a quarter millennium, would have been in better position to afford.

The law went nominally out of effect during the decade known as Reconstruction, when the North took control of the former Confederacy, but it returned in spirit and custom after the North retreated and the former enslavers took power again, ready to avenge their defeat in the Civil War. In North Carolina, during slavery and into the era of sharecropping, people in the lowest caste were forbidden to sell or trade goods of any kind or be subject to thirty-nine lashes. This blocked the main route to earning money from their own farm labors and forced them into economic dependence on the dominant caste.

"The caste order that followed slavery defined the Negroes as workers and servants of the whites," wrote the scholar Edward Reuter. "The range of occupations was narrow, and many of those outside the orbit of common labor were closed to the Negroes."

The South foreclosed on them any route to a station higher than that assigned them. "Anything that causes the negro to aspire above the plow handle, the cook pot, in a word the functions of a servant," Gov. James K. Vardaman of Mississippi said, "will be the worst thing on earth for the negro. God Almighty designed him for a menial. He is fit for nothing else."

Those who managed to go north after the Civil War and in the bigger waves of the Great Migration, starting in World War I, found that they could escape the South but not their caste. They entered the North at the bottom, beneath southern and eastern Europeans who might not yet have learned English but who were permitted into unions and into better-served neighborhoods that barred black citizens whose labor had cleared the wilderness and built the country's wealth. While there was no federal law restricting people to certain occupations on the basis of race, statutes in the South and custom in the North kept lower-caste people in their place. Northern industries often hired African-Americans only as strikebreakers, and unions blocked them from entire trades reserved for whites, such as pipe fitters or plumbers. City inspectors would refuse to sign off on the work of black electricians. A factory in Milwaukee turned away black men seeking jobs as they walked toward the front gate. In New York and Philadelphia, black people were long denied licenses merely to drive carts.

"Every avenue for improvement was closed against him," wrote William A. Sinclair, author of a history of slavery and its aftermath, of the fate of the subordinate-caste man.

There were exceptions—those select enslaved people, often the children of slaveholders, who were permitted to serve as carpenters or blacksmiths or in other trades as would be required on large plantations like Thomas Jefferson's at Monticello.

Even in India, where there are thousands of castes within castes, within the four main *varnas*, "no one occupation has but one caste assigned to it," wrote the anthropologists W. Lloyd Warner and Allison Davis. "While in theory caste demands occupational specialization, in practice even the most ideally organized of the several castes, the Brahmans, have a great variety of occupations." The French anthropologist and philosopher Célestin Bouglé wrote that, in the Indian caste system, "one can distinguish six merchant castes, three of scribes, forty of peasants, twenty-four of journeymen, nine of shepherds and hunters, fourteen of fishermen and sailors, twelve of various kinds of artisans, carpenters, blacksmiths, goldsmiths and potters, thirteen of weavers, thirteen of distillers, eleven of house servants."

Thus, the caste lines in America may have at one time been even starker than those in India. In 1890, "85 percent of black men and 96 percent of black women were employed in just two occupational categories," wrote the sociologist Stephen Steinberg, "agriculture and domestic or personal service." Forty years later, as the Depression set in and as African-Americans moved to northern cities, the percentages of black people at the bottom of the labor hierarchy remained the same, though, by then, nearly half of black men were doing manual labor that called merely for a strong back. Only 5 percent were listed as white-collar workers—many of them ministers, teachers, and small business owners who catered to other black people.

North and south, the status of African-Americans was so well understood that people in the dominant caste were loath to perform duties they perceived as beneath their station. A British tourist in the 1810s noted that white Americans well knew which tasks were seen as befitting only black people. White paupers in Ohio, "refused to carry water for their own use," wrote the historian David R. Roediger, "for fear of being considered 'like slaves.' "

The historic association between menial labor and blackness served to further entrap black people in a circle of subservience in the American mind. They were punished for being in the condition that they were forced to endure. And the image of servitude shadowed them into freedom.

As the caste system shape-shifted in the twentieth century, the dominant caste found ever more elaborate ways to enforce occupational hierarchy. "If white and colored persons are employed together," wrote the historian Bertram Doyle in the 1930s, "they do not engage in the same tasks, generally, and certainly not as equals. . . . Negroes are seldom, if ever, put into authority over white persons. Moreover, the Negro expects to remain in the lower ranks; rising, if at all, only over other Negroes." No matter how well he does his job, Doyle wrote, "he cannot often hope for promotion."

Your place was preordained before you were born. "A Negro may become a locomotive fireman," Doyle wrote, "but never an engineer."

Thus, caste did not mean merely doing a certain kind of labor; it meant performing a dominant or subservient role. "There must be, then, a division of labor where the two races are employed, and menial labor is commonly supposed to be the division assigned to Negroes," Doyle wrote, "and he must look and act the part."

A black man in the 1930s was on his way to pay a visit to a young woman he fancied, which occasioned him to go into the town square. There, some white men approached him and "forced him to procure overalls, saying he was 'too dressed up for a weekday.'"

Slavery set the artificial parameters for the roles each caste was to perform, and the only job beyond the plow or the kitchen that the caste system openly encouraged of the lowest caste was that of entertainment, which was its own form of servitude in that world. It was in keeping with caste notions of their performing for the pleasure of the dominant caste. It affirmed the stereotypes of innate black physicality, of an earthiness based on animal instinct rather than human creativity and it presented no threat to dominant-caste supremacy in leadership and intellect.

Making enslaved people perform on command also reinforced their subjugation. They were made to sing despite their exhaustion or the agonies from a recent flogging or risk further punishment. Forced good cheer became a weapon of submission to assuage the guilt of the dominant caste and further humiliate the enslaved. If they were in chains and happy, how could anyone say that they were being mistreated? Merriment, even if extracted from a whip, was seen as essential to confirm that the caste structure was sound, that all was well, that everyone accepted, even embraced their station in the hierarchy. They were thus forced to cosign on their own degradation, to sing and dance even as they were being separated from spouses or children or parents at auction. "This was done to make them appear cheerful and happy," wrote William Wells Brown, a speculator's assistant before the Civil War, whose job it was to get the human merchandise into sellable condition. "I have often set them to dancing," he said, "when their cheeks were wet with tears."

African-Americans would later convert the performance role that they were forced to occupy—and the talent they built from it—into prominence in entertainment and in American culture disproportionate to their numbers. Since the early twentieth century, the wealthiest African-Americans—from Louis Armstrong to Muhammad Ali—have traditionally been entertainers and athletes. Even now, in a 2020 ranking of the richest African-Americans, seventeen of the top twenty—from Oprah Winfrey to Jay-Z to Michael Jordan—made their wealth as innovators, and then moguls, in the entertainment industry or in sports.

Historically, this group would come to dominate the realm carved out for them, often celebrated unless they went head to head against an upper-caste person, as did the black boxer Jack Johnson when he unexpectedly knocked out James Jeffries in 1910. The writer Jack London had coaxed Jeffries out of retirement to fight Johnson in an era of virulent race hatred, and the press stoked passions by calling Jeffries "the Great White Hope." Jeffries's loss on that Fourth of July was an affront to white supremacy, and triggered riots across the country, north and south, including eleven separate ones in New York City, where whites set fire to black neighborhoods and tried to lynch two black men over the defeat. The message was that, even in an arena into which the lowest caste had been permitted, they were to know and remain in their place.

For centuries, enslaved people had been ordered to perform at the whim of the master, either to be mocked in the master's parlor games or to play music for their balls, in addition to their hard labors in the field. "Menial and comic roles were the chief ones allotted to Negroes in their relationships with white people," wrote the anthropologists W. Lloyd Warner and Allison Davis of slavery-based caste relations that worked their way into American culture.

The caste system took comfort in black caricature as it upheld the mythology of a simple, court jester race whose jolly natures shielded them from any true suffering. The images soothed the conscience and justified atrocities. And thus minstrelsy, in which white actors put burnt cork on their faces and mocked the subordinate caste, became a popular entertainment as the Jim Crow regime hardened after slavery ended. Whites continued the practice at fraternity parties and talent shows and Halloween festivities well into the twenty-first century.

At the same time, black entertainers have long been rewarded and often restricted to roles that adhere to caste stereotype. The first African-American to win an Academy Award, Hattie McDaniel, was commended for her role as Mammy, a solicitous and obesely desexed counterpoint to Scarlett O'Hara, the feminine ideal, in the 1939 film *Gone with the Wind*. The Mammy character was more devoted to her white family than to her own, willing to fight black soldiers to protect her white enslaver.

That trope became a comforting staple in film portrayals of slavery, but it was an ahistorical figment of caste imagination. Under slavery, most black women were thin, gaunt even, due to the meager rations provided them, and few worked inside a house, as they were considered more valuable in the field. Yet the rotund and cheerful slave or maidservant was what the dominant caste preferred to see, and McDaniel and other black actresses of the era found that those were the only roles they could get. Because many of these women had been raised in the North or the West, they knew little of the southern Negro vernacular that scripts called for and had to learn how to speak in the exaggerated, at times farcical, way that Hollywood directors imagined that black people talked.

This mainstream derision belies the serious history of arbitrary abuse of African-Americans under slavery when their degradation was entertainment for the dominant caste. In one case, two planters in South Carolina were dining together at one of their plantations. The two were passing the time, discussing their slaves and debating whether the slaves had the capacity for genuine religious faith. The visiting planter said he didn't much believe they did.

The planter who was hosting begged to differ.

"I have a slave who I believe would rather die than deny his Saviour," he said.

The guest ridiculed the host and challenged him to prove it. So the host summoned an enslaved man of his and ordered him to deny his faith in the Lord Jesus Christ. The enslaved man affirmed his faith in Jesus and pleaded to be excused. The master, seeking to drive home his point to the fellow slaveowner, kept asking the man to deny Jesus, and the man, as expected, kept declaring his faith. The host then whipped the enslaved man, now for disobedience, and continued to whip him, the whip cord cutting to bone. The enslaved man of faith "died in consequence of this severe infliction."

Similarly, soldiers of the Third Reich used weakened and malnourished Jewish prisoners for entertainment. An SS squad leader, who oversaw the construction of the firing range at Sachsenhausen, forced prisoners to jump and turn like dancing bears around a shovel for his amusement. One of them refused to dance and, for this, the SS squad leader took the shovel and beat him to death with it.

Every act, every gesture, was calculated for the purpose of reminding the subordinate caste, in these otherwise unrelated caste systems, of the dominant caste's total reign over their very being. The upper caste, wrote the nineteenth-century author William Goodell, made "the claim of absolute proprietorship in the human soul itself."

Dehumanization and Stigma

Dehumanization is a standard component in the manufacture of an out-group against which to pit an in-group, and it is a monumental task. It is a war against truth, against what the eye can see and what the heart could feel if allowed to do so on its own.

To dehumanize another human being is not merely to declare that someone is not human, and it does not happen by accident. It is a process, a programming. It takes energy and reinforcement to deny what is self-evident in another member of one's own species.

It is harder to dehumanize a single person standing in front of you, wiping away tears at the loss of a loved one, just as you would, or wincing in pain from a fall as you would, laughing at an unexpected double entendre as you might. It is harder to dehumanize a single individual that you have gotten the chance to know. Which is why people and groups who seek power and division do not bother with dehumanizing an individual. Better to attach a stigma, a taint of pollution to an entire group.

Dehumanize the group, and you have completed the work of dehumanizing any single person within it. Dehumanize the group, and you have quarantined them from the masses you choose to elevate and have programmed everyone, even some of the targets of dehumanization, to no longer believe what their eyes can see, to no longer trust their own thoughts. Dehumanization distances not only the out-group from the in-group, but those in the in-group from their own humanity. It makes slaves to groupthink of everyone in the hierarchy. A caste system relies on dehumanization to lock the marginalized outside of the norms of humanity so that any action against them is seen as reasonable.

Both Nazi Germany and the United States reduced their outgroups, Jews and African-Americans, respectively, to an undifferentiated mass of nameless, faceless scapegoats, the shock absorbers of the collective fears and setbacks of each nation. Germany blamed Jews for the loss of World War I, for the shame and economic straits that befell the country after its defeat, and the United States blamed African-Americans for many of its social ills. In both cases, individuals were lumped together for sharing a single, stigmatizing trait, made indistinct and indistinguishable in preparation for the exploitation and atrocities that would be inflicted upon them. Individuals were no longer individuals. Individuality, after all, is a luxury afforded the dominant caste. Individuality is the first distinction lost to the stigmatized.

We are sorrowfully aware of the monstrously swift murder of 6 million Jews and 5 million others during the Holocaust. What we may not be as familiar with are the circumstances leading up to that horror and the millions who suffered in the labor camps of the Third Reich, the process of dehumanization before any of those atrocities could be conducted and the interconnectedness not just of humanity but of evil within it.

Held hostage in labor camps in different centuries and an ocean apart, both Jews and African-Americans were subjected to a program of purposeful dehumanization. Upon their arrival at the concentration camps, Jews were stripped of the clothing and accoutrements of their former lives, of everything they had owned. Their heads were shaved, their distinguishing features of sideburns or mustaches or the crowns of lush hair, were deleted from them. They were no longer individuals, they were no longer personalities to consider, to engage with, to take into account.

During the morning and evening roll calls, they were forced to stand sometimes for hours into the night as the SS officers counted the thousands of them to check for any escapees. They stood in the freezing cold or summer heat in the same striped uniforms, with the same shorn heads, same sunken cheeks. They became a single mass of self-same bodies, purposely easier for SS officers to distance themselves from, to feel no human connection with. Loving fathers, headstrong nephews, beloved physicians, dedicated watchmakers, rabbis, and piano tuners, all merged into a single mass of undifferentiated bodies that were no longer seen as humans deserving of empathy but as objects over whom they could exert total control and do whatever they wanted to. They were no longer people, they were numbers, a means to an end.

Upon their arrival at the auction blocks and labor camps of the American South, Africans were stripped of their given names and forced to respond to new ones, as would a dog to a new owner, often mocking names like Caesar or Samson or Dred. They were stripped of their past lives and identities as Yoruba or Asante or Igbo, as the son of a fisherman, nephew of the village priest, or daughter of a midwife. Decades afterward, Jews were stripped of their given and surnames and forced to memorize the prison numbers assigned them in the concentration camps. Millennia ago, the Untouchables of India were assigned surnames that identified them by the lowly work they performed, forcing them to announce their degradation every time they introduced themselves, while the Brahmins, many quite literally, carried the names of the gods.

In the two more modern caste systems, at labor camps in central and eastern Europe and in the American South, well-fed captors forced their hostages to do the heaviest work of inhuman exertion, while withholding food from those whose labors enriched the captors, providing barely enough to sustain the human metabolism, the bare minimum for human subsistence. The Nazis approached human deprivation as a science. They calculated the number of calories required for a certain task, say, chopping down trees and digging up stumps, and fed those laborers one or two hundred calories fewer as a cost savings and to keep them too weak to fight back as they slowly starved to death.

Southern planters provided their African captives, who were doing the hardest labor in the hierarchy, the least nutrients of anyone on the plantation. Both groups were rarely allowed protein, restricted to feed rather than food, some taunted with the extravagance of their captors' multi-course feasts.

They were under the complete control and at the whim of their captors who took every chance to reassert their debasement. Jews were given prison uniforms of coarse fabric in sizes that were purposely too big or too small. Enslaved African-Americans were allotted garments of coarse gray cloth, a cross between an "undergarment and an ordinary potato bag," that was made "without regard to the size of the particular individual to whom it was allotted, like penitentiary uniforms."

Beyond all of this, the point of a dehumanization campaign was the forced surrender of the target's own humanity, a karmic theft beyond accounting. Whatever was considered a natural human reaction was disallowed for the subordinate caste. During the era of enslavement, they were forbidden to cry as their children were carried off, forced to sing as a wife or husband was sold away, never again to look into their eyes or hear their voice for as long as the two might live.

They were punished for the very responses a human being would be expected to have in the circumstances forced upon them. Whatever humanity shone through them was an affront to what the dominant caste kept telling itself. They were punished for being the humans that they could not help but be.

In India, Dalits, suffering the deprivations of their lowly status, were nonetheless beaten to death if ever they stole food for the sustenance denied them. As with African-Americans during the time of enslavement, it was a crime for Dalits to learn to read and write, "punishable by cutting off their tongue or by pouring molten lead into the ear of the offender," wrote V. T. Rajshekar, editor of *Dalit Voice*.

In the United States, African-Americans, denied pay for their labors during slavery and barely paid afterward in the twentieth century, were whipped or lynched for stealing food, for the accusation of stealing seventy-five cents, for trying to stand up for themselves or appearing to question a person in the dominant caste. In Nazi labor camps, one of the many cruel details a prisoner could be assigned was to work in the bakery. There, day in and day out, starving captives, forced to subsist on rations of watery nettle or beet soup, kneaded and baked the breads and pastries for their SS tormenters. They were surrounded by the scent of fresh-rising dough but risked a beating or worse if caught taking a crust of bread.

In America, slave auctions became public showcases for the dehumanization project of caste-making. As the most valuable liquid assets in the land, combined, worth more than land itself, enslaved people were ordered to put on a cheery face to bring a higher profit to the dominant-caste sellers who were breaking up their families. Women were forced to disrobe before the crowd, to submit to hours of physical probing by roughhousing men who examined their teeth, their hands, or whatever other parts of their bodies the potential bidders decided to inspect. Their bodies did not belong to them but to the dominant caste to do whatever it wished and however it wished to do it. At auction, they were to answer any question put to them with "a smiling, cheerful countenance" or be given thirty lashes for not selling themselves well enough to the seller's satisfaction.

"When spoken to, they must reply quickly and with a smile on their lips," recalled John Brown, a survivor of slavery, who was sold away from his own mother and subjected to these scenes many times thereafter. "Here may be seen husbands separated from their wives, only by the width of the room, and children from their parents, one or both, witnessing the driving of the bargain that is to tear them asunder for ever, yet not a word of lamentation or anguish must escape from them; nor when the deed is consummated, dare they bid one another good-bye, or take one last embrace."

————

In the United States, there developed two parallel worlds existing on the same plane with flagrant double standards to emphasize the purposeful injustices built into the system. Presaging the disparities that led to mass incarceration in our era, the abolitionist minister William Goodell observed the quandary of black people in antebellum America. "He is accounted criminal for acts which are deemed innocent in others," Goodell wrote in 1853, "punished with a severity from which all others are exempted. He is under the control of the law, though unprotected by the law, and can know law only as an enemy."

In Virginia, there were seventy-one offenses that carried the death penalty for enslaved people but only imprisonment when committed by whites, such as stealing a horse or setting fire to bales of grain. Something as ordinary to most humans as a father helping a son with his lessons was prohibited. A black father in Georgia could "be flogged for teaching his own child" to read. Free black people were forbidden to carry firearms, testify against a white person, or raise a hand against one even in self-defense.

"Richmond required that Negroes and mulattoes must step aside when whites passed by, and barred them from riding in carriages except in the capacity of menials," the historian Kenneth Stampp wrote. "Charleston slaves could not swear, smoke, walk with a cane, assemble at military parades, or make joyful demonstrations."

Just as enslaved and malnourished Africans had to drain the swamps, chop down the trees, clear the land to build the plantations and infrastructure of the South, the starving captives of the Third Reich had to drain the swamps, chop down the trees, dig up the tree roots, carry the logs to build the infrastructure of their tor-ment. They worked the clay pits and quarries to make bricks for the Reich. Under both regimes, the hostages built the walls that would imprison them and often died as they did so.

Each day during the early years of Nazi expansion, some two thousand prisoners were marched through the village of Oranien-burg, north of Berlin, over the canal bridge, from the concentra-tion camp to the clay pits, and would often return that evening with a cart filled with the people who had died of exhaustion or had been killed that day.

———

At the depths of their dehumanization, both Jews and African-Americans were subjected to gruesome medical experimenta-tion at the hands of dominant-caste physicians. In addition to the horrifying torture of twins, German scientists and SS doctors con-ducted more than two dozen types of experiments on Jews and others they held captive, such as infecting their victims with mus-tard gas and testing the outer limits of hypothermia.

In the United States, from slavery well into the twentieth century, doctors used African-Americans as a supply chain for experimen-tation, as subjects deprived of either consent or anesthesia. Sci-entists injected plutonium into them, purposely let diseases like syphilis go untreated to observe the effects, perfected the typhoid vaccine on their bodies, and subjected them to whatever agoniz-ing experiments came to the doctors' minds.

These amounted to unchecked assaults on human beings. One plantation doctor, according to the medical ethicist Harriet A. Washington in her groundbreaking book *Medical Apartheid*, made incisions into a black baby's head to test a theory for curing sei-zures. The doctor opened the baby's skull with cobbler's tools, puncturing the scalp, as he would later report, "with the point of a crooked awl."

That doctor, James Marion Sims, would later be heralded as the

founding father of gynecology. He came to his discoveries by acquiring enslaved women in Alabama and conducting savage sur-
geries that often ended in disfigurement or death. He refused to
administer anesthesia, saying vaginal surgery on them was "not
painful enough to justify the trouble." Instead, he administered
morphine only after surgery, noting that it "relieves the scalding
of the urine," and, as Washington writes, "weakened the will to
resist repeated procedures."

A Louisiana surgeon perfected the cesarean section by experimenting on the enslaved women he had access to in the 1830s.
Others later learned how to remove ovaries and bladder stones.
They performed these slave cabin experiments in search of break-
throughs for their white patients who would one day undergo
surgery in hospitals and under the available anesthesia.

Their total control over black bodies gave them unfettered access to the anatomy of live subjects that would otherwise be closed
to them. Sims, for example, would force a woman to disrobe and
get on her knees on a table. He would then allow other doctors to
take turns with the speculum to force her open, and invite leading
men in town and apprentices in to see for themselves. He later
wrote, "I saw everything as no man had seen before."

———

We would all like to believe that we would resist the impulse to
inflict such horror on fellow members of our own species, and
some of us very likely would. But not as many as we might like to
believe.

In a famous though controversial 1963 study of people's threshold for violence when ordered to inflict it, college students were
told to administer electric shocks to a person in an adjoining room.
The people "receiving" the shocks were unharmed but yelled out
and banged on the walls as the intensity of the shocks increased.
The conductor of the study, the psychologist Stanley Milgram,
found that a majority of participants, two out of three, "could be
induced to deliver the maximal voltage to an innocent suffering

subject," wrote the scholar David Livingstone Smith, who specializes in the study of dehumanization.

In a similar experiment, conducted at Stanford University in 1975,
the participants did not have to be ordered to deliver the shocks.
They needed only to overhear a single negative comment about the
students facing potential punishment. The participants were led
to believe that students from another college were arriving for a
joint project. Some participants overheard the experimenters, presumably by accident, make neutral or humanizing comments
about the visiting students (that they seemed "nice"). Other participants heard dehumanizing comments (that they seemed like
"animals"). Participants gave the dehumanized people twice the
punishment of the humanized ones and significantly more than
those they knew absolutely nothing about. The participants were
willing to go to maximum intensity on the dehumanized group.

"Dehumanization is a joint creation of biology, culture and the
architecture of the human mind," Smith wrote. "The human story
is filled with pain and tragedy, but among the horrors that we
have perpetrated on one another, the persecution and attempted
extermination of the Jewish people, the brutal enslavement of Africans, and the destruction of Native American civilizations in
many respects are unparalleled."

———

In America, a culture of cruelty crept into the minds, made violence and mockery seem mundane and amusing, built as it was
into the games of chance at carnivals and county fairs well into
the twentieth century. These things built up the immune system
against empathy. There was an attraction called the "Coon Dip,"
in which fairgoers hurled "projectiles at live African Americans."
There was the "Bean-em," in which children flung beanbags at
grotesquely caricatured black faces, whose images alone taught
the lesson of caste without a word needing to be spoken.

And enthusiasts lined up to try their luck at the "Son of Ham"
shows at Coney Island or Kansas City or out in California, "in

which white men paid for the pleasure of hurling baseballs at the head of a black man," Smith wrote.

A certain kind of violence was part of an unspoken curriculum for generations of children in the dominant caste. "White culture desensitized children to racial violence," wrote the historian Kristina DuRocher, "so they could perpetuate it themselves one day."

Terror as Enforcement,
Cruelty as a Means of Control

The only way to keep an entire group of sentient beings in an artificially fixed place, beneath all others and beneath their own talents, is with violence and terror, psychological and physical, to preempt resistance before it can be imagined. Evil asks little of the dominant caste other than to sit back and do nothing. All that it needs from bystanders is their silent complicity in the evil committed on their behalf, though a caste system will protect, and perhaps even reward, those who deign to join in the terror.

Jews in Nazi-controlled Europe, African-Americans in the antebellum and Jim Crow South, and Dalits in India were all at the mercy of people who had been fed a diet of contempt and hate for them, and had incentive to try to prove their superiority by joining in or acquiescing to cruelties against their fellow humans.

Above all, the people in the subordinate caste were to be reminded of the absolute power the dominant caste held over them. In both America and in Germany, people in the dominant caste whipped and hanged their hostages for random and capricious breaches of caste, punished them for the natural human responses to the injustice they were being subjected to. In America, "the whip was the most common instrument of punishment," the historian Kenneth Stampp wrote. "Nearly every slaveholder used it, and few grown slaves escaped it entirely."

In Germany, the Nazis forced and strapped Jews and political prisoners onto a wooden board to be flogged for minor infractions like rolling cigarettes from leaves they gathered or killing rats to augment their bare rations. The captives were forced to count out each lash as it was inflicted upon them. The Nazis claimed a limit of twenty-five lashes, but would play mind games by claiming that the victim had not counted correctly, then extend the torture even longer. The Americans went to as many as four hundred lashes, torture that amounted to murder, with several men, growing exhausted from the physical exertion it required, taking turns with the whip.

In the New World, few living creatures were, as a class of beings, subjected to the level of brute physical assault as a feature of their daily lives for as many centuries as were the subjects of American slavery. It was so commonplace that some overseers, upon arriving at a new plantation, summarily chose "to whip every hand on the plantation to let them know who was in command," Stampp wrote. "Some used it as incentive by flogging the last slave out of the cabin in the morning. Many used it to 'break in' a young slave and to 'break the spirit' of an insubordinate older one."

A teenager endured a whipping that went on for so long, he passed out in the middle of it. "He woke up vomiting," the historian Edward Baptist recounted. "They were still beating him. He slipped into darkness again."

One enslaver remarked "that he was no better pleased than when he could hear . . . the sound of the driver's lash among the toiling slaves," for then, Baptist wrote, "he knew his system was working."

———

Human history is rife with examples of inconceivable violence, and as Americans, we like to think of our country as being far beyond the guillotines of medieval Europe or the reign of the Huns. And yet it was here that "Native Americans were occasionally skinned and made into bridle reins," wrote the scholar Charles Mills. Andrew Jackson, the U.S. president who oversaw the forced removal of indigenous people from their ancestral homelands during that Trail of Tears, used bridle reins of indigenous flesh when he went horseback riding. And it was here that, into the twentieth century, African-Americans were burned alive at the stake, as seventeen-year-old Jesse Washington was in Waco, Texas, in 1916 before a crowd of thousands.

The crimes of homicide, of rape, and of assault and battery were felonies in the slavery era as they are today in any civil society. They were seen then as wrong, immoral, reprehensible, and worthy of the severest punishment. But the country allowed most any atrocity to be inflicted on the black body. Thus twelve generations of African-Americans faced the ever-present danger of assault and battery or worse, every day of their lives during the quarter millennium of enslavement.

Advertisements for runaways record a catalog of assaults upon them. A North Carolina enslaver took out an ad for the return of Betty and reported having burnt her "with a hot iron on the left side of her face; I tried to make the letter M." A warden in Louisiana reported that he had just taken custody of a runaway and noted that "he has been lately gelded and is not yet well." Another Louisianan reported his disgust for a neighbor who had "castrated 3 men of his."

An order from the justices went out in New Hanover County, North Carolina, in the search of a runaway named London, granting that "any person may KILL and DESTROY the said slave by such means as he or they may think fit." This casual disregard for black life and the deputizing of any citizen to take that life would become a harbinger of the low value accorded African-Americans in the police and vigilante shootings of unarmed black citizens that continued into the early decades of the twenty-first century.

Some argue in hindsight that people who were enslaved were seen as too valuable to be hurt or killed. That argument disregards the many instances of humans trashing their own property, of absentee slumlords who get by with the least maintenance of their buildings, for example, with often catastrophic consequences. But more important, it misinterprets violence as merely damage to one's property, presumably rare and against the interest of the "owner," when it was actually a terror mechanism that was part of the regular maintenance of an unnatural institution, part of the calculus of American slavery. A Louisiana planter once left his plantation in the care of an overseer and staff. Upon returning after a year's absence, the planter discovered the overseer and his men had beaten and starved the enslaved people while the planter was away and that his inventory had shrunk. On that one family plantation, "at least twelve slaves had died at the overseer's hands," Stampp wrote. The planter would have to factor that "loss" into the cost of doing business.

————

Nazi Germany and the American South devised shockingly similar means of punishment to instill terror in the subordinate caste. Hostages in Nazi labor camps were subjected to public hangings, in front of a full assemblage of camp prisoners, for any minor offense or merely to remind the survivors of the power of their captors. In the special prisons inside the concentration camps, there stood a lynching post designed to draw out the agony of the captive being killed. Across the ocean, in the same era, lynchings, preceded by mutilation, were a feature of the southern landscape.

Both the Germans in the Nazi era and the descendants of the Confederacy used ritualized torture for arbitrary infractions, some as minor as stealing shoes or pocket change or, in the case of the American South, for acting out of one's place.

It was during the era of enslavement that Americans in the South devised a range of horrors to keep human beings in the unnatural state of perpetual, generational imprisonment. Fourteen-pound chains and metal horns radiating two or three feet from the skull were locked onto the heads of people who tried to escape. Slave pens had flogging rooms in the attics where rows of wooden cleats for the reaving cords were screwed into the floor to tie people down for their floggings for "not speaking up and looking bright and smart" to their potential buyers. "Every day there was flogging going on," wrote John Brown, a survivor of slavery.

The tortures were elaborate enough to be given names. One was called "bucking," in which the person was stripped naked, hands and feet tied, forced into a sitting position around a stake and rotated for three hours of flogging with a cowhide, as other enslaved people were forced to watch. The person was then washed down with salt and red pepper. An enslaved man named John Glasgow was punished in this way for having slipped away to see his wife on another plantation. Then there was "the picket," which involved iron cleats, pulleys, and cords that formed a gallows, along the crossbeam of a whipping post, and the sharp end of a stake. John Glasgow suffered this, too, after attempting to see his wife again. His fellow captives were made to take turns whipping him or face the same punishment themselves. "He was left to die or recover, as might be," Brown said. "It was a month before he stirred from his plank, five months more elapsed ere he could walk. Ever after he had a limp in his gait."

After slavery ended, the former Confederates took power again, but now without the least material investment in the lives of the people they once had owned. They pressed down even harder to keep the lowest caste in its place. African-Americans were mutilated and hanged from poplars and sycamores and burned at the courthouse square, a lynching every three or four days in the first four decades of the twentieth century.

A slaveholder in North Carolina seemed to speak for the enforcers of caste throughout the world. "Make them stand in fear," she said.

The dominant caste demonstrated its power by forcing captives to perform some of the more loathsome duties connected to the violence against their fellow captives. People in the upper caste did not often trouble themselves with the dirty work, unless specifically hired for the job of enforcement, as were the plantation overseers in the American South. It was caste privilege to order the lowest caste to do their bidding and dirty work.

It was part of the psychological degradation that reinforced one's own stigma and utter subjugation, so dominated that they were left with little choice but to cooperate if they were to save themselves for one more day. The Nazis in Germany and the planters in the authoritarian South sowed dissension among the subordinate caste by creating a hierarchy among the captives, rewarding those who identified more with the oppressor rather than the oppressed and who would report back to them any plots of escape or uprising. They would select a captive they felt they could control and elevate that person above the others.

In Nazi labor camps, it was the *kapo,* the head Jew in each hut of captives, whose job it was to get everyone up by five in the morning and to exact discipline. In exchange, he would get a bunk of his own or other meager privileges. In the American South, it was the slave driver, the head Negro, who served this role, setting the pace for the work at hand and elevated with the task of watching over the others and disciplining them when called to do so.

The dominant caste often forced its captives to exact punishment on one another or to dispose of the victims as their tormenters watched. In Nazi Germany, the SS guards were not the ones who put the prisoners into the ovens. The captives were forced into that grim detail. It was not the SS who collected the bodies of the people who had died the night before. That was left to the captives. In the American South, black men were made to whip their fellow slaves or to hold down the legs and arms of the man, woman, or child being flogged. Later, when lynchings were the primary means of terror, it was the people who had done the lynching who told the family of the victim or the black undertaker when they would be permitted to take down what was left of the body from the lynching tree.

———

One day in the mid-eighteenth century, an elder of the Presbyterian Church was passing through a piece of timbered land in a slaving province of the American South when he heard what he called "a sound as of murder." He rode in that direction and discovered "a naked black man, hung to the limb of a tree by his hands, his feet chained together and a pine rail laid with one end on the chain, between his legs, and the other upon the ground to steady him." The overseer had administered four hundred lashes on the man's body. "The miserably lacerated slave was then taken down and put to the care of a physician," the Presbyterian elder said.

The elder asked the overseer, one of the men who had inflicted this upon another human being, "the offence for which all this was done." He was told that the enslaved man had made a comment that was seen as beyond his station. It began when the owner said that the rows of corn the enslaved man had planted were uneven. The enslaved man offered his opinion. "Massa, much corn grow on a crooked row as a straight one," the enslaved man replied. For that, he was flogged to the brink of death.

"This was it, this was enough," the Presbyterian elder said. The overseer boasted of his skill in managing the master's property. The enslaved man "was submitted to him, and treated as above."

A century later, slavery was over, but the rules, and the consequences for breaking them, were little changed. A young white anthropologist from Yale University, John Dollard, went south to the Mississippi Delta in 1935 for his research into the Jim Crow caste system. He noticed how subservient the black people were, stepping aside for him, taking their hats off, and calling him "sir" even if they were decades older.

One day he was out riding with some other white men, southern white men, who were checking out some black sharecroppers.

The black people were reluctant to come out of their cabins when the car with the white men pulled up. The driver had some fun with it, told the sharecroppers he was not going to hang them. Later, Dollard mentioned to the man that "the Negroes seem to be very polite around here."

The man let out a laugh. "They have to be."

Inherent Superiority versus
Inherent Inferiority

The Hollywood still is from a 1930s movie released during the depths of the Jim Crow era. A black woman, ample in frame and plain of face, wears a headscarf and servant's uniform. Her arms are wrapped around a white woman, slender, cherubic, and childlike, her golden hair and porcelain, air-brushed skin pops against the purposely unadorned darkness of the black woman. When they begin to speak, the dark woman will utter backward syllables of servility and ignorance. The porcelain woman will speak with the mannered refinement of the upper caste. The fragile frame of Mary Pickford is in direct contrast to the heft of Louise Beavers in a set piece of caste played out in a thousand films and images in America, implanting into our minds the inherent superiority in beauty, deservedness, and intellect of one group over another.

As it happens, the black actress, Louise Beavers, was nothing like the image she was given little option but to play. She grew up in California and had to learn and to master the broken dialect of southern field hands and servants. She was frequently under stress in the narrow box she was confined to, which led her to lose weight on set. The filmmakers made her attach padding to her already full frame, to ensure that she contrasted all the more with the waifish white ingenues who were the stars of whatever film she was in.

Beneath each pillar of caste was the presumption and continual reminder of the inborn superiority of the dominant caste and the inherent inferiority of the subordinate. It was not enough that the designated groups be separated for reasons of "pollution" or that they not intermarry or that the lowest people suffer due to some religious curse, but that it must be understood in every interaction that one group was superior and inherently deserving of the best in a given society and that those who were deemed lowest were deserving of their plight.

For the lowest-caste person, "his unquestioned inferiority had to be established," wrote the anthropologists Audrey and Brian Smedley, and that alleged inferiority would become the "basis for his allocation to permanent servile status."

At every turn, the caste system drilled into the people under its spell the deference due those born to the upper caste and the degradation befitting the subordinate caste. This required signs and symbols and customs to elevate the upper caste and to demean those assigned to the bottom, in small and large ways and in everyday encounters.

"He must be held subject, like other domestic animals," observed the nineteenth-century abolitionist William Goodell, "to the superior race holding dominion over him."

African-Americans during the century of the Jim Crow regime and Jews during the murderous twelve years of the Third Reich were often prohibited from sidewalks and were forced instead to give way to the dominant caste or to walk in the gutter as a reminder of their degraded station.

"If a Negro, man or woman, met a white person on the street in Richmond, Virginia," for example, wrote the historian Bertram Doyle, they were "required to 'give the wall,' and if necessary to get off the sidewalk into the street, on pain of punishment with stripes on the bare back."

During the height of the caste systems in America, in India, and in the Third Reich, the lowest caste was not permitted to bear the symbols of success and status reserved for the upper caste. They were not to be dressed better than the upper caste, not to drive better cars than the upper caste, not to have homes more extravagant than the upper caste should they manage to secure them.

In India, the caste system dictated the length and folds of a Dalit woman's saris. Dalits were not to wear the clothing or jewelry of upper-caste people but rather tattered, rougher clothing as the "marks of their inferiority."

In America, the South Carolina Negro Code of 1735 went so far as to specify the fabrics enslaved black people were permitted to wear, forbidding any that might be seen as above their station. They were banned from wearing "any sort of garment or apparel whatsoever, finer, other or of greater value than Negro cloth, duffels, coarse kerseys, osnabrigs, blue linen, check linen, or coarse garlix, or calicoes," the cheapest, roughest fabrics available to the colony. Two hundred years later, the spirit of that law was still in force as African-American soldiers were set upon and killed for wearing their army uniforms.

In Germany, one of the characteristics that enraged the Nazis was the wealth and success of German Jews and any public display of it. Late in the Second World War, a young Jewish woman in Berlin had on a fur coat when the Gestapo rounded her and others up and shoved them onto cattle cars to the concentration camps. Upon arrival, the SS were incensed to see a Jewish woman in fur that their wives could likely not afford, and, out of hatred, forced her into the camp's pigsty and rolled her in her fur coat, over and over, in the icy muck, leaving her to die in the bitter cold. But this was just days before the Allied forces reached them, and this was how she survived, eating the food scraps thrown into the sty. She huddled beside the pigs and stayed warm until liberation.

———

From the beginning, the power of caste and the superior status of the dominant group was perhaps never clearer than when the person deemed superior was unquestionably not. Given that intelligence is distributed in relatively similar proportions among individuals in any subset, it was a special form of human abuse that everyone in a particular group, regardless of intellect, morality, ethics, or humaneness, was automatically accorded control over everyone in another group, regardless of their gifts.

The historian Kenneth Stampp described the arbitrary nature of life for enslaved people in the caste system, the terrifying forced submission to individuals who were unfit for absolute power over the life and death of another. "They were owned by a woman 'unable to read or write,'" Stampp wrote, "'scarcely able to count to ten,' legally incompetent to contract marriage," and yet had to submit to her sovereignty, depend upon her for their next breath. They were owned by "drunkards, such as Lilburne Lewis, of Livingston County, Kentucky, who once chopped a slave to bits with an ax," Stampp wrote; "and by sadists, such as Madame Lalaurie, of New Orleans, who tortured her slaves for her own amusement."

In order to survive, "they were to give way to the most wretched white man," observed *The Farmers' Register* of 1834.

For much of the time that African-Americans have been in this land, they have had to find ways to stay alive in a structure that required total submission, a close reading of their betters and the performance of that submission in order to avoid savage punishment. "They must obey at all times, and under all circumstances, cheerfully and with alacrity," said a Virginia slaveholder. They had to adjust themselves to the shifting and arbitrary demands of whatever dominant person they happened to be encountering in that moment.

This created a nerve-jangling existence, given that "any number of acts," according to a North Carolina judge during the time of slavery, could be read as "insolence," whether it was "a look, the pointing of a finger, a refusal or neglect to step out of the way when a white person is seen to approach."

To these, the nineteenth-century orator Frederick Douglass added the following gestures that could incite white rage and violence. "In the tone of an answer," Douglass wrote, "in answering at all; in not answering; in the expression of countenance; in the motion of the head; in the gait, manner and bearing." Any one of these, "if tolerated, would destroy that subordination, upon which our social system rests," the North Carolina judge said.

This code extended for generations. Years after the Nazis were defeated across the Atlantic, African-Americans were still being brutalized for the least appearance of stepping out of their place. Planters routinely whipped their sharecroppers for "trivial offenses," wrote Allison Davis and Burleigh and Mary Gardner in 1941. A planter in Mississippi said that, if his tenant "didn't stop acting so big, the next time it would be the bullet or a rope. That is the way to manage them when they get too big." In 1948, a black tenant farmer in Louise, Mississippi, was severely beaten by two whites, wrote the historian James C. Cobb, "because he asked for a receipt after paying his water bill."

The most trivial interaction had to be managed with ranking in mind. Well into the 1960s in the American South, the mere boarding of a public bus was a tightly choreographed affair devised for maximum humiliation and stigma to the lowest caste. Unlike dominant-caste passengers who climbed aboard, paid their bus fare, and took a seat, black passengers had to climb up, pay their fare, then get off the bus so as not to pollute or disturb the white section by walking through it. Having been forced to disembark after paying, they then had to run to the back door of the bus to board in the colored section. It was not uncommon for the bus to drive off before they could make it to the back door. The passengers who had the least room for error, the least resources to lose the benefit of the ticket they had paid for, the least cushion to weather a setback, would now be humiliated as the bus pulled off without them, now likely to arrive late for work, thus putting already tenuous jobs at further risk.

"The Negro occupies a position of inferiority and servility, of which he is constantly reminded when traveling, by restriction and by the attitudes of his white neighbors," wrote the historian Bertram Doyle.

The laws and protocols kept them both apart and low. The greater the chasm, the easier to distance and degrade, the easier to justify any injustice or depravity.

"The human meaning of caste for those who live it is power and vulnerability, privilege and oppression, honor and denigration, plenty and want, reward and deprivation, security and anxiety," wrote the preeminent American scholar of caste, Gerald Berreman. "A description of caste which fails to convey this is a travesty."

In the slaveholding South, some in the dominant caste grew so accustomed to the embedded superiority built into their days, and the brutality that it took to maintain it, that they wondered how they might manage in the afterlife. "Is it possible that any of my slaves could go to Heaven," a dominant-caste woman in South Carolina asked her minister, "and I must see them there?"

———

A century after the slaveholder spoke those words, the caste system had survived and mutated, its pillars intact. America was fighting in World War II, and the public school district in Columbus, Ohio, decided to hold an essay contest, challenging students to consider the question "What to do with Hitler after the War?"

It was the spring of 1944, the same year that a black boy was forced to jump to his death, in front of his stricken father, over the Christmas card the boy had sent to a white girl at work. In that atmosphere, a sixteen-year-old African-American girl thought about what should befall Hitler. She won the student essay contest with a single sentence: "Put him in a black skin and let him live the rest of his life in America."

Part Four

The Tentacles
of Caste

Brown Eyes versus Blue Eyes

The third-graders fidgeted in their seats and rested their chins on their folded forearms as their teacher, Mrs. Elliott, told them the rules of a class experiment she wanted to try with them. This was in the farm town of Riceville, Iowa, in the late 1960s, and all of the children, the descendants of immigrants from Germany and Scotland and Ireland and Scandinavia, had roughly the same skin color as their teacher and, from afar, little by which to distinguish one from another. But after the assassination of Martin Luther King, Jr., and the turmoil that followed beyond the cornfields that surrounded them, Jane Elliott decided she needed to do something out of the ordinary to teach her dominant-caste students how it felt to be judged on the basis of an arbitrary physical trait—the color of their eyes.

She announced to the children that they would do things differently that day. She laid out arbitrary stereotypes for a neutral trait that, for now, in her classroom, would put a student with that trait in essentially the lowest caste. She told the children that brown-eyed people are not as good as blue-eyed people, that they are slower than blue-eyed people, not as smart as blue-eyed people, that, until she said otherwise, the brown-eyed students would not be allowed to drink from the water fountain, that they had to use paper cups instead. She told the children that the brown-eyed people could not play with the blue-eyed people on the playground and would have to come in early, but that the blue-eyed students would get to stay out longer for recess.

The students looked confused at first. Then, in a matter of minutes, a caste hierarchy formed. It started as soon as the teacher told the children to open their books to a certain page to begin their lesson.

"Everyone ready?" Mrs. Elliott asked the class. One little girl was still turning the pages in her book to get to the right one. The teacher looked at the girl, her eyes judging and impatient. "Everyone but Laurie," Mrs. Elliott said with exasperation. "Ready, Laurie?"

A blue-eyed boy interjected. "She's a brown-eyed," he said, having caught on instantly to the significance of what had never mattered for as long as he had known the girl.

When lunchtime approached, the teacher told the blue-eyed children they would get to eat first and would be permitted a second helping, but the brown-eyed children weren't allowed to.

"They might take too much," the teacher told them.

The brown-eyed children looked downcast and defeated.

One boy got into a fight at recess because one of the blue-eyed boys had called him a name.

"What did he call you?" the teacher asked him.

"Brown eyes," the boy said, tears at the surface of those eyes.

An otherwise neutral trait had been converted into a disability. The teacher later switched roles, and the blue-eyed children became the scapegoat caste, with the same caste behavior that had arisen the day before between these artificially constructed upper and lower castes.

"Seems when we were down on the bottom, everything bad was happening to us," one girl said. "The way you're treated you felt like you didn't want to try to do anything," said another.

Classroom performance fell for both groups of students during the few hours that they were relegated to the subordinate caste. The brown-eyed students took twice as long to finish a phonics exercise the day that they were made to feel inferior.

"I watched my students become what I told them they were," she told NBC News decades later.

When the brown-eyed children were put on a pedestal and made dominant, Elliott told the network, she saw "little wonderful brown-eyed white people become vicious, ugly, nasty, discriminating, domineering people in the space of fifteen minutes."

With the blue-eyed children scapegoated and subordi-

nated, "I watched brilliant, blue-eyed, white Christian children become timid and frightened and angry and unable to learn in the space of fifteen minutes," she said.

"If you do that with a whole group of people for a lifetime," she said, "you change them psychologically. You convince those who are analogous to the brown-eyed people that they are superior, that they are perfect, that they have the right to rule, and you convince those who take the place of the blue-eyed students that they are less than. If you do that for a lifetime, what do you suppose that does to them?"

CHAPTER TEN

Central Miscasting

I arrived in London on a slate-gray morning in December 2017 for a major conference on the topic that had begun to consume my waking hours: caste. Unlike many events I attend, I was going there to listen, to gain a greater understanding of that which I did not know rather than to speak myself. I would be surrounded by people who studied what seemed to be the missing codes to human ruptures. The issue of caste was, to my mind, the basis of every other *ism*. These researchers were now my intellectual tribe. These were people who could see past the hierarchies and false divisions that undermined the species.

The auditorium was packed with sociologists, political scientists, anthropologists, graduate students, and I could barely contain myself as I took a seat in the front. A woman who appeared to be of East Asian descent removed her jacket and nodded. There was no flinching or scooting away, there were no quizzical side-eyes as might happen in a similar setting in the States. I was feeling better already.

I took a measure of the crowd and noticed that, here at the crossroads of the world, there was no one else at the conference who looked like me. Most everyone appeared to be descended from South Asia, meaning India, or from Europe, primarily the United Kingdom. Not one person of African descent, from what I could tell, only two or three Americans, all of them white and based in Europe or India. I alone had crossed the Atlantic for this single day of attempting to understand the forces that had shaped the course of my life and those of my ancestors and of many other people before me.

While I had studied the unspoken caste structure in the United States, I had not yet spent time on the original caste system of India. As with many conversations about injustice, the talks turned almost exclusively on the victims and consequences of societal ills rather than on their origins. Panel after panel looked through a different lens at the suffering of the lowest castes, which in India have been called the "scheduled castes" or, shocking to American ears, the "backward castes." I began to see parallels with America, heard stories that could have been taken from the headlines in the United States about African-Americans and indigenous people.

Both countries had abolished legal discrimination, and yet, according to the panels and keynotes, Dalits were being brutalized by Indian authorities, as African-Americans were being brutalized by police in the United States. And a people known as the Adivasi were fighting to retain their lands and culture in India, as have the indigenous people in America. Two different countries, oceans apart, had found parallel ways to contain the subordinate groups within them. I could close my eyes, change the names as I listened to these reports and feel that I was back in the United States. "Another Dalit murdered by police, another Adivasi murdered by the police," a woman said. "Why do we not face up to the outrage of state-sanctioned violence?"

At the first break, I was anxious to get a copy of the papers the scholars had read that morning. I had decided early on that I was not going to lean on any recognition that might accrue to me from my first book. In fact, I purposely kept a quiet profile so as not to attract attention to this new project that was then still germinating in my head. I was there on the strength of my own personal presentation, there to be accepted for what people could see—a well-dressed woman, an American, an African-American, well-spoken and focused.

I went up to a professor, an Indian woman, an upper-caste woman, as I would come to realize, who seemed to be in charge. I asked if I might get a copy of the papers that were presented. Would they be made available? She said no.

"You'll have to wait. Why do you need a copy?"

"I'm a writer, and I have come all the way from America just for this," I told her. I thought that this level of dedication might impress her. It did not. She directed me to an Englishman who was her senior, and it seemed that, even here among people who studied caste, there might be traditional hierarchy at work. The woman was then pulled away by the press of people, and the Englishman was swamped as well. As in any human grouping, there were cliques and fraternities of people who had known one another or worked together, and, rather than an open conference, this was starting to feel like a family reunion to which I had been admitted by accident.

At the lunch break, I spotted a gentleman who was sitting alone, across from other men who were talking to one another. He was Indian, like three-quarters of the attendees, but he was different. He was carrying a black briefcase, all business and purposeful amid the backpacks surrounding us. Like me, he seemed an outsider among insiders. I felt an immediate kinship.

His name, he told me as I took a seat next to him, was Tushar. He was born in Bengal and was a geologist now living in London. He was more formally dressed than everyone else, blue Oxford shirt collar peeking above his gray tweed jacket, a side part in his thick gray hair, his eyes smiling in quarter moons on his warm, kind face as he talked.

"According to the caste system," he said, as if informing me of the status of someone he once knew, "I belong to the second upper caste. The warrior-soldier caste."

I looked at this man who was not much taller than I, small-boned, narrow-shouldered, gentle of face, self-effacingly modest in bearing and wondered on what planet would this man be seen as a natural-born warrior? Here was living proof of the miscasting of caste. This had long ago registered to him as well, and he took the caste ascription with so little solemnity that he was not at first able to give the exact spelling of the caste, or, in Sanskrit, the *varna*, to which he was born. I did not yet know the four *varnas* at the time, or that castes were even called *varnas*, so I asked him to write it down for me. He wrote the words *Khatriya* and then *Kayastras* in my notepad.

"I think it is *Kshatriya*," he said, as if to disregard its significance by misremembering how to spell or pronounce it. "It's an issue not well understood. I was raised with social privilege. You are told you are second upper caste, the ruling caste, and that you are to be happy that there are many below you."

But as a young boy on the way to school, he passed the beggars on the streets asking for money and people crying out that they had no food. His own family sat down to meals with four or five courses—dal and amaranth, mutton and chutney, while less well-off families subsisted on rice and potatoes, and those beneath them on even less.

It was hard to enjoy one's privilege when so few people had it. When he was eleven or twelve, he began asking why his family had so much and others so little. "Don't discuss about these things," the elders told him. "Do your studies. Caste is created by God."

The afternoon sessions were about to begin, discussions of Dalit protests and corporate encroachment on the land of the Adivasis. Tushar and I headed back to the auditorium, each of us on our respective missions.

As this was England, there was a break for tea, and I gravitated to Tushar again in the crowd. He looked forlorn and impatient now. "They haven't answered my questions," he said. "All my life I have lived with this. I am looking for answers about how this began. I will stay to hear more."

He asked me why I had come all the way from America for this conference. I told him I wanted to understand caste because I lived with it, too. I told him most people don't think of America as having a caste system, but it has all the hallmarks of one. He listened and did not judge.

"Caste defines everything in India," he said. "It is the Hindu religion that maintains the caste system. That is why Ambedkar became a Buddhist. It was not an escape for him, it was a liberation. Casteism is another form of racism. God knows how long it will take for people to let it go."

"I am wondering then, are you still a Hindu?" I asked him.

"I am atheist," he said. "No religion. Since I was thirteen."

"What does your family think of that?"

"They think, you are born a Hindu, you die a Hindu. You do not escape caste. But I believe what I believe. Who cares what they think?"

He appeared to have given some consideration to what I had told him about the hierarchy in America. It had puzzled him and intrigued him.

"If you have caste in the U.S.," he asked me, "where are you in the caste system?"

That is the question that many Indians ask, in one form or another, upon meeting a fellow Indian. It is a line of inquiry that those in the lowest caste know is coming and that they dread. Indians will ask the surname, the occupation of one's father, the village one is from, the section of the village that one is from, to suss out the caste of whoever is in front of them. They will not rest until they have uncovered the person's rank in the social order.

Tushar had waited quite some time to ask me this, and would not likely have done so, or thought of it at all, if I hadn't mentioned caste in America. The idea seemed a wonderment to him. He seemed to want to know how things worked, and where I fit into what, to him, was an alien hierarchy.

I had not expected this question. Nobody had ever asked me before. How could he not know? Was he merely being polite? Hollywood and the news media have exported demeaning images of African-Americans for generations, which means our reputations often precede us, and not for the better. So I was, in fact, strangely grateful for his giving me an option. Even without the language of caste, most any American would know the ranking of the group to which I was born.

But here was a man born upper-caste in India and a skeptic of inherited status, seeing me as an individual who might be of any rank. He was not putting me in a box nor making the assumptions that I labor under every day.

His question was liberating in its innocent lack of judgment. Yet it brought to mind Dr. King's epiphany nearly sixty years before in India.

"Well," I told Tushar, "in America, I am assigned to the lowest caste, the American Untouchables. I am an American Dalit. And I am living proof that caste is artificial."

He gave a look of recognition. My answer was further confirmation of what he considered a disease. We would have other conversations in the following months whenever I visited London. He would share more of the absurdities he had witnessed in the caste system back home.

He remembered the Dalit students whose exams went ungraded. "The tests were not marked," he said, "because the teacher was upper caste and would not touch the paper touched by a Dalit. So you laugh or you cry."

He told me about the upper-caste woman in an office where he once worked. She would get up from her desk and walk the length of the office, down the hall and around the corner, to ask a Dalit to get her water.

"The jug was there next to her desk," he said. "The Dalit had to come to where she was sitting and pour it for her. It was beneath her dignity to get the water herself from the desk beside her. This is the sickness of caste."

He recalled the heartbreak of the Indian fixation on skin color, which was caste within caste, and the hatred of darker Indians, who tend to be lower caste but not always, and how they suffer for this accident of fate, as do African-Americans and other people of color in the United States and in other parts of the world.

His older sister happened to be darker than most of his siblings, and, when she reached courting age, she was told she would have to boil milk and skim the skin from the boiled milk and spread it on her face prior to sleep every night before the young men came to interview her for marriage. "Imagine," he said. "Week after week. Night after night. She knew she would be rejected, and she would close the door to her room and cry. I was twelve. I remember to this day. She got married, but that's not the point. She should not have to go through all of this. The cruelty of it."

We had both been miscast, each in our own way, and could see through the delusion that had shaped and restricted us from the other side of our respective caste systems. We had broken from the matrix and were convinced that we could see what others could not, and that others could see it, too, if they could awaken from their slumber.

We had defied our caste assignments: He was not a warrior or ruler. He was a geologist. I was not a domestic. I was an author. He had defied his caste from on high and I, from below, and we had met at this moment in London at our own Maginot Line of equality, standing on different sides of the same quest to understand the forces that had sought to define us but had failed.

CHAPTER ELEVEN

Dominant Group Status Threat
and the Precarity of the Highest Rung

In late 2015, two economists at Princeton University announced the startling revelation that the death rates of middle-aged white Americans, especially less-educated white Americans at midlife, had risen for the first time since 1950. The perplexing results of this study on mortality rates in the United States sounded alarms on the front pages of newspapers and at the top of news feeds across the nation.

The surge in early deaths among middle-aged white people went counter to the trends of every other ethnic group in America. Even historically marginalized black and Latino Americans had seen their mortality rates fall during the time period studied, from 1998 to 2013. The rise in the white death rate was at odds with prevailing trends in the rest of the Western world.

Americans had enjoyed increasing longevity the previous century, with each succeeding generation, due to healthier lifestyles and advancements in medicine. But starting just before the turn of the twenty-first century, the death rates among middle-aged white Americans, ages forty-five to fifty-four, began to rise, as the least educated, in particular, succumbed to suicide, drug overdoses, and liver disease from alcohol abuse, according to the authors of the seminal study, Anne Case and the Nobel laureate Angus Deaton. These "deaths of despair," as the economists called them, accounted for the loss of some half a million white Americans during that period, more than the number of American soldiers who died during World War II. These are people who might still be alive had this group kept to previous generational trends.

"These are deaths that do not have to happen," Case said at a conference on inequality. "These are people who are taking their lives, either slowly or quickly."

The worsening numbers were "persistent and large enough" to drive up white mortality rates overall and to outweigh the gains in longevity from advances in the treatment of cancer and heart disease. The turnabout reversed "decades of progress in mortality and was unique to the United States," Case and Deaton wrote. "No other rich country saw a similar turnaround."

For this group of Americans, mortality rates rose at a time when rates in other Western countries had not merely dipped but had plummeted. The rate for middle-aged white Americans rose from about 375 per 100,000 people in the late 1990s to about 415 per 100,000 in 2013, as against a fall in the United Kingdom, for example, from about 330 per 100,000 to 260 per 100,000 over the same period. A graphic of the mortality rates for leading Western nations shows an upward line for the death rates of middle-aged white Americans against the plunging lines for their counterparts in fellow Western countries.

What could account for the worsening prospects of this group of Americans, unique in the Western world and singular even in the United States?

The authors noted that, since the 1970s, real wages had stagnated for blue-collar workers, leading to economic insecurity and to a generation less well off than previous ones. But they acknowledged that similar stagnation had occurred in other Western countries. They noted that comparable Western countries had a more generous safety net that could offer protections not available in the United States. Yet white Americans would not be the only group affected by wage stagnation and a thin safety net. Blue-collar workers of other backgrounds would be equally at risk from the uncertainties of the economy, if not more so. Black death rates have been historically higher than those of other groups, but even their mortality rates were falling, year by year. It was white Americans at midlife who were dying of despair in rising numbers.

In caste terms, these are the least well off, most precariously situated members of the dominant caste in America. For generations, they could take for granted their inherited rank in the hierarchy and the benefits that accrued from it.

We may underestimate, though, the aftershocks of a shift in demographics, the erosion of labor unions, the perceived loss of status, the fears about their place in the world, and resentment that the kind of security their fathers could rely upon might now be waning in what were supposed to be the best years of their lives. Rising immigration from across the Pacific and the Rio Grande and the ascendance of a black man as president made for an inversion of the world as many had known it, and some of them might have been more susceptible to the calls to "take our country back" after 2008 and to "make America great again" in 2016.

In America, political scientists have given this malaise of insecurities a name: dominant group status threat. This phenomenon "is not the usual form of prejudice or stereotyping that involves looking down on outgroups who are perceived to be inferior," writes Diana Mutz, a political scientist at the University of Pennsylvania. "Instead, it is born of a sense that the outgroup is doing too well and thus, is a viable threat to one's own dominant group status."

The victims of these deaths of despair are in the same category of people whom, centuries ago, the colonial elites elevated as they created the caste system. The planters bestowed higher status on European yeomen and those of the lower classes to create a new American category known as white. In earlier times, even those who owned no slaves, wrote the white southern author W. J. Cash, clung to the "dear treasure of his superiority as a white man, which had been conferred on him by slavery; and so was determined to keep the black man in chains."

By the middle of the twentieth century, the white working-class

American, wrote the white southern author Lillian Smith, "has not only been neglected and exploited, he has been fed little except the scraps of 'skin color' and 'white supremacy' as spiritual nourishment."

Working-class whites, the preeminent social economist Gunnar Myrdal wrote, "need the demarcations of caste more than upper class whites. They are the people likely to stress aggressively that no Negro can ever attain the status of even the lowest white."

In a psychic way, the people dying of despair could be said to be dying of the end of an illusion, an awakening to the holes in an article of faith that an inherited, unspoken superiority, a natural deservedness over subordinated castes, would assure their place in the hierarchy. They had relied on this illusion, perhaps beyond the realm of consciousness and perhaps needed it more than any other group in a forbiddingly competitive society "in which downward social mobility was a constant fear," the historian David Roediger wrote. "One might lose everything, but not whiteness."

In the midst of the Great Depression, the scholar W.E.B. Du Bois observed that working-class white Americans had bought into the compensation of a "public and psychological wage," as he put it. "They were given public deference and titles of courtesy because they were white." They had accepted the rough uncertainties of laboring class life in exchange for the caste system's guarantee that, no matter what befell them, they would never be on the very bottom.

The American caste system, which co-opted this class of white workers nearly from the start, "drove such a wedge between black and white workers that there probably are not today in the world two groups of workers with practically identical interests" who are "kept so far apart that neither sees anything of common interests," Du Bois wrote.

These insecurities extend back for centuries. A Virginia slaveholder remarked in 1832 that poor whites had "little but their complexion to console them for being born into a higher caste." When a hierarchy is built around the needs of the group to which one happens to have been born, it can distort the perceptions of one's place in the world. It can create an illusion that one is innately superior to others if only because it has been reinforced so often that it becomes accepted as subconscious truth.

"Nobody could take away from you this whiteness that made you and your way of life 'superior,'" Lillian Smith wrote. "They could take your house, your job, your fun; they could steal your wages, keep you from acquiring knowledge; they could tax your vote or cheat you out of it: they could by arousing your anxieties make you impotent, but they could not strip your white skin off of you. It became the poor white's most precious possession, a 'charm' staving off utter dissolution."

Given that the hierarchy was designed for the benefit of the caste that created it, "the basic restrictions upon marriage, occupation and public gatherings separate the two groups into two self-perpetuating castes, in such a way that the white group is assured the higher privileges and fuller opportunities," wrote the anthropologists W. Lloyd Warner and Allison Davis of the bipolar caste system exemplified by the Jim Crow South. This affords the dominant caste "a tremendous gain in psychological security . . . as a result of their categorically defined superiority of status."

Things began to change in the 1960s when civil rights legislation opened labor markets to women of all races, to immigrants from beyond Europe, and to African-Americans whose life-and-death protests helped unlock doors for all of these groups. New people flooded the labor pool at the precise moment that manufacturing was on the decline, and every worker now faced greater competition.

"In the span of a few cruel years," wrote the *New York Times* columnist Russell Baker in the 1960s, of the white Anglo-Saxon Protestant, "he has seen his comfortable position as the 'in' man of American society become a social liability as the outcasts and the exploited have presented their due bills on their conscience."

Some people from the groups that were said to be inherently inferior managed to make it into the mainstream, a few rising to the level of people in the dominant caste, one of them, in 2008, rising to the highest station in the land. This left some white working-class Americans in particular, those with the least education and the material security that it can confer, to face the question of whether the commodity that they could take for granted—their skin and ascribed race—might be losing value.

There had always been a subordinate caste, and everyone knew who the subordinate caste was and had positioned themselves accordingly. "Always [the Negro] was something you had to prove you were better than," Lillian Smith wrote of the white working-class dilemma, "and you couldn't prove it, no, you couldn't prove it." The beliefs and assumptions had all contributed to a "collective madness—and it is that—which feeds on half-lies and quarter-truths and dread."

Those in the dominant caste who found themselves lagging behind those seen as inherently inferior potentially faced an epic existential crisis. To stand on the same rung as those perceived to be of a lower caste is seen as lowering one's status. In the zero-sum stakes of a caste system upheld by perceived scarcity, if a lower-caste person goes up a rung, an upper-caste person comes down. The elevation of others amounts to a demotion of oneself, thus equality feels like a demotion.

If the lower-caste person manages actually to rise above an upper-caste person, the natural human response from someone weaned on their caste's inherent superiority is to perceive a threat to their existence, a heightened sense of unease, of displacement, of fear for their very survival. *"If the things that I have believed are not true, then might I not be who I thought I was?"* The disaffection is more than economic. The malaise is spiritual, psychological, emotional. Who are you if there is no one to be better than?

"It's a great lie on which their identity has been built," said Dr. Sushrut Jadhav, a prominent Indian psychiatrist, based in London, who specializes in the effects of caste on mental health.

Thus, a caste system makes a captive of everyone within it. Just as the assumptions of inferiority weigh on those assigned to the bottom of the caste system, the assumptions of superiority can burden those at the top with unsustainable expectations of needing to be several rungs above, in charge at all times, at the center of things, to police those who might cut ahead of them, to resent the idea of undeserving lower castes jumping the line and getting in front of those born to lead.

"His whole life is one anxious effort to preserve his caste," wrote the Dalit leader Bhimrao Ambedkar of the dominant caste. "Caste is his precious possession which he must save at any cost."

When people have lived with assumptions long enough, passed down through the generations as incontrovertible fact, they are accepted as the truths of physics, no longer needing even to be spoken. They are as true and as unremarkable as water flowing through rivers or the air that we breathe. In the original caste system of India, the abiding faith in the entitlement of birth became enmeshed in the mind of the upper caste and "hangs there to this day without any support," Ambedkar wrote, "for now it needs no prop but belief—like a weed on the surface of a pond."

The anxieties of the least secure in the dominant caste are not unlike those of a firstborn child expected to take over the family business. He may have neither the interest nor the specialized aptitude for it but feels duty-bound, pressured to take the reins, even though a younger sibling, say, a sister, is the one who was always good with numbers and has the temperament to run things but is not considered because of the family hierarchy of who goes first and who inherits what. This creates unsustainable expectations in a culture that proclaims to be egalitarian but was set up for certain people to dominate by birth.

Custom and law segregated the white working and middle classes for so long that most would not have been in a position to see firsthand the headwinds confronting disfavored Americans. The hand of government in the lives of white citizens has often been made invisible and has left distortions as to how each group got to where they are, allowing resentments and rivalries to fester. Many may not have realized that the New Deal reforms of the

1930s, like the Social Security Act of 1935 (providing old age insurance) and the Wagner Act (protecting workers from labor abuse), excluded the vast majority of black workers—farm laborers and domestics—at the urging of southern white politicians.

Further tipping the scales, the Federal Housing Administration was created to make homeownership easier for white families by guaranteeing mortgages in white neighborhoods while specifically excluding African-Americans who wished to buy homes. It did so by refusing to back mortgages in any neighborhood where black people lived, a practice known as redlining, and by encouraging or even requiring restrictive covenants that barred black citizens from buying homes in white neighborhoods.

Together, these and other government programs extended a safety net and a leg-up to the parents, grandparents, and great-grandparents of white Americans of today, while shutting out the foreparents of African-Americans from those same job protections and those same chances to earn or build wealth.

These government programs for the dominant caste were in force during the lifetimes of many current-day Americans. These programs did not open to African-Americans until the late 1960s, and then only after the protests for civil rights. The more recent forms of state-sanctioned discrimination, along with denying pay to enslaved people over the course of generations, has led to a wealth gap in which white families currently have ten times the wealth of their black counterparts. If you are not black and "if you or your parents were alive in the 1960s and got a mortgage," wrote Ben Mathis-Lilley in *Slate*, "you benefited directly and materially from discrimination."

The very machinery upon which many white Americans had the chance to build their lives and assets was forbidden to African-Americans who were still just a generation or two out of enslavement and the apartheid of Jim Crow, burdens so heavy and borne for so long that if they were to rise, they would have to work and save that much harder than their fellow Americans.

Rather than encouraging a greater understanding of how these disparities came to be or a framework for compassion for fellow Americans, political discourse has usually reinforced prevailing stereotypes of a lazy, inferior group getting undeserved handouts, a scapegoating that makes the formal barriers all the more unjust and the resentments of white working-class citizens all the more tragic. The subordinate caste was shut out of "the trillions of dollars of wealth accumulated through the appreciation of housing assets secured by federally insured loans between 1932 and 1962," a major source of current-day wealth, wrote the sociologist George Lipsitz. "Yet they find themselves portrayed as privileged beneficiaries of special preferences by the very people who profit from their exploitation and oppression."

Once labor, housing, and schools finally began to open up to the subordinate caste, many working- and middle-class whites began to perceive themselves to be worse off, by comparison, and to report that they experienced more racism than African-Americans, unable to see the inequities that persist, often in their favor.

Unconscious Bias: A Mutation in the Software

Toward the end of the twentieth century, social scientists found new ways to measure what had transformed from overt racism to a slow boil of unspoken antagonisms that social scientists called unconscious bias. This was not the cross-burning, epithet-spewing biological racism of the pre-civil-rights era, but rather discriminatory behaviors based on subconscious prejudgments by people who professed and believed in equality.

By adulthood, researchers have found, most Americans have been exposed to a culture with enough negative messages about African-Americans and other marginalized groups that as much as 80 percent of white Americans hold unconscious bias against black Americans, bias so automatic that it kicks in before a person can process it, according to the Harvard sociologist David R. Williams. The messaging is so pervasive in American society that a third of black Americans hold anti-black bias against themselves.

"All racial ethnic minority groups are stereotyped more negatively than whites," Williams said. "Blacks are viewed the worst, then Latinos, who are viewed twice as negatively as Asians. There is a hierarchy of rank."

What kind of person is likely to carry this kind of unconscious bias? "This is a wonderful person," Williams said, "who has sympathy for the bad things that have happened in the past. But that person is still an American and has been fed the larger stereotypes of blacks that are deeply embedded in the culture of this society. So, despite holding no explicit racial prejudices, they nonetheless hold implicit bias that's deep in their subconscious. They have all these negative images of African-Americans so that when they meet an African-American, although self-consciously they are not prejudiced, the implicit biases nonetheless operate to shape their behavior. This discriminatory behavior is activated more quickly and effortlessly than conscious discrimination, more quickly than saying, 'I've decided to discriminate against this person.'

"This is the frightening point," he said. "Because it's an automatic process, and it's an unconscious process, people who engage in this unthinking discrimination are not aware of it. They are not lying to you when they say, 'I didn't treat this person differently, and I treat everyone the same.' They mean it because, consciously, that is the way they see themselves. These implicit biases shape their behavior in ways they are not even aware of. The research suggests that about 70 to 80 percent of whites fall into this category."

These autonomic responses contribute to disparities in hiring, in housing, in education, and in medical treatment for the lowest-caste people compared to their dominant-caste counterparts and, as with other aspects of the caste system, often go against logic. For example, a pioneering study by the sociologist Devah Pager found that white felons applying for a job were more likely to get hired than African-Americans with no criminal record.

In the life-and-death world of medicine, African-Americans and other marginalized people are granted fewer procedures and poorer-quality care than whites across every therapeutic intervention, said Williams, who specializes in biases in public health. Of the sixty most common procedures reimbursed by Medicare, he said, "African-Americans receive fewer procedures than white patients even though they have a higher rate of illness." The only procedures that African-Americans receive at higher rates than whites, Williams said, are shunts for renal disease, the removal of stomach tissue for ulcers, leg amputation, and the removal of testicles.

Bias does not contain the damage it inflicts to one group, however. One tragic form of unconscious bias has had the unintended effect of unwittingly protecting the disfavored castes of African-Americans and Latinos from a scourge that has brought untold heartache to many white Americans. Empirical studies have found that physicians often disregard the reports of pain from black and Latino patients, wrongly believing that African-Americans in particular have higher pain thresholds. This has led physicians to undertreat or to deny pain medication to black patients—even those with metastatic cancer—while readily prescribing medication to white patients reporting equivalent levels of pain. The disparity is so severe that African-Americans as a group receive pain medication at levels beneath the thresholds established by the World Health Organization.

Just as pollutants don't confine themselves to the air around a factory, this single caste inequity has spared no one. The undertreatment of the subordinate caste leaves them to suffer needlessly, and the overtreatment of the dominant caste may have contributed to the rising mortality rate for white Americans who become addicted to opioids.

Worse still, society was less prepared for the opioid crisis than it might have been had it not missed the chance to build a comprehensive framework for dealing with substance abuse in the 1990s, when it was the subordinate caste that was in need of help. The crack cocaine epidemic of that era was dismissed as an urban crime problem rather than addressed as a social and health crisis, considered a black problem rather than a human one. The response was to criminalize addiction when the abusers were subordinate caste, which swelled the rate of mass incarceration, broke up families, and left the country ill-equipped for the incoming tragedy of opioid addiction. Caste assumptions created devastation on both sides of the caste divide and have made for a less generous society overall.

Exclusion costs lives, up and down the hierarchy. The physician Jonathan M. Metzl, who has conducted research into the health of disaffected whites in middle America, has measured the life-and-death consequences of state decisions to withhold benefits seen as helping presumably undeserving minority groups. In the state of Tennessee, for example, he found that restrictive health policies may have cost the lives of as many as 4,599 African-Americans between 2011 and 2015, but also cost the lives of as many as 12,013 white Tennesseans, more than double the loss sustained by black residents.

In his book *Dying of Whiteness*, Metzl told of the case of a forty-one-year-old white taxi driver who was suffering from an inflamed liver that threatened the man's life. Because the Tennessee legislature had neither taken up the Affordable Care Act nor expanded Medicaid coverage, the man was not able to get the expensive, lifesaving treatment that would have been available to him had he lived just across the border in Kentucky. As he approached death, he stood by the conviction that he did not want the government involved.

"No way I want my tax dollars paying for Mexicans or welfare queens," the man told Metzl. "Ain't no way I would ever support Obamacare or sign up for it. I would rather die."

And sadly, so he would.

CHAPTER TWELVE

A Scapegoat to Bear the Sins of the World

E very year, on the day of atonement, the ancient Hebrews took two male goats and presented them before the Lord at the entrance to the tent of meeting. Then the high priest cast lots to determine the fate of each goat.

One they would kill as a sacrifice to the Lord to cleanse and make sacred the sanctuary. The other, the scapegoat, they would present to the Lord alive.

The high priest would lay both hands on the head of the live goat and confess upon its head all the guilt and misdeeds of the Israelites. All of their sins he would transpose to the goat, and the goat was then banished to the wilderness, carrying on its back the weight of the faults of the Israelites, and thus freeing the Israelites to flourish in peace.

The goat was cast out to suffer for the sins of others and was called the scapegoat.

This was the ritual according to Leviticus that was passed down through the ages, adopted by the ancient Greeks. It survives not only in individual interactions but within nations and castes. For the ancients, the scapegoat served as the healing agent for the larger whole. In modern times, the concept of the scapegoat has mutated from merely the bearer of misfortune to the person or group blamed for bringing misfortune.

"This serves to relieve others," wrote the Jungian psychologist

Sylvia Brinton Perera, to free "the scapegoaters, of their own responsibilities, and to strengthen the scapegoaters' sense of power and righteousness."

In a caste system, whether in the United States or in India or in World War II Germany, the lowest caste performed the unwitting role of diverting society's attention from its structural ills and taking the blame for collective misfortune. It was seen, in fact, as misfortune itself.

Thus the scapegoat unwittingly helps unify the favored castes to be seen as free of blemish as long as there is a visible disfavored group to absorb their sins. "Scapegoating, as it is currently practiced," Perera wrote, "means finding the one or ones who can be identified with evil or wrongdoing, blamed for it and cast out of the community in order to leave the remaining members with a feeling of guiltlessness, atoned (at one)."

A scapegoat caste has become necessary for the collective wellbeing of the castes above it and the smooth functioning of the caste system. The dominant groups can look to those cast out as the cause of any fate or misfortune, as representing the worst aspects of society. "The scapegoater feels a relief in being lighter," Perera wrote, "without the burden of carrying what is unacceptable to his or her ego ideal, without shadow." The ones above the scapegoat can "stand purified and united with each other, feeling blessed by their God."

In the American South, the designated scapegoat was expelled not to the wilderness but to the margins of society, an attempted near banishment from the human race. Many men and women in the dominant caste blamed the people they enslaved for poor harvests or for meager returns, called the people who worked as many as eighteen hours a day for the enrichment of others lazy, and took out their frustrations on the bodies of those they held captive.

The caste system spared no one in the scapegoat caste. When pregnant women were to be whipped, "before binding them to the stakes, a hole is made in the ground to accommodate the enlarged form of the victim," a Mr. C. Robin of Louisiana wrote in describing what he had witnessed.

"The Negro becomes both a scapegoat and an object lesson for his group," the anthropologist Allison Davis wrote. "He suffers for all the minor caste violations which have aroused the whites, and he becomes a warning against future violations."

After the Civil War, Confederates blamed the people they had once owned for the loss of the war. Well into the twentieth century, into the lifetimes of people among us today, lynchings served as a form of ritual human sacrifice before audiences sometimes in the thousands. People drove in from neighboring states, schools let out early so that white children could join their parents to watch men in the dominant caste perform acts of sadism on people from the subordinate caste before hanging them from the limb of a sycamore. Lynchings almost always occurred "at the hands of persons unknown," performed "in a collective way so that no one person could be blamed."

"Whites were unified in seeing the Negro as a scapegoat and proper object for exploitation and hatred," wrote Gunnar Myrdal, a leading social economist in the 1940s. "White solidarity is upheld and the caste order protected."

As scapegoats, they are seen as the reason for societal ills. The scapegoats are blamed for a crime rate that they alone do not cause and for drugs that they are no more likely to use than the dominant caste, but for which they are incarcerated at six times the rate as whites accused of similar offenses. Thousands of African-Americans are behind bars for having been in possession of a substance that businessmen in the dominant caste are now converting to wealth in the marijuana and CBD industry.

In the United States and in India, people in the dominant caste have blamed stagnant careers or rejections in college admissions on marginalized people in the lower caste, even though African-Americans in the United States and Dalits in India are rarely in positions to decide who will get hired at corporations or admitted to universities. In the United States, it is a numerical impossibility for African-Americans to wreak such havoc in employment and higher education: there are simply not enough African-Americans to take the positions that every member of the dominant caste dreams of holding.

Notably, while affirmative action grew out of the civil rights movement fought by lowest-caste people and their white allies, decades of analysis show that it is white women, and thus white families, rather than African-Americans, who became the prime beneficiaries of a plan intended to redress centuries of injustice against the lowest-caste people. Scapegoating nimbly obscures the structural forces that make life harder than it has to be for many Americans for the benefit of a few, primarily in the dominant caste. It blames societal ills on the groups with the least power and the least say in how the country operates while allowing the larger framework and those who control and reap the dividends of these divisions to go unchecked. It worsens during times of economic tensions when the least secure in the dominant group attacks a group in the minority "for structural economic problems that actually harmed both," one social scientist observed, "and that neither caused."

———

The human impulse to blame a disfavored outsider group puts the lives of both the favored and disfavored in peril.

On an autumn evening in October 1989, a suburban Boston couple, expecting their first child that December, were driving home from a childbirth class. The husband, twenty-nine-year-old Charles Stuart, was the reserved and ambitious store manager at a luxury furrier downtown. His wife, thirty-year-old Carol DiMaiti Stuart, was a petite and gregarious attorney. They had bought a split-level house in the suburbs and had already decided that if that baby was a boy, they would name him Christopher. They were both children of the dominant caste, who had risen from modest, blue-collar backgrounds. They had just celebrated their fourth wedding anniversary.

That evening, they were driving home through the neighborhood of Roxbury, which had been the landing place for waves of European immigrants and, after World War II, became mostly black, poor and working class, ravaged by the war on drugs. The husband was behind the wheel of their Toyota and had taken a somewhat circuitous route. At a traffic light in the Mission Hill section, shots were fired, hitting the wife in the head and the husband in the abdomen, both at close range. The husband was in better shape than the wife, and he called police dispatch from his car phone. His wife died at the hospital of the massive wounds she sustained. Their baby was delivered in the wife's final hours, two months premature, and named Christopher as his parents had wished. He lived for only seventeen days.

The night of the shooting, Charles Stuart told police that a black man with a raspy voice and wearing a jogging suit had forced his way into the car and had mugged and shot them. The tragedy triggered every deep-seated fear and horror in Boston and across the nation. The husband's desperate call to police dispatch aired repeatedly on television, as did video footage of paramedics pulling the mortally wounded wife from the Toyota.

Outraged over an incomprehensible tragedy, the city went into action and began a massive manhunt. Mayor Raymond Flynn vowed to "get the animals responsible" and ordered every available detective diverted to the case. Officers combed Roxbury and stopped and strip-searched every man who fit the description, which meant almost any black man on the streets, hundreds of them. The hunt for a suspect became the near singular fixation for weeks. The dragnet yielded a thirty-nine-year-old unemployed black man with a criminal record whom Charles picked out in a police lineup. People began calling for the death penalty.

For months, officials had paid little notice to inconsistencies in the husband's behavior, distracted as they were by a storyline tailored to their expectations. The night of the shooting, Charles had driven around aimlessly for thirteen minutes while talking to dispatch, rather than heading back to the hospital that the couple had just left, claiming not to recognize any landmarks in the city he had lived in all his life. "He never tried to comfort his wife, never called her name," according to *Time* magazine. "In the ambulance to the hospital, he only asked about the seriousness of his own wound, and never about his wife's condition."

Not long before, he had taken out several insurance policies on his young and healthy wife. After his release from the hospital, he collected on one of them and promptly bought a new car, a Nissan Maxima, and a thousand-dollar pair of women's diamond earrings. It turned out that he had been staying out late on Friday evenings and into the early morning hours to the consternation of his wife in the months before her death. He had been seen with a young blond woman who worked summers at the furrier and whom he had arranged to phone him at the hospital, though she vehemently denied a relationship as the story broke. He had told friends he did not want the baby, that it would disrupt his climb up the social ladder.

Those contradictory details were not powerful enough to dislodge the fixed assumptions about the case. But there had been a third person involved on the night of the shooting, and as Christmas approached, that person began to crack. It was the husband's brother, Matthew. Charles had planned ahead for Matthew to meet the car at a rendezvous site the night of the shooting. Before the brother arrived, Charles had stopped the car and shot his wife in the head, after which Charles pointed the gun at himself, intending to shoot his foot but misfiring into his torso instead. Charles told his brother to take and dispose of Carol's jewelry and purse and the gun that Charles had used to kill her. This would make it look like the robbery he would later report to the police.

But afterward, the brother's conscience began to plague him, and he told other members of the family. He said he thought he was helping his brother in an insurance scam when he got the purse and gun, not in a murder plot. Word got back to Charles Stuart that his brother was planning to go to the police and testify against him in exchange for immunity. With the investigation closing in on him, the husband jumped to his death from the Tobin Bridge into the Mystic River that January. His brother, Matthew, later pleaded guilty to conspiracy and possession of a firearm, among other charges, and served three years in prison.

In the end, the husband alone was responsible for the death of his wife, but the caste system was his unwitting accomplice. He knew that he could count on the caste system to spring into action as it is programmed to do, that people would readily accept his account if the perpetrator were black, believe the dominant-caste man over subordinate people, focus on them rather than him, see the scapegoat caste as singularly capable of any depravity, and would deflect any suspicion away from him. The story didn't even have to be airtight to be believed. It needed only to be plausible. Any sympathy would accrue to him and not the scapegoat caste, which bears the burdens of someone else's sins, no matter the protestations.

The caste system had given Charles Stuart cover and endangered the life of Carol DiMaiti Stuart, as it had for white women in the Jim Crow South, where husbands and lovers knew that a black man could be blamed for anything that befell a white woman if the dominant caste chose to accuse him. This is not to say that any group is more prone to criminality or subterfuge than another. It is to say that one of the more disturbing aspects of a caste system, and of the unequal justice it produces, is that it makes for a less safe society, allowing the guilty to shift blame and often to go free. A caste system gives us false comfort, makes us feel that the world is in order, that we automatically know the good guys from the bad guys.

It is possible that nothing could have saved Carol Stuart's life, given the man she was married to. We will never know. Had the husband not been able to depend upon the universal decoy of black criminality, had he not been able to count on the instinctive reviling of the lowest caste and the corresponding presumption of virtue of the dominant caste, had he not been able to correctly assume that the caste system would act on his behalf, perhaps he might not have been as brazen, perhaps he might have tried something else, divorce, for instance. Perhaps he might not have felt as free to attempt something so heinous. Perhaps the wife might not have been killed, their son not been lost, at least not that night and not in that way, if he thought the suspicion would rightly be trained on the actual perpetrator from the start.

————

Decades later, in the years of anxiety after the 2016 election, Anthony Stephan House, a thirty-nine-year-old project manager in Austin, Texas, was getting ready to take his eight-year-old daughter to school. It was just before seven in the morning on March 2, 2018. Something prompted him to go to his front door, and when he stepped over the threshold, he noticed a package on the porch. As he picked it up, it exploded. He died shortly after his arrival at the hospital.

His death was ruled a homicide for obvious reasons at first, but the investigation quickly pivoted away. House was African-American, living on the working-class black and Latino east side of Austin with its aging ranch houses and ramblers. The police figured that the bombing might be drug-related. Maybe it was intended as retribution for a drug dealer but left at the wrong house. They considered another possibility, that maybe he had detonated the bomb himself, a theory that blamed the victim for his own death.

"We can't rule out that Mr. House didn't construct this himself and accidentally detonate it, in which case it would be an accidental death," Assistant Police Chief Joseph Chacon said.

"Based on what we know right now," Brian Manley, then interim police chief, told reporters the day of House's death, "we have no reason to believe this is anything beyond an isolated incident that took place at this residence and in no way this is linked to a terroristic attack."

Those assumptions would prove to be tragically misdirected. Ten days later, seventeen-year-old Draylen Mason, a high school senior who was a beloved bass violinist with the Austin Youth Orchestra, discovered a package outside his family's door. When he brought it inside, it exploded in the kitchen, killing him, and leaving his mother critically wounded. They, too, were African-American. Later that morning, a few miles away, a seventy-five-year-old Latina, Esperanza Herrera, was critically injured when a package left at her mother's house detonated when she picked it up.

It was only then, ten days after the first bombing, that the Austin police began warning citizens to take precautions with unknown packages. A serial bomber was at large in Austin, had been at large from the first bomb attack. The bombings were now being considered a possible hate crime. The fact that the victims were black and Latina meant that some people could distance themselves from the bombings if they chose. Until the bomber expanded his reach. Less than a week later, on the other side of Austin, two white men in their twenties were walking in a well-to-do white neighborhood when a bomb triggered by a trip wire detonated in the street and seriously injured them.

Two days after that, a bomb exploded on a conveyor belt at a FedEx warehouse, and another was discovered at a FedEx before it could detonate. The police now raced at warp speed. Surveillance cameras caught images of the man who had dropped off the last package bombs and recorded the license plate on his car. The police began tracking him by the location of his cellphone. They discovered that the suspect was a twenty-three-year-old unemployed white man named Mark Conditt, who was from a conservative Christian family. The day after the explosion at the FedEx warehouse, a SWAT team closed in on him. Cornered by officers, Conditt detonated a bomb inside his car and blew himself up.

Spectacular police work had brought the bomber down within twenty-four hours, aided in no small part by the suspect's own change in tactics but also by their taking swift action once the caste blinders were removed. The police chief apologized to black citizens and to the family of the first victim, who had been portrayed as a suspect in his own death. But African-American residents, the scapegoat caste, were left with lingering questions, questions whose answers they lived with every day: Why had the police paid little heed when the first bombs killed or harmed people of color? Why had they disregarded the potential threat? Why did authorities wait ten days to warn the public? Why did they let precious time pass, blaming the first victim for his own death?

"How messed up is it that police can make it seem like the person did it themself?" Fatima Mann, an advocate for poor families in Austin, told *The Washington Post.* "It's insulting and offensive and tiring."

A scapegoat, like the man who was the first to die in Austin, is seen by definition as expendable. People can come to disregard the predicaments facing people deemed beneath them, seeing their misfortunes as having no bearing on their own lives, seeing whatever is happening to them as, say, a black problem, rather than a human problem, unwittingly endangering everyone.

———

In late 2013, a wicked contagion resurfaced in the coastal nations of West Africa. An eighteen-month-old boy died in a village in Guinea. His mother, grandmother, and sister soon died after suffering the same hemorrhagic symptoms of Ebola, among the most dreaded diseases known to man.

Mourners who flocked to the grandmother's funeral carried the virus back to their own villages, and from there, Ebola began decimating families and hamlets in Liberia, Guinea, and Sierra Leone, and killing the doctors who were treating the sick. Anyone with the least exposure had to follow an elaborate hazmat protocol virtually out of science fiction and still fear that the exposed tip of a finger cut might condemn them to a virus that assured an agonizing death and for which there was then no widely proven vaccine.

It raged through West Africa as the Western world looked on mostly with pity and detachment. What a continent of sorrow, through the Western lens. These were countries siphoned of their populations during the transatlantic slave trade, then conquered and colonized and now still recovering from the destabilization and wars that these upheavals had wrought.

To those at a distance, the sad circumstances of these countries, from primeval health systems to ancient burial rites, had brought this plague upon them. The virus spread through contact with the bodily fluids of an infected person who was showing symptoms, and people infected were to be quarantined in isolation wards. But some villagers despaired of being apart from their loved ones in their last days and chose to stay with them or, unable to get them to a hospital from the villages, had tried to care for sick loved ones themselves. There was an admirable closeness in their family ties that transcended disease. For this, they were blamed as well.

Far from the villages, dehumanizing photos of dying patients, images that at times deprived them of dignity in their final hours, stretched across the pages of Western newspapers. It was a distant sadness for many Westerners if any emotion registered at all from the safe comfort and buffer of sea and ocean. Thousands of people were dying, and courageous Westerners like Doctors Without Borders flew in to help. But the full artillery of Western science had not stirred to action. This was a problem for Africa, seen as a place of misfortune filled with people of the lowest caste, not the primary concern of the Western powers.

But the virus did not recognize race or geography, and in the late summer of 2014, several American aid workers contracted the virus while in the afflicted region. Alerted to the existential threat, the United States sent millions in aid and three thousand troops to help with infrastructure and security.

Then in September 2014, a man boarded a flight from Liberia to Brussels en route to Dallas, to reunite with his partner and son. Unbeknownst to him, he was carrying the virus. He became the first case of Ebola in the United States.

A Dallas hospital, unprepared for a virus identified with another hemisphere, sent the man home with antibiotics when he showed up complaining of symptoms. He later returned in worsened condition, and he died within ten days of his eventual diagnosis. Soon afterward, two of the nurses who had cared for him contracted the virus. Panic set in as news reports retraced the whereabouts of one of the nurses in the days preceding her diagnosis, after it was discovered that she had been on a commercial plane and had traveled to and from Cleveland. Days later, cable news channels interrupted regular programming to show her being transported on live television to a flight from Dallas to Atlanta for specialized treatment. The scourge that had seemed a problem of another planet was now in the United States.

That October, shortly after the first diagnosis on American soil and nearly a year after West Africans had been left to manage largely on their own with the help of volunteer health workers, the Food and Drug Administration arranged for an American pharmaceutical company to begin emergency research into an antivirus for Ebola. Eight more people would be diagnosed within months in the United States, their care and condition closely monitored in the news.

The 2014 epidemic struck 28,000 people and killed more than 11,000 in the largest outbreak of Ebola the world had ever seen. The virus brought the interconnectedness of the planet into vivid, terrifying relief. Distance and geography could contain Ebola for a time, but Ebola did not recognize race or color or caste or national origin. A human being was a human being and a prospective new host to a frighteningly efficient virus. The contagion had initially not been seen as the global human crisis it was. Those suffering were West Africans with ill-equipped health systems, a hemisphere away. But Ebola, and potentially planet-wide catastrophes like it, as the world would discover beyond imagining six years later, have a way of reminding human beings that we are all indeed one species, all interwoven, more alike than different, more interdependent on one another than we might otherwise want to believe. Ebola had been merely a whispered forewarning of what was to come.

CHAPTER THIRTEEN

The Insecure Alpha and the Purpose of an Underdog

The West Highland terrier had been acting up since the divorce. He was just over a year old and had begun nipping and snarling once the presumed pack leader, the first husband, was no longer around. The Westie had not taken the upset to the social order in the household very well, feared his world had collapsed, his survival in danger, and had communicated his displeasure to the old alpha, the first husband, by nipping his nose once during a brief visit. I had to figure out what to do if I were to keep the Westie, which, to me, was the only option.

I decided I had nothing to lose by consulting a canine behaviorist and found a Westie specialist who lived in California. I was expecting a list of instructions from her on how to better manage my terrier. What I got was a brief lesson in canine hierarchy and in how canines interact with one another, exert dominance or submission, for the survival and wellness of the pack.

The social hierarchy and vocabulary of wolves and canines runs throughout our culture: alpha male, underdog, lone wolf, pack mentality—in part due to our observations of the dogs we may have owned and to the seeming parallels between ourselves and this companion species of social animals. Current-day canine specialists have sought to correct the distortions of the term *alpha* male—the king-of-the-world chest-beater of popular imagining—that have worked their way into our psyches.

True alphas, the behaviorist told me, are fearless protectors against outside incursions, but they rarely have to assert themselves within the pack, rarely have to act with aggression, bark orders, or use physical means of control. While I would never strike a dog or yank a choke chain as I have seen other would-be alpha humans treat their dogs, my forbearance alone was not working and neither were the shrieks of "No! No! No!" when I found Chi-Chi chewing on another pair of slingbacks.

"See, that's what humans do," the behaviorist said. "We treat them like children, but as pack animals, they respond to the cues of an alpha in a pack structure. A human alpha should never have to raise her voice. Dogs don't understand that.

"If you are having to raise your voice to get their attention," she said, "a dog will not see you as the leader. You have already lost. A true alpha does not behave like that and doesn't have to. If a so-called alpha resorts to that, they are signaling that they are not in control at all."

True alphas command authority through their calm oversight of those who depend upon them. They establish their rank early in life and communicate through ancient signals their inner strength and stewardship, asserting their power only when necessary. An alpha generally eats first, decides when and who will eat afterward, inspires trust through firm shepherding for the safety and well-being of the pack. An alpha is not necessarily the biggest or fastest but usually the innately self-assured one who can chastise a pack member with a mere look or a low voice. A true alpha wields quiet power judiciously apportioned.

You know that you are not seeing a true alpha, or, put another way, you have encountered an insecure alpha, if he or she must yell, scream, bully, or attack those beneath them into submission. That individual does not have the loyalty and trust of the pack and endangers the entire group through his or her insecurities, through his or her show of fear and lack of courage.

The behaviorist gave me a set of assignments to establish my role, and assured me that once my Westie saw me as the alpha, the relationship would be reset, very likely for good. The main goal was to bring order and consistency, firmness to my compassion.

The first exercise was to let him know who controlled the means of his survival—the food. At the next feeding, I was to set the food bowl down, holding on to it, and then remove the bowl to let him know my role before setting it down again for him to eat. He was at first unsettled by this new move but adjusted to it. For the next exercise, I was to keep my hand on the food bowl the entire time he was eating. This he settled into as well. The last exercise was for me to set the food bowl down, hold the bowl, and then put my hands in the food as he ate, to let him know that I was not afraid of him or of what he might do. This, I was not looking forward to.

"You have seen the size of a Westie's teeth, haven't you?" I asked when she gave me this instruction.

"I know," she said. "He will not bite the hand that feeds him."

When the time came for that last exercise, I set the bowl down and kept my hands in the bowl as he ate, and I discovered that there's a reason why dog behavior is built into our language. Dogs, for sure, and people, if they are wise, do not bite the hand that feeds.

The behaviorist also recommended that I consider getting another dog. Westies are a particularly social breed, and he would fare better with a companion. As much as I love Westies, I felt one spirited terrier was enough and looked for a gentle, easygoing breed. Enter Sophie, the Havanese. She was a three-pound mop of fur that, as a puppy, could fit inside my purse.

I took Chi-Chi with me when I went to get Sophie, and he was fine with her at first. Until we got her home. Uncertain as to what this intruder meant for the household structure, he began asserting himself as the alpha. If ever I looked away, he hunted her down under dressers and cabinets. At feeding time, he pushed her from her food bowl.

One day, he went to shove her from her food bowl, and she stiffened, on alert, and glared at him looming above her, and she let out a tinny, barely audible growl, the first sounds ever to escape from her. Chi-Chi jumped, startled by this turnabout. His ears and ego flattened, he slinked back to his own food bowl with his tail between his legs. From that day forward, Sophie was in charge.

From then on, it was she who would eat first, walk through doors first, remain a pace ahead of him at all times on walks. Though she was only half his size once full grown, she could pin him to the wall to keep him in line if she chose to, and whenever she corrected or corralled him, he stepped back and submitted and then nudged her to play. The Westie had been an unconvincing and ill-suited alpha but made for a relaxed and contented beta, tail bouncing, lighthearted and free. He came to adore Sophie and was watchful of her. Now that the hierarchy between them was settled and everyone was in positions that suited their strengths, there was order and peace in the household.

———

We owe our misperceptions about alpha behavior to studies of large groupings of wolves placed into captivity and forced to fight for dominance or to cower into submission. In nature, wolf packs are more likely to consist of extended family systems, packs of between five and fifteen wolves, led by an alpha male and an alpha female, whom the pack trusts and has reason to trust for the survival of them all.

"The main characteristic of an alpha male wolf is a quiet confidence, quiet self-assurance," Richard McIntyre, a researcher of wolf behavior at Yellowstone National Park, told the ecologist Carl Safina. "You know what's best for your pack. You lead by example. You're very comfortable with that. You have a calming effect."

The other members of the pack, the various beta and gamma wolves, can thus go about their tasks with greater reassurance in the wisdom of the alpha. At the bottom of the hierarchy is the omega, the underdog, the lowest-ranking wolf, arising from natural personality traits in relation to others in the pack. The omega generally eats last and serves as a kind of court jester who acts as an escape valve, often picked on by the other wolves. He bears the brunt of the tensions they face in the wild, where they are subject to attack from predators or from rival packs and during lean times in the hunt for prey.

The omega acts as "a kind of social glue, allowing frustration to be vented without actual acts of war," wrote a wolf conservationist. The omega is so critical to the pack structure that when a pack loses its omega, it enters "into a long period of mourning," the conservationist observed, "where the entire pack stops hunting and just lays around looking miserable," as if there were no longer a reason to go on.

The loss of the omega can threaten social cohesion and put the entire pack at risk. Depending on the composition of the pack, an omega might not be easily replaced. The new omega would mean a demotion for one of the lower to mid-level pack members. Either way, the pack is destabilized. After all, these roles are not artificially assigned based upon what an individual wolf looks like, as with a certain other species, but emerge as a consequence of internal personality traits that surface naturally in the forming of a pack.

Humans could learn a lot from canines. The great tragedy among humans is that people have often been assigned to or seen as qualified for alpha positions—as CEOs, quarterbacks, coaches, directors of film, presidents of colleges or countries—not necessarily on the basis of innate leadership traits but, historically, on the basis of having been born to the dominant caste or the dominant gender or to the right family within the dominant caste, the assumption being that only those from a certain caste or gender or religion or national origin have the innate capacity or deservedness to be leaders.

This is a tragedy not just for the many overlooked alphas from marginalized groups whose talents have gone untapped or unrecognized, who have had to watch organizations founder under insecure or ill-suited alphas. It is a tragedy not only for the misplaced alphas who may be in over their heads and who struggle to lead disgruntled staffs that may not respect them. It is a tragedy for humankind, which is deprived of the benefit of natural alphas who might lead the world with the compassion and courage that are the hallmarks of a born leader, male or female, of whatever religion or background or caste, the actual intended alphas of the species.

CHAPTER FOURTEEN

The Intrusion of Caste in Everyday Life

A father and his young son were out at a restaurant in Oakland on one of their precious days together, now that the mother and father had separated. The little boy ordered what he thought he wanted, but when the food came, he said he just wanted to drink his juice. The father had been worried about the effect the disruption in the family might be having on his son and wanted to keep the same stability and order in his little boy's life.

He wanted to hold to the same standards they had always had, of showing gratitude for the blessing of food, and eating what the universe had seen fit to put before you, of keeping to the manners they had established when they were all together. Mainly he wanted his son to get his nourishment, didn't want to return him to his mother hungry, as he surely would be if he filled his little stomach with sweet juice and snacks. He remembered the times he'd filled up on sweets and had no space left for mealtime.

What he couldn't tell his son at the moment, but would have to tell him later, when he was big enough to understand, was that he would have to grow up respecting authority. One day, he would no longer be an adorable little toddler but would be a black teen-ager or grown man, and respecting authority, following the rules, could mean his very life.

This was his only child, the most precious human in the world to him. The boy was so sweet-faced, innocent, and free. How could he tell him that the world, his country, saw him as a threat? When exactly is the best time to break a child's heart?

Should a parent clip them a little at a time, spread it out to spare them the pain of a single blow? Should a parent sit them down and get it over with? You could argue that the sooner a child knows, the safer, more prepared he will be. Maybe a parent should hold off as long as he can, give his child the longest possible chance to be . . . a child. He'll have the rest of his life, decades, to live with reality, adjust himself to the truth.

Maybe the most loving thing to do is to wait, wait until something happens, somebody drops the n-word on him at the playground or a teacher checks him for running down the hall but not his white schoolmates, and he knows it's wrong and wants to know why.

Back in 2014, Tamir Rice was twelve when officers shot him within seconds of their arrival as he stood in a Cleveland park playing with a pellet gun, despite the fact that Ohio was an open carry state, and it is a common occurrence for boys to have toy guns, an all-American thing to do. Tamir Rice happened to be the same age as the fictional Jem when the beloved fictional father Atticus Finch gave him an air rifle in *To Kill a Mockingbird,* the very scene from which the title comes. Lots of American boys play with guns, are given guns, and aren't killed for it. Tamir Rice died before he could ask why.

This father in Oakland didn't believe in guns, and that wasn't the issue anyway. The issue was his son's life and what the father could do to protect it. The challenge for a parent in the subordinate caste is to calculate the precise and optimal moment to break the truth to a child before the caste system does it for him, to figure out how to stretch their innocence until the last possible moment before it is too late.

Another father, an immigrant from West Africa, had to find a way to push past his sorrow to break the news to his little boy that he could no longer be a child, that he could not jump and dart and shriek like the other children. He would have to tell his son that it was too dangerous. They were in America now.

The father in Oakland was a respected professor at a local college. In fact, African-American history was his field. He would figure it out when the time came. That moment was weighing on him, but that day was not today. The father looked back at his son and told him he needed to go ahead and eat his vegetables first, like Daddy said, and then he could drink his juice. The little boy scrunched his face and shook his head and began to cry.

A woman at a nearby booth had been listening to their exchange. She was an older, grayish-blond woman from the dominant caste. She scooted from her booth and walked over to the table where the father and son were sitting. The father could see the shadow of her form moving toward them. The woman stopped and stood over them. She leaned toward the little boy and told him: "You drink your juice if you want to. It's okay to drink your juice."

The woman did not address or acknowledge the father. She focused her attention on the little boy as she stood there. The father was beside himself. A perfect stranger had gotten up, disregarded a parent, and told a child to disobey the parent right in the parent's face.

The woman had crossed so many boundaries it was hard to process. Something had made her feel entitled enough to enter into the private space of people she did not know and veto a father's decision regarding his own son. This was Oakland, bright blue home of Huey and Tupac, where such phrases as *gender nonconformity* and *micro-aggressions* are part of everyday language. The woman would not have gotten up if she didn't perceive she had a right to. Had she done this to other parents? Would she have breezed past a white father, ignored him to tell his son to do precisely what the father had just told him not to?

The father held up his hand like a traffic officer signaling a car to stop.

"Ma'am, you need to go sit down," the father said. "Don't come to my table. I don't know you."

The woman looked stunned at the rejection but turned around and went back to her booth. The father had a hard time enjoying his own food after that. He would remember this moment long afterward.

The United States has a centuries-old history of people in the upper caste controlling and overriding the rightful role of lower-caste parents and their children, the most extreme of which was selling off children from their parents, even infants who had yet to be weaned from their mothers, as with fillies or pups rather than human beings. "One of them," remarked an enslaver, "was worth two hundred dollars . . . the moment it drew breath." This routine facet of slavery prevailed in our country for a quarter millennium, children and parents denied the most elemental of human bonds.

Even when children were permitted to remain with their parents, caste protocols undermined their authority and punished them if they tried to protect their own children. A mother in Louisiana was administered twenty-five lashes for "countermanding an order" given her son by the white mistress who owned them. Several of the most gruesome whippings and tortures were administered on enslaved men who intervened in cases of violence against their wives or children at the hands of an enslaver or overseer.

Thus enslaved parents could offer their children little "shelter or security from the frightening creatures" that lorded over them, historian Kenneth M. Stampp wrote. Nor could they protect themselves. But if the upper caste did not see the evil in this, the lowest-caste children could see it. Once, when an overseer tied a woman up and whipped her in front of her children, "the frightened children pelted the overseer with stones," Stampp wrote, "and one of them ran up and bit him in the leg," as they cried for him to let her go. The caste system may have treated them as cattle or machinery, but the children responded instantly as the human beings the dominant caste refused to see.

It was only in the mid-twentieth century, with the protections arising from the civil rights era, that black parents had legal and political recourse to shield their children from abuse, or to call into account harm done to their children at the hands of the state. But the essential contours of the hierarchy remained intact, the modes of expression having mutated with the times.

Modern-day caste protocols are less often about overt attacks or conscious hostility and can be dispiritingly hard to fight. They are like the wind, powerful enough to knock you down but invisible as they go about their work. They are sustained by the muscle memory of relative rank and the expectations of how one interacts with others based on their place in the hierarchy. It's a form of status hyper-vigilance, the entitlement of the dominant caste to step in and assert itself wherever it chooses, to monitor or dismiss those deemed beneath them as they see fit. It is not about luxury cars and watches, country clubs and private banks, but knowing without thinking that you are one up from another based on rules not set down in paper but reinforced in most every commercial, television show, or billboard, from boardrooms to newsrooms to gated subdivisions to who gets killed first in the first half hour of a movie. This is the blindsiding banality of caste.

———

Every day across America, wherever two or more are gathered, caste can infect the most ordinary of interchanges, catching us off guard, disrupting and confusing and potentially causing mayhem for anyone in the hierarchy.

These are scenes of caste in action:

The doorbell rang at the home of an accountant from the dominant caste in a wealthy suburb of a midwestern city. The accountant and his family had only recently moved into the neighborhood. Through the glass sidelights of his front door, he could see a woman, an African-American woman, there on his landing.

He knew exactly what this meant. The dry cleaner in town offered its customers pickup and drop-off, so he went to get the clothes that needed cleaning and then opened the door to hand the armload of tousled clothes to the woman waiting out front.

The woman stepped back. "Oh, I'm not the dry cleaner," the woman said. "I'm your next-door neighbor. I came over to introduce myself and welcome you to the neighborhood."

The woman was the fashionable wife of a prominent cardiologist, exceedingly upper class, yet labeled subordinate caste on sight, still, to someone who had just moved next door to her. They would both have to recover from that one.

•

A college professor in Chicago had just returned from a bike ride and picked up his mail in the lobby of his apartment building off Michigan Avenue. He was African-American, in his thirties, patrician of face, still in his helmet and cycling gear. He stepped onto the elevator en route to his floor and, barely noticing the other man on the elevator with him, began going through his mail. He saw something of interest and unsealed one of his envelopes.

The other man was horrified.

"You're supposed to be delivering the mail, not opening it."

This seemed to have come out of nowhere, and the college professor looked up and saw that the other man was white, but didn't fully register the accusation, was just going about his day, and gave an honest reply.

"Oh, I want to see what's inside," the professor said.

The other man looked even more stricken now, shaking his head in disgust, mistakenly believing he was witnessing a crime in progress.

The professor got off on his floor and only later did it occur to him that he had been taken for a delivery boy in his own building, an assumption so ludicrous he hadn't bothered to consider it in the moment, which left the dominant-caste man convinced that he had just seen a black messenger brazenly break open an "actual" resident's mail in full view of another resident. This is the self-perpetuating mischief of caste.

•

The phone kept ringing at the civil engineer's desk. He had deadlines to meet and projects bearing down on him. But, over and over, the phone broke his concentration and wasted his limited time. The engineer was from the dominant caste, and so, too, was the man pestering him. On the face of it, the intrusion would seem to have nothing to do with caste. Here was a white contractor calling a white engineer for answers about a project under way.

The engineer was a supervisor with a general idea of the project, but the project was not his. It belonged to another engineer on the team, as the contractor well knew, one who happened to be African-American and a woman.

The white contractor had been told to go to her with any questions he had. But the contractor had ignored her, ignored protocol, and had gone to the dominant-caste engineer instead. The white engineer answered the contractor's questions at first, to be polite and move things along. But the phone kept ringing, and it was disrupting his own work, and it was hindering the project in question.

The black engineer could hear this unfold in front of her from her cubicle next to the white engineer's. From her desk, she could hear it every time his phone rang, while hers sat mute and silent. She could hear the white engineer's impatient replies to questions that both of them knew should have come to her.

The white engineer grew agitated with disbelief. When the contractor called the next time, the white engineer let him have it. "I indicated to you from the beginning that you need to talk to D. about day-to-day matters," the white engineer said. "If you have a problem with that, we'll have to find another contractor for the job."

The minute the white engineer hung up, the black engineer's phone rang.

On an ordinary workday, the caste system had pulled a

dominant-caste man into its undertow. It had drained him
of time and disrupted the operation. He found himself in an
unexpected fight against an invisible foe, forced to take a
stand for his colleague and against, perhaps unbeknownst
to him on a conscious level, the caste system itself.

———

If there is anything that distinguishes caste, however, it is, first, the policing of roles expected of people based on what they look like, and, second, the monitoring of boundaries—the disregard for the boundaries of subordinate castes or the passionate construction of them by those in the dominant caste, to keep the hierarchy in place.

After the 2016 election, the surveillance of black citizens by white strangers became so common a feature of American life that these episodes have inspired memes of their own, videos gone viral, followed by apologies from management or an announcement of company-wide diversity training. People in the dominant caste have been caught on video inserting themselves into the everyday lives of black people they do not know and calling the police on them as they wait for a friend at a Starbucks in Philadelphia or try to enter their own condo building in St. Louis. It is a distant echo of an earlier time when anyone in the dominant caste was deputized, obligated even, to apprehend any black person during the era of slavery.

With the resurgence of caste after the 2016 election, people in the dominant caste have been recorded calling the police on ordinary black citizens under a wide range of ordinary circumstances, with videos cropping up almost daily at one point:

In New Haven, Connecticut, a woman called campus police on a graduate student at Yale University who had fallen asleep while studying in the common area of her dormitory. Officers demanded her identification even after she unlocked the door to her dorm room. "You're in a Yale building," an officer said, "and we need to make sure that you belong here."

In Milwaukee, a woman called the police on a corrections officer whose key fob had malfunctioned as he tried to open his own car door. A man called the police on a software engineer who was waiting for a friend outside a condo building in San Francisco. As the white man briefed the authorities from his cellphone, the man's little boy, uncomfortable with his father's actions, begged him to hang up and let it go.

A woman walking her dog stood and blocked a marketing consultant from getting into his own condo building in St. Louis. She demanded that he show proof that he lived there before she would step aside. When he walked past her, she followed him into the elevator and onto his floor to see if he in fact lived there. In the video that the man took as a precaution, she can be seen tracking him all the way to his apartment, checking whether he was a resident even after he unlocked his door to go inside.

And a woman began to stalk a black man in Georgia when she saw him out with two white children. From her car, the woman trailed Corey Lewis, their babysitter, as he drove from a Walmart to a gas station and to his home after he did not permit the woman, a complete stranger, to talk with the children alone to see if they were all right. Lewis, a youth pastor who runs an after-school program, started recording the situation on his cellphone. In it, the children can be seen calm and unfazed, buckled in their seatbelts in the back of his car.

His voice is strained and disbelieving. "This lady is following me," he says in the video, "all because I got two kids in the back seat that do not look like me."

The woman called 911 and asked if she should keep following him. She continued to trail him even though she was told not to. By the time Lewis got home, a patrol car had pulled up behind him, an officer heading toward him.

"Jesus have mercy—what is wrong with this country?" a woman outside of the camera frame cried. The officer told the children, a six-year-old boy and a ten-year-old girl, to step out of the car, and Lewis's voice grew tense. The outcome of this police encounter and his very safety depended on what those children said, and he asked them to please tell the officer who he was.

"Please," he said to them.

Satisfied that Lewis was, in fact, their babysitter and that the children were okay, the officer, just to be safe, called the parents, who were out at dinner.

"It just knocked us out of our chair," the children's father, David Parker, told *The New York Times*.

Afterward, a reporter asked one of the children, ten-year-old Addison, what she would tell the woman who followed them that day. Her father told the *Times* her response: "I would just ask her to, next time, try to see us as three people rather than three skin colors, because we might've been Mr. Lewis's adopted children."

———

These intrusions of caste would seem to harm the targets more than anyone. Given the widely publicized attacks and shootings of black citizens at the hands of police, most Americans know by now that calling the police on a black person can carry life-and-death consequences. Frivolous calls squander public resources and distract police from actual, serious crime to the detriment of us all.

Beyond that, when any citizen is disrupted in the midst of everyday life and responsibilities, it is, in fact, a societal disruption, a tear in the daily workings of human interaction. These people are part of the American economy, and when they are interrupted, schools and business and institutions suffer an invisible loss in output as their workers get blindsided from their tasks.

These intrusions serve to reinforce caste by derailing lower-caste people, subverting their work lives in an already competitive society, imposing additional burdens not borne by their dominant-caste colleagues as they go about their work, as occurred to me in Michigan some years ago.

I could hear footsteps behind me but paid little attention. This was an airport, and there were footfalls and roller bags all around. I had just landed in Detroit on an early-morning flight from Chicago for interviews I needed to conduct as a national correspondent for *The New York Times*.

I'd already lost an hour going from Central to Eastern time, and I was thinking of all I'd have to do in the space of the next eight hours. If the first interview was at ten-thirty, and if it took me forty minutes to get downtown, maybe more since this was rush hour, I needed to get straight to the rental car to make this work.

Any delays in the day's interviews and I might not make the flight back to Chicago that evening. I thought to myself that I'd worry about that later and just get to the Avis bus as soon as I could. I thought about how it always seems that the shuttle you're looking for is the one that has just pulled off, and no matter what company you've booked, the one you need is always the last to show up.

I was walking fast, because I always walk fast, and I was heading to the sliding-glass doors in the direction of the shuttle stop when I heard them. The footsteps were closer and faster and heading toward me. Why would anybody be heading toward me? It was a man and a woman. It happened to be a white man and a white woman, the woman's light brown hair swinging just above her shoulders as she ran. They had a parka-and-corduroy look about them, and both were out of breath as they reached me.

"We need to talk to you," they said, walking alongside me.

I could see the shuttle bus lane through the sliding-glass doors, and buses pulling up, and was not fully registering whatever it was they were saying.

"Why are you in Detroit? What are you here for?"

"I'm on business. I'm here for work."

I was thinking that I did not have time for whatever travel survey they were conducting. And now I could see that Avis was on schedule. The shuttle bus was pulling to the curb. People were queuing up to board.

"I have to catch my shuttle bus," I told them as I walked out of the terminal doors.

"Where are you coming from?" they asked, one on each side of me now.

"I just flew in from Chicago," I said, nearing the clot of people in suits and overcoats boarding the shuttle bus.

"Is that where you live?"

"Why are you asking me this? I need to get on the bus."

"We need to know if you live in Chicago, and what you're doing in Detroit."

The last of the passengers were climbing on board. The doors of the bus were wide open. The driver was looking down at me and at them. The man and the woman stood there holding up the bus, holding up the passengers, holding up me.

"What is this for?"

"We're DEA. We need to know where you live, how long you will be in Detroit, and exactly what you're doing here."

This was too preposterous to comprehend. The Drug Enforcement Administration? Why in the world were they stopping me, out of all the travelers at the airport? This was a day trip, so I didn't have luggage, like a lot of business travelers between cities close to each other. I was in a suit like everyone else, Coach bag slung over my shoulder. Covering the Midwest as I was at the time, I used to tell people that I catch planes like other people catch the subway. Airports were a second home to me. How could they not see that I was like every other business traveler boarding the shuttle?

The people on the bus were checking their watches and glaring down at me through the windows as I stood at the steps. The driver shifted in his seat, and I could hear the shake of the engine, the snort of the brakes, transmission about to shift, the driver's impatient hand on the door pull.

I blurted out what they wanted to know so that they would leave me alone.

"I live in Chicago. I'm here for the day. I'm a reporter for *The New York Times*. I need to get on this bus."

"We will allow you to board. We will have to ride with you."

I was shaking now as I climbed onto the shuttle, its air thick with the scorn of fellow travelers. I looked for an empty seat, people pulling away as I sat down. This whole exchange had delayed everyone on the bus, and for all that anyone could see, it was because of a woman, a black woman who probably didn't even belong with real business travelers and might be a criminal to boot.

The two agents took seats directly in front of me, staring and assessing, their eyes never leaving me. Twitter did not exist, and there were no cameras on cellphones to go into video mode. The bus was filled with business people, white people, or, I should say, white business people. I was the only African-American on the bus and one of the few women, and there were two agents surveilling me and my every move.

The other passengers glared at me and at the two agents and back again at me. I was in utter disbelief, too shocked even to register fear. It was a psychic assault to sit there, accused and condemned, not just by the agents but by everyone on the bus who looked with contempt and disdain, seeing me as not like them, when I was exactly like them—a frequent flyer on business like anyone else on the bus, early on a weekday morning, having just flown into a major American city and needing to focus on the work that I, like them, was there to do. I wanted to proclaim my innocence of whatever it was that all of them were thinking.

When you are raised middle class and born to a subordinated caste in general, and African-American in particular, you are keenly aware of the burden you carry and you know that working twice as hard is a given. But more important, you know there will be no latitude for a misstep, so you must try to be virtually perfect at all times merely to tread water. You live with the double standard even though you do not like it. You know growing up that you cannot get away with the things that your white friends might skate by with—adolescent pranks or shoplifting on a dare or cursing out a teacher. You knew better, even if you were so inclined, which I wasn't and never have been.

I needed to regain my composure and clear myself of the accusation of their presence. They hadn't believed I was a reporter, so I decided to be conspicuously what I was. I fished my pen and notebook out of my bag. I figured nobody could stop me from taking notes. It was a natural and protective reflex for me, like breathing. I had a captive audience bearing witness to my performance of emergency journalism.

In silence, I looked across at the agents and, with my quaking right hand, made notes of what they were wearing, what they looked like, how they were looking at me. They hadn't expected this, and they turned to look out of a window and down at the floor.

It was a long ride to the car rental lot. Now they felt the sting of inspection as I jotted down everything I could about them, and, in that moment, I took back some fraction of the power they had taken from me, proved who and what I was to anyone watching, or at least that was how it felt to me at the time.

Soon the bus pulled into the Avis lot, and I took a deep breath. They had ridden all the way from the airport, trailing me, and I had no idea what the next step would be. When the bus came to a stop, I stood up like the other passengers. The agents looked up from their seats.

"Have a nice day," they said. And it was over just like that.

Except it wasn't. I somehow made it to the rental counter and somehow got the keys to a car, but I don't remember any of it. What I recall is getting turned around in a parking lot that I had been to dozens of times, going in circles, not able to get out, not registering the signs to the exit, not seeing how to get to Interstate 94, when I knew full well how to get to I-94 after all the times I'd driven it.

Now, in the car, away from the agents, I was beginning to comprehend the seriousness of that encounter, only now able to admit my terror. The other business travelers were likely well on their way to their appointments, perhaps annoyed at the delay but able to make preparations in their heads for their meetings, maybe get a coffee on the way.

This was the thievery of caste, stealing the time and psychic resources of the marginalized, draining energy in an already uphill competition. They were not, like me, frozen and disoriented, trying to make sense of a public violation that seemed all the more menacing now that I could see it in full. The quiet mundanity of that terror has never left me, the scars outliving the cut.

We are told over and over again in our society not to judge a book by its cover, not to assume what is inside before we have had a chance to read it. Yet humans size up and make assumptions about other humans based upon what they look like many times a day. We prejudge complicated breathing beings in ways we are told never to judge inanimate objects.

CHAPTER FIFTEEN

The Urgent Necessity of a Bottom Rung

It turns out that the greatest threat to a caste system is not lower-caste failure, which, in a caste system, is expected and perhaps even counted upon, but lower-caste success, which is not. Achievement by those in the lowest caste goes against the script handed down to us all. It undermines the core assumptions upon which a caste system is constructed and to which the identities of people on all rungs of the hierarchy are linked. Achievement by marginalized people who step outside the roles expected of them puts things out of order and triggers primeval and often violent backlash.

The scholar W.E.B. Du Bois recognized this phenomenon in his research into what happened after the end of the Civil War: "The masters feared their former slaves' success," he wrote, "far more than their anticipated failure."

Decades after the Civil War, the entire world was at war and well into a fourth year of trench combat that was tearing Europe apart. The year was 1918, after the Americans had finally sent in their troops. The French welcomed the reinforcement during World War I, had badly needed it. The French began commanding some of the American troops, and it was then that the problems began. The French were treating the soldiers according to their military rank rather than their rank in the American caste system.

They were treating black soldiers as they would white soldiers, as they would treat other human beings, having drinks with them, patting their shoulders for a job well done. This rankled the white soldiers in an era of total segregation back home, and this breach had to be put to a stop.

American military command informed the French of how they were to treat the black soldiers, clarified for them that these men were "inferior beings," no matter how well they performed on the front lines, that it was "of the utmost importance" that they be treated as inferior.

The fact that military command would take the time in the middle of one of the most vicious wars in human history to instruct foreigners on the necessity of demeaning their own countrymen suggests that they considered adherence to caste protocols to be as important as conducting the war itself. As it was, the white soldiers were refusing to fight in the same trenches as black soldiers and refusing to salute black superiors.

The American military communicated its position, and French commanders, in turn, had to convey the rules to their soldiers and officers who had come to admire the black soldiers and had developed a camaraderie with them. "This indulgence and this familiarity," read the announcement, "are matters of grievous concern to the Americans. They consider them an affront to their national policy."

In apprising their officers of the new protocols, French command noted the contradictions given that "the (black American) soldiers sent us have been the choicest with respect to physique and morals." Still, in trying to translate the rules of the American caste system, the French command gave this directive: "We cannot deal with them on the same plane as with the white American officers without deeply wounding the latter. We must not eat with them, must not shake hands or seek to talk or meet with them outside of the requirements of military service."

More pointedly, the French officers were told: "We must not

commend too highly the black American troops, particularly in the presence of (white) Americans. It is all right to recognize their good qualities and their services, but only in moderate terms."

Later, in the final months of the war, an African-American soldier, Pvt. Burton Holmes, was grievously wounded in a hail of machine gun fire and heavy German artillery in an ambush of his unit in September 1918. He managed to make his way back to the command post to exchange rifles because the one he had been given was malfunctioning.

Commanders wanted to get him to the hospital for treatment, but he refused and rejoined the fight with a backup rifle. He continued to fire upon the enemy until his last breath. Another African-American in Company C, Freddie Stowers, crawled into enemy shelling and led the assault on German trenches. He, too, died on the front lines defending France and America.

White officers who had witnessed their bravery broke with caste and nominated both men for the Medal of Honor. But this was the height of the eugenics era, when black inferiority was near universal convention in American culture. The government refused to grant the medal to either soldier. The award intended for Holmes was downgraded to a lesser citation, and the recommendation for Stowers was lost for half a century.

These actions were in keeping with societal norms that people in the lowest caste were not to be commended even in death, lest the living begin to think themselves equal, get uppity, out of their place, and threaten the myths that the upper caste kept telling itself and the world.

"Imagine," Dr. Jeff Gusky, a physician who, decades later, took an interest in the case, told the *Army Times* in 2018, "how powerful this would have been in the American press . . . if word got out that there were two black soldiers who died in this ambush and were both nominated for the Medal of Honor."

A generation later, during the Second World War, there was continued resistance to the lowest caste rising from its assigned place even in the most mundane of endeavors. One day in the spring of 1942, white army officers happened to assign black soldiers to direct traffic in Lincolnton, Georgia, as an Army convoy passed through. It caused an uproar in town. The sight of black men in uniform, standing at an intersection, "halting white motorists, apparently sent some residents over the edge," wrote the historian Jason Morgan Ward.

After the war ended, in February 1946, Sgt. Isaac Woodard, Jr., was riding a Greyhound bus home to North Carolina from Augusta, Georgia, where he had been honorably discharged, having served in the Pacific theater. At a stop along the way, Woodard asked the bus driver if he could step off the bus to relieve himself. The driver told him to sit down, that he didn't have time to wait. Woodard stood up to the driver and told him, "I am a man just like you." Woodard had been out of the country and away from Jim Crow for three years, had served his country and taken on "a degree of assertiveness and self-confidence that most southern whites were not accustomed to nor prepared to accept," in the words of the southern author and judge Richard Gergel.

The driver backed down for the time being, told him to "go ahead then and hurry back." But at the next stop, outside Aiken, South Carolina, the bus driver notified the police.

There the police chief arrested Woodard on charges of disorderly conduct. At the bus stop and later in jail, the police chief beat him and jabbed his eyes with a billy club, blinding him. The next day a local judge found him guilty as charged, and, though he asked to see a doctor, the authorities did not get him one for several more days. By the time he was finally transferred to an army hospital, it was too late to save his eyesight. He was blind for the rest of his life.

The NAACP brought the case to the attention of President Harry S. Truman, a midwestern moderate who was incensed to learn that authorities in South Carolina had taken no action in the maiming of an American soldier. He ordered the Justice Department to investigate based on the fact that Woodard was in uniform at the time he was beaten and that the initial assault occurred at a bus stop on federal property.

But the federal trial ran into caste obstructions in South Carolina. The local prosecutor relied solely on the testimony of the bus driver who had called the police, the defense attorney hurled racial epithets in open court at the blinded sergeant, and, when the all-white jury returned a not-guilty verdict for the police chief, the courtroom broke out in cheers.

It had been revealed during the trial that Woodard had apparently said "yes" instead of "yes, sir" to the police chief during the arrest. This, combined with the elevated position his uniform conveyed, was seen as reason enough for punishment in the caste system. After the trial, the police chief who had admitted to jabbing Woodard in the eyes went free. Woodard went north to New York as part of the Great Migration. The northern white judge assigned to the case lamented, "I was shocked by the hypocrisy of my government."

The message was clear to those whose lives depended on staying in their place, or appearing to. "If a Negro rises, he will be careful not to become conspicuous, lest he be accused of putting on airs and thus arouse resentment," wrote the ethnographer Bertram Schrieke. "Experience or example has taught him that competition and jealousy from the lower classes of whites often form an almost unsurpassable obstacle to his progress."

———

It was largely black efforts to rise beyond their station that set off the backlash of lynchings and massacres after Reconstruction following the Civil War, that sparked the founding of the Ku Klux Klan and the imposition of Jim Crow laws to keep the lowest caste in its place. A white mob massacred some sixty black people in Ocoee, Florida, on Election Day in 1920, burning black homes and businesses to the ground, lynching and castrating black men, and driving the remaining black population out of town, after a black man tried to vote. The historian Paul Ortiz has called the Ocoee riot the "single bloodiest election day in modern American history."

It occurred amid a wave of anti-black pogroms in more than a dozen American cities, from East St. Louis to Chicago to Baltimore, as black southerners arrived north during the Great Migration and many tried to make their claims to citizenship after risking their lives in the Great War. One thing these rampages had in common: the mobs tended to go after the most prosperous in the lowest caste, those who might have managed to surpass even some people in the dominant caste. In the 1921 riot in Tulsa, Oklahoma, a mob leveled the section of town that was called black Wall Street, owing to the black banking, insurance, and other businesses clustered together and surrounded by well-kept brick homes that signaled prosperity. These were burned to the ground and never recovered.

Decades before, in the early 1890s, a black grocery and a white grocery sat across the street from each other at an intersection just outside Memphis, Tennessee. The black store, known as People's Grocery, was a cooperative that was thriving even as the walls of Jim Crow closed in. Its owner, Thomas H. Moss, was an upright figure in a three-piece suit and bow tie with a side part in his close-cropped hair, who did double duty delivering mail and running the grocery. Both he and his grocery store drew the resentment of his white competitor.

One day, two boys, one black and one white, were playing marbles in front of People's Grocery and got into an argument. The white boy's father began to thrash the black boy, at which point two clerks from the black grocery ran out to rescue him. A crowd gathered, and tensions rose.

Seizing on the discord and angered by the competition from the black store to begin with, the white grocer, William Barrett, showed up at People's Grocery, looking for one of the store clerks who had intervened in the fracas. But the clerk on duty, Calvin McDowell, refused him any information. The white grocer struck McDowell with a pistol for his perceived insolence. McDowell managed to wrestle the gun from the white grocer and fired, barely missing him. Under the protocols of the caste system, it was the black store clerk who was arrested. Though he was released, the caste system had only begun to stir. The black owner, Thomas Moss, tried to prepare for it. He stationed several black men to guard the grocery.

On March 5, 1892, six white men stormed People's Grocery. The black grocer and his supporters fired upon the intruders, wounding two of them. The white men happened to have been the sheriff and five men he had just deputized. After the shooting, a hundred more whites were deputized to hunt down the black store owner and other black men he knew. The three black storekeepers—the owner, Moss, and the two clerks, McDowell and Will Stewart—were arrested. In the early morning hours of March 9, 1892, a mob stormed the jail and tortured and lynched all three men. The next day, a white mob ransacked People's Grocery, and, within months, Moss's white competitor bought the store for pennies on the dollar.

One of Moss's dear friends was the journalist Ida B. Wells, and this lynching is what set her on her lifelong mission to awaken the country to the terror of lynching. "A finer, cleaner man than he never walked the streets of Memphis," Wells wrote. "He was murdered with no more consideration than a dog. . . . The colored people feel that every white man in Memphis who consented in his death is as guilty as those who fired the guns which took his life."

The irony of the quest of the lowest caste is that it is the very uprightness embodied by Moss, attested to by Wells, and applauded when shown by most every other group, that incites the greatest backlash. The effort to escape stigma is what can trigger the punishment.

"Moss was murdered for running a better business than his white competitor," wrote Nathaniel C. Ball, a historian at the Hooks Institute at the University of Memphis. "McDowell for forgetting his place in the hierarchy in the white world he lived in; and Stewart for being in the wrong place at the wrong time."

———

The lowest caste was to remain in its place like an ill-fitting suit that must constantly be altered, seams and darts re-sewn to fit the requirements of the upper caste, going back to the enslavers who resented displays of industriousness and intellect in the people they saw themselves as owning. "When slaves earned money they became 'vain and arrogant,'" wrote the historian Kenneth Stampp, "and felt 'more independent.'"

They were not to be credited for their ideas or innovations, even at the risk of progress for everyone. Crediting them would undermine the pretext for their enslavement, meaning their presumed inferiority in anything other than servitude. In the summer of 1721, an epidemic of smallpox, one of the deadliest afflictions of the era, besieged the city of Boston. It sent stricken people into quarantine, red flags signaling to all who might pass, "God have mercy on this house."

Cotton Mather was a Puritan minister and lay scientist in Boston and had come into possession of an African man named Onesimus. The enslaved African told of a procedure he had undergone back in his homeland that protected him from this illness. People in West Africa had discovered that they could fend off contagions by inoculating themselves with a specimen of fluid from an infected person. Mather was intrigued by the idea Onesimus described. He researched it, and decided to call it "variolation." It would become the precursor to immunization and "the Holy Grail of smallpox prevention for Western doctors and scientists," wrote the medical ethicist and author Harriet A. Washington.

During the 1721 outbreak, Mather tried to persuade Bostonians to protect themselves with this revolutionary method, but did not anticipate the resistance and rage, the "horrid Clamour," that arose from Bostonians. The idea sounded outlandish to them. They feared it could spread smallpox all the more, and they also wanted nothing to do with a practice that had come from Africa and had been suggested by an African slave. Physicians dismissed the procedure out of hand and "resented being told by a gaggle of ministers that Africans had devised the panacea they had long sought," Washington wrote. Rage turned to violence when someone hurled a lighted grenade into Mather's house. Mather escaped serious injury, but wrote that he could see no difference between adopting the African solution for smallpox and using the Native Americans' antidote for snake venom, which the colonists had readily taken up.

Only one physician, Zabdiel Boylston, was willing to try the new method. He inoculated his son and the enslaved people he owned. In the end, the epidemic would wipe out more than 14 percent of Boston's population. But of the 240 people that Boylston had inoculated, only six died—one in forty, as against one in seven people who forwent inoculation.

By 1750, vaccinations, based on the method introduced by Onesimus, would be standard practice in Massachusetts and later in the rest of the country. "What is clear is that the knowledge he passed on saved hundreds of lives—and led to the eventual eradication of smallpox," wrote the author Erin Blakemore. "It remains the only infectious disease to have been entirely wiped out."

For his contribution to science, Onesimus does not appear even to have fully won his freedom. What little that is known is that Mather grew sour on him, and Onesimus managed to buy partial freedom by paying Mather money toward the purchase of another slave. He had gone well beyond what would have been expected of a man of the lowest caste, and, as often happens, does not appear to have reaped the rewards for a role that was beyond his station.

————

Instead, the rewards and privileges flowed from upholding the caste order. Doing so could boost the prospects of those who knew to stay in their place, the more conspicuous, the better. Two centuries after Onesimus's day, the Jim Crow regime would make a single exception to its iron law of segregation between blacks and whites. It was for black maids who had shown themselves sufficiently faithful to be entrusted with the care of white children. These women alone could ride in the whites-only section of a train or bus if they were out taking care of a white child. This exception served several purposes: It enshrined the white child as the ticket to a first-class seat for a black person. It reinforced the servile role, the natural place, of the subordinate caste. It elevated the black nursemaid by fiat of the dominant caste. It made domestics superior to even the likes of the great orator Frederick Douglass, who was once reduced to sitting on top of cargo on a train journey. It protected the children of the dominant caste from enduring for a single trip the taint and discomforts of the colored car. And it reminded everyone in the subordinated caste that they would only rise with the permission of the dominant caste, and on its terms, and only as long as they kept to the role assigned them.

They were to be given no quarter, no latitude to imagine themselves in any place other than the bottom rung. From Reconstruction to the civil rights era, southern school boards spent as little as one-tenth the money on black schools as for white schools, openly starving them of resources that might afford them a chance to compete on level ground. School terms for black students were made shorter by months, giving them less time in class and more time in the field for the enrichment of the ruling caste.

In hiring black teachers for segregated schools during Jim Crow, a leading southern official, Hoke Smith, made a deliberate decision: "When two Negro teachers applied to a school, to 'take the less competent.'" It was a nakedly creative way to cripple black prospects for achievement. It put black children under the instruction of the least qualified teachers. It passed over the brightest, most accomplished applicants—in fact, punished excellence—while elevating the mediocre in a purposeful distortion of meritocracy. All of this created dissension in the lowest caste over the patent unfairness and worked to crush the ambitions of those with the most talent. In these and other ways, the caste system trained the people in the lowest caste that the only way to survive was to play the comforting role of servile incompetent. The caste system all but ensured black failure by preempting success.

In a caste system, there can be little allowance for the disfavored caste to appear equal, much less superior at some human endeavor.

In the early years of the Third Reich, the Nazis made a point of excluding Jews from any position or circumstance in which they might outshine Aryans. This extended to classrooms in which the Berlin Gestapo went to the trouble of ordering that "everything must be done to put an end to the appearance that Aryan students are receiving assistance from Jews in preparing their exams." These were the ways that, irrespective of the natural range of intelligence and talent arising in any human subset, the people in the dominant caste were artificially propped up as superior in all things, a setup for disillusionment not of their own making.

If one of the requirements of a hierarchy is that the lowest caste must remain the scapegoat, on the bottom, the culture works to keep it that way by playing up the stereotypes that affirm their lowliness and minimizing indications to the contrary. In America, news outlets feed audiences a diet of inner-city crime and poverty so out of proportion to the numbers that they distort perceptions of African-Americans and of societal issues as a whole. Little more than one in five African-Americans, 22 percent, are poor, and they make up just over a quarter of poor people in America, at 27 percent. But a 2017 study by Travis Dixon at the University of Illinois found that African-Americans account for 59 percent of the poor people depicted in the news. White families make up two-thirds of America's poor, at 66 percent, but account for only 17 percent of poor people depicted in the news.

These generations-old distortions shape popular sentiment. A political scientist at Yale, Martin Gilens, found in a 1994 study that 55 percent of Americans believed that all poor people in America were black. Thus, a majority have come to see *black* as a synonym for *poor*, a stigmatizing distortion in a country that glorifies afflu-ence. Like poverty, crime, too, receives coverage out of proportion to the numbers. Crimes involving a black suspect and a white vic-tim make up 42 percent of the crimes reported on television news even though crimes with white victims and black suspects make up a minority of crimes, at 10 percent, according to the Sentencing Project, an advocate for criminal justice reform.

For generations, the culture has decried the alarming rate of births among black teenagers, often accompanied by depictions of welfare dependency, even though the majority of teenage mothers of all races are unmarried and likely to require help. But one might not know from news coverage that the rate of black teenagers giv-ing birth has plummeted in recent decades, from 118 per 1,000 black teenagers in 1991 to 28 per 1,000 in 2017, according to a 2019 analysis by the nonprofit research institute Child Trends.

This should be considered great news for society. The turnabout in birth rates for black and Latina teenagers has helped bring the overall teenage pregnancy rate to the lowest levels recorded in the modern era. Yet what little media coverage there has been has tended to revert to familiar caste tropes about unemployment and poverty, language of the 1990s, rather than looking into the rea-sons for the historic decline.

These numbers are clearly telling us something, and they do not fit caste assumptions. "The long-term downward trends," the researchers wrote, "may reflect that teenagers are increasingly likely to delay sex, and, if sexually active, to use contraception more carefully." Meaning that black and Latina teenagers are tak-ing precautions at a rate that is bringing them closer to the main-stream, an outcome contrary to societal expectations and thus largely disregarded.

———

The investment in the established hierarchy runs sufficiently deep that people in the dominant caste have historically been willing to forgo conveniences to themselves to keep the fruits of citizenship within their own caste.

After the Supreme Court outlawed segregation in public schools in *Brown v. Board of Education* in 1954, the white-run school board in Prince Edward County, Virginia, delayed integrating as long as it could and then shut down the school system entirely rather than allow black students into classrooms with white students. The county had no public schools for five years, from 1959 to 1964, forcing parents of both races to find alternatives for their children. Local whites diverted government funds to private academies for white students, while black parents, whose tax dollars were now going to the white students, had to make do on their own.

Around the same time, civil rights legislation outlawed segregation in public facilities, and, in response, cities in the South closed, auctioned off, or poured concrete into their whites-only pools so that nobody could swim, rather than sharing the water with black people. But those in the dominant caste had the means and resources, acquired over generations of collective income and wealth disparities, to build private pools behind gated communities for themselves and their children, leaving the lowest caste locked out again.

It is in these ways that a caste system shape-shifts and protects its beneficiaries, a workaround emerges, provisions are made, and the hierarchy remains intact, even in the face of challenges from the highest authority in the land. This is how a caste system, it seems, manages always to prevail.

In-group–out-group tensions remain a feature of American life. When black teenagers attended a pool party in a predominantly white, gated community in McKinney, Texas, in 2015, white residents called the police on them for trespassing.

Afterward, as shown in a video that drew international attention, an officer who responded to the call yanked a fifteen-year-old girl from the sidewalk, slammed her to the ground facedown, and pinned her with his full weight. Here was a grown man with his knees bearing down on her slight, bikini-clad frame, as she sobbed, helpless, beneath him. When black boys instinctively rushed to help her, the officer pointed his gun at them and they backed away, the full power of the state treating them not as children but as threats to society.

It was a scene that would be hard to imagine occurring with a young girl from the same caste—the dominant caste—as the officer. Within days, the officer resigned, but the incident demonstrated the depth of assumptions about who belongs where in a caste society, and the instantaneous walls erected and punishments meted out for breaching those boundaries even in our era.

CHAPTER SIXTEEN

Last Place Anxiety:
Packed in a Flooding Basement

Caste puts the richest and most powerful of the dominant caste at a remove, in the penthouse of a mythical high-rise, and everyone else, in descending order, on the floors beneath them. It consigns people in the subordinate caste to the basement, amid the flaws in the foundation and the cracks in the stonework that it appears others choose not to see.

When those in the basement begin rising to the floors above them, surveillance begins, the whole building is threatened. Thus caste can pit the basement-dwellers against themselves in a flooding basement, creating an illusion, a panic even, that their only competition is one another.

It can lead those down under to absorb into their identities the conditions of their entrapment and to do whatever it takes to distinguish themselves as superior to others in their group, to be first among the lowest.

"The stigmatized stratify their own," wrote the anthropologist J. Lorand Matory, "because no one wants to be in last place."

Over the generations, they learn to rank themselves by their proximity to the random traits associated with the dominant caste. Historically, the caste system has granted privileges to some in the subordinated group with the use of a toxic tool of caste known as colorism.

Among marginalized Americans, the closer they have been to

the dominant caste in skin color and in hair and facial features, the higher on the scale they have generally ranked, the women in particular, and the more value attached to them even by those whose appearance is further from the caste-driven ideal. This distortion in human value is especially insidious in America, owing to the historic means by which most African-Americans acquired their range in color and facial features—the rape and sexual abuse of enslaved African women at the hands of their masters and of other men in the dominant caste over the centuries.

With few other outlets for control and power, people on the bottom rung may put down others of their own caste to lift themselves up in the eyes of the dominant. They may feel more deeply wounded and deprived personally when someone of their shared lower rank rises or pushes past them than when the already chosen move ahead.

When someone from the already favored group moves up, it can seem preordained, in line with expectations, more easily accepted because this is how things have always been. Those in the dominant caste were above ground anyway. The rise of a favored person can seem less a commentary on you or your own deficiencies than a reflection of the way the world is.

"Conspicuously outperforming one's fellows is sometimes resented, as it makes people who are already feeling inferior feel even more inferior," Matory wrote. "Honor is a zero-sum game, with particularly intense implications for the discredited, because . . . there is so little honor to go around."

The caste system thrives on dissension and inequality, envy and false rivalries, that build up in a world of perceived scarcity. As people elbow for position, the greatest tensions arise between those adjacent to one another, up and down the ladder. In India, the uppermost castes have historically at times found themselves rubbing against one another. "They even quarrelled over such petty questions as to who should salute first," observed Bhimrao Ambedkar, "as to who should give way first, the Brahmins or the Kshatriyas, when the two met in the street."

If there are anxieties at the top, so much more so at the bottom. The caste system has historically rewarded snitches and sellouts among the lowest caste, as with the enforcers in the concentration camps of the Third Reich and the slave drivers on southern plantations. This was such a common device that, in America, there are several names for such a person, among them Uncle Tom or HNIC, short for Head Negro in Charge. People in the lowest caste came to resent these stooges of the caste system as much as if not more than they resented the dominant caste itself.

Even as others in the lowest caste try to escape the basement, those left behind can tug at the ones trying to rise. Marginalized people across the world, including African-Americans, call this phenomenon "crabs in a barrel." Many of the slave rebellions or the later attempts at unionizing African-American laborers in the South were thwarted because of this phenomenon, people subverting those who tried to get out, the spies paid with an extra peck of privilege for forewarning the dominant caste of unrest. These behaviors unwittingly work to maintain the hierarchy that those betraying their brethren are seeking to escape.

But this universal impulse may not always be caused by rank envy. A group already under siege may feel that "the team just cannot afford losing any member," wrote Sudipta Sarangi, an Indian specialist in organizational management. "If a certain member of the group starts climbing up—by doing better in life—the sheer fear of that individual's exit pushes everyone to pull him down."

––––––

Success in the American caste system requires some level of skill at decoding the preexisting order and responding to its dictates. The caste system instructs us all as to whose lives and opinions should bear the most weight and take precedence in most any encounter. One of its teachers is the criminal justice system, which descends from the criminal codes of the slavery era.

There, we learn, for instance, that it is the race of the victim, rather than just the perpetrator, that is "the greatest predictor of who gets the death penalty in the United States," the acclaimed legal justice advocate Bryan Stevenson observed, citing a study on death penalty cases. "Offenders in Georgia were eleven times more likely to get the death penalty if the victim was white than if the victim was black. These studies were replicated in every other state where studies about race and the death penalty took place."

The lesson teaches everyone, for instance, whose lives are considered expendable and whose are sacrosanct. It forces everyone to tithe to whatever degree to the supremacy of the ruling caste in order to flourish. Upon entry to the American caste system, immigrants learn to distance themselves from those in the basement, lest they land there themselves.

Though it was the protest movements of the subordinated caste that helped open the door to nonwhite immigrants in 1965, immigrants of color, like immigrants throughout American history, face the dilemma of adhering to the unwritten rules of caste. They face the painful dilemma of either rejecting the lowest caste of indigenous African-Americans or making common cause with those who fought so that they could enter the country to begin with.

But caste inverts the path to acceptance in America for people of African descent. Immigrants from Europe in the previous century were often quick to shed their names and drop the accents and folkways of the old country. They played down their ethnicity to gain admission to the dominant caste. Black immigrants discover that because they look like the people consigned to the lowest caste, the caste system rewards them for doing the opposite of the Europeans. "While white immigrants stand to gain status by becoming 'Americans,'" wrote the sociologist Philip Kasinitz, "by assimilating into the higher status group—black immigrants may actually lose social status if they lose their cultural distinctiveness."

Many recent African immigrants are better educated, better traveled than many Americans, may be fluent in multiple languages, and do not wish to be demoted to the lowest caste in their adopted homeland. The caste system encourages black immigrants to do everything they can to build distance between themselves and the subordinated caste they might be taken for. Like everyone else, they are exposed to the corrosive stereotypes of African-Americans and may work to make sure that people know that they are not of that group but are Jamaican or Grenadian or Ghanaian.

A Caribbean immigrant told Kasinitz: "Since I have been here, I have always recognized that this is a racist country, and I have made every effort not to lose my accent."

It is a clever, self-perpetuating tool of the caste system to keep those at the bottom divided in a manufactured fight to avoid last place. This has led to occasional friction between people descended from Africans who arrived in America at different points in our history. Some immigrants from the Caribbean and Africa, like their predecessors from other parts of the world, may show a wariness of African-Americans, warn their children not to "act like African-Americans" or not to bring one home to date or marry. In so doing, they may fall into the trap of trying to prove, not that the stereotype is false, but that they do not fit the lie.

Up and down the hierarchy, Ambedkar noted, "each caste takes its pride and its consolation in the fact that in the scale of castes it is above some other caste."

Try as it may to entice newcomers to take sides in upholding the hierarchy, the caste system fails to reach some people. Some children of immigrants from the Caribbean, people like Eric Holder, Colin Powell, Malcolm X, Shirley Chisholm, and Stokely Carmichael, among many others, have shared in the common plight of those in the lowest caste, become advocates for justice, and transcended these divisions for the greater good.

———

Caste helps explain the otherwise illogical phenomenon of African-Americans or women or other marginalized people who manage to rise to authority only to reject or diminish their own. Caught in a system that grants them little true power or authority, they may bend to the will of caste and put down their own if they wish to rise or to be accepted or merely to survive in the hierarchy. They learn that they may not be held accountable because of the low status of those they betray or neglect.

Many cases of mistreatment of people in the lowest caste occur at the hands of those of their same caste, as in the case of Freddie Gray, who died of spinal injuries at the hands of police officers in Baltimore. Gray was handcuffed in the back of a police van but not secured with safety belts, according to court testimony. The van swerved and curved, knocking Gray around the cargo area, handcuffed and unable to keep himself from crashing into the interior walls of the van. Three of the officers involved were black, including the driver of the van. This combination of factors allowed society to explain away Gray's death as surely having nothing to do with race, when in fact it was likely caste at work. All of these officers were either acquitted or had their charges dropped.

It is in keeping with caste protocols that, of the few officers who have been prosecuted for police brutality in recent high-profile cases, a notable number of them were men of color—a Japanese-American officer in Oklahoma, a Chinese-American officer in New York City, and a Muslim-American officer in Minneapolis. These are cases in which men of color pay the price for what upper-caste men often have gotten away with.

This phenomenon runs across levels of marginalization. The supervisor of the officers at the chokehold death of Eric Garner was a black woman. The people hardest on women employees can sometimes be women supervisors under pressure from and vying for the approval of male bosses in a male-dominated hierarchy in which fewer women are allowed to rise. Each of these cases presents a complicated story that presumably dismisses race or sex as a factor, but one that makes perfect sense, and maybe only makes sense, when seen through the lens of a caste system.

The enforcers of caste come in every color, creed, and gender. One does not have to be in the dominant caste to do its bidding. In fact, the most potent instrument of the caste system is a sentinel at every rung, whose identity forswears any accusation of discrimination and helps keep the caste system humming.

CHAPTER SEVENTEEN

On the Early Front Lines of Caste

In the fall of 1933, a distinguished black couple, newly returned from their studies in Europe, headed south from Virginia in the direction of Nashville and then, with both dread and anticipation, passed a symbolic iron curtain into the heart of Jim Crow Mississippi. They were anthropologists embarking on a perilous two-year study of the social hierarchy of the South. They were entering hostile and alien territory where they would have to learn to sublimate their upright bearing and submit to the humiliations of the social order, knowing that any slipup could cost them their lives.

They could not reveal the true nature of their mission at their final destination of Natchez, Mississippi. They would have to watch their every step in a world that preferred to keep its feudal conventions to itself and to keep people who looked like them in their place. They were driving headlong into a region where a black person was lynched every four days for some breach, large or small, of those conventions. They would soon discover that, just weeks before their arrival, a black man had been lynched in the county next to Natchez, under accusation of raping a white woman that even many local whites did not believe.

Allison Davis was an impeccably tailored academic with the sculpted, square-jawed face of a film star, and his wife, Elizabeth, was a model of refinement. But their path had been a twisting obstacle course. Just the previous spring, they had cut short their advanced studies at the University of Berlin and fled Germany when Hitler took power. They had seen the Nazis burn books and jail teachers, and this gave him new insight into the nature of hate, and combined with the burdens he bore in his own country, further inspired him to examine injustice.

Davis was a young anthropologist with two degrees from Harvard University and a wealth of experience abroad, but, once in Mississippi, he could not in any way act like it. He would have to conceal his inner self to survive. The couple had chosen to make the personal sacrifice for the greater good of documenting the structure of human division, a mission that would practically render them undercover agents. Urbane and bespectacled though he was, he decided it best to keep a gun in the car to protect himself and his wife if it came to it.

In Natchez, they would be joining the other half of their team, a white couple named Burleigh and Mary Gardner, two other Harvard anthropologists, who, in keeping with the plan, had preceded the Davises to Mississippi. The mission was quietly revolutionary. Together, they would embed themselves in a closed and isolated southern town from both sides of the caste divide. Coming from the North, neither couple could fully know what they were getting themselves into. This was in the depths of the Jim Crow caste system, and they would find their every move dictated by the very phenomenon that they were studying.

This would be among the first studies of its kind and a groundbreaking experiment in interracial scholarship. They would have to plan every detail of their interaction with the local people and come up with plausible reasons for the four of them to be together in this alien landscape. Given the dangers, they would not be able to tell the local people the full intention of their project—that they were seeking to infiltrate the white and black worlds to accurately render how caste, class, and race operated in the region.

The two couples were to report back to a senior professor who was overseeing the project from Cambridge. The pioneering anthropologist W. Lloyd Warner anticipated the dangers the team would face and went to Natchez himself ahead of the two couples to scout out the area and to prepare the town for their arrival.

Warner met with the mayor and law enforcement officials and with editors of the local newspaper before leaving the team on its own. He told town officials that they had chosen Natchez to represent a typical southern town and that the researchers would be collecting data to compare it with a town in the North. This was not altogether untrue. Warner had completed research on social stratification in Newburyport, Massachusetts, and could find the comparison useful.

The officials in Natchez were delighted to share the history of their town with the white husband-and-wife team. But it was harder for the team to come up with a credible reason for African-American scholars to come into town doing research.

They made the decision to tell the locals that the black researchers were there to study the black church, a safe enough subject for the town fathers to accept. As a measure of how far ahead of society the researchers were and of the proficiency of Allison Davis, it was he, the black anthropologist, who was chosen to lead the team on the ground in Natchez. They were two different castes studying caste in the belly of the caste system.

In order for the mission to work, the white couple went in first to get established before the black couple showed up. The Gardners rented rooms in an old country mansion as their base of operations and began gaining acceptance in Natchez society. But they had to give more forethought into where the Davises would live. The mansion was isolated, and the Davises would be uncomfortably, perhaps dangerously, conspicuous in that rural setting. Finding housing for them was a challenge in a region where most African-Americans were sharecroppers living in lean-to cabins. The team finally moved the project into the town itself, and the Davises rented rooms from a black doctor, who opened the way to the town's few black elites.

The couples soon found themselves embedded in their respective and separate castes, but that restricted them in other ways.

The team needed to study the layers within each caste—the elite and the lowly. But the social hierarchy drew such stark lines that even within one caste, fraternizing with those not seen as on one's level invited scrutiny and potential ostracism. To reach poor white residents—the lower class of the dominant caste—Mary Gardner took a position as a government caseworker in a New Deal program, which allowed her to meet poorer whites and to visit their homes.

That was not an option available to Elizabeth Davis as the Davises sought to meet with poorer black residents. At the time, few African-American women were permitted to hold those government jobs in Mississippi, and the federal relief that Mary Gardner was in a position to extend to the whites she met was not then being extended to poor blacks in Mississippi.

So Allison Davis sought to recruit a fifth researcher, St. Clair Drake, a former student of his who, decades later, would become a renowned scholar of mid-twentieth-century life in Chicago. The northern-bred Drake was not keen on spending months or years in the Jim Crow South, where, only a few years before, nine young black men, known as the Scottsboro Boys, had been imprisoned in neighboring Alabama, accused of attacking two white women, who later recanted their stories. Davis convinced him of the transcendent purpose of the mission. "You can't really smash the system if you don't understand how it works," Davis told him.

Drake agreed to come, and he spent his time with sharecroppers and domestics that the Davises, now seen as part of the sliver of upper-middle-class blacks in Natchez, no longer had readily explainable access to. They were all locked in the roles into which they had been accepted, having to do whatever their subcaste did, or compromise their foothold in their research setting.

Their lives depended upon obeying the rules they had come to study and proving themselves loyal to the caste to which they were ascribed. Mary Gardner, the white woman researcher, went so far as to climb into a hoop skirt and to serve as hostess at a mansion tour to which she had been invited. It was perilous to step out of character, perilous for the white couple to be seen as too closely aligned with the Davises, with whom, in that world, the dominant caste would have had minimal contact.

Out in public, they had to remain in character at all times, with the Davises required to show deference to the Gardners and never give the appearance that they were, in fact, friends and colleagues in the trenches. The two women found that they could not be seen together in public at all, had to conceal how well they knew each other, the caste system disallowing that kind of camaraderie between women of different castes. "Their encounters were limited to an occasional chance meeting at the chain grocery store in the center of town," Davis and the Gardners wrote in their paper "The Natchez Research," as quoted in David A. Varel's biography of Davis, *The Lost Black Scholar.* "There they exchanged only a polite, restrained greeting."

Over time, the white researchers came to see firsthand the barriers that African-Americans faced. Wherever they went, if they were together, there were no guarantees of food or restrooms for the Davises. Every move had to be thought out in advance with consideration of caste protocol. There were times when Gardner, the white researcher, had to request the bathroom key if Davis were to be allowed to use it.

Davis was the leader of the team, but they could not let the locals know that. They had to keep to their caste performance. It was a revolutionary concept, this idea of an educated black man working with a white man in this way to begin with, a spectacle the likes of which the townspeople would never have seen before.

They couldn't pretend that they weren't working together, but "it was explained to them, and generally understood by others, that Allison was working for Burleigh: this was the only acceptable relationship between a white man and a Negro," Davis and the Gardners wrote.

Just to meet and discuss their findings required an elaborate choreography. They had no outside office and could not go to each other's homes without arousing suspicions or causing discomfort. It did not sit well with the caste system for a white person to visit a black person, so Gardner could not visit Davis. It would have been permissible, and in fact, expected, for a subordinate-caste person to go to the dominant-caste person's location for the convenience of the upper-caste person. But for purposes of morale and dignity, it would have been unacceptable for Davis, as the team leader, to walk through the back door of his colleague's home. "It was not enough to *say* that Allison was working for Burleigh," Davis and the Gardners wrote. "Each of them was expected to *behave* strictly according to his caste role."

So they created a protocol for themselves whenever they needed to meet. One would telephone the other to make an appointment. Davis would arrive at an agreed-upon corner. Gardner would pick him up, and they would drive to a rural back road to go over their work in the car without bringing undue attention to themselves. Even this, they knew, was a breach of the caste system but it was their only option if they were to get their work done.

Later, Gardner happened to learn that "both the chief of police and the sheriff were informed of each meeting," Davis and the Gardners wrote. The sheriff and police chief did not intervene, but it was so serious a violation that, David Varel noted in *The Lost Black Scholar*, "the sheriff felt compelled to keep tabs on the two men."

This surveillance was a reminder that, at any given moment, the authorities could shut down their project, or worse. "The sheriff could seize their notes at any time, exposing the true nature of the larger study and destroying the data that they were gathering," Varel wrote.

To protect their research, they made frequent mailings to Warner back in Cambridge. But Allison had to be careful in doing so. "Frequent mailings by a Negro, especially an educated Negro, would have aroused suspicion in the middle-aged, middle-class white postal clerk," Davis and the Gardners wrote.

"The whole Negro-white research," Warner once said, was "delicate and filled with dynamite."

———

In 1941, as the United States prepared to enter the Second World War, the Davis and Gardner team emerged with perhaps the most comprehensive study to date of the American caste system. The volume was 538 pages long and titled *Deep South: A Social Anthropological Study of Caste and Class*. It described the layers of social classes within the two major castes in America—white and black people.

Davis and the Gardners determined that caste was "the fundamental division" in the Jim Crow town they studied, built on economic interdependence, in which "the caste system and the economic system reinforce each other." They documented the multiple rungs within the two castes, the layers of classes within each caste, the social control employed to keep the castes separate, and the slave-like conditions and power structure on the plantations in America as it approached the middle of the twentieth century.

They chronicled the rigid codes of conduct required to maintain the hierarchy. A black landlord, for instance, had to walk to the back door of his own building to collect the rent from his white tenants. The team described the terror campaign against the subordinate caste, the daily menace to the sharecroppers who were subject to ambush in the planters' whipping parties and the risks to the Davises themselves as they documented the assaults on other African-Americans.

It had taken them eight years to publish their findings, and even then, the researchers were bedeviled with setbacks and the disadvantages of both caste and timing in getting it out to the world. They had begun the work in the midst of the Great Depression and thus faced the ongoing challenge of financing a project that seemed risky from the start.

Two years in, with the Depression worsening and the project taking longer than expected, the Davises, who had borne the brunt of the humiliation that confronted their caste and with the least personal resources, found themselves so strapped for money that they had to take on teaching duties at Dillard University, an underfunded, historically black institution in New Orleans. There, Allison Davis was weighed down with a teaching load of five courses each semester while trying to complete the larger caste

study. Worn down by the isolation and indignities, having to perform in character over the course of several years, he fell into a
depression over their circumstances.

At the same time, competition arrived on the scene. The Mississippi Delta got crowded with young social scientists investigating
this feudal country-within-a-country, as the Depression had raised
interest in rural and southern poverty. And while the interracial
Davis and Gardner team had spent far longer—years, in fact—
living under the caste rules they were studying, two Yale anthropologists, both white and working in the same area in two separate
studies, spent several months in Mississippi and, with their shorter
timelines, were able to beat the Davises' and the Gardners' more
comprehensive study to publication.

John Dollard of Yale spent five months in Indianola. Hortense
Powdermaker, also of Yale, spent nine months there in the 1932–33
school year and another three months in 1934.

Dollard's 1937 book, *Caste and Class in a Southern Town,* was the
first of the three major works to be published. It received wide ac-
claim and defined the emerging field. Dollard was hailed as a pio-
neer while the Davises and the Gardners were still analyzing their
volumes of data. Dollard acknowledged the limits of his work,
conceded that, as a white Yankee in the southern caste system, he
ran headlong into caste taboos that restricted his access to African-
Americans. The local whites he needed to rely on couldn't understand why he would be interested in black residents. When he told
some white residents of his plan to visit a black woman's home, he
said he was "ostracized from the town."

Hortense Powdermaker's *After Freedom: A Cultural Study in the
Deep South* was published next, in 1939. Both Dollard's and Powdermaker's books were met with spirited reviews and came to
dominate the field of southern caste scholarship. Even decades
later, the journal *American Anthropologist,* in 2004, described the
two books as "canonical" "landmark studies," consigning the
Davis and Gardner book to the footnotes.

Deep South was published in 1941 and has long been overshadowed by the two earlier works produced by scholars from the dominant caste. The Davis and Gardner project seemed to meet the same fate of marginalization as the subordinate caste that they had studied.

———

Neither Davis nor Gardner made the claim that the Indian caste system and the American one were identical. Yet, criticism of the idea of caste in America followed a pattern in caste relations that the team documented in Mississippi. They found that African-American workers, trained in the subordinated behavior and perspective necessary to survive in a caste system, were more likely to show respect for people in the dominant caste and to disregard or feel freer to criticize those from their own subordinated caste.

For a range of complex reasons, some leading African-American social scientists of the early to mid-twentieth century objected to Davis and others applying the notion of caste to the plight of African-Americans, even as they were living under one of the purest forms of it in American history. Restricted as they were, locked behind the walls of caste with no end in sight, they did not want to give credence to the possibility that the system might indeed be closed forever. If their status was seen as a fixed one, there might be no hope of rising above it.

They were deep in a caste wilderness, before *Brown v. Board of Education,* before the Montgomery bus boycott, before the 1963 March on Washington and the civil rights legislation of the 1960s that would formally prohibit the caste restrictions they were then living under. In the middle of the twentieth century, no one could have dreamt of a member of the subordinate caste sitting on the Supreme Court, becoming secretary of state, being in the Oval Office as president rather than as a butler.

The lowest caste had yet to break free and disprove the assumptions of group inferiority that were the justification of the caste system, show that its members were as capable as anyone else in any endeavor, from singing Verdi at the Metropolitan to orbiting space to winning Nobel Prizes. These things were inconceivable because the caste system had disallowed any possibility of them. Thus there was an understandable fear that invoking the fixed and formal, millennia-long caste system of India could forestall the few hard-earned gains they had managed to achieve.

Any success that Davis might see was itself a challenge to the caste system. And as one of the few African-Americans given the chance to conduct this kind of research, he walked a narrower path, had put his life on the line in a way others had not, and was in line for more criticism than dominant-caste researchers might receive. The white researchers who were published before *Deep South* had the chance to seize on the novelty of the idea were more readily embraced by the mainstream and accorded more authority due in part to their position in the dominant caste.

Despite their immersion and mastery of the subject, Davis and Gardner fell under greater scrutiny and faced more obstacles just to complete their book. Publication was delayed in part because a leading black sociologist, Charles Johnson, trained in a different discipline, raised lengthy questions about the manuscript, which required Davis and Gardner to embark upon a significant revision. Davis, as lead researcher, was an easier target for criticism, particularly from peers in the subordinated caste who were under pressure to uphold the hierarchy if they wished to succeed and who would have been wary of calling into question the work of dominant-caste scholars. The resistance to Davis's work inadvertently proved the very theories Davis had devoted his life to exposing.

The concept of caste grew only more contentious as it was applied to the United States at midcentury. One leading sociologist, the Caribbean-born Oliver Cromwell Cox, assembled a cantankerous critique of this school of thought in his landmark 1948 book, *Caste, Class and Race: A Study in Social Dynamics*. He devoted a hundred pages to his reading of the Indian caste system and later chapters to the differences between the hierarchies of the two countries.

An underlying argument of his contrarian view was that the caste system in India was singular because it was considered stable and unquestioned, because even the lowest castes embraced their degraded lot as the fate of the gods. The fact that black Americans resisted their condition, both in slavery and afterward, and aspired to equality was evidence, to Cox, that the term *caste* could not be applied to this country. "If, for instance, the Negro-white relationship were a caste relationship," he wrote, "Negroes would not be aspiring toward the upper social position occupied by whites. "

In India, however, "caste barriers in the caste system are never challenged," he wrote in a bafflingly misguided observation. From his perspective, up and down the Indian caste system, "regardless of his position in the society, a man's caste is sacred to him; and one caste does not dominate the other."

Despite his brilliance, he disregarded both the injustices inflicted upon Dalits by castes that most certainly dominated them and the basic human will to be free. And he overlooked the fiery resistance and leadership of Bhimrao Ambedkar and other Dalits who were challenging the caste system at the very moment of his writing.

Before Cox's excoriation of the notion of caste, the findings of Davis and the Gardners got reinforcement from perhaps the most ambitious work ever attempted on race in America, the monumental two-volume *American Dilemma*, published in 1944. It was based on the research of a team of scholars, including Davis and his contemporary Johnson, and was overseen by the Swedish social economist Gunnar Myrdal. In this analysis of race, Myrdal described intergroup relations in the United States as a caste system, a term he returned to time and again.

"The caste system," Myrdal wrote, "is upheld by its own inertia and by the superior caste's interest in upholding it."

———

Davis would go on to get a Ph.D. in anthropology at the University of Chicago and join the faculty there, thus becoming the first black tenured professor at a major white American university. But he would suffer additional indignities. Faculty colleagues openly debated whether he should be allowed to teach white students, and he was prohibited from eating in the faculty dining room for a time.

Of the major scholars of the American South in the first half of the twentieth century, he and his wife were among the only field researchers who labored under the cloud of caste subordination themselves. Their work would end up inspiring St. Clair Drake, Stokely Carmichael, and Martin Luther King, Jr., among others, all of whom read his work as undergraduates and saw themselves in his analysis.

Allison Davis was nearly lost to history, but he has become a champion to current-day researchers who seek to understand the infrastructure of our divisions. He brought a singular depth of commitment to understanding the caste system in hopes of defeating it. He had taken on the challenge as if his life had depended upon it, because in a very real way, it did.

CHAPTER EIGHTEEN

Satchel Paige and the Illogic of Caste

His fastball shot toward home plate like a pistol bullet, once was clocked at 103 miles an hour, fast enough to "tear the glove off the catcher," in the words of the sportswriter Robert Smith. LeRoy "Satchel" Paige was one of the greatest baseball pitchers ever to step onto a mound. Yet, coming of age in the early twentieth century, when Jim Crow was at its cruelest, he never had the chance to become all that he could have been. And the world of baseball forwent a talent that surely would have changed the fate of matchups and pennant races, perhaps entire teams, and the sport itself.

Here was a man who threw so hard and so fast that "catchers had to cushion their gloves with beefsteak so that their hands wouldn't be burning after the game," his biographer Larry Tye told National Public Radio.

Here was a man so confident that he told whoever was paying him that he would strike out the first nine batters with a money-back guarantee and told the outfielders to just take a seat.

The beloved Yankee center fielder Joe DiMaggio, who went to bat against Paige at exhibition games before Paige was hired by the majors, called him the best pitcher he had ever faced. In his day, Paige "may well have been the fastest pitcher in the nation," wrote Smith in *Pioneers of Baseball*, "or even in history."

He didn't get the chance to make the most of it. The distorting lens of caste can cloud the senses, make the dominant group willing to deprive itself of the benefit of talent outside its ranks, allow the gifts of those from groups deemed inferior to languish, as it did with Satchel Paige, to keep the castes separate or to uphold the fiction that all talent resides within one favored group.

It happened that Paige was not only fast but threw with such precision that teammates let him practice knocking lit cigarettes out of their mouths with his fastballs. "That we know of, he never knocked out a ballplayer," Tye told NPR. "He knocked out one cigarette after another, and that was extraordinary faith."

For more than half a century, America's pastime was rigidly segregated, the very best players of either caste rarely getting to meet on the field and never in an official game. Paige got into baseball in the late 1920s and thus spent most of his career playing on all-black teams that were every bit as talented but lacking in the resources and infrastructure of the all-white majors. The full measure of his and his teammates' talents cannot truly be known because of the incomplete record-keeping and scant media coverage in the devalued world of the Negro Leagues.

Paige was widely considered superior not solely because of his innate talent and ingenuity but because he worked so long and hard at it—a work ethic that had him barnstorming the country, pitching for the Negro Leagues and then for whoever else was willing to pay him. He pitched nearly every day, all year long, not just during the traditional baseball season and without the luxury of the relief pitchers in the majors. He gave his pitches names like the bat dodger and the midnight crawler and the hesitation pitch, where he would pause after planting his left foot, psyching the batter into swinging prematurely.

Though he was one of the greatest pitchers in baseball history, the limits of the caste system reduced him at one point to picking up spare change by pitching batting practice for white players in the minor leagues. By the time major league baseball opened up to African-Americans in 1946, when Jackie Robinson signed with the

Brooklyn Dodgers, Satchel Paige was already forty and considered too old for the game.

But two years later, the Cleveland Indians were in the midst of one of the tightest pennant races in American League history, and the owner thought Paige might put them over the top now that the color bar had been lifted. The owner, Bill Veeck, approached Paige in the middle of the 1948 season and signed him as a free agent.

Paige was well past his peak when he finally got his shot at the majors. At forty-two, he was the oldest rookie in baseball, old enough to be his teammates' father. Still, at one of his first starting games in the big league, fans stormed the turnstiles to see him play at Comiskey Park. There, he pitched a 5–0 shutout for Cleveland over the Chicago White Sox, helping Cleveland make it to the playoff, and ultimately to the World Series, just as the team owner had hoped.

That year, Paige would become the first African-American to pitch in the World Series, though given the assumptions about his age and the politics of a championship season, he was assigned as a relief pitcher. When it was his turn at the mound, he pitched for two-thirds of an inning while the Indians were trailing the Boston Braves and did not allow a hit. The Cleveland Indians won the World Series that year.

He would go on to pitch in the majors for a few more seasons, but his best years were behind him, the career he should have had in a fairer world deprived of him, and there was nothing that anyone could do to make up for what had been withheld. The majors turned to him one more time, in the fall of 1965, to pitch at the age of fifty-nine. By then he was older than most of the managers. The Kansas City Athletics were last in the standings, and attendance had plummeted. The owner got the idea to recruit Paige, who had always been a showman, to pitch for the A's to fill the stands as a publicity stunt.

The fans turned out. They loaded onto the stands for the spectacle. But Paige came to play. The oldest pitcher in baseball history threw three scoreless innings that day against the Red Sox. Paige left the field with his team in the lead, a lead that the Athletics blew after he returned to the dugout, losing the game in the end. He had salvaged the team momentarily and was serenaded by the audience, who had come out mostly to see him pitch one last time.

Afterward, reporters asked him how it felt to pitch at nearly sixty years old to batters who could be his grandsons. "It was no big deal for me to come back up here," he said, "because I had no business being out. Now folks can see that I must have had a lot more going for me, and I deserved to be in the big leagues when I was in my prime."

Satchel Paige was cheated by a caste system at the height of its injustice and absurdity. But he was not the only loser to the illogic of caste. "Many critics agree that it was actually American baseball that was the loser in the Paige saga," wrote the sportswriter Mark Kram. "Any number of major league teams would have done better with Paige in their ranks when he was in his prime. Marginal teams might have won pennants; championship teams might have extended their domination."

Under the spell of caste, the majors, like society itself, were willing to forgo their own advancement and glory, and resulting profits, if these came at the hands of someone seen as subordinate.

Part Five

The Consequences of Caste

CHAPTER NINETEEN

The Euphoria of Hate

The film footage, black and white, rough against the wall onto which it is projected, unfolds in a continuing loop in a cave of a viewing room at a Berlin museum. It shoves/ heaves/spits you back in time to Saturday, July 6, 1940, at precisely three P.M. There is no commentary explaining the footage. You are forced to absorb the horror of it, in all of its banal pageantry, on your own.

Hitler is returning to Berlin after the Germans have seized Paris in the Battle of France. The camera captures his arrival at Anhalter Station and follows the flower-strewn Strasses along the parade route to the Reich Chancellery. Hitler's motorcade winds past people who are not just hurling confetti but are so tightly packed together that they themselves look like mounds of confetti thrown by the wind. Soldiers have to hold back the smiling, crying women, as would happen at Beatles concerts a generation from this moment. The roar of the crowd is not recognizably human but the rolling crash of ocean waves that recede and then batter the shore again. Church bells ring in the distance. The children and the men and the women flutter their own Nazi flags like bird wings.

The camera closes in, and you can begin to make out the individual Heils—the male Heils from the high-pitched female Heils. A boy is hoisted on a street sign waving and heiling. A little girl is on a parent's shoulder heiling. Soldiers' heels press against the soil to keep their footing against the crowd, their jackboots braced against women's pumps, the women swooning and pushing, the soldiers grinning at the futility of holding back Hitler's screaming fans in a lighthearted tussle between pant cuffs and stockinged calves.

The camera cuts to the balcony and to the object of the throng's uncontained rapture. You see him first from behind, the silhouette of Hitler set against a million dots that are his jubilant fans. He stands like a statue, arms rigidly forward. He leans over the balcony and lets escape a smile of satisfaction. You recall that you have never seen an image of evil smiling, a quarter second of human emotion. He surveys the waving, cheering base of his power, and nods. "This is good," the look on his face is saying.

People laugh in reverie, jubilation all around, from the balcony and along the parade route and on the packed Platz where it appears that every German alive has managed to squeeze themselves in. So many that they are fairly holding one another up and jumping and waving their Nazi flags, a million Nazi flags. The motorcade had only minutes ago wound beneath Nazi banners a story high, blowing from above on both sides of the street, every few feet a Nazi banner, rows and rows for miles. This is the worship service of the true believers, looking now like mounds of pebbles on a beach, a million indistinguishable bees in a hive.

The film played in a loop on the wall without comment. None was necessary. I sat mesmerized and repulsed, sickened but unable to get up. Perhaps if I stayed long enough, I might begin to comprehend it. In that moment, you are face-to-face with the force of willing susceptibility to evil. The Nazis could not have risen to power and done what they did without the support of the masses of people who were open to his spell. I could not stop watching it. The smiling, shining faces in this carpet of exuberant humanity—this massive number of people could not all be what we would consider evil. They are husbands, wives, mothers, fathers, children, uncles, nephews, all gathered at a ticker-tape parade on a brilliant, sunny day celebrating what we know to be a horror.

I thought to myself, Did the German people know the carnage they were celebrating? Yes, it turns out, clips of bombing raids were shown during news reels before the feature film at the cinema. They knew that the French had been violently defeated. It was two years past Kristallnacht. They knew that Jewish friends and neighbors had been rounded up, publicly humiliated, taken away, never seen again. And the people in the crowd were smiling and happy. Everything that happened to the Jews of Europe, to African-Americans during the lynching terrors of Jim Crow, to Native Americans as their land was plundered and their numbers decimated, to Dalits considered so low that their very shadow polluted those deemed above them—happened because a big enough majority had been persuaded and had been open to being persuaded, centuries ago or in the recent past, that these groups were ordained by God as beneath them, subhuman, deserving of their fate. Those gathered on that day in Berlin were neither good nor bad. They were human, insecure and susceptible to the propaganda that gave them an identity to believe in, to feel chosen and important.

What would any of us have done had we been in their places? How many people actually go up against so great a tide of seeming inevitability? How many can see the evil for what it is, as it is occurring? Who has the courage to stand up to the multitudes in the face of a charismatic demigod who makes you feel better about yourself, part of something bigger than yourself, that you have been primed to believe?

Every last one of us would now say to ourselves, I would never have attended such an event, I would never have attended a lynching. I would never have stood by, much less cheered, as a fellow human was dismembered and then set on fire here in America. And yet tens of thousands of everyday humans did just that in the lifetime of the oldest among us in Germany, in India, in the American South. This level of cold-hearted disconnection did not happen overnight. It built up over generations of insecurities and resentments.

Some of the witnesses and participants who heiled Hitler and laughed at humans being tortured in the Jim Crow South are still alive, cradling grandchildren to their bosom. The camera in Berlin panned the crowd and fixed its lens on the children, a little girl with a blond pageboy and a barrette in her hair, heiling Hitler, hoisted on her parent's shoulders. She would be about eighty now, and this could be one of the earliest memories she carries inside her as a human being.

Germany bears witness to an uncomfortable truth—that evil is not one person but can be easily activated in more people than we would like to believe when the right conditions congeal. It is easy to say, If we could just root out the despots before they take power or intercept their rise. If we could just wait until the bigots die away . . . It is much harder to look into the darkness in the hearts of ordinary people with unquiet minds, needing someone to feel better than, whose cheers and votes allow despots anywhere in the world to rise to power in the first place. It is harder to focus on the danger of common will, the weaknesses of the human immune system, the ease with which the toxins can infect succeeding generations. Because it means the enemy, the threat, is not one man, it is us, all of us, lurking in humanity itself.

CHAPTER TWENTY

The Inevitable Narcissism of Caste

Through no fault of any individual born to it, a caste system centers the dominant caste as the sun around which all other castes revolve and defines it as the default-setting standard of normalcy, of intellect, of beauty, against which all others are measured, ranked in descending order by their physiological proximity to the dominant caste.

They are surrounded by images of themselves, from cereal commercials to sitcoms, as deserving, hardworking, and superior in most aspects of American life, and it would be the rare person who would not absorb the constructed centrality of the dominant group. It would be the rare outliers who would go out of their way to experience the world from the perspective of those considered below them, or even to think about them one way or the other, and the caste system does not require it of them.

Society builds a trapdoor of self-reference that, without any effort on the part of people in the dominant caste, unwittingly forces on them a narcissistic isolation from those assigned to lower categories. It replicates the structure of narcissistic family systems, the interplay of competing supporting roles—the golden-child middle castes of so-called model minorities, the lost-child indigenous peoples, and the scapegoat caste at the bottom.

The centrality of the dominant caste is not lost on those considered beneath them in the hierarchy. The highest and lowest rungs are seen as so far apart as to seem planted in place, immovable. Thus those straddling the middle may succumb to the greatest angst and uncertainty as they aspire to a higher rung.

Everyone in the caste system is trained to covet proximity to the dominant caste: an Iranian immigrant feeling the need to mention that a relative had blond hair as a child; a second-generation child of Caribbean immigrants quick to clarify that they are Jamaican and categorically not African-American; a Mexican immigrant boasting that one of his grandfathers back in Mexico "looked just like an American"—blond hair and blue eyes—at which point he was reminded by an African-American that Americans come in all colors of hair and eyes.

Those accustomed to being the measure of all that is human can come to depend on the reassurance that, while they may have troubles in their lives, at least they are not at the bottom. As long as the designated bottom dwellers remain in their designated place, their own identities and futures are secure.

"No matter how degraded their lives, white people are still allowed to believe that they possess the blood, the genes, the patrimony of superiority. No matter what happens, they can never become 'black,'" wrote the sociologist Andrew Hacker. "White Americans of all classes have found it comforting to preserve blacks as a subordinate caste: a presence that despite all its pain and problems still provides whites with some solace in a stressful world."

———

We are accustomed to the concept of narcissism—a complex condition of self-aggrandizing entitlement and disregard of others, growing out of a hollow insecurity—as it applies to individuals. But some scholars apply it to the behavior of nations, tribes, and subgroups. Freud was among the earliest psychoanalysts to connect a psychiatric diagnosis to Narcissus of Greek mythology, the son of the river god who fell in love with his own image in a pool of water and, not realizing that it was he who was "spurning" his affection, died in despair. "Narcissus could not conceive that he was in love with his own reflection," wrote the psychologist Elsa Ronningstam. "He was caught in an illusion."

So, too, with groups trained to believe in their inherent sovereignty. "The essence of this overestimation of one's own position and the hate for all who differ from it is narcissism," wrote the psychologist and social theorist Erich Fromm. "He is nothing," Fromm wrote, "but if he can identify with his nation, or can transfer his personal narcissism to the nation, then he is everything."

A person deeply invested in his group's dominance "has a euphoric 'on-top-of-the-world' feeling, while in reality he is in a state of self-inflation," Fromm wrote. "This leads to severe distortion of his capacity to think and to judge. . . . He and his are over-evaluated. Everything outside is under-evaluated." And underneath may lie the fear that he cannot live up to the constructed ideal of his own perfection.

History has shown that nations and groups will conquer, colonize, enslave, and kill to maintain the illusion of their primacy. Their investment in this illusion gives them as much of a stake in the inferiority of those deemed beneath them as in their own presumed superiority. "The survival of the group," Fromm wrote, "depends to some extent on the fact that its members consider its importance as great or greater than that of their own lives, and furthermore that they believe in the righteousness, or even superiority, of their group as compared to others."

Thus, when under threat, they are willing to sacrifice themselves and their ideals for the survival of the group from which they draw their self-esteem. The social theorist Takamichi Sakurai wrote bluntly: "Group narcissism leads people to fascism. An extreme form of group narcissism means malignant narcissism, which gives rise to a fanatical fascist politics, an extreme racialism."

In modern times, this kind of group narcissism has gripped two nations in particular, according to Fromm: "the racial narcissism which existed in Hitler's Germany, and which is found in the

American South," he wrote in 1964, at the height of the civil rights movement.

Fromm well knew the perils of group narcissism from both his training in psychoanalysis and his personal experience. He was a German Jew who fled to Switzerland after the Nazis took power in Germany, and then to the United States in 1934. He saw first-hand the Nazi appeals to the fears and insecurities of everyday Germans in the lead-up to the Nazi takeover.

"If one examines the judgment of the poor whites regarding blacks, or of the Nazis in regard to Jews," Fromm wrote, "one can easily recognize the distorted character of their respective judgments. Little straws of truth are put together, but the whole which is thus formed consists of falsehoods and fabrications. If the political actions are based on narcissistic self-glorifications, the lack of objectivity often leads to disastrous consequences."

In both instances, Fromm found the working class to be among the most susceptible, harboring an "inflated image of itself as the most admirable group in the world, and of being superior to another racial group that is singled out as inferior," he wrote. A person in this group "feels: 'even though I am poor and uncultured I am somebody important because I belong to the most admirable group in the world—I am white'; or 'I am Aryan.'"

A group whipped into narcissistic fervor "is eager to have a leader with whom it can identify," Fromm wrote. "The leader is then admired by the group which projects its narcissism onto him."

The right kind of leader can inspire a symbiotic connection that supplants logic. The susceptible group sees itself in the narcissistic leader, becomes one with the leader, sees his fortunes and his fate as their own. "The greater the leader," Fromm wrote, "the greater the follower. . . . The narcissism of the leader who is convinced of his greatness, and who has no doubts, is precisely what attracts the narcissism of those who submit to him."

———

Caste behavior is essentially a response to one's assigned place in the hierarchy. According to the script that the culture hands us all, the dominant caste (whether man over woman, rich over poor, white over black, Brahmin over Dalit) is not to take instructions or even suggestions from the lower caste. The script decrees that the dominant caste must be right, more informed, more competent, first in all things. The caste system primes the dominant caste to experience discomfort, unfairness at the sight of a lower-caste person in a position above their perceived station and more particularly above them, and may feel the need to restore equilibrium by putting the lower-caste person in their place.

The dominant caste tends to resist comparison to lower-caste people, even the suggestion that they have anything in common or share basic human experiences, as this diminishes the dominant-caste person and forces the contemplation of equality with someone deemed lower. A comparison forces the contemplation of that person's humanity, a source of internal conflict when confronted with injustice that society deems appropriate if the target is not seen as fully human as themselves.

Years ago, a colleague fretted to me about his and his wife's worries about his father-in-law, who had recently had a health setback. The father-in-law lived in another state and was not as sharp as he once had been, might have fallen recently or suffered some other worrisome though not life-threatening development. My colleague lamented to me that his wife was going to have to make a trip many miles away to check on him, and she would perhaps have to look into assisted living. It was weighing on her, and him.

He was speaking directly to me, but his words seemed a general lament to the universe. He was facing an existential disruption that I could identify with. In the past, I had mentioned to him the challenges I had had managing the care of my mother, who had been disabled years before. He had listened at the time with the detachment of those who have not yet faced the inevitable, who tell themselves, as we all do, that somehow we will escape what we know is coming.

I told him I was sorry to hear that his family was going through this. I can understand, I told him. As you know, I said, I have been having to take care of my mother while being on the road, and I, too, had to look into assisted living for her. He seemed taken aback at the very suggestion that the situations might have anything whatsoever in common, as if this were tantamount to equating a giraffe with a kangaroo. The statement was seen as an insult to him and activated a deep-seated programming. "Why, you can't compare my father-in-law," he said of the preposterousness of the idea, "to *your mother*."

———

In the unspoken rules of caste, the people in the dominant caste are expected to be first or in the superior station. Historically, their job is to correct, direct, discipline, and police the people in the lowest caste. They are to be ever vigilant to any rise or breach on the part of those beneath them.

I had borne witness to this in the American caste system, but the more time I spent among Indians, the more these caste rules became apparent to me, predictive even, in my interactions with people from the world's original caste system. I learned to recognize almost immediately the differences between dominant-caste Indians and Dalits, even without the starker physical cues of dominant and subordinated castes in America.

Indians wondered how I, as an outsider from a completely different culture, was able to distinguish them so quickly. I spoke none of the Indian languages, knew nothing of the *jatis*, and was in no position to query anyone as to the section of village from which they came or recognize early the surnames that conveyed one's place in the caste system.

I noticed, first, upper-caste people tended to be lighter in complexion and sharper in features, though that is not an ironclad indicator. Secondly, I noticed that they were more likely to speak English with British diction, although that could be a sign of education and class as much as caste hierarchy. More revealingly and more consistently, I began to be able to distinguish people from their bearing and demeanor, in accord with the universal script of caste. It was no accident that my caste radar worked more efficiently when there was a group of people interacting among themselves. Caste is, in a way, a performance, and I could detect the caste positions of people in a group but not necessarily a single Indian by himself or herself. "There is never caste," the Dalit leader Ambedkar once said. "Only castes."

And so, at gatherings of Indians of different castes, I could see that the upper-caste people took positions of authority, were forthright, at ease with being in charge, correcting and talking over the lower-caste people. It echoed a similar dynamic in the United States, an expectation that an upper-caste person must assert superiority of knowledge and intellect in all things, having been socialized to be first and to be central, a pressure to be right and the need to remind the lower-caste person, subtly or not, of their historic, cultural, spatial, and familial inferiority.

At a panel or seminar, they were often the ones leading the discussion or doing most of the talking. They tended to speak more formally, giving direction, heads held high. On the other hand, the Dalits, as if trained not to bring attention to themselves, sat in the shadows, on the periphery at a conference seminar, asking few questions, daring not, it seemed, to intrude upon an upper-caste domain or conversation even if the discussion was about them, which in fact it was.

Even in the rarefied space of a scholarly presentation, when an upper-caste person was correcting a lower-caste person, the Dalit listened and took their admonishment without questioning, head often down or nodding that, *yes, you are correct, I will go back now and do what you have said.* I winced as I watched people talk down to scholars from the subordinate caste in an open forum.

In India, it was Dalits who gravitated toward me like long-lost relatives, surrounding me and propping themselves on a sofa near me for an impromptu subordinate-caste tête-à-tête. I discovered that they wanted to hear from me, or, I should say, commune with someone they recognized as a kindred spirit who shared a common condition. "We read James Baldwin and Toni Morrison because they speak to our experiences," a Dalit scholar said to me. "They help us in our plight."

I was standing during a lunch break at a conference in Delhi. A Dalit scholar and I were communing about our kindred perspectives when an upper-caste woman walked up and broke into the conversation to tell the Dalit woman what she should have included in her presentation, a point that she missed and which she would do well to include the next time.

The upper-caste woman interrupted us with a sense of entitlement, without excusing herself for breaking in, disregarding the conversation in progress, disregarding me, the person with whom the Dalit woman was talking, as if whatever we were saying could wait. She chided the Dalit scholar with an air of condescension and superiority and proceeded to instruct the Dalit scholar on the Dalit behavior that the Dalit scholar had researched and written about. She castigated her in front of me, a complete stranger to both of them. I was there on a mission of my own, and an upper-caste woman was making herself the center of someone else's conversation and was keeping me from my task.

It evoked a convention of the American caste system that often places the word of a dominant-caste person above the word of a subordinate-caste person even in matters that the subordinated person would be more likely to know about. For most of American history, African-Americans were not permitted to sit on juries, for example, or to testify against a white person. Even in more recent times, accusations of racial discrimination often carry more weight if a dominant-caste person vouches for it.

Now, on the other side of the world, a dominant-caste woman in India was presuming the same privilege in a parallel universe. In American social justice circles, her castigation of the Dalit woman would be seen as a kind of Brahmin-splaining, as with mansplaining and whitesplaining—a dominant-caste person lecturing a subordinate-caste person about something on which the subordinate-caste person may, in fact, be an authority.

When the upper-caste woman left after making her points, it was hard to get our footing again. She had jarred us from our parallel caste communing. I asked the Dalit woman if she knew the woman who had just interrupted us, because she had spoken with such familiarity and comfort. "No," the Dalit scholar said. "You see, that is what happens. She just let me know that she was upper caste and above me."

————

Though they may not recognize it on a conscious level, dominant-caste Americans often show nearly as much curiosity about the ethnic, and thus caste, origins of their fellow Americans as do people in India. When Americans seek to locate themselves in the hierarchy, the line of inquiry may be more subtle and may not have the same life-or-death consequences as in India. But it is there.

They will question a person whose race is ambiguous until they are satisfied of an origin. If descended from western Europe, they might query an Italian-American about their roots—what part of Italy, north or south, countryside or city—out of genuine interest or because they have visited or wish to, but also perhaps to locate them in the southern European hierarchy. If a person is part Irish and part Czech, they might emphasize, upon meeting someone, the Irish grandfather rather than the Czech grandmother. A white person might describe him- or herself as a mutt or as a "Heinz 57," which handily obscures lineage outside of northwestern Europe.

The old eugenics hierarchy of presumed value still lurks beneath the surface. A woman whose grandparents immigrated from Poland might say to an Irish-American—whose status is perceived as higher than hers—that they came from Austria (justifying it to herself by recalling the shifting borders in the twentieth century). But the same woman might "admit" that they came from Poland to an African-American of presumed lower rank, whom she had no need to impress, her higher status secure and under-stood.

Not long ago, in Boston and Chicago and Cleveland, people spoke of "white ethnics" from southern and eastern Europe as po-litical voting blocs. They distinguished the "lace-curtain Irish" from the "shanty Irish." Once, at the end of a meeting in the North-east a few years ago, a young white assistant in a room with black professionals was asked the routine question of how her name was spelled, which could have been Kathryn, Catherine, Kather-ine, or maybe Katharine. She straightened her back and answered pertly, "The English spelling," which seemed no answer at all and a curious bid to set herself apart from everyone else in the room, to pull rank with Anglo-Saxony, which no actual Anglo-Saxon would need to do. I thought to myself, *And exactly what spelling would that be?*

Three white women were once catching up over dinner about people they had known for years, their conversation flowing along caste lines beyond conscious awareness. One woman, of Irish descent, brought up someone whose family, she pointed out, had arrived from Germany in the first half of the twentieth cen-tury. This prompted a second woman to chime in that her family had come from Germany earlier. They arrived in the 1860s. The third woman brought up someone who had an unusual last name. The other two immediately asked its origin. "Is it German?" "No, Danish," came the answer. They moved on to another acquain-tance. "Isn't his wife Spanish?" one woman asked another. "Oh, she's from a country in South America," another said, "like Co-lombia or Venezuela."

The conversation turned to the third woman and the strawberry-colored hair of some of her relatives. The German-American woman said they looked Irish.

"No," the third woman said. "We're Nordic."

The other two, the Irish-American and the German-American, fell silent. The conversation paused. Somehow everyone in the room realized the power of the word *Nordic* in all of its ambiguous specificity, ambiguous because it's not a country, specific in that it is language inherited from early twentieth-century eugenics, passed down through culture and lore. No one asked which country her family had come from—Sweden? Norway? Finland? Iceland?—or when they had arrived. If one was Nordic, it did not matter.

Nordic was the kind of label that in earlier decades preceded the word *stock,* as with *Alpine* stock or *Iberic* stock, on a now-debunked scale of European "races." Nordics and Anglo-Saxons were the two groups that had always been welcome in America. Nordic was what the drafters of the 1924 immigration law coveted. Nordic had inspired an entire ideology, *Nordicism,* which declared Nordics the most superior of all the Aryans. Nordic was the region of Europe on which the forty-fifth president of the United States seemed fixated nearly a century after the eugenics movement and whose people he wished would immigrate to America instead of Mexicans, Muslims, or Haitians.

The word shut down conversation momentarily. Nordic has long been at the top of the hierarchy. And after all these decades, it still trumped everyone in the room.

CHAPTER TWENTY-ONE

The German Girl
with the Dark, Wavy Hair

There came a time during World War II that most every Jewish resident had vanished from German life. They were abducted or forced underground, and their absence left a vacuum and a paranoia among the Aryans who remained. Without a scapegoat to look down upon, the people had only themselves to regard and to distinguish, one from the other, and they scanned their countrymen for someone else to be better than.

The fixation on purity had put everyone on high alert, and, in the north of the country, in a village near Hanover, someone made a passing remark to a young German girl, raising suspicions about her appearance and, by extension, her lineage, and thus her worth.

The air was dense with nervous surveillance, a hunting hyperawareness of the least sign of difference. People had noticed that the girl's hair was darker than most, closer to that of Iberians to the south of them than to many Germans. Of course, the *Führer* himself had pitch-dark hair, and, for this, dark-haired Germans could console themselves if they happened to have this trait in common with their leader. But his hair was bristle straight, and on this score, too, the German girl near Hanover strayed from Aryan convention.

People thought it curious that this girl from a solid German family looked, to them, as if she could be from the Middle East, that she looked, as best they could tell from their limited knowledge, Persian. It was not clear that villagers had actually known any Persians, but the idea somehow got embedded in their minds. Did the family have any Persian blood or the blood of people from that part of the world in their background? More ominously, and implied if not said outright, any Jewish blood?

People noticed, and took the time to comment, that her hair curved in waves, fell in dark ripples rather than the flaxen silk that flowed straight down the backs of many Aryan girls. Not only that, people noticed that her skin was perceptibly if ever so slightly darker than that of many Germans, leaning golden and olive, one might say, rather than ivory and alabaster like the people around her, even those in her own family, as if a buried trait had somehow surfaced in her.

These are the minute distinctions that can take on greater significance when there are fewer distinctions to make. Under the Nazis, these distinctions carried graver consequences than idle chatter. This was an explosive observation at a time when Reich citizens were under threat to live up to Aryan ideals in order to survive.

The comments, or rather, in that era, accusations, rattled the German teenager. And so she went to a mirror with a measuring tape and measured the width and length of her eyes, her forehead and nose to see if they were within some standard that people spoke of in the era of eugenics and Aryan conformity. She had pictures taken of herself gauging the features of her face to find some reassurance beyond her hair and skin.

The mere mention of perceived deviations from the Aryan standard brought unwanted, potentially dangerous scrutiny. As it was, Germans knew to have a "racial passport" on hand in the event that their Aryan status came into question. Even priests and nuns were arrested after a Jewish ancestor was uncovered.

The family grew concerned enough to make a discreet search into their family tree. Genealogists did brisk business in the Third Reich. Germans combed family Bibles and church records and government offices in case they were called upon to defend their origins. So, before they could be further accused, the family went back three generations to see for themselves if something other than Aryan blood had somehow slipped into their veins, some unwelcome intruder that a forebear might have adored but whose presence was now cause for shame.

The family happened to have found themselves in the clear and maintained their status as good Germans. The girl with the dark, wavy hair survived the war. She married and had children and grandchildren but spoke little of the Reich or the war that had defined her adolescence.

Decades later, a granddaughter would find a photograph of her. It shows a teenage girl holding a measuring tape to her face, a relic of the paranoia of the dominant caste. Even the favored ones were diminished and driven to fear in the shadow of supposed perfection.

CHAPTER TWENTY-TWO

The Stockholm Syndrome and the Survival of the Subordinate Caste

O ver the centuries, people at the margins have had to study those at the center of power, learn their invisible codes and boundaries, commit to memory the protocols and idiosyncrasies, because their survival depends upon knowing them as well as if not better than their own dreams and wishes. From the sidelines, they learn to be watchful of the needs and tempers of the dominant caste. They decode how those in power are getting along with one another or not, who is gaining or losing favor, as women historically have watched their men, or as a child watches for signs of discord in their parents' marriage, intertwined as they are with those who are in charge of the household.

They must develop powers of perception if they are to navigate from below.

"Knowledge without wisdom is adequate for the powerful," wrote the sociologist Patricia Hill Collins, "but wisdom is essential to the survival of the subordinate."

To thrive, they must somehow adjust themselves to the expectations of the dominant caste, to play out their role upon the stage, and, while they may choose not to fully submit, they find that things go easier for them if they default to the script handed down through the ages, if they accept their assignment of serving and entertaining, comforting and consoling, forgiving any trespass without expectation of atonement from their trespassers.

"The first moral duty is resignation and acceptance," wrote the social anthropologist Edmund Leach of the expected behavior of the lowest caste in India. "The individual gains personal merit by fulfilling the tasks which are proper to the station into which he has been born. . . . The rewards for virtue will come in the next life."

The ancient code for the subordinate caste calls upon them to see the world not with their own eyes but as the dominant caste sees it, demands that they extend compassion even when none is forthcoming in exchange, a fusion of dominant and subordinate that brings to mind the Stockholm Syndrome.

Though the syndrome has no universally accepted definition or diagnosis, it is generally seen as a phenomenon of people bonding with those who abuse or hold them hostage. It takes its name from a 1973 bank robbery in Stockholm, Sweden, where the hostages came to feel empathy for the men who held them captive during the six-day siege. It is regarded as a survival mechanism in which people must become attuned to the people with power over them and learn to adjust themselves to their expectations to please them.

———

In the fall of 2019, a Dallas courtroom became a set piece for the display of the interlocking roles and power imbalances of caste. In a rare case in American history, a white former police officer was convicted of killing a black man who had been having ice cream and watching television in his own apartment, an apartment the officer argued she had mistaken for her own. The conviction carried a sentence of up to ninety years. The prosecutor recommended twenty-eight years, the age the victim would have been at the time had the defendant not killed him. In the end, the former officer was sentenced to ten years, with eligibility for parole in five.

The brother of the slain man extended his forgiveness to the dominant-caste woman who had killed his brother, and he hugged her in a scene that went all over the world. As the dominant-caste woman was sobbing over her conviction, the bailiff, a black woman, went over to her and began stroking the blond hair of a woman who had killed an innocent man of the bailiff's own caste. Had the inverse occurred and a black man taken the life of a white woman under similar circumstances, it is inconceivable that the murder sentence would have been ten years or the felon been hugged and his hair stroked, nor would it be remotely expected.

Many observers in the dominant caste were comforted by the bailiff's gesture, which they saw as an act of loving, maternal compassion. Many in the subordinate caste saw it as a demeaning fetishization of a dominant-caste woman who was being extended comfort and leniency that are denied African-Americans, who are treated more harshly in an era of mass incarceration and in society over all. Was the bailiff showing empathy for a fellow officer? Was she patting her down, as some thought, and if so, why did she not wear gloves or have the convict stand, and why stroke only her hair? Was the bailiff channeling the convict's pain, responding to ancient cues to protect the upper caste at all times, thus fulfilling the unspoken role assigned the subordinate caste for generations?

The judge was also a woman from the subordinate caste, and she stepped down from the bench to give the convicted killer a Bible. Then she held the dominant-caste woman close to her bosom and prayed on her and with her. No one could remember ever seeing such a thing, a judge or an officer of the court hugging and consoling a newly convicted felon. The judge's embrace seemed not so far removed from the comfort black maids extended to the disconsolate white children in their care as they wiped away their tears over the centuries.

"It's almost impossible to imagine the same level of compassion," wrote the journalist Ashley Reese, "being extended toward a black person who was just charged with murder."

Around the same time, in fact, a twenty-one-year-old black man in Florida was sentenced to ten days in jail for the crime of arriving late to jury duty. The judge, a man from the dominant caste, showed none of the compassion shown a dominant-caste woman who had killed a man in his own home. The judge excoriated the young juror, threw the full weight of the law at him for a single misstep rather than show mercy.

The judge even took the young man, Deandre Somerville, to task over the composition of the jury, saying that the man was needed at the trial because he was the only black juror. Somerville was, in effect, singled out and held to a different standard from white jurors—he alone was being blamed for inadequacies of a system that happened not to have enough people who looked like him. He had not had a criminal record, and now, on the cusp of life, due to the one-way expectation of empathy from the powerless toward the empowered, he did.

"This expectation feels fueled by a perverse need to see harmed people demonstrate nobility," the poet Hanif Abdurraqib wrote in *Pacific Standard*, "because that's how we can believe the myths that political suffering builds character, and that righteousness rather than power will inevitably triumph."

———

From the moment I saw the pictures, they rattled me. It was November 2014, in the middle of the post-Ferguson protests against police brutality. At a rally in Portland, Oregon, there appeared a melancholy black boy in front of a crowd of protesters, holding a sign in the direction of the officers that said, "Free hugs."

There was something deeply unsettling about that image that I could not figure out at first. For one thing, the boy's face looked more like that of a man's on a child's small frame. His face was contorted in anguish, tears glistening down his cheeks, a wrenching emotion out of sync with the circumstances. He was wearing a fedora that seemed of another century. He did not have the carefree look of a child nor the affectionate cheer of someone offering hugs to strangers.

A white police officer responded to the sign and hugged the boy. The photograph went viral, shown on every television network. It comforted many in the dominant caste to see this gesture of compassion and grace. Here was a black child wanting to hug someone from a group that had been in contention with young black males in the months before this encounter. They were moved by the way the boy hugged the officer long and deep, as if clutching him for dear life.

What was disturbing about that picture could only be seen if one applied the same standards of human behavior to subordinated people as to others. Few black mothers, or mothers in general for that matter, would insist that their sons, and especially their black sons, go over and hug a police officer or any stranger they didn't know. And few children would willingly do so. The boy's face showed far more than discomfort but a despair of someone older than he appeared to be.

The world would not know the tragedy beneath that moment until years later. Two white women in Minnesota had adopted the boy, Devonte Hart, and five other black children from Texas, receiving more than $2,000 a month from the state for doing so. Over the course of ten years, the women essentially held the children captive, keeping them isolated in remote locations, withholding food from them.

They used them as props to attract a social media following with staged videos of the children forced to dance and sing for their captors. Off-camera, the women beat the children with belts and closed fists and held one girl's head under cold water as punishment after the women found a penny in the girl's pocket. When the children sought help and food from neighbors and teachers, the women defaulted to caste stereotypes, told the other adults not to feed them, that the children were playing the "food card," that they were lying, that they were "drug babies," whose birth mothers, they told people, were addicted while pregnant.

Authorities in multiple states inquired into reports of abuse but seemed unable to protect the children. Even after one of the women pleaded guilty in Minnesota in 2010 to misdemeanor assault of one of the daughters, the children remained in their custody. After that, whenever anyone got close enough to intervene, the women pulled the children out of school and moved to a different jurisdiction. They were able to rely on both the patchwork of disconnected social service agencies and their own caste privilege—the presumptions of competency and the benefit of the doubt accorded them—to evade state investigations and to deflect the children's pleas for help.

That day in November 2014, they posted pictures of Devonte hugging the police officer and got adulation from people all over the world. People saw what they wanted to see and not the agony in the face of a twelve-year-old boy who had the body of an eight-year-old due to starvation, his hug, on some level, a bid to be rescued. People saw a picture of black grace when what the world was actually looking at was an abused hostage.

On March 26, 2018, with caseworkers closing in, the two women put the children in their SUV and drove off a cliff in Northern California along the Pacific Coast Highway, killing themselves and the children they had held captive. Blindness to the depth of pain in the boy's face, the latitude granted these white saviors to abuse children seen as throwaways, the collective desire to solve tribal wounds with superficial gestures of grace from the wounded—all of these things contributed to this tragedy and haunt many of us still. We were all witness to a crime that ended in horror.

————

Years before, in 2015, nine black parishioners were massacred in a Charleston church, and the families of the victims almost immediately extended forgiveness to the unrepentant white killer of their loved ones. It was an act of abiding faith that captivated the world but was also in line with society's expectation that the subordinate caste bear its suffering and absolve its transgressors.

Black forgiveness of dominant-caste sin has become a spiritual form of having to be twice as good, in trauma, as in other aspects of life, to be seen as half as worthy.

"White people embrace narratives about forgiveness," wrote the essayist and author Roxane Gay after the massacre, "so they can pretend the world is a fairer place than it actually is and that racism is merely a vestige of a painful past instead of this indelible part of our present."

The act of forgiveness seems a silent clause in a one-sided contract between the subordinate and the dominant. "Black people forgive because we need to survive," Gay wrote. "We have to forgive time and time again while racism or white silence in the face of racism continues to thrive. We have had to forgive slavery, segregation, Jim Crow laws, lynching, inequity in every realm, mass incarceration, voter disenfranchisement, inadequate representation in popular culture, microaggressions and more. We forgive and forgive and forgive and those who trespass against us continue to trespass against us."

In 2018, as every week seemed to bring a new case of dominant-caste people calling the police on black people going about their daily lives, a middle-aged white woman in Brooklyn called the police on a nine-year-old boy who she said had sexually assaulted her as he passed her at the register at a corner deli. The boy said he had not done such a thing, had not touched her, and began to cry. What saved the boy from further action was the store video, which later went viral. It shows the boy passing the woman in the crowded deli and his bag brushing against her, unbeknownst to him as he walked by.

The woman was shamed into apologizing for the false accusation. Afterward, people wanted to know, had he forgiven her? The boy had not learned all the rules of caste yet, had not lived long enough to have read the whole script or have it completely downloaded to his subconscious. He was thinking with the still-free mind of an innocent who had not yet faced the consequences of breaking caste. "I don't forgive the woman," he said, "and she needs help."

The little boy had the X-ray vision of childhood. He had not accepted the inversion of right and wrong, had not been willing to concede a privilege that should not be extracted but granted freely at the discretion of the aggrieved.

"What white people are really asking for when they demand forgiveness from a traumatized community is absolution," Gay wrote. "They want absolution from the racism that infects us all even though forgiveness cannot reconcile America's racist sins."

———

One cannot live in a caste system, breathe its air, without absorbing the message of caste supremacy. The subordinated castes are trained to admire, worship, fear, love, covet, and want to be like those at the center of society, at the top of the hierarchy. In India, it is said that you can try to leave caste, but caste never leaves you. Most immigrants to the United States from India are among the most accomplished and well-to-do from their mother country, and thus few Dalits have the resources to get to America. By some estimates, Dalits are less than 2 percent of people of Indian descent in America. For those who manage to make it across the ocean, caste often migrates with them.

And so a brilliant Dalit from India, a Ph.D. at a prestigious university on the East Coast, paced and shifted his weight from one foot to the other, growing agitated, triggered, in the common parlance of early-twenty-first-century America, at the very mention of the surnames of his upper-caste countrymen. These are names that might have little meaning to most Americans but which signify rank and privilege in India. The names Gupta and Mehta and Mukherjee, common among Indian immigrants in America, are among the most revered in their homeland.

"These names," the Dalit scholar said, shaking his head and looking down toward the carpet. "I can't look them straight in the face. I can't look them in the eye. I don't know what to say. These were our masters. My grandfathers were the workers of their grandfathers. I would never be invited inside their homes. In India, they would not speak to me. Man, I could not imagine talking with them even here in America. They are of a completely different caste from me."

He began pacing again. "The trauma to cross that line," he said.

"I have been here three years. I still do not have the confidence to talk with them."

At the bottom of the hierarchy, the message of inferiority comes at you in whispers and billboards. It burrows into your identity. The violence and terror used to maintain the hierarchy keep you in your place without signage.

"It is a feeling of danger," the Dalit scholar said, just the thought of upper-caste people. "They are a danger to me. I feel danger with them."

Caste is more than rank, it is a state of mind that holds everyone captive, the dominant imprisoned in an illusion of their own entitlement, the subordinate trapped in the purgatory of someone else's definition of who they are and who they should be.

The Dalit Ph.D. was the only one in his entire family who had a passport, the only one to ever step outside of India. The others had no passport and saw no need of a passport. "Where would they go?" he asked. The caste system had deprived them of the need or the use of a basic human trait, one's imagination.

The first to break through from a family in a marginalized caste, he bears the weight of the dreams of everyone back home and the stigma and expectation of failure from the larger society. "If I make a mistake, my community makes a mistake," he said. "If I fall, the community falls. I walk a very thin line."

Back home in India, when the scholar goes into a store, they watch him and hound him like a thief, as with a black person in a store in America. He has absorbed that expectation and adjusted to it to survive. "I never ask about the quality of an item," the scholar said. "I ask the price. If I ask the quality, they will say, 'You can't afford this, why are you wasting my time?' If I say I want to see it, they will say, 'Get out. I will call the police.' So I come back with friends who are not Dalit, who can speak their language and get it for me."

It is for that reason that he stood there in the lobby of a high-end hotel after a dinner near campus and pointed to his shoes, his leather-clad sneakers. He bent down and pressed the empty toe box of his sneakers. "These shoes I bought," he said, "they are not my size. They are too big for me. I bought them because I did not want to trouble the salesman. I did not have the confidence to ask for another size. So I bought what he gave me."

He, like subordinate-caste people wherever there is caste, has had to create an entire protocol to protect himself from insult. "If I go into a store and stay thirty minutes, I have to buy something," he said. "I have so many things that I was afraid to return."

Dalits have suffered brutal assaults for caste infractions, forbidden even today in the rural precincts from walking the same roads as the dominant caste. A family in the Vellore district was forced to carry a deceased loved one along the back roads to reach the funeral pyre. The men had to lower the body, wrapped in cloth and leaves, by a rope from a bridge, the body dangling on descent, as the men below stretched their arms up to receive it. They had been denied access to public roads that they would have been seen as polluting.

They do what they must to avoid further insult.

"For us, it is dignity," he said. "If I go someplace, they might say, you can't afford this, you are wasting my time. So when I go to a restaurant, I don't want to take up the waiter's time. They might attack us, and then they say that we are hostile, when for us it is a matter of dignity. Our dignity is under assault."

He once accompanied two white American women to a store and was astonished at their behavior. "They took up the owner's time and did not buy anything," he said. "I could not imagine doing that."

The fear runs deep within his soul.

I asked him, "Is this fear of anticipated rejection or the actual rejection itself?"

"It is the former caused by the latter," he answered.

"What would help you feel better in these situations?" I asked him.

"What I need is to feel better inside my own skin," he said.

CHAPTER TWENTY-THREE

Shock Troops on the Borders of Hierarchy

A t the dinner hour on a nineteenth-century steamboat in the antebellum South, the caste ritual went as follows: At the first bell, the white passengers were seated with the captain for their meal. After they finished, the second bell rang for the white crewmen—the engineers, the pilot, the servants. Only after all of the white people on board, of every class and status, completed their meals would the third bell ring, and the black crewmen, slave or free, be permitted to eat.

A problem arose, however, if there happened to be free black passengers in their midst. Free blacks paid their fare and were on paper in the same category as the white passengers. They were likely middle-class, but what mattered was that they were lowest caste. And historically, caste trumps class.

It was taboo for blacks and whites to sit, stand, or eat in the same space at the same time or even to use the same utensils. So they were not going to eat with their white counterparts or with the white crewmen who were presumably lower in class than they.

But there was more to it than that. Free blacks were an affront to the caste system, always brushing against its borders. By their very existence, moving about as equals to the dominant caste, having the means to enter spaces considered the preserve of their betters, and having had the ingenuity to gain their freedom and to walk around in it, they threw the entire caste belief system into question. If people in the lowest caste had the capacity to be equal, why were they being enslaved? If they were smart enough to do something other than pick cotton or scrub floors, why then were they picking cotton and scrubbing floors? It was too mind-twisting to contemplate.

After the dinner service was cleared away and everyone else aboard had eaten and retired to their cabins or posts, the small group of black passengers, all women in this case, were permitted to eat in the pantry, "standing at the butler's table."

From the start of the caste system in America, people who were lowest caste but who had managed somehow to rise above their station have been the shock troops on the front lines of hierarchy. People who appear in places or positions where they are not expected can become foot soldiers in an ongoing quest for respect and legitimacy in a fight they had hoped was long over.

———

Public conveyances and recreational spaces have been the sound-stage for caste confrontation precisely because they bring together in a confined space, for a limited time and purpose, groups that have historically been kept apart. They become test tubes of caste interaction, with its written and unwritten codes, its unspoken but understood rules of engagement.

In 2015, the members of a black women's book club were traveling by train on a wine tour of Napa Valley. They were laughing and chatting as were other tourists, given the nature of the outing and what all the passengers had been imbibing. But they alone seemed to attract the notice of the maître d'. "When you laugh," the maître d' told them, "I see it on the [other] passengers' faces." Soon the train stopped, and the black women, some of them senior citizens, were ejected and met by police, "as if we were criminals," they later said.

In 2018, the owner of a Pennsylvania golf club ordered black women club members to leave and called the police on them after white golfers complained that they were not moving fast enough. The women described themselves as experienced players aware of the game's protocols and said they had paced themselves according to the groups behind and in front of them. They said they noted that the men behind them were on break and were not ready to tee up. After arriving on the scene, the police determined that no charges were warranted. But the women said the confrontation had put them on edge, and they left to avoid further humiliation.

My work has required me to spend many, many hours in settings where I am often the only person of my ethnicity and gender, most often on planes. A flight attendant once commented on the miles I log year in and year out, "You fly more than we do." Because I fly so often, I frequently have cause to be seated in first or business class, which can turn me into a living, breathing social experiment without wanting to be. The things that have happened to me are far from the most grievous a person might suffer when traveling in a domain that can bring out the worst in most anyone. But some have stood out as a commentary on caste in action and can be demoralizing in the unexpected moment of intrusion.

For a flight out of Denver, I happened to be one of the first to board the plane, along with others in the front cabin. I could see the lead flight attendant greeting passengers at the boarding door. He was a man in his late twenties or early thirties, short blondish hair, and behind him was a second flight attendant, her brunette hair in a French twist.

The tendinitis in my wrist had been flaring up, and, as I stepped onto the plane with a splint on my forearm, I looked over to the lead flight attendant for help with my carry-on.

"Sir," I said, "I'm having a problem with my wrist, and I wondered if you would help me get my bag in the bin."

He looked past me to the men behind me at the boarding door, the kind of men who would come to mind when you think of first class. He waved me along as if I were holding up the line, though no one was moving at the moment. He seemed insulted even to have been asked, as if I was not aware of how the boarding process worked.

"There are two flight attendants in the back," he said. "They can help you when you get back there."

With those curt instructions, it was as if he had pulled me out of a lineup, singled me out from the other business travelers as the one who, on sight, did not belong, the one trespassing and now seeking special treatment to which I was not entitled. Marginalized people have a hard enough time moving about in a world built for others. Now it was as if I were taking up space that belonged to its rightful passengers. It came as a shock to me, perhaps because this clipped dismissal came from a man whose generation would not be expected to hold such retrograde assumptions. Somehow the air had turned confrontational. I had asked for something he did not believe I deserved.

"But I'm in first," I said.

That seemed only to make things worse. He had been caught in his moment of stereotyping and in front of others. He had disregarded all information inputs to the contrary, that I was boarding early, that luggage tags dangling from the bag I was seeking help with proclaimed that I had reached the highest possible level of loyalty to his airline. He could only have come to the conclusion he made on the basis of one thing alone: what I looked like.

He tried to recover from the faux pas of an openly dismissive caste assumption, for what is caste if not where one belongs in a hierarchy? He had to find a way to retain his own caste position, now that a flight attendant under him in the airline's hierarchy had heard him speak so brusquely to a passenger, wherever she happened to be seated.

"Well, leave it here, and we'll have to see what to do with it," he said, sighing as if it were a bass violin instead of a rolling bag.

The woman flight attendant who stood there during the exchange stepped forward and tried to set things right, cover for him, her superior.

"Here," she said, "let me help you with it. What seat are you in?"

She walked me to the seat and helped me hoist the bag into the bin. I thanked her for her kindness.

It was uncomfortable the rest of the flight. He was the only attendant in that cabin, and each time he passed through the aisle, the tension rose. I could feel the edge of it. He had been outed, and he punished me with a curt hostility until we landed.

———

It was a late-night flight from Portland, Oregon, to the East Coast. I had just boarded, and the flight attendant and I were looking for space to fit my roller bag into the haphazardly filled overhead compartments. Every time the flight attendant and I touched a bag to turn it on its side or to move it to the next bin, someone said, "No, you can't touch that one, that's my bag."

The man in the aisle seat behind me had two carry-ons overhead, taking up more space than allowed. I was anxious to get seated and out of this uncomfortable testing of wills. I offered to let him put his bag under my seat so that it would not take up space in front of him, anything to get the bag stored and get on our way.

"I'd be glad to do it," I told him and the flight attendant.

He let out a heavy breath.

"I put my bag where I wanted it. I don't want it under another seat."

He took the bag from the flight attendant and shoved it under his own seat. He then began complaining to the man in the window seat beside him, a man, like him, from the dominant caste, seated directly behind me.

"That's what happens when they let just anybody in first class," the owner of the bag said to the man next to him, loud enough for anyone around us to hear. "They should know better how to treat paying customers. I paid for my first-class ticket, and this is how they treat you."

The two men commiserated the whole flight, having found common cause and united by a shared resentment. It was a night flight, and I was exhausted from a long day of lectures. I needed to sleep. I let down the seat back. What did I do that for?

The man in the window seat behind me, who had been grousing about the unfairness of it all with the man whose bag had been moved, let out a howl.

"What do you think you're doing!" he yelled. "I'm trying to work here! Look what you've done. I've got my laptop out and you've shoved it into me!"

He slammed the back of my seat and pounded the tray forward, jostling me as he continued to hit from behind.

"I had no control over the seatback," I told him, looking back. "I'm just trying to get some rest." I looked over at the white man next to me, who had seen all of this, who would have felt the shudder of my seat being pushed from behind. He would not return a glance, isolating me further.

The men behind me continued to talk about the intrusions into first class. The air was thick with venom and made it impossible to sleep. I got up to tell the flight attendant to see if she might be able to help.

"I am desperately tired, and I need to sleep," I told her. "The man behind me is shoving my seat and making it impossible to get rest. Is there anything you could do? Could you explain the rules to him to defuse the situation?"

"Frankly, I don't know if it would help," she said. "Why don't you stay up here the rest of the flight?"

"I need to rest," I told her. "I can't sleep standing up here, and besides, I have a seat, and I should be able to sit in it."

"I know," she said. "I don't know what to tell you. It's up to you if you want to stay up here or go back."

I went back and sat up straight, across the length of the country. The caste system had put me in my place.

———

I had been up since before five in the morning for the flight out of Idaho Falls. The original flight was canceled, the second one delayed, and now, finally, I was on the last leg of the journey, the connecting flight out of Salt Lake City that would not get me in until ten-thirty P.M. I was in seat 2D, a window in first, the only passenger in that cabin who was African-American.

The lead attendant was a black man, small in frame, cheerful, and efficient.

"What are you having, my friend?" he asked the male passengers as he chatted them up.

"And you?" he said, terse and impatient, when he got to me.

Upon landing, the mad shuffle began for everyone's respective bag in the overhead compartments. Passengers crowded into the aisle, and I was standing behind a man who looked to be in his thirties, his light hair in a buzz cut. He asked a woman next to him if she needed help with her bag. He pulled it down for her, and she thanked him.

Then he began to reach for his own bag. It was in the compartment above and behind me. He did not speak nor gesture in my direction. Instead, he reached back and up and over me, wordlessly leaned farther and farther, his body at a backward angle against mine, pinning me under his torso and leaving me no escape because of the wall of passengers packed behind me.

I was in disbelief, forced to arch my body back, as he rammed himself harder against me, heavy and sweaty, shifting his feet now, shoving his thick arm across my face and against the side of my neck to unloosen the bag from the compartment. He thrust his full weight, his entire frame, into mine, his back muscles crushing my breasts, his buttocks protruding into my pelvis, violating my body in full view of other passengers, and no one was saying or doing a thing.

"Hey, I can't go back any further!" I told him in a plea for help, loud enough for everyone around me to hear.

He said nothing, as if I were not there, as if nobody were there, as if the laws of physics or privacy did not apply. I tried to hold my head away from his shoulder blades so that I could breathe. It was taking the ground crew forever to open the boarding door. I looked around for whoever would recognize the horror of a complete stranger forcing himself onto you. I looked over to the two young women who were inches away and who could see what he was doing. I gave them a look of distress and shock at the man's aggression. I was needing empathy. They were standing so close, they could share a sense of womanly outrage at what was happening. But their faces were blank. They looked into space, returned no glance.

A silence of complicity had overtaken the entire first-class cabin, and I was alone in a packed compartment. Not one of these passengers would have lost their job or a promotion, lost money or privilege, had they stood up that day. Very likely they would never see these other passengers again in their lives, and stepping up would have had no material consequences. But that day, with so very little at stake to themselves, they chose caste solidarity over principle, tribe over empathy.

The boarding door finally opened. The passengers filed out. And the man finally eased his behind off of me. The black flight attendant, who had seen all of it, had not come to my aid nor spoken up, though he was the flight attendant in charge.

As I approached the door, he looked up at me, sheepish and shamefaced.

"I'm really sorry," he said.

"Thanks, I know," I said, shaking my head.

He hadn't intervened. He, too, seemed powerless. He couldn't likely have taken the risk. This was an upper-caste man assaulting a lower-caste woman, and the lead attendant was lower caste himself. The lead attendant very likely had no idea what the man's position might be, what power and influence he might have had. Why should he stick his neck out for me and get on the bad side of heaven knows who? The man had bullied me, out in the open, with witnesses all around who pretended not to see. The lead attendant likely felt it would do him no good to get involved. In a caste system, things work more smoothly when everyone stays in their place, and that is what he did.

I was shaking and livid. Once off the plane and out in the terminal, the man who had forced me into a vertical spoon with him, in front of an audience, was walking with a brisk swagger several paces ahead of me. He knew full well what he had done. Cocking his head back at me, he spat out a curt "Sorry," and kept walking with the entitlement that comes from knowing he could get away with it. There would be no consequences; not one person had stepped to my defense or shown a blink of compassion.

A host of factors might have made things different. Perhaps it was the lateness of the hour that inured some people. Maybe it was just the singular combination of personalities that left me without anyone to stand up to it. Change one or two seats with different people, and there might have been a different outcome.

One thing seems certain: had an African-American man pressed his body against a white woman the way this man had, it is hard to imagine that no one on board would have intervened, if only to say to him, "I'll get your bag for you so you can get off of her." Over the course of American history, black men have died for doing far less to white women than what he did to me that night.

You might say, *Why didn't you complain to the airline? Why didn't you tell him off?* Those questions belie the situation. This was not the fault of the airline. As for the man who did this, he ignored my protests of his behavior. This happened because good people were silent and let it happen. I was too disgusted to reply as the man swaggered ahead of me. I made my way to the other side of the passenger walkway and continued until he was out of my sight.

———

Incursions such as these are more than personal insults and unfortunate misunderstandings. Fighting convention, fighting to be seen and treated for who you truly are, diminishes the human contract, demeans everyone, and worsens the well-being of people on all sides of these caste skirmishes. The most brazen cases lead to violence, a hallmark of a caste system at the breaking point. In 2013, on a flight into Atlanta, a white passenger actually slapped a black baby in the face because the baby was crying due to the change in altitude upon descent. Such an assault would be virtually inconceivable had a baby from the dominant caste been crying, no matter his decibel level.

In 2017, a Vietnamese-American passenger was dragged off a United Airlines plane in Chicago, suffering injuries to his head and knocking out some of his teeth. The airline had discovered that it had overbooked the flight, and no passenger took the airline up on offers of compensation in exchange for giving up their seats. The airline chose four passengers, at random by computer, to be ejected.

The first three passengers left the plane without incident, but the Vietnamese-American man, a physician named David Dao, said he had an urgent need to get back to his patients. He said he had paid his fare and should not have to give up his seat. The airline called security to remove him, and he was dragged by his legs in front of stunned passengers. Captured on a video that quickly went viral, the incident drew outrage across the country and in Asia.

Dao said he was convinced that his ethnicity was a factor in his treatment, that this would not have happened to a white man of his or most any other stature. The ordeal, he said, was more horrifying than when he fled Vietnam. Even three years later, watching the video of his violent removal again, he told ABC News, "I just cried."

CHAPTER TWENTY-FOUR

Cortisol, Telomeres, and the
Lethality of Caste

A young man emigrated from Nigeria at the age of seventeen to attend college in the United States. His father paid the tuition, and at the end of the first semester, the young man went to pick up the refund at the bursar's office.

"You speak very good English," the clerk told him.

The Nigerian man excoriated the clerk.

"Of course I speak good English," he said. "I speak English better than many Americans. I speak other languages as well. Don't ever say that again."

He discovered that in America he was not seen for his skills or his education. He was seen as black before anything else. It was an identity he was unaccustomed to, that had no meaning back home where everyone had similar coloring. Now it seemed to mean everything. The African-Americans were always talking about being profiled and mistreated, and he hadn't paid it much attention at first. But the longer he was in the United States, the more he shed his accent, as immigrants often do, and the more Americanized he became, the more he began to experience life not as an immigrant, not solely as a Nigerian, but as a black man in a hierarchy that disfavored people who looked like him.

Women clenched their purses as he approached, shrank from him on the elevator, crossed the street to avoid passing near him. He was followed in stores as if he were a felon, and the authorities questioned him more intensely than he was accustomed to, more intensely than the white men, he noticed. A white driver locked her door when he merely drove up in traffic one day. He went and locked his door, too, to show that he was as concerned for his safety as she was.

He found himself passed over for promotions as a compliance officer, and despite his seniority and experience, he was laid off, and he wondered, as many people assigned to the subordinate caste cannot help but consider, if race had anything to do with it. Before coming to America, he would have thought it preposterous. *Maybe the African-Americans were not working hard enough, were not educated enough.* Now, having lived longer in the United States than in Nigeria, he knew better than to dismiss what they said out of hand.

Once when he pulled into a parking space, an older white woman, whose car he had parked next to, turned and stared, then recoiled backward in her driver's seat. "I see her," he told the passenger in the car with him. "I don't give a shit."

Except, actually, he did, or rather his physiology did. Modern medicine has long sought to attribute the higher rates of disease in African-Americans relative to white Americans to genetics. But it turns out that sub-Saharan Africans do not have high rates of high blood pressure, diabetes, and heart disease, while African-Americans have the highest rates of those conditions of all ethnic groups in the United States.

The Nigerian man now in America was living this, too. "My father lived to ninety years old," the man said. "He had no high blood pressure until the last day of his life.

"I just went to the doctor, and he tells me I have high blood pressure and early signs of diabetes," he said. "And I am just fifty-four. The effects of spending my entire adult life as a black man in this country are making me sick forty years ahead of my own father back in Nigeria."

———

The friction of caste is killing people. Societal inequity is killing people. The act of moving about and navigating spaces with those whom society has trained us to believe are inherently different from us is killing people, and not just the targets. Studies are showing that prejudice itself can be deadly.

Neuroscientists have found that harboring this kind of animus can raise a person's blood pressure and cortisol levels, "even during benign social interactions with people of different races," wrote the neuropsychologist Elizabeth Page-Gould. Prejudice itself can be deadly. These physical reactions can put the person at greater risk for stroke or diabetes or heart attacks and premature death.

A study of white Americans who scored high on a measure of automatic prejudice, meaning the degree to which they associate certain ethnic groups with negative stereotypes at the level of the unconscious, found that when they were put into situations where they were, for example, to be interviewed for a job by an African-American or to have social interaction with Latinos, they perceived the people of a different ethnicity as a threat, even in a safe laboratory setting.

The threat they perceived as a result of their prejudice set off their body's alarm system. Their panic produced automatic physiological responses as would occur if they were in combat or confronting an oncoming car—restricted blood flow to the heart, the flooding of the muscles with glucose as the body releases cortisol, the hormone useful in the rare moment when one might need to escape danger, but damaging to the body on a regular basis. The combination of reduced blood flow, constrictions to the circulatory and digestive systems, and the breakdown of muscle by cortisol can lead to life-threatening damage to the heart and the immune system and to death before one's time.

Even the briefest exposure is all it takes to activate the body's response. Among whites, the sight of a black person, even in faded yearbook photographs, can trigger the amygdala of the brain to perceive threat and arm itself for vigilance within 30 milliseconds of exposure, the blink of an eye, researchers have found. When whites have a bit more time for the conscious mind to override the automatic feeling of threat, the amygdala activity switches to inhibition mode. When whites are prompted to think of the black person as an individual, imagine their personal characteristics, the threat level falls.

This shows that it is "possible to override our worst impulses and reduce these prejudices," wrote the psychologist Susan Fiske. But to do so in a meaningful way requires forethought, an awareness of the unconscious biases passed down through the generations, and the chance for people different from one another to work together as equals, on the same team, with shared goals that "require cooperation to succeed," Fiske said. Outside of sports and the military, American society provides few such opportunities.

This leaves many Americans at risk without knowing it. As they go about their days interacting with co-workers, neighbors, contractors, or other ordinary people perceived as unlike themselves, they can be in danger of worsened health and premature illness due to the threat signals triggered by the person's own unaddressed prejudice.

———

On the other side of the caste system, scientists have connected a key indicator of health and longevity—the length of human telomeres—to one's exposure to inequality and discrimination, primarily focusing on the telomere lengths of African-Americans.

A telomere is a repeating sequence of double-stranded DNA at the end of a chromosome. The more frequently a cell divides, the shorter the telomeres become, wearing out the cell in a process that public health scientist Arline Geronimus, in her pioneering 1992 work, termed *weathering*. It is a measure of premature aging of the cells, and thus of the person bearing those cells, and of the early onset of disease due to chronic exposure to such stressors as discrimination, job loss, or obesity.

These studies initially focused on the accelerated aging of the telomeres of African-Americans. But expanded research is finding that this kind of cell damage results from one's exposure to social inequity and difficult life conditions, rather than merely one's race and ethnicity. Thus, the telomeres of poor whites, for example, are shorter than those of wealthier whites, whose resources might better help them weather life's challenges.

The opposite is true for people in the lower castes in America. Socioeconomic status and the presumed privilege that comes with it do not protect the health of well-to-do African-Americans. In fact, many suffer a health penalty for their ambitions. "Middle class African American men and women are *more* likely to suffer from hypertension and stress than those with lower incomes," wrote the sociologist George Lipsitz. The stigma and stereotypes they labor under expose them to higher levels of stress-inducing discrimination in spite of, or perhaps because of, their perceived educational or material advantages.

The pattern applies to another marginalized group, Mexicans in America. It turns out that poorer Mexican immigrants have longer telomeres, meaning healthier, younger cells, than better-off Mexican-Americans. Poorer Mexicans are likely to be newer to this country and to cluster together in closer support networks. Their isolation from the mainstream and the language barrier could inadvertently insulate them from the discrimination that more affluent Mexicans may face as they navigate the caste system on a daily basis. Those who were born in the United States or have lived in the country for many years would have greater exposure to the damaging effects of stereotyping and stigma.

All of these groups appear to be paying a price when they step outside of the roles assigned them in the hierarchy. "High levels of everyday discrimination contribute to narrowing the arteries over time," said the Harvard social scientist David R. Williams. "High levels of discrimination lead to higher levels of inflammation, a marker of heart disease."

People who face discrimination, Williams said, often build up a layer of unhealthy fat, known as visceral fat, surrounding vital organs, as opposed to subcutaneous fat, just under the skin. It is this visceral fat that raises the risk of diabetes and cardiovascular disease and leads to premature death. And it can be found in people of all ethnicities based on their experience of discrimination.

"Black women experience higher levels of discrimination than white women do," Williams said. "But when white women experience discrimination, the effects are the same. So discrimination leading to higher levels of visceral fat, that is true for African-American women and for white women. When whites report higher levels of discrimination, their health is also hurt. It really says something about the nature of human interaction."

When it comes to life expectancy, middle-aged and less educated white Americans are experiencing a downward trend, as we have seen. But people of color at the bottom of the caste system, who bear the brunt of societal stigma, still have an overall lower life expectancy than their white counterparts at every level of education, according to Williams.

The average white American at age twenty-five is likely to live five years longer than the average African-American. While white high school dropouts have a lower life expectancy than their more educated white counterparts, they live three years longer than African-American high school dropouts. And white college graduates live four years longer than African-American college graduates.

Thus, people of color with the most education, who compete in fields where they are not expected to be, continually press against the boundaries of caste and experience a lower life expectancy as a result. The more ambitious the marginalized person, the greater the risk of what evolutionary biologist Joseph L. Graves calls "the out-of-place principle of social dominance." Graves found that hypertension rates of blacks and whites are roughly the same when affluent African-Americans are deleted from the equation. The caste system takes years off the lives of subordinate-caste people the more they find themselves in contention with it.

"There is a black tax that we pay that hurts our health, and the gap is larger among the college-educated than it is among high school dropouts," Williams said. "We still carry that burden, to engage in a heightened vigilance, which means you're careful of how you look, how you appear, how you dress."

Williams had a friend, a middle-class black businessman, who would never leave the house in the sweats and sneakers that his white neighbors wore without a moment's thought. He couldn't afford to. He took great care whenever he left the house, and it took more time and more forethought for even the most casual errand.

"If his wife needed a gallon of milk and he needed to run to the supermarket to get that gallon of milk, he would run into the house to get a jacket and tie," Williams said. "It was his way of trying to minimize the likelihood that he's going to be perceived as criminal because he's a young black male. That is what we live with, and it is taking a toll on our lives."

It seems that people in the dominant caste know in their bones that the playing field tilts toward the group they happened to have been born to. Years ago, back in the 1990s, the political scientist Andrew Hacker posed a theoretical question to his white undergraduates at Queens College in New York. He asked them how much they would have to be paid to live the next fifty years as a black person. The students thought it over and came back with a figure. Most said they would need $50 million—$1 million for every year that they would have to be black. They felt they would need it, he said, to "buy protection from the discriminations and dangers white people know they would face once they were perceived to be black."

Part Six

BACKLASH

CHAPTER TWENTY-FIVE

A Change in the Script

The greatest departure from the script of the American caste system was the election of an African-American to the highest office in the land. History has shown that there would be consequences to this disruption of the social order, and there were. What follows is not an analysis of the presidency of Barack Obama, but rather a look into the caste system's response to his ascension and the challenges it would place in his path.

First, to break more than two centuries of tradition and birthright, it would take the human equivalent of a supernova—a Harvard-trained lawyer, a U.S. senator from the land of Lincoln, whose expertise was the Constitution itself, whose charisma and oratory matched or exceeded that of most any man who had ever risen to the Oval Office, whose unusual upbringing inclined him toward conciliation of the racial divide, who famously saw the country as not blue states or red states but as the United States, whose wife, if it could be imagined, was also a Harvard-trained lawyer with as much star power as her husband, who, together with their two young daughters, made for a telegenic American dream family, and who, beyond all this, ran a scrupulous, near-flawless campaign, a movement really. It would take an idealist, who believed what most Americans would have sworn was impossible, for a black man to make it to the White House.

Secondly, his opponent, a beloved and aging war hero from Arizona, a wise and measured moderate Republican in a party that had grown more conservative, ran a less-than-energetic campaign and made several misjudgments, the most significant of which was choosing an unpredictable former governor of Alaska, a woman prone to gaffes and to quirky, word-salad misstatements, as his running mate.

Then, in the months leading up the election, a once-in-a-generation financial catastrophe descended on a country that seemed on the brink of financial ruin under the Republican administration then in power. Wall Street firms collapsed before our eyes, and the value of American homes, the primary source of many citizens' wealth, plunged in value, leaving millions of voters underwater.

In October 2008, a few weeks before the election, envelopes arrived in the mailboxes of millions of American households, mailings that became inadvertent leaflets in favor of the Democrat: the quarterly 401(k) statements that showed losses of as much as 40 percent of people's savings in the last year under the Republican president. By that November, some 12 million homeowners owed more on their mortgages than their houses were worth in what was now being called the Great Recession, among the worst economic downturns since the Great Depression.

People in the dominant caste who might have been on the fence about taking a chance on an African-American candidate were looking at massive losses with no end in sight. *Hope* had been Obama's mantra during times that badly needed it. A record tide of people from the lower and middle castes, people who swelled with pride and whose votes now felt like a mission, came out for him, and, along with just enough dominant-caste voters who believed in him, too, swept Obama into the White House. The world was so joyous that a committee in Norway awarded him the Nobel Peace Prize within months of his inauguration. "Only very rarely has a person to the same extent as Obama captured the world's attention," the Nobel committee said, "and given its people hope for a better future."

———

Over the course of American history, the idea of a black man in the Oval Office was virtually unthinkable. But from a caste perspective, and beyond his own personal gifts, his singular origin story was one that the caste system would be more willing to accept, if any. His growing up in Hawaii, the son of an immigrant from Kenya and of a white woman from Kansas, was free from the heaviness of slavery and Jim Crow and the hard histories of regular African-Americans. His story did not trigger the immediate discomfort in the dominant caste, unlike those of everyday black people, who, if you scratch their family trees long enough, you run into a sharecropper cheated at settlement or an ancestor shut out of a neighborhood because of redlining, people for whom these injustices were not history, but their own or their foreparents' actual *lives*.

Rather, his origin story freed people in the dominant caste from having to think about the unsavory corners of American history. They could regard him with curiosity and wonderment and even claim him as part of themselves, if they chose. They could perhaps feel a connection to his mother and to his mother's mother, who tragically died just before Election Day. Both women were from the dominant caste and would not get to see how very far he would go in this world. The Delaware senator who would become his running mate, though, seemed to be speaking, however awkwardly, for some others in the ruling majority. "You've got the first sort of mainstream African-American who is articulate and bright and clean and a nice-looking guy," said Joe Biden. "I mean, that's a storybook, man."

After the election, white Americans in both parties extolled the progress the country had made in the past generation, relieved to be able to say that racism was a thing of the past. "We have a black president, for heaven's sakes," they would say, by way of example. The fact is, though, this was a development that the majority of the dominant caste was not truly in a position to claim. The majority of white voters did not support him in either of his presidential bids. He had star power and a way with babies and pensioners, but no matter how refined and inspirational, well-spoken and conciliatory he was, Obama's victory did not occur because most voters in the dominant caste had become more open-minded and enamored of him. As with other recent Democrats running for president, he won despite the bulk of the white electorate.

Even as they proclaimed a new post-racial world, the majority of white Americans did not vote for the country's first black president. An estimated 43 percent went for him in 2008. Thus, a solid majority of white Americans— nearly three out of every five white voters—did not back him in his first election, and fewer still—39 percent—voted for him in 2012. In the former Confederate state of Mississippi, only one in ten white voters pulled the lever for Obama. For much of his presidency, he was trying to win over people who did not want him in the Oval Office and some who resented his very existence.

As a measure of the enduring role of caste interests in American politics, the shadow of the Civil War seemed to hang over the 2008 election. It turned out that Obama carried every state that Abraham Lincoln had won in 1860, an election with an almost entirely white electorate but one that became a proxy for egalitarian sentiment and for the future of slavery and of the Republic. "The cultural divides of the Civil War on racial grounds," wrote the political scientist Patrick Fisher of Seton Hall University, "can thus still be considered to be influencing American political culture a century and a half later."

Lyndon B. Johnson, after signing the 1964 Civil Rights Act, is said to have predicted that the Democrats would lose the South for a generation for having stood up for the citizenship rights of African-Americans. That prophecy would prove to be correct but also an understatement. The Democrats would lose more than just the South and for well longer than a generation. From that moment forward, white Americans overall moved rightward toward the Republicans as the country enacted more egalitarian policies.

In the more than half century since that prophecy of 1964, no Democrat running for president has ever won a majority of the white vote. Lyndon Johnson was the last Democrat to win the presidency with a majority of the white electorate. Since that time, the Democrat who came closest, who attracted the largest percentage of white voters—at 48 percent—was fellow southerner Jimmy Carter in 1976. Only three Democrats have made it to the Oval Office since the Johnson and the civil rights era—Carter, Obama, and Bill Clinton, who won with 39 percent of the white vote in 1992 and 44 percent in 1996.

With whites pulling away from the Democrats and accustomed to prevailing in presidential elections through their sheer numbers, the outcome of the 2008 election was seen not merely as the defeat of John McCain, but perhaps a defeat of the historic ruling majority itself, "a challenge to the absoluteness of whites' dominance," wrote the political scientist Ashley Jardina of Duke University, who specializes in the behavior of the white electorate.

Combined with census projections of an end of the white majority by 2042, Obama's victory signaled that the dominant caste could undergo a not altogether certain but still unthinkable wane in power over the destiny of the United States and over the future of themselves and their children, and their sovereign place in the world. "The symbolism of Obama's election was a profound loss to whites' status," Jardina wrote.

This was something that no one in the dominant caste, or any other group in the country, for that matter, had ever had to contemplate. It meant that people who had always been first now had to consider the potential loss of their centrality. For many, "the ability of a black person to supplant the racial caste system," wrote the political scientist Andra Gillespie of Emory University, was "the manifestation of a nightmare which would need to be resisted."

That sense of fear and loss, however remote, "brought to the fore, for many whites," Jardina wrote, "a sense of commonality, attachment, and solidarity with their racial group," a sense of needing to band together to protect their place in the hierarchy.

The caste system sprang into action against this threat to the preexisting order. "The single most important thing we want to achieve," said Senate Majority Leader Mitch McConnell, Republican of Kentucky, on the eve of the midterm elections in 2010, "is for President Obama to be a one-term president."

———

The opposition party would not succeed in denying him a second term but would obstruct virtually every proposal he made and force him to resort to executive orders to accomplish his aims. Within nine months of his inauguration, the president was addressing a joint session of Congress on his healthcare plan when a heckler interrupted an ordinarily staid affair of pomp and ritual by yelling, "You lie!" The outburst came from a Republican congressman from South Carolina, Joe Wilson. It was considered so out of order that the House of Representatives passed a resolution of disapproval against Wilson, and Sen. John McCain, the Republican who lost to Obama in 2008, declared that there was "no place for it in that setting or any other."

In early 2012, Air Force One landed just outside Phoenix for a presidential visit to a manufacturing plant in Arizona, a routine stop at the start of an election year in which the president would be seeking a second term. There on the tarmac to greet the president was Jan Brewer, the state's Republican governor. The encounter quickly turned tense for such a moment of formality. As the wind rustled the tarmac, the governor, blond and slight of build, handed the president an envelope, and soon she was looking stern and agitated at him. She jabbed her finger at the leader of the free world, inches from his nose, her mouth in mid-yell, like a principal scolding a child facing detention. In the photograph of their encounter, the president appears calm and stoic, if slightly bemused, which had been his usual demeanor, as she sticks her finger in his face, as if to be saying, *"And another thing . . ."* In some countries, and with previous presidents, this might be seen as an act of aggression, a threat to a nation's head of state, a display of profound disrespect, were it to happen at all.

The photograph would become one of the defining images of the opposition and resentment President Obama faced in office. The difference in the accomplishments of these two people would not have been apparent from the optics of who was chastising whom. While the president was a graduate of Columbia and of Harvard Law School and had made a methodical march from state senator to U.S. senator to the Oval Office, the woman with the temerity to point her finger in his face had a two-year certificate as a radiology technician, and had risen to the governor's mansion by accident of succession, after having been secretary of state. She was now a governor, one out of fifty, compared to the U.S. president, the highest office in the land and the most powerful in the world.

But Gov. Brewer was from the dominant caste, her birth-ascribed status seen as inherently above his, and she did not shrink from a gesture that had the look of putting a man from the subordinate caste in his place, no matter his station. The disagreement on the tarmac had presumably arisen over a passage in a book she had written, in which she described a meeting the two of them had had some time before, a depiction that he considered inaccurate. In it, she had complained that he "thought he could lecture me, and I would learn at his knee." The envelope she handed him was an invitation to see the Arizona border with Mexico, given that they had differing views on border security.

Afterward, Governor Brewer denied what everyone could see. "I was not hostile," she told reporters. "I was trying to be very, very gracious." She went as far as to say that it was, in fact, she who felt unsafe. "I felt a little bit threatened, if you will, in the attitude that he had," she said, even though the exchange had been in full view of cameras and Secret Service and elected officials, and despite the fact that it was she, after all, who was wagging her finger in his face, not the other way around.

The encounter put the governor in the spotlight for the moment, and she used it to raise money for her political action committee, according to news reports at the time, and to fire up her base. She told potential donors that the message she was really giving the president that day was: "You have ONE more year."

———

An entire machinery had moved into place upon the arrival of the first head of state from the subordinate caste. A new party of right-wing detractors arose in his wake, the Tea Party, vowing to "take our country back." A separate movement of skeptics, who would come to be known as birthers, challenged the legitimacy of his citizenship and required him to produce an original birth certificate that they still chose to disbelieve. His opponents called him the "food stamp" president and depicted the president and the First Lady as simians. At opposition rallies, people brandished guns and bore signs calling for "Death to Obama."

In response to his election, Republicans began changing election laws, making it harder to vote. They did so even more vigorously after the Supreme Court overturned a section of the Voting Rights Act, removing federal election oversight that the states, each with a history of obstructing the minority vote, said was no longer needed.

Between 2014 and 2016, states deleted almost 16 million people from voter registration lists, purges that accelerated in the last years of the Obama administration, according to the Brennan Center for Justice. States enacted new voter ID laws even as they created more barriers to obtaining this newly required ID. Together, these actions had the cumulative effect of reducing voter participation of marginalized people and immigrants, both of whom were seen as more likely to vote Democrat. "A paper found that states were far more likely to enact restrictive voting laws," wrote the commentator Jonathan Chait, "if minority turnout in their state had recently increased."

Contrary to the wistful predictions of post-racial harmony, the number of hate groups in the United States surged from 602 to more than 1,000 between 2000 and 2010, the middle of Obama's first term in office, according to the Southern Poverty Law Center. A 2012 study found that anti-black attitudes and racial stereotyping rose, rather than fell, as some might have hoped, in Obama's first term. The percentage of Americans who expressed explicit anti-black attitudes ticked upward from 48 percent in 2008 to 51 percent in 2012, but the percentage expressing implicit bias rose from 49 percent to 56 percent. The study found that higher percentages of white respondents now saw African-Americans as violent, irresponsible, and, most especially, lazy, after his victory, despite, or perhaps because of, the studiously wholesome black family in the White House headed by two Ivy League–educated parents.

With rising resentments, it would not be surprising that attacks on African-Americans might not only not have abated but would worsen under the unprecedented reversal of the social hierarchy. By the second term of the administration, in 2015, police were killing unarmed African-Americans at five times the rate of white Americans. It was a trend that would make police killings a leading cause of death for young African-American men and boys, these deaths occurring at a rate of 1 in 1,000 young black men and boys.

Early on, Obama had taken symbolic steps to bridge the racial divide. He held a "beer summit" with Henry Louis Gates, Jr., and the officer who had arrested Gates as he tried to enter his home near Harvard, having called the summit after the uproar over his comments that the police had "acted stupidly" in arresting the Harvard professor. When Trayvon Martin was killed, Obama observed that if he had had a son, the son would have looked like Trayvon. But the caste system rose up and his approval ratings fell after even these benign gestures. The opposition party stood firm against many of his ambitions and nominees, shutting down the government time and again, refusing to confirm or even consider his Supreme Court nominee Merrick Garland.

The caste system had handcuffed the president as it had handcuffed the African-Americans facedown on the pavement in the videos that had become part of the landscape. It was as if the caste system were reminding everyone of their place, and the subordinate caste, in particular, that no matter how the cast of the play was reshuffled, the hierarchy would remain as it always had been.

In a paradox of caste, many whites seemed to have known this, studies show, seemed to have trusted on some unconscious level that the caste system would hold the first black president, and the subordinate caste with which he had come to be associated, in check. As deeply as some people resented a black man presiding in the Oval Office, "most whites in the United States were not overwhelmingly concerned," Jardina writes, "that Obama would favor blacks over their own group."

Thus, within the parameters in which he was forced to maneuver, he made more headway with race-neutral goals. In so doing, he managed to reshape the country's healthcare system and lead on such issues as climate change, clean energy, gay marriage, sentencing reform, and investigations into police brutality that other administrations might have ignored altogether, while guiding the country out of recession.

But accomplishments from those considered to have stepped out of their place often only breed more resentment, in this case inciting the tremors of discontent among those feeling eclipsed by his very existence.

"Any upheaval in the universe is terrifying," James Baldwin once wrote, "because it so profoundly attacks one's sense of one's own reality."

Which is why Obama's presidency and his high approval ratings "masked an undercurrent of anxiety about our changing nation," according to Jardina. "It hid a swell of resistance to multiculturalism, and a growing backlash to immigration."

In November 2012, on the day after the first black president won reelection to a second term, Rush Limbaugh, the conservative radio talk show host, went on the air and lamented to his listeners. "I went to bed last night thinking we're outnumbered," Limbaugh said. "I went to bed last night thinking we've lost the country. I don't know how else you look at this."

That same day, a troubled sixty-four-year-old man in South Florida took the most extreme action imaginable. In the time leading up to the election, according to police, Henry Hamilton, owner of a tanning salon in Key West, told friends, "If Barack gets reelected, I'm not going to be around." He kept his word. His body was found in his condominium a day and a half after the returns came in. Two prescription bottles sat empty in his dining room. Beside him was a handwritten note demanding that he not be revived and cursing the newly reelected president.

CHAPTER TWENTY-SIX

Turning Point and the Resurgence
of Caste

In the final breaths of 2015, an influential gathering of political insiders in Washington were seeing in the New Year. It was the eve of an election season that was considered of great significance before it had even begun. I felt out of my orbit whenever I was in official Washington, and so I gravitated toward Gwen Ifill, whom I had known for years and had not seen in some time. Back during our days at *The New York Times,* I had been a narrative writer focused on everyday people rather than the halls of power as she had been, the intuitive empath to her political savant.

I went straight up to her.

"So," I began, "what are you thinking?"

The first seconds of 2016 were approaching, and she knew exactly what I meant. I hesitated to proffer my own opinion at first. Gwen was the beloved co-host of the *NewsHour* on PBS. She was a long-standing, clear-eyed Washington sage whom I, along with millions of others, admired for her brilliance and sixth sense, for how she had taken to the sharky waters of the capital as if born to it, always rising above it somehow. She was an embed in a political ecosystem that I had little patience for. I didn't know if what I was feeling compelled to say would sound wildly off base or preposterous to someone as steeped in establishment Washington as she was.

For some reason, I felt the need to whisper. This was supposed to be a party, after all, champagne pouring all around us, a celebration to ring in 2016. There were people from the current administration and perhaps people in the Democratic front-runner's campaign, for all I knew, or, in any case, certainly people supporting the front-runner and expecting a continuing through line of the forward-thinking perspectives carried forth by what would soon be the outgoing administration. So I leaned in and lowered my voice.

"People are not paying attention," I said. "I believe he could win."

I didn't say his name, and I didn't have to. It was still early, the primaries had yet to begin. But momentum had been building for the celebrity billionaire from the time he announced his candidacy the previous June from the escalator of his tower in Manhattan, accusing Mexicans of bringing crime, drugs, and rape across the border and vowing to build a wall. Most journalists and media outlets were not taking him seriously, so I wondered what Gwen thought.

"No question," she said. "Of course. He could absolutely win."

I was not a political animal by any measure, but what I did know was the caste system, so I went on.

"I think it's all about 2042," I said.

"Exactly," she said, her face firm and resolute.

Her response, forthright and assured, was as unsettling as it was affirming of my own instincts, because if she, with her impeccable radar, was thinking this, then it was very likely to be true. We exchanged knowing glances of acceptance of the otherwise inconceivable, as if it were already settled, whether the rest of the country realized it or not, because it was bigger than him, had always been bigger than him, and now all that was left to do was to watch it play out.

Gwen lived just long enough to see her predictions come true and tragically passed away the week after the election. This was a loss to the country at the precise time that it could have benefited from her even-tempered analysis. That prophetic conversation was the last I would have with her, and it now seems all the more powerful in the years that followed.

———

Spring 2016, and into the summer, the election was virtually all that anyone could talk about. One banner headline after another, one time-honored norm shattered after another—a presidential candidate who blew off a major debate in the primaries, a presidential candidate caught on tape boasting about grabbing women by the genitals, a presidential candidate mocking a disabled reporter, arms and hands flailing, face jerking as might a middle schooler's, a presidential candidate deriding the grieving parents of an American war hero who happened to be Muslim. A presidential candidate demeaning an American war hero, John McCain, because he had been captured. The latest breaking news report would be announced before we had even absorbed the last one, a new lexicon forming before our eyes.

"Surely you don't think he has a chance of winning?" a French intellectual asked me when I happened to be in Paris months before the election. "Well, yes, he could," I told her. "He's on the ballot. He could very well win."

"America would never do that," she said, dismissively.

———

Caste does not explain everything in American life, but no aspect of American life can be fully understood without considering caste and embedded hierarchy. Many political analysts and left-leaning observers did not believe that a Trump win was possible and were blindsided by the outcome in 2016 in part because they had not figured into their expectations the degree of reliable consistency of caste as an enduring variable in American life and politics.

The liberal take was that working-class whites have been voting against their interests in supporting right-wing oligarchs, but that theory diminishes the agency and caste-oriented principles of the people. Many voters, in fact, made an assessment of their circumstances and looked beyond immediate short-term benefits and toward, from their perspective, the larger goals of maintaining dominant-caste status and their survival in the long term. They were willing to lose health insurance now, risk White House instability and government shutdowns, external threats from faraway lands, in order to preserve what their actions say they value most—the benefits they had grown accustomed to as members of the historically ruling caste in America.

Trump channeled insecurities and disaffection that went deeper than economics, researchers have found. "White voters' preference for Donald Trump," wrote the political scientists John Sides, Michael Tesler, and Lynn Vavreck, ". . . was weakly related to their own job security but strongly related to concerns that minorities were taking jobs away from whites."

The tremors within the dominant caste had been building long before Trump announced his candidacy. "Defections accelerated over the course of Obama's presidency," Sides, Tesler, and Vavreck wrote. "This is why racial attitudes appear the more likely culprit."

In fact, "no other factor predicted changes in white partisanship during Obama's presidency as powerfully and consistently as racial attitudes," they said.

The researchers consider this kind of group hypervigilance to be what they call "'racialized economics': the belief that undeserving groups are getting ahead while your group is left behind."

The precarity of their lives and the changing demographics of the country induced a greater need to maintain whatever advantages they had come to expect and to shore up the one immutable characteristic that has held the most weight in the American caste system.

"Whites' racial attitudes are not merely defined by prejudice," writes Ashley Jardina of Duke University. "Many whites also possess a sense of racial identity and are motivated to protect their group's collective interests and to maintain its status. . . . Whiteness is now a salient and central component of American politics. White racial solidarity influences many whites' worldview and guides their political attitudes and behavior."

Consciously or not, many white voters "are seeking to reassert a racial order in which their group is firmly at the top."

The 2016 election thus became a cracked mirror held up to a country that had not been forced in this way to search its origins in more than a generation and was now seeing itself perhaps for the first time as it truly was. It was the culmination of forces that had been building for decades.

In a caste context, the two main political parties bear the advantages and burdens of the castes they most attract and with which they are associated. At times, the stigma and double standard attached to disfavored minorities have accrued to the Democrats, while the privilege and latitude accorded the dominant caste has accrued to the Republicans, who have come to be seen as proxies for white America. This in part explains the unforgiving scrutiny and obstructions faced by Democrats like Barack Obama and Hillary Clinton, and before them John Kerry and Al Gore, as white support has intensified for Republicans, now seen as the party of an anxious but powerful dominant-caste electorate.

Clinton, the former secretary of state, was widely viewed as having won the presidential debates, despite her opponent's stalking of her at the podium and calling her a "nasty woman." She was seen as having carried herself with dignity and exhibiting a polished, if stiff, mastery of domestic and foreign affairs. Yet in polling she rarely managed to pull much beyond the margin of error against a man considered by some to be the least qualified person ever to run for president.

There were many factors at work in the 2016 election, among them foreign interference and barriers to voting that disproportionately affected marginalized voters. Still, Clinton's loss in the Electoral College seems shocking until one considers caste, and the historic challenges that subordinate-caste candidates, meaning African-American candidates, have often faced on Election

Day despite favorable polling. Seen from a caste perspective, Clinton perhaps suffered from a version of the Bradley Effect—inflated polling numbers that do not materialize on Election Day due to people telling pollsters what they believe is the socially acceptable answer about their voting plans but then choosing differently in the voting booth. This is what happened to Los Angeles mayor Tom Bradley when he ran for governor of California in 1982. That would have made an inability to rise above the margin of error a harbinger of a tough Election Day.

Caste gives insights, too, into the Democrats' wistful yearning for white working-class voters that they believe should respond in higher numbers to their kitchen table appeals. Why, some people on the left kept asking, why, oh, why, were these people voting against their own interests? The questioners on the left were unseeing and yet so certain. What they had not considered was that the people voting this way were, in fact, voting their interests. Maintaining the caste system as it had always been was in their interest. And some were willing to accept short-term discomfort, forgo health insurance, risk contamination of the water and air, and even die to protect their long-term interest in the hierarchy as they had known it.

———

When you are caught in a caste system, you will likely do whatever it takes to survive in it. If you are insecurely situated somewhere in the middle—below the very top but above the very bottom—you may distance yourself from the bottom and hold up barriers against those you see as below you to protect your own position. You will emphasize the inherited characteristics that rank higher on the caste scale.

In the voting booth, many people make an autonomic, subconscious assessment of their station, their needs and wishes, and the multiple identities they carry (working class, middle class, rich, poor, white, black, male, female, Asian, Latino). They often align themselves not with those whose plight they may share, but with those whose power and privilege intersect with a trait of their own. People with overlapping self-interests will often gravitate toward the personal characteristic that accords them the most status. Many make an existential, aspirational choice. They vote up, rather than across, and usually not down. They believe they know who will protect the interests of the trait that gives them the most status and that matters most to them.

In the pivotal election of 2016, whether consciously or not, the majority of whites voted for the candidate who made the most direct appeals to the characteristic most rewarded in the caste system. They went with the aspect of themselves that grants them the most power and status in the hierarchy. According to *New York Times* exit polling of 24,537 respondents, 58 percent of white voters chose the Republican Donald Trump and only 37 percent went for the Democrat Hillary Clinton. While she won nearly 3 million more votes than Trump by the popular count, she attracted a smaller share of the white vote than any Democratic candidate other than Jimmy Carter in his failed bid for reelection against Ronald Reagan in 1980.

"The parties have grown so divided by race," writes the political scientist Lilliana Mason, "that simple racial identity, without policy content, is enough to predict party identity."

There was perhaps no clearer measure of white solidarity than the actions of white women in 2016. The majority of them—53 percent—disregarded the common needs of women and went against a fellow white woman to vote with their power trait, the white side of their identities to which Trump appealed, rather than help an experienced woman, and themselves, make history.

"Trump was ushered into office by whites concerned about their status," Jardina writes, "and his political priorities are plainly aimed at both protecting the racial hierarchy and at strengthening its boundaries." These are people who feel "that the rug is being pulled out from under them—that the benefits they have enjoyed because of their race, their group's advantages, and their status atop the racial hierarchy are all in jeopardy."

A subliminal awareness of the power of caste (though the word would rarely, if ever, be used) appears also to be at work, to whatever degree, in how the parties respond to their respective bases. The Republican reverence for its base of white evangelicals stands in stark contrast to the indifference often shown the Democratic base of African-Americans, who are devalued for a host of reasons, among them their suppressed status at the bottom of the social hierarchy.

For the Republicans, the singularity of focus, the sense of rallying around an existential threat, combined with the inherent caste advantages of the collective wealth and influence of its voters overall, gives the GOP a seeming advantage in firing up its supporters against Democratic opposition. For their part, Democrats constitute a diffuse majority of the electorate, but seem at times lukewarm toward a base that the party has often lectured to or taken for granted, chided, if ever there is lower-than-expected turnout, despite voter suppression, sadly buying into caste assumptions rather than bolstering their most loyal voters as do the Republicans with theirs. Democrats expend energy and weaken their power pining for the die-hard voters of their opponents, the homecoming queens of the electorate, while taking for granted the majority that they already have.

As the most loyal voters of their respective parties, white evangelicals are to Republicans what African-Americans are to Democrats, though each makes up a minority of the total electorate. But the foremost concerns of the Democrats' most reliable voting bloc—affordable housing, clean water, police brutality, the racial wealth gap, and reparations for state-sanctioned discrimination (as has been accorded other groups discriminated against in the United States)—have remained on the back burner, or have even been considered radioactive issues for the party that African-Americans help to sustain. To those who say that this would be impractical, it would be the duty of the party representing and dependent on the subordinate caste to open the eyes of their fellow Americans and make the case for a more egalitarian country.

Meanwhile, the priorities of white evangelicals—ending abortion, restricting immigration, protecting gun rights, limiting government, and, more recently, the disdain for science and the denial of climate change—have become the menu of belief systems for the Republican Party.

"What most distinguishes white American evangelicals from other Christians, other religious groups, and nonbelievers is not theology but politics," writes Seth Dowland, associate professor of religion at Pacific Lutheran University and author of *Family Values and the Rise of the Christian Right*. "Over the course of the 20th century, the evangelical coalition entwined theology, whiteness, and conservative politics. . . . To identify as evangelical in the early 21st century signals commitments to gun rights, the abolition of legal abortion, and low taxes."

People identifying as white evangelicals, regardless of their personal religiosity, "rallied around Trump to defend a white Protestant nation," Dowland writes. "They have proven to be loyal foot soldiers in the battle against undocumented immigrants and Muslims. The triumph of gay rights, the persistence of legal abortion, and the election of Barack Obama signaled to them a need to fight for the America they once knew."

———

The 2016 election became a remarkable blueprint of caste hierarchy in America, from highest to lowest status, in a given group's support of the Republican: White men voted for Trump at 62 percent. White women at 53 percent. Latino men at 32 percent. Latina women at 25 percent. African-American men at 13 percent, and black women at 4 percent. Unlike the majority of white voters, every other group of voters supported the Democrat in 2016. The Democratic vote went as follows: White men, 31 percent. White women, 43 percent. Latino men, 63 percent. Latina women, 69 percent. African-American men, 82 percent. African-American women, whose race and gender together put them at the bottom of the country's artificial hierarchy, supported the white female Democrat by 94 percent. While CNN did not break down the Asian vote by gender, Asians, like other nonwhites, voted overwhelmingly for Clinton, at 65 percent versus 27 percent for Trump, tracking the Latino vote overall.

Trump fared well against Clinton with all categories of white voters, at every age and education level, though his percentages were higher for whites who had no college degree (66 percent for Trump, 29 percent for Clinton) than for those who had a college degree (48 percent for Trump, 45 percent for Clinton). Contrary to popular assumptions that economic insecurity was a driver of the 2016 outcome, Trump beat Clinton in most every income level except those who were least economically secure—those making less than $50,000 per year. This could be seen as a reflection of the fact that marginalized voters in general, and black voters in particular—those more likely to support the Democrat—make up a disproportionate share of voters with lower incomes.

With these stark racial patterns, the 2016 election seemed a consolidation of rank among the historic ruling caste. "Even though white Americans still comprise a clear political majority and continue to possess most of the country's wealth," observed the legal scholar Robert L. Tsai, "it is possible to stoke outlandish fears of a coming reckoning where racial and ethnic minorities will seek to subjugate white citizens."

———

The sense of perceived injury found a voice in 2016. "These aggrieved whites are a potentially untapped well," Jardina wrote, "one whose resentments are primed, ready to be stoked by politicians willing to go down a potentially very dark path."

For this reason, the ruptures exposed in 2016 transcend a single election or candidate and go well beyond the initial theories of economic insecurity as the driver of the white vote. "In many ways, a sense of group threat is a much tougher opponent than an economic downturn," wrote the political scientist Diana Mutz, "because it is a psychological mindset rather than an actual event or misfortune."

Once in office, the forty-fifth president made no secret of his laser focus on the desires of his base. "Whether out of personal animus, political calculation, philosophical disagreement or a conviction that the last president damaged the country, Mr. Trump has made clear that if it has Mr. Obama's name on it, he would just as soon erase it from the national hard drive," wrote the *New York Times* White House correspondent Peter Baker.

Those susceptible to "dominant group status threat," Mutz wrote, will do whatever they can to protect the hierarchy that has benefited them, to "regain a sense of dominance and wellbeing."

The election outcome alone had his base feeling better. A couple of days after the election, two middle-aged white men with receding hairlines and reading glasses took their seats in first class on a flight from Atlanta to Chicago. They suspected by looking at each other, and knowing the polling results, that they were likely on the same team. It didn't take them long to confirm that they were.

"Last eight years," one of them said, "worst thing that ever happened, I'm so glad it's over."

"It was bigger than an election," the other one said. "It was one of the most amazing events I think we'll ever witness. I stayed up all night to watch it."

"Yeah, well, I went to bed that night thinking I'd be crying the next morning. Woke up. Best news I ever heard."

"There is justice in this world. They made a bad, bad choice with her," one said.

"The current president was a bad choice," the other said.

"He was in over his head. It's a beautiful day!"

"Yep, finally got it right. Yessiree."

CHAPTER TWENTY-SEVEN

The Symbols of Caste

The Confederate general who led the war against the United States over the right to hold human beings hostage for all their natural-born days, Robert E. Lee, or, more precisely, a bronze sculpture of Robert E. Lee, rose two stories high on its granite pedestal in the center of a village green in Charlottesville, Virginia. On this day in the late summer of 2017, the statue in honor of a hero of the former slaveholding states was now covered with a thin black tarp that had taken two men positioned in cranes something like an hour to stretch across the length and width of it, over the general's head and the American Saddlebred horse he sat astride.

The statue was under a shroud while city leaders tried to figure out what to do with it. The monument had drawn the attention of the world after a rally of white supremacists turned deadly just weeks before. The rally brought together disaffected members of the dominant caste in protest of the city's plan to remove the statue. It was as if the passions of the Civil War had been resurrected and had merged with a resurgent Nazism, which the forefathers of the young Americans at the rally had fought to vanquish back in the middle of the previous century. The heirs to the Confederates and the heirs to the Nazis could see how much they and their histories had in common even if ordinary Americans did not.

On that day in August 2017, Confederate flags and swastikas interfused above the ralliers, men mostly, some with haircuts as severe as their faces. Together, the night before, they had marched through the campus of the University of Virginia, extending Nazi salutes, chanting, "Sieg Heil," and "White lives matter," and "Jews will not replace us." They held tiki torches in the night air, reenacting the torchbearers' rivers of light at the old processions for Hitler. The following day, at the rally itself, the neo-Confederates and the neo-Nazis arrived well armed, which in turn drew counterprotesters bearing signs of peace. Then a white supremacist rammed a car into a crowd of counterprotesters, killing one of them, a paralegal named Heather Heyer, and wounding dozens of others.

Now the city was trying to keep the statue from public view, but every time the city covered it, someone would come and remove the tarp, releasing Lee's likeness in protest. The city would again send in the cranes to put the tarp back over it. The day I happened to visit Charlottesville, shortly after the rally, the city was prevailing.

From the center of the green, in the very middle of town, rose a jagged black trapezoid tied at the base like a giant chifforobe wrapped for protection until the movers arrive. It looked for all the world like a giant trash bag from which you could make out the crown of the general's head and the nose and tail of the horse at opposite ends. The whole effect of the giant trapezoid in the middle of a stately park brought more attention to the general, and to the monuments to the Confederacy, not less, though the tarp had been a short-term compromise to keep it from public view. Tourists came in search of it.

"Guess that's him right there," a man said, crossing the street to take a closer look. The tourists waited their turn to take their picture in front of the cloaked general. Then they made the pilgrimage to the street across from the statue, the street where Heather Heyer had been killed. It had become a block-long memorial to her, piles of dying roses and sunflowers, heartbroken messages scrawled in the pavement and on the sides of brick walls, a plea for humanity.

We are witness

Never forget

The minute we look away,
the minute we stop fighting, bigotry wins

There is no more room for hate

That all men are created equal

Across the United States, there are more than seventeen hundred monuments to the Confederacy, monuments to a breakaway republic whose constitution and leaders were unequivocal in declaring the purpose of their new nation. "Its foundations are laid," said Alexander Stephens, the vice president of the Confederacy, "its corner-stone rests upon the great truth that the negro is not equal to the white man; that slavery subordination to the superior race is his natural and normal condition. This, our new government, is the first, in the history of the world, based upon this great physical, philosophical, and moral truth. . . . With us, all of the white race, however high or low, rich or poor, are equal in the eye of the law. Not so with the negro. Subordination is his place. He, by nature, or by the curse against Canaan, is fitted for that condition which he occupies in our system."

The Confederacy would lose the war in April 1865, but in the succeeding decades would win the all-important peace. The Confederates would manage to take hold of the public imagination with gauzy portrayals of the Lost Cause. Two of the most influential and popular films of the early twentieth century—*Birth of a Nation* and *Gone with the Wind*—fed the country and the world the Confederate version of the war and portrayed the people of the degraded lowest caste as capable only of brute villainy or childlike buffoonery.

Even though the Thirteenth Amendment in 1865 ended slavery, it left a loophole that let the dominant caste enslave people convicted of a crime. This gave the dominant caste incentive to lock

up lowest-caste people for subjective offenses like loitering or va-
grancy at a time when free labor was needed in a penal system
that the dominant caste alone controlled. After a decade of Reconstruction, just as African-Americans were seeking entry to mainstream society, the North abandoned its oversight of the South,
pulled its occupying troops out of the region, and handed power
back to the former rebels, leaving the survivors of slavery at the
mercy of supremacist militias nursing wounds from the war. The
federal government paid reparations not to the people who had
been held captive, but rather to the people who had enslaved
them.

The former Confederates reinscribed a mutation of slavery in the
form of sharecropping and an authoritarian regime that put people who had only recently emerged from slavery into a world of
lynchings, night riders, and Klansmen, terrors meant to keep them
subservient. As they foreclosed the hopes of African-Americans,
they erected statues and monuments everywhere to the slave-
owning Confederates, a naked forewarning to the lowest caste of
its subjugation and powerlessness.

It was psychic trolling of the first magnitude. People still raw
from the trauma of floggings and family rupture, and the descendants of those people, were now forced to live amid monuments
to the men who had gone to war to keep them at the level of live-
stock. To enter a courthouse to stand trial in a case that they were
all but certain to lose, survivors of slavery had to pass statues of
Confederate soldiers looking down from literal pedestals. They
had to ride on roads named after the generals of their tormenters
and walk past schools named after Klansmen.

Well into the twentieth century, heirs to the Confederacy built a
monument with Lee, Stonewall Jackson, and Jefferson Davis
carved in granite, bigger than Mount Rushmore, in Stone Mountain, Georgia. If the Confederacy had lost the war, the culture of
the South and the lives of the lowest caste did not reflect it. In fact,
the return to power of the former Confederates meant retribution
and even harder times to come.

By the time of the rally in Charlottesville, there were some 230 memorials to Robert E. Lee in the United States, including the Robert E. Lee Hotel in Lexington, Virginia, Robert E. Lee Park in Miami, Florida, and Robert E. Lee Creek in Boise National Forest in Idaho, two thousand miles from the old Confederacy. There are scores of plaques, busts, schools, and roadways throughout the country—a Robert E. Lee *Street* in Mobile, Alabama, a Robert E. Lee *Drive* in Tupelo, Mississippi, a Robert E. Lee *Boulevard* in Charleston, South Carolina, a General Robert E. Lee *Road* in Brunswick, Georgia, and a Robert E. Lee *Lane* in Gila Bend, Arizona.

Students take classes at Robert E. Lee High School in Jacksonville, Florida, and in Tyler, Texas, among others, and at Lee Junior High School in Monroe, Louisiana. Eight states in the Union have a county named after Robert E. Lee: Alabama, Arkansas, Florida, Kentucky, Mississippi, North Carolina, South Carolina, and Texas. The third Monday in January is Robert E. Lee Day in both Mississippi and Alabama.

Robert E. Lee was a well-born graduate of West Point Academy, a pragmatic and cunning military strategist, a political moderate, for his times and his region, and a Virginia slaveholder who saw slavery as a necessary evil that burdened the owners more than the people they enslaved. "The blacks are immeasurably better off here than in Africa, morally, socially & physically," he once wrote. "The painful discipline they are undergoing, is necessary for their instruction as a race, & I hope will prepare & lead them to better things. How long their subjugation may be necessary is known & ordered by a wise merciful Providence."

Like other slaveholders, he made full use of the "painful discipline" of which he spoke. In 1859, three of the people he enslaved on his Virginia plantation—a man named Wesley Norris and his sister and cousin—fled north and were captured near the Pennsylvania border. They were forced back to Lee's plantation. Upon their arrival, Lee told them that "he would teach us a lesson we would never forget," Wesley Norris later recounted. Lee ordered his overseer to strip them to the waist, tie them to posts, and whip the men fifty lashes and the woman twenty, on their bare backs. When the overseer resisted, Lee got the county constable and told him to "lay it on well," which the constable did. "Not satisfied with simply lacerating our naked flesh," Norris recalled, "Gen. Lee then ordered the overseer to thoroughly wash our backs with brine, which was done."

This was common practice and standard procedure during much of the 246 years of slavery. Had these and even more gruesome atrocities occurred in another country, at another time, to another set of people other than the lowest caste, they would have been considered crimes against humanity in violation of international conventions. But the slaveholders, overseers, and others in the dominant caste who inflicted atrocities upon millions of African-Americans over the centuries were not only not punished but were celebrated as pillars of society.

Lee was never called to account for what he did to the Norrises nor to the many families he broke apart as an enslaver, the children he separated from parents, the husbands from wives. Even after leading the war of southern secession that ended with more casualties than any other on this soil, Lee faced few penalties associated with treason. President Andrew Johnson, the Tennessee Democrat and onetime slaveowner who succeeded Abraham Lincoln after Lincoln's assassination, granted amnesty to most of the Confederates in a bid to move on from sectional tensions and to put the matter to rest. Lee did no jail time and suffered little censure, though he was no longer permitted to vote, and he was forced to relinquish his plantation, which the government coveted and converted into Arlington National Cemetery.

It turned out that, after the war, many white northerners felt a greater kinship with the former Confederates who had betrayed the Union than with the people whose free labor built the country's wealth and over whose freedom the Civil War had been fought. The North's conciliatory embrace of the former Confederates compelled Frederick Douglass to remind Americans that "there was a right side and a wrong side in the late war which no sentiment ought to cause us to forget," adding that "it is no part of our duty to confound right with wrong, or loyalty with treason."

Robert E. Lee went on to become president of a college that would later add his name to its own, Washington and Lee University in Virginia. This granted him social standing and a worshipful legacy, and allowed him a platform to weigh in on issues of the day with authority if he chose.

His reputation only grew after his death in 1870. As the country embraced segregation, north and south, with redlining and restrictive covenants keeping black people out of white neighborhoods and the races separate, he became not just a southern hero, but a national one. He is interred at a chapel named after him on the campus of Washington and Lee, Confederate flags flanking, up until recently, a mold of the general in repose. Among the memorials in his honor well beyond the South, there came to be plaques and busts of him in the Bronx and in Brooklyn, elementary schools named after him in Long Beach and San Diego, and five different Robert E. Lee stamps issued by the U.S. Postal Service. Usually, it is the victors of war who erect monuments and commemorations to themselves. Here, an outsider might not be able to tell which side had prevailed over the other.

———

At two o'clock in the morning on April 24, 2017, a SWAT team positioned its sharpshooters at strategic locations at a dangerous intersection in downtown New Orleans. K-9 units patrolled the grounds and perimeter. At the center of the targeted area, men in face masks and bulletproof vests went about their perilous duty in the darkness. Others had refused to risk their lives for this, declined even to attempt the operation, after the death threats and firebombing that preceded this moment. These men in face masks were the only ones willing to take up the mission. They were removing the first of four Confederate monuments in the city of New Orleans.

Tensions had been building since 2015 when Mayor Mitch Landrieu, a fifth-generation Louisianan whose ancestors had been in the state since before the Civil War, decided it was time for the Confederate statues to go. That June, a gunman inspired by the Lost Cause of the Confederacy massacred nine black parishioners as they prayed at the end of Bible study at Emanuel African Methodist Episcopal Church in Charleston, South Carolina. Under international pressure, the South Carolina state legislature and Gov. Nikki Haley agreed to remove the Confederate flag from the state capitol and put it in the Confederate Relic Room in the State Museum. South Carolina had been the first state to secede from the Union in the run-up to the Civil War, and this gesture opened the way for other states to follow if they could gather the will.

Landrieu was moved by this and was further awakened by his friend, the jazz trumpeter Wynton Marsalis, to the perspective of the descendants of enslaved people who had been terrorized under the Confederate banner.

The monuments in question included one for Confederate president Jefferson Davis and one for Gen. Robert E. Lee, the latter of whom had no direct connection to New Orleans but whose statue was erected by the city as the Jim Crow regime took hold after the end of Reconstruction.

Now, more than a century later, the city was within its right to remove its own property, and Mayor Landrieu thought it would be a fairly straightforward process of public hearings and a vote by a city council as progressive as the city it represented. With the country newly reminded of the enduring nature of white supremacy, supporters came forward, including an influential citizen who pledged to donate $170,000 toward the cost of removing the monument as long as he could be assured of anonymity.

The city tested the idea with the public. At one hearing, a Confederate sympathizer had to be escorted out by police after he cursed and gave the middle finger to the audience. A retired lieutenant colonel in the Marine Corps, Richard Westmoreland, came at it from the other side. He stood up and said that Erwin Rommel was a great general, but there are no statues of Rommel in Germany. "They are ashamed," he said. "The question is, why aren't we?"

As time wore on, though, things got ugly. The city had trouble finding a contractor to remove the statues. Every contractor who considered the city's request got threatening attacks at home, at work, and on social media. It turned out that not one construction company in New Orleans wanted to touch it. Finally a contractor in Baton Rouge agreed to do it, but he pulled out, too, after his car was firebombed. The Confederate sympathizers made it clear that "any company that dared step forward," Landrieu wrote, "would pay a price."

The faithful of the old Confederacy held candlelight vigils at the monuments and clogged the city hall switchboard, cursing and threatening the receptionists. Soon the benefactor backed out of his promise of donating money for the removal effort. If it were ever discovered, he said, "I'll get run out of town."

The issue was now dividing all of New Orleans. "People who had served for years on civic boards quit," Landrieu said. "There was a "deep, mean chill we felt when we entered a room for a public event." Some of the mayor's own neighbors and some of the people he thought of as friends averted their gaze when they saw him. He had not anticipated "the ferocity of the opposition."

Finally, the city found a construction company willing to take on what had become hazard duty in a virtual war zone. It could be seen as karma that the only construction crew willing to risk their lives to remove the Confederate statues was African-American. Due to the dangers of the operation, the company charged four times what the city had anticipated to remove the three largest monuments, and said the company would only go in if there was police protection. By now, the city had few other options if it wanted the statues gone.

The mayor decided first to remove a monument to a supremacist organization called the White League because white citizens seemed to have the least attachment to that one. Still, the city took no chances.

That night, the men wore long sleeves and masks both to protect their identities and to conceal their skin color. Cardboard covered the company name on its trucks and cranes and hid the vehicle license plates. Still, the pro-Confederate forces poured sand in the gas tank of one of the cranes. As the workers proceeded to remove the obelisk in pieces, drones lurked above them taking unauthorized photographs of the operation. People in the crowd trained high-definition cameras on the workers to try to identify them. Finally, the pieces of the obelisk were down and driven to a storage shed.

The next month, the Robert E. Lee monument, a larger-than-life bronze likeness, arms crossed, standing on a sixty-foot marble column in a manicured circle in the center of town, was the last of the four to be removed. His figure dangled from a crane in full daylight and, this time, to cheering crowds.

Mayor Landrieu gave a speech that day to remind citizens of why this needed to happen. "These monuments celebrate a fictional, sanitized Confederacy," he said, "ignoring the death, ignoring the enslavement, ignoring the terror that it actually stood for."

They were more than mere statuary. "They were created as political weapons," he would later write, "part of an effort to hide the truth, which is that the Confederacy was on the wrong side not just of history, but of humanity."

The day that New Orleans wrested Robert E. Lee from his column, the Alabama state legislature sent a bill to the Alabama governor, Kay Ivey. As in most of the former Confederacy after the post-civil-rights realignment, Republicans now dominated Alabama. They were now fighting to keep monuments to the very cause that the one-time party of Lincoln had fought in the Civil War. The new Alabama bill sent to the governor that day made it illegal to remove any monument that had been in place for twenty years or more, which in effect meant that nobody could lay a hand on a single Confederate statue in Alabama.

————

An ocean away, in the former capital of the Third Reich, Nigel Dunkley, a former British officer and now a historian of Nazi Germany, drove along a curve of what is left of the Berlin Wall. He pointed to the neoclassical buildings of the old Weimar Republic that were for a time run by the Nazis and have been reclaimed since the reunification of Germany. We drew near the Brandenburg Gate, which survived the Allied bombing in the Second World War, and then reached a wide-open space in the very center of downtown.

The office towers and government buildings came to a halt and gave way to a modernist Stonehenge on 4.7 acres, the size of three football fields, where once there had been the death strip to catch defectors in the Cold War. Two thousand seven hundred eleven concrete rectangles, as if a field of chiseled coffins of varying heights, stand in formation, separated by just enough space for people to walk between them and to contemplate their meaning. The stones undulate and dip toward the center, where the ground hollows out, so that when a visitor reaches the interior, the traffic noise dies away, the air grows still, and you are trapped in shadow, isolated with the magnitude of what the stones represent. This is the Memorial to the Murdered Jews of Europe who perished during the Holocaust. There is no sign, no gate, no fence, no list of the 6 million. The stones are as regimented as the Nazis and as anonymous as the captives shorn of identity in the concentration camps. Since 2005, the memorial has borne mute witness to anyone who wishes to come, day or night.

The designer of the memorial, Peter Eisenman, a New York architect, chose not to explain the meaning of the number 2,711, or very much else about the installation. "I wanted people to have a feeling of being in the present and an experience that they had never had before," Eisenman told *Der Spiegel* the year it opened. "And one that was different and slightly unsettling."

The company that once produced cyanide gas for the concentration camps now provides the protectorate applied to the concrete stones to prevent graffiti and defacement, which might be seen as either an act of atonement from the perspective of some or the very least they could do from the perspective of others. The installation is the most imposing of a series of memorials to the people killed under Hitler's reign. "We have a memorial to everyone victimized by the Nazis," Dunkley said. "There is a memorial to homosexuals who perished. There is a memorial to the Sinti and Roma right outside the Reichstag. We have lesser memorials to lesser groups. And then we have the stumbling stones."

These are the micro-memorials of discreet brass squares the size of one's palm inscribed with the names of Holocaust victims and placed throughout the city. More than seventy thousand of these stumbling stones, known as *Stolpersteine*, have been forged and installed in cities across Europe. They are embedded among the cobblestones in front of houses and apartment buildings where the victims whose names are inscribed on them are known to have last lived before being abducted by the Gestapo. "Here lived Hildegard Blumenthal, born 1897, deported 1943, died in Auschwitz," reads a stumbling stone clustered among others outside an apartment building in western Berlin. Nearby are the stones for Rosa Gross and Arthur Benjamin, who were deported in 1942 and who perished in Riga.

The stumbling stones force the viewer to pause and squint to read the inscription, force the viewer to regard the entry doors the people walked through, the steps they climbed with their groceries and toddlers, the streets they strolled that were the everyday life of real people rather than abstractions of incomprehensible millions. Each one is a personal headstone that gives a momentary connection to a single individual. Leaning over to read the names on the stumbling stones forces you to bow in respect.

Nigel Dunkley made a slow turn near the site of the Reich Chancellery in the Mitte of Berlin and pulled his old Volvo up to a parking lot off Wilhelmstrasse. It was an asphalt square at the base of some concrete office and apartment buildings, and it had a low guardrail around it, like parking lots everywhere.

"You see that blue Volkswagen parked next to the white minivan?" he asked me.

From the car window, I looked past a recycling bin on the sidewalk and then over to the asphalt lot, the white lines separating each car, and saw the Volkswagen he was pointing to. It was parked in front of the low, straggled branches of untended barberry bushes.

"Right there, underneath that Volkswagen, was Hitler's bunker," Nigel said. The hideout had been built thirty feet underground and protected by two meters of reinforced concrete, in the event that Hitler should ever need a secure location. This is where Hitler spent the last weeks and hours of his life, hiding out from enemy shelling as the Allies closed in on them, where he heard that Mussolini had been executed and his Wehrmacht overcome on every front, where he married Eva Braun at the last minute as his closest confidants turned on him, where he shot himself in the head after biting into a cyanide pill, and where his hours-long wife had bitten into a cyanide pill just before him, on April 30, 1945. His body was unceremoniously dragged to a nearby lot and set afire.

In America, the men who mounted a bloody war against the United States to keep the right to enslave humans for generations went on to live out their retirement in comfort. Confederate president Jefferson Davis went on to write his memoirs at a plantation in Mississippi that is now the site of his presidential library. Robert E. Lee became an esteemed college president. When they died, they were both granted state funerals with military honors and were revered with statues and monuments.

An American author living in Berlin, who happens to be Jewish and to have been raised in the South, often gets asked about Germany's memorials to its Nazi past. "To which I respond: There aren't any," Susan Neiman, author of *Learning from the Germans: Race and the Memory of Evil,* has written. "Germany has no monuments that celebrate the Nazi armed forces, however many grandfathers fought or fell for them."

Rather than honor supremacists with statues on pedestals, Germany, after decades of silence and soul-searching, chose to erect memorials to the victims of its aggressions and to the courageous people who resisted the men who inflicted atrocities on human beings.

They built a range of museums to preserve the story of the country's descent into madness. They converted the infamous villa at Wannsee, where fifteen men worked out the details of the Final Solution to kill the Jews of Europe, into a museum examining the consequences of that fateful decision. The country converted the Gestapo headquarters into a museum called the Topography of Terror, a deep dive into the founding of the Third Reich. As for the man who oversaw these atrocities, Germany chose quite literally to pave over the *Führer*'s gravesite. There could be no more pedestrian resolution than that.

––––––

In Germany, displaying the swastika is a crime punishable by up to three years in prison. In the United States, the rebel flag is incorporated into the official state flag of Mississippi. It can be seen on the backs of pickup trucks north and south, fluttering along highways in Georgia and the other former Confederate states. A Confederate flag the size of a bedsheet flapped in the wind off an interstate in Virginia around the time of the Charlottesville rally.

In Germany, there is no death penalty. "We can't be trusted to kill people after what happened in World War II," a German woman once told me. In America, the states that recorded the highest number of lynchings, among them the former Confederate States of America, all currently have the death penalty.

In Germany, few people will proudly admit to having been related to Nazis or will openly defend the Nazi cause. "Not even members of Germany's right-wing Alternative for Germany party," wrote Neiman, "would suggest glorifying that part of the past."

The Germans who may "privately mourn for family members lost at the front," Neiman wrote, "know that their loved ones cannot be publically [*sic*] honored without honoring the cause for which they died."

In America, at Civil War reenactments throughout the country, more people typically sign up to fight on the side of the Confederates than for the Union, leaving the Union side sometimes struggling to find enough modern-day conscripts to stage a reenactment.

In Germany, some of the Nazis who did not kill themselves were tracked down and forced to stand trial. Many were hanged at the hands of the Allies for their crimes against humanity. The people who kidnapped and held hostage millions of people during slavery, condemning them to slow death, were not called to account and did not stand trial.

In Germany, restitution has rightly been paid, and continues to be paid, to survivors of the Holocaust. In America, it was the slaveholders who got restitution, not the people whose lives and wages were stolen from them for twelve generations. Those who instilled terror on the lowest caste over the following century after the formal end of slavery, those who tortured and killed humans before thousands of onlookers or who aided and abetted those lynchings or who looked the other way, well into the twentieth century, not only went free but rose to become leading figures—southern governors, senators, sheriffs, businessmen, mayors.

———

On a gray November afternoon, couples with strollers, tailored women with their shopping totes, commuters in wool and tweed, all make their way to the Wittenbergplatz subway station off

Kurfürstendamm, the buzzy, neon-lit Fifth Avenue of Berlin, on the west side of the city.

They converge at the front doors to the station, and there to the right of them is the sign, nearly a story high, for every commuter, every shopper, every store clerk, every couple on a date, every backpacked student and tourist to see. Translated from German, it reads: *Places of Horror That We Should Never Forget.* Then it lists the places never to be forgotten: Auschwitz, Dachau, Bergen-Belsen, Treblinka, Buchenwald, Sachsenhausen, and half a dozen other concentration camps.

It was through these station doors that thousands of Jews took their last look at their beloved Berlin before being forced onto trains that would carry them to their deaths. This fact, this history, is built into the consciousness of Berliners as they go about their everyday lives. It is not something that anyone, Jew or Gentile, resident or visitor, is expected to put behind them or to just get over. They do not run from it. It has become a part of who they are because it is a part of what they have been. They incorporate it into their identity because it is, in fact, them.

It is a mandatory part of every school curriculum, even for grade school students, and it is never far from view for any citizen. This is not to say that everyone is in agreement as to the lengths to which the country goes to reinforce this history. What seems not in contention is the necessity of remembering. A former member of the German parliament was once talking with Nigel Dunkley and thought out loud about his discomfort with the massive stone installation to the European Jews near the Brandenburg Gate, which some have compared to a cemetery in the middle of downtown. "Why can't we have a nice park with grass and trees and a proper monument?" the former parliamentarian said. "Every time I drive past, I feel I am being punished by this higgly-piggly mess."

"If that is what you really think," Dunkley said to him, "that you're being punished, then you are being punished."

When Dunkley takes German students on tours of the history of the Third Reich, he asks them their reaction to what they have seen.

"Do you as Germans feel any guilt for what the Germans did?" he will ask them.

They will go off into groups and have heated discussions among themselves, and then come back to him with their thoughts.

"Yes, we are Germans, and Germans perpetrated this," some students once told him, echoing what others have said. "And, though it wasn't just Germans, it is the older Germans who were here who should feel guilt. We were not here. We ourselves did not do this. But we do feel that, as the younger generation, we should acknowledge and accept the responsibility. And for the generations that come after us, we should be the guardians of the truth."

CHAPTER TWENTY-EIGHT

Democracy on the Ballot

It was nearing the sesquicentennial of the end of the Civil War, and the turmoil in America had doubled over on itself through the summer of 2014 and into 2015, a metronome of unfiltered videos, one after another, of police attacking unarmed citizens from Staten Island to Los Angeles. Then came the mass demonstrations, protesters converging by the thousands to shut down FDR Drive in Manhattan and Lake Shore Drive in Chicago at rush hour, protesters dropping to the ground as had the victims in those shootings. And we could see on Twitter or cable news the office workers and undergraduates splayed together on the tile floor at the cosmetics counters at Macy's or at Grand Central Terminal or the University of Michigan Medical School, the die-ins as they were called, under the tragically obvious rallying cry of Black Lives Matter.

By June of 2015, the first black president was delivering a eulogy at the funeral of the pastor killed in the Charleston church massacre. The president, looking grim-faced and stricken, sought to bring the country to a hoped-for redemption by leading the sanctuary through the refrain of "Amazing Grace," the song itself a quest for absolution by the captain of a slaving ship.

It was shortly thereafter that the Confederate flag finally came down from the state capitol in Columbia after it had flown for fifty-four years. At the same time, Harper Lee's second novel, *Go Set a Watchman*, was released, and the country discovered that the most beloved hero in American fiction, Atticus Finch, had actually been an unreconstructed bigot.

The country was being unmasked, it seemed. It moved me enough to write an op-ed about what appeared to be a moment of truth. I decided to reach out to a friend, Taylor Branch, the esteemed historian of the civil rights movement, to hear his thoughts. He was translating this through the lens of Martin Luther King, Jr.'s thirteen-year campaign for social justice. He believed then that the country had been hurled back to the 1950s, which he said he found hopeful, actually, because it could be the beginning of a breakthrough.

"It is building up to a crisis for those who want to will this away," he told me, and I included him in my opinion piece in *The New York Times* that July.

Three years later, we were catching up over coffee, with a different president and the concentric circles of hate seeming to radiate outward to Muslims, Mexican immigrants, nonwhite immigrants overall, and now to Jews. It was November 2018. The month before, eleven Jewish worshippers had been gunned down as they prayed at the Tree of Life Synagogue in Pittsburgh.

"With everything going on, where do you think we are now?" I asked him. "Are you still thinking 1950s? I'm thinking 1880s."

"Well, that's awfully bleak," he said. "There was a total exclusion of the black vote, total exclusion from political life. People were being lynched openly. That is not happening now. The 1880s was the start of a long period of suppression."

I could see his point, and I told him I fervently hoped to be wrong. That era, the decades roughly between the end of Reconstruction and the start of World War II, was called the Nadir by the black historian Rayford Logan. Many black historians see the current era, starting roughly with the shooting of Trayvon Martin and other unarmed black people, combined with the rollbacks in voting rights protections, as the Second Nadir.

"We're seeing the twenty-first-century version of the backlash," I said. "The tools will be different than before."

We both well knew that grandfather clauses had faded with the previous century, but now states were purging tens of thousands of voters for missing a single election, shutting down polling stations at the last minute in Democratic-leaning precincts. They were now requiring state ID just to vote, but were rejecting IDs that didn't match the voter list to the letter or that were missing a single apostrophe. Since 2010, twenty-four states had passed one or all of these restrictions.

Then there were the shootings of unarmed African-Americans at the hands of authorities that, despite viral videos, often went without prosecution.

"The purpose of the lynchings was to keep black people in their place," I said. "In both eras, people were killed with impunity. And now, the mass shootings."

"Based on what you're saying," Taylor said, "that sounds like we're at the end of the Weimar Republic!"

"It grieves me to think that," I said.

"Donald Trump brought to the surface what had been there all along, and now that it is out, there is no denying it. So it should be easier to defeat."

"I think what we're looking at is South Africa."

"They are more out front with their racism than here," he said.

"By that, I mean the demographics and the dynamics of their demographics."

"Yes," he said of the predictions for 2042. "People were angry when the projections came out. People said they wouldn't stand for being a minority in their own country."

"Now there are troops at the border," I said, "and shootings of black and brown and Jewish people."

Taylor nodded. He contemplated the meaning of that. "So the real question would be," he said finally, "if people were given the choice between democracy and whiteness, how many would choose whiteness?"

We let that settle in the air, neither of us willing to hazard a guess to that one.

CHAPTER TWENTY-NINE

The Price We Pay for a Caste System

L eon Lederman was an American physicist who won a Nobel Prize in 1988 for his groundbreaking contributions to our understanding of the particles of nature. Decades afterward, when he was in his early nineties, he began to suffer memory loss and to require additional care. In 2015, he took the extraordinary step of auctioning off his Nobel Prize medal for $765,000 to cover medical bills that were mounting. In 2018, he died in a nursing home, his Nobel Prize in the hands of someone else.

Compared to our counterparts in the developed world, America can be a harsh landscape, a less benevolent society than other wealthy nations. It is the price we pay for our caste system. In places with a different history and hierarchy, it is not necessarily seen as taking away from one's own prosperity if the system looks out for the needs of everyone.

People show a greater sense of joint responsibility to one another when they see their fellow citizens as like themselves, as in the nations of western Europe or in Australia, a diverse country with a looser hierarchy. Societies can be more magnanimous when people perceive themselves as having an equal stake in the lives of their fellow citizens.

There are thriving, prosperous nations where people do not have to sell their Nobel Prizes to get medical care, where families don't go broke taking care of elderly loved ones, where children exceed the educational achievements of American children, where drug addicts are in treatment rather than prison, where perhaps the greatest measure of human success—happiness and a long life—exists in greater measure because they value their shared commonality.

In a video that went viral at the end of 2019, British citizens are shown being asked to guess what they think routine medical procedures, covered by their own healthcare system, would cost in the United States. Time and again, the interviewees woefully underestimate the cost to Americans, some bellowing, gobsmacked, at the actual prices, some refusing to believe that anyone would have to pay that much for basic, necessary care.

"Ten grand?" one woman asks when told the average cost of childbirth. "For a baby? Mad!"

One man is asked how much he thinks it costs for an ambulance to take you to the hospital. "There's a price for that?" he asks. "Why?"

"I'm genuinely speechless," one woman says.

The majority of America's peer nations have some form of free or low-cost healthcare coverage. The writer Jonathan Chait noted America's singular indifference, unique among developed nations, toward helping all of its citizens. He connected this hardheartedness to the hierarchy that arose from slavery. He found that even conservatives in other wealthy nations are more compassionate than many Americans.

"Few industrialized economies provide as stingy aid to the poor as the United States," he observed in *New York* magazine in 2014. "In none of them is the principle of universal health insurance even contested by a major conservative party. Conservatives have long celebrated America's unique strand of anti-statism as the product of our religiosity, or the tradition of English liberty, or the searing experience of the tea tax. But the factor that stands above all the rest is slavery."

A caste system builds rivalry and distrust and lack of empathy toward one's fellows. The result is that the United States, for all its wealth and innovation, lags in major indicators of quality of life among the leading countries in the world.

There are more public mass shootings in America than in any other country, and the United States has one of the highest rates of gun deaths in the developed world, according to the World Health Organization. Americans own more guns per capita than any other nation. Americans own nearly half of the guns in the world owned by civilians.

The United States has the highest incarceration rate in the world, higher than that of Russia and China, with a rate of 655 per 100,000. The United States imprisons more people, 2.2 million, than any other nation. The incarceration rate in America is so high that the line representing the United States extends well off the page in graphics of the prison rates in the developed world. If the U.S. prison population were a city, it would be the fifth largest in America.

American women are more likely to die during pregnancy and childbirth than women in other wealthy nations. With fourteen deaths per 100,000 live births, the maternal mortality rate in America is nearly three times the rate in Sweden, according to the Commonwealth Fund. Part of this reflects the woeful maternal death rates for black and indigenous women in the United States.

Life expectancy in the United States is the lowest among the eleven highest-income countries (United Kingdom, Canada, Germany, Australia, Japan, Sweden, France, the Netherlands, Switzerland, and Denmark). The life expectancy in America is 78.6 years, as against a combined average of 82.3 years and against 84.2 for Japan, the country with the longest life expectancy, based on a 2019 analysis.

Infant mortality in the United States is highest among the richest nations, 5.8 deaths per 1,000 live births, as against a combined average of 3.6 per 1,000 live births for the richest countries, as against about 2 per 1,000 in Japan and Finland.

American students score near the bottom in industrialized nations in mathematics and reading. Fifteen-year-olds in the United

States scored well below students in peer nations on math literacy, below Latvia and the Slovak Republic, among the dozens of countries that exceed U.S. test scores. By the time that the first woman major-party candidate ran for president in 2016, some sixty other countries had already had a woman head of state, including India, Germany, Australia, and the United Kingdom, and smaller countries such as Iceland, Norway, Burundi, and Slovenia. And, in perhaps the most important measure of all for citizens anywhere, the United States ranked eighteenth in happiness in the world, just above the Czech Republic, according to the consortium of organizations, including Gallup, that publishes the results each year. The United States has fallen seven spots since 2012, a testimony to our continuing discontents.

———

In the winter of 2020, the one year in human history that would hold the promise of perfect insight, an invisible life-form awakened in the Eastern Hemisphere and began to spread across the oceans.

The earth's most powerful nation watched as faraway workers in hazmat gear tested for what no one could see, and deluded itself into believing that American exceptionalism would somehow grant it immunity from the sorrows of other countries.

Yet the virus arrived on these shores, and it planted itself in the gaps of disparity, the torn kinships and fraying infrastructure in the country's caste system, just as it exploited the weakened immune system in the human body.

Soon, America had the largest coronavirus outbreak in the world. Governors pleaded for basic supplies and test kits, were reduced to bidding against one another for ventilators. "As Usual," read a headline in *The Atlantic*, "Americans Must Go It Alone."

The virus exposed both the vulnerability of all humans and the layers of hierarchy. While anyone could contract the virus, it was Asian-Americans who were scapegoated for it merely because they looked like the people from the part of the world that the virus first struck.

And as the crisis wore on, it was African-Americans and Latino-Americans who began dying at higher rates. Preexisting conditions, often tied to the stresses on marginalized people, contributed to the divergence. But it was the caste-like occupations at the bottom of the hierarchy—grocery clerks, bus drivers, package deliverers, sanitation workers, low-paying jobs with high levels of public contact—that put them at greater risk of contracting the virus in the first place. These are among the mudsill jobs in a pandemic, the jobs less likely to guarantee health coverage or sick days but that sustain the rest of society, allowing others to shelter in place.

As the number of deaths climbed to the highest in the world, America—and those looking to it for leadership—had to come to terms with the untested fragilities of its social ecosystem.

"To a watching world," wrote *The Guardian*, "the absence of a fair, affordable US healthcare system, the cut-throat contest between American states for scarce medical supplies, the disproportionate death toll among ethnic minorities, chaotic social distancing rules, and a lack of centralised coordination are reminiscent of a poor, developing country, not the most powerful, influential nation on earth."

The pandemic, and the country's fitful, often self-centered lack of readiness, exposed "a failure of character unparalleled in US history," in the words of Stephen Walt, a professor of international relations at Harvard University. The pandemic forced the nation to open its eyes to what it might not have wanted to see but needed to see, while forcing humanity to contemplate its impotence against the laws of nature.

"This is a civilization searching for its humanity," Gary Michael Tartakov, an American scholar of caste, said of this country. "It dehumanized others to build its civilization. Now it needs to find its own."

Part Seven

AWAKENING

CHAPTER THIRTY

Shedding the Sacred Thread

Near the sacred waters of the alluvial plains, east of the Thar Desert, a man born to the highest caste in India had awakened slowly to a privileged despair. He had a position of rank in civil society and a high-born wife and family. He was a Brahmin, of the priestly caste, above even kings and warriors. He was the Indian equivalent of the bluest of blood in America. Unlike ordinary men, he was twice born—first, of his mother's womb and then of the temple during the rite of passage for boys of the upper castes. The Brahmin, the Kshatriya, and the Vaishya alone have historically been granted this singular elevation. It is one of the many things—perhaps the most prized, transcendent thing—that set upper-caste men apart from lower ones as the most favored by the gods.

Many years before, on the day that he, as a young Brahmin boy, went through his second birth, his head had been shaved, and he was bathed in a ritual cleansing. The Brahmin priest read from holy text and called upon the god Vishnu for his strength and protection. At the appointed hour, they slipped a sacred thread around his neck that fell over his bare shoulders and draped it across his chest, three interwoven threads representing the body, the mind, and the tongue with which to speak wisdom. This was his initiation into Brahmin manhood, and, henceforth, he was to wear the sacred thread at all times, under his clothing by day, to sleep in it by night, and to wash in it, as it remained one with his skin. He was to keep it clean and pure as a Brahmin was to remain clean and pure, and to replace it if it became frayed or polluted, if, for example, he were by chance touched by anyone of the lower castes. When he became old enough to shave, he would have to tuck it behind his ear, or hold it under his chin as he washed, to protect it. The sacred thread was an extension of his Brahmin body, the purest of all human bodies, and a signal to everyone of his high rank in the land. He was now permitted to take meals with the men in the family and village and learn his place among the men of high caste.

But on a Sunday thereafter, his father was out surveying his land. The father came across a farmworker on his land, but the farm worker did not bid the father the respect due a Brahmin lord in the father's eyes. The laborer was a Dalit, the lowest of the castes, one whose very shadow was polluting to the boy and his father's caste. The Dalits were trained to bend in fear at the sight of their superiors. Untold thousands of Dalits had lost their lives for offending the upper castes and were at their mercy.

The boy's father took a stick and charged after the Dalit laborer. The Dalit pulled the limb of a tree to protect himself from the father. Seeing this, the father gathered his senses and retreated from the Dalit and ran away from him. But a group of fellow Brahmins witnessed the father running, saw him permit an Untouchable to chase away his master. The father had not upheld his superiority over the Dalit. He had brought dishonor to his caste by allowing an inferior to prevail over him.

The caste system had a way of policing the behavior of everyone in its wake to keep everyone in their assigned places. Now he had brought shame and humiliation to himself, to his line, and to his caste in that one moment. Seeing no option to retain his honor, the father fled the village. His family searched and searched for him and finally found him chanting in a room surrounded by images of the gods.

"I lost my father that day," the Brahmin recalled many decades

later, "and I lost my childhood." Perhaps his father had been mentally unwell from the start. Perhaps the pressures to live out a role
that one was born to but did not choose for oneself, and to which
one's temperament was unsuited, had been too much for the father.

The Brahmin grew up and had a family of his own. He put his
father's humiliation behind him. But in the anonymity of the big
city, he began to see the hardships and inequities all around him,
the dust rising from the streets and into the thick air, the street
sweepers and the scavengers who he had been told accepted their
lot beneath him. But he knew from the Dalit who had stood up to
his father that they did not accept their lot, that they were not the
docile, lazy creatures of caste mythology.

The Brahmin came to know and to admire the few Dalits who
crossed his path in his work, who had pushed through the walls
of caste to become educated, professional. He came to realize that
they were as capable as he was, and, in fact, that because they had
to come so far, they knew things about the world that his privilege
had not required him to know. He saw that the caste system created a smooth path for some and broken-glass shoals for others,
that creativity and intellect were not restricted to one group alone.
These were the people whose very sight and touch was said to
be polluting, and yet here he was sitting across from them, sharing
and learning from them. He was the beneficiary of their gifts
rather than the other way around, and he came to see what had
been lost by one not getting to know the other for his lifetime and
all the lifetimes before his. He began to see himself differently, to
see the illusion of his presumed superiority, that he had been told
a lie, and that his father had been told a lie, and that trying to live
up to the lie had taken some part of his father away. For this, he
bore a heavy guilt and shame over the tragedy that had befallen
the family and a memory that would not leave him. He wanted to
be free of it.

He shared this realization with a Dalit he had come to know
and told him of a decision he had made. "I have ripped off my

sacred thread," he told the Dalit, a professional man. "It was a poisonous snake around my neck, and its toxic venom was getting inside of me."

For most of his life, he had worn the sacred thread as if it were strands of hair from his head. Removing it amounted to renouncing his high caste, and he considered the consequences, that his family might reject him if they knew. He would have to determine how to manage their knowing when the time came.

He was now born a third time, the shades lifted in a darkened room in his mind.

"It is a fake crown that we wear," he came to realize.

He wished every dominant-caste person could awaken to this fact. "My message would be to take off the fake crown. It will cost you more to keep it than to let it go. It is not real. It is just a marker of your programming. You will be happier and freer without it. You will see all of humanity. You will find your true self."

And so he had discovered. "There was a stench coming from my body," he said. "I have located the corpse inside my mind. I have given it a decent burial. And now my journey can begin."

The Radicalization of the Dominant Caste

We had sat down for dinner, a family friend and I, at a chic restaurant in a hip section of a major American city. I did not know her well, but I knew that she was an artsy free spirit, kindhearted, well traveled.

She was also from the dominant caste and had grown up in a neighborhood surrounded mainly by people like herself. As we sat catching up on each other's lives, lives that each of us had known only from afar, several waiters passed by, and it was unclear which one was ours.

Finally, a waiter stopped at our table. He was blond, curt, and matter-of-fact. I ordered fish, she ordered pasta. We both ordered drinks, an appetizer or two.

While we waited for the drinks to arrive, a couple from the dominant caste, same caste as her, sat down at the table next to us. Our waiter rushed over to take their order, now charming and effusive, filling them in on the specials, chatting them up. Seconds later, he brought a basket of bread to their table. He brought them their drinks shortly thereafter, while we sipped water and waited for ours.

The family friend was growing impatient, seething actually, and turned to see where he was. She was trying to process an unaccustomed disregard. The waiter rolled around to check on the people next to us yet again and to deliver drinks and bread to other tables down the row.

Trying to keep calm, she motioned for him to come over. "We haven't gotten our drinks yet," she said. "Can you bring us our drinks, please? And we'd like bread, too," she added, looking over at the couple who had arrived after us. They were now dipping theirs in olive oil, as we stared at an empty table.

He nodded and said sure, but stopped to check on several other tables on his way back to the kitchen, which delayed him further. He reappeared later with dishes on his tray, but these were now the appetizers for the couple at the next table.

The family friend motioned to him again. "Our drinks? And we never got the bread."

"Oh, right, sure," he said, turning back again.

It was now hard for her to concentrate on whatever it was she was saying. The people next to us were remarking on how good the appetizers were and had all but finished their bread. Their table was laden, and ours was empty, and she seemed exquisitely aware of the couple beside us, that they were passing us on the escalator of dining attention.

On one of his many rounds past our table, the waiter at

last brought the drinks but not the bread, and the exclusion was now impossible to ignore. Finally, he showed up with the entrées. The people next to us were on to their desserts, which were lovely apparently, from what they were saying. She stared at the pasta and jostled it with her fork, tasted it, and set the fork down.

"Pasta's cold. It's not even good. How's your fish?"

"It's okay. Not great. Mine's cold, too."

"I'm getting the waiter."

Her face was now approaching crimson. She fidgeted in her seat and looked around for him, shaking her head in disbelief. She was barely able to keep it together.

"Can you come here a second?" she called out to him as he passed again. "I know exactly what this is about. This is about racism!"

Her voice was rising, she was loud enough for the whole restaurant to hear.

"You're a racist! This restaurant is racist! We sat here all this time, and you served all these other people at all these other tables, and you ignored us this whole time just because she's African-American."

People at other tables were now looking over at me, when I had not wanted the attention. I had no interest in making a federal case out of this. If I responded like that every time I was slighted, I'd be telling someone off almost every day.

But she was just getting started. "I want your name, I want the manager's name. I will turn this place out."

She pushed the bowl of pasta to the center of the table. "The pasta's cold," she said. "I can't even eat it. Her fish is cold. She can't eat hers. I'm not paying, we're not paying. I'm telling everybody I know not to come here. This is crap."

With all of the ruckus, the manager came out to see what was going on. As it happened, the manager was a petite African-American woman, who seemed cowed by the ferocity of this newly minted anti-racist, anti-casteist, upper-caste woman, standing before her enraged at the unaccustomed humiliation. The manager apologized profusely, but my friend was having none of it.

She stormed out of the restaurant, and I walked out with her. It took a while for her to calm down.

Part of me wanted to say to her, "Imagine going through something like this almost every day, not knowing when or how it might happen. You wouldn't last very long. We can't afford to be blowing up every time we're slighted and ignored. We stand up when we need to, but we have to find a way not to go off every time and still get through the day."

Part of me resented that she could go ballistic and get away with it when I might not even be believed. It was caste privilege to go off in the restaurant the way she did. It was a measure of how differently we are treated that she could live for over forty years and not experience what is a daily possibility for any person born to the subordinate caste, that it was so alien to her, it so jangled her, that she blew up over it.

But part of me wished that every person in the dominant

caste who denies and deflects, minimizes and gaslights African-Americans and other marginalized people could experience what she did. She had been radicalized in a matter of minutes. She knew full well that this was not how people treated her when she was out with others in the dominant caste. She had come to the realization on her own.

And part of me, the biggest part of me, was happy to see her righteous indignation on my behalf, on her own behalf, and on behalf of all the people who endure these indignities every day. It would be a better world if everyone could feel what she felt for once, and awaken.

CHAPTER THIRTY-ONE

The Heart Is the Last Frontier

December 2016, One Month After the Election

He smelled of beer and tobacco. He was wearing a cap like the men at the rallies who wanted to make America great again, the people who had prevailed in the election the month before. His belly extended over his belt buckle. The years had carved lines into his face, and stubble was poking through his chin and cheeks. He let out a phlegmy cough.

I had called the plumbing company because I had discovered water in the basement, and he was the one they sent. He was standing at the threshold of my front door and seemed not to have expected someone who looked like me to answer. It's a predominantly white neighborhood, with joggers and cyclists and purposeful moms in yoga sweats pushing baby strollers, ponytails bouncing, maybe a labradoodle trotting behind. Landscapers' trucks and housekeeping crews squeeze past each other on every side street. I was used to that reaction.

"Is the lady of the house at home?" a leafleteer or survey-taker will ask me—the only lady in sight, standing right there in front of them. The assumption doesn't inspire me to indulge them. I could correct them if I wanted, and they might try to play it off, or I could just spare them the embarrassment.

"No, she's not here," I'll say. They never press me, never seem to suspect.

"Do you know when she'll be back?"

"No, no, I don't," I'll say. "Who shall I say is calling?" They will hand me a card or a flyer, and I will give it a glance as they go on their way.

So the plumber checked to see if this was, in fact, the right house, then walked in with a let's-get-this-over-with look on his face. "Where's the basement?"

I was reliant on this man and others like him, now that I was both widowed and motherless, having lost the two most important people in my life within a span of eighteen months. I was having to depend on contractors to fix things in this house, people who might resent me for being here and might or might not be inclined to help me or even to do their job. And now the air had shifted after the election.

He followed me into the basement and stood there as I moved boxes to make space for him to better inspect it. I moved my mother's portable wheelchair, the one she would not be needing anymore, and a lampshade, stacks of my late father's engineering books, and an old bucket, as the plumber watched, never reaching over to help. I began sweeping water toward the sump pump as he looked down at the wet floor.

I told him that there had been three or four inches of water, that the HVAC man had helped get the sump pump restarted to drain most of the water out, that this had never happened before.

"I hardly ever come into the basement," I told him. "We had that drought, so I didn't think about water in the basement. My husband was the one who came down here." He was the one who checked the filter on the furnace, checked the fuse box, patched things in his workshop, which was exactly as he had left it, the sawhorse and drill bits untouched from whenever he'd last come down to fix something before he died. He died last year, I told the plumber. The magnitude of that statement seemed not to register. The plumber just shrugged and said uh-huh.

I was sweeping the water with him standing there, and I was remembering what had happened in the last week. I had been trying to get as far away from the grief as I could over the holidays. I would have left the planet if that had been an option, but that was not yet possible, so I had planned the next best, most convenient recourse to detach from the gravity of loss, which was a ticket to Buenos Aires. I had never been to Buenos Aires, so there were no memories to surface there, nothing to make me think of having seen or done this or that with anyone I had lost. As I was preparing to go, the HVAC contractor arrived for the semiannual check of the furnace and discovered water in the basement. He was an immigrant from Central America, and, though it was not his job, he helped to drain it as best he could.

———

The plumber was now surveying the boxes and stepped around a few of them, knocking a lampshade and wreath to the wet floor and not reaching over to pick them up. I kept sweeping. It appeared as if there was nothing further for him to do, or at least I would say he wasn't doing anything.

He pointed to the sink. "That's where the water is coming in," he said, looking to wrap this up.

"But the sink's never overflowed before," I said. "It had to be more than that."

"How long's it been since the water came?"

"Maybe since the rains last week. There's a drain here somewhere. I wonder if it's clogged."

I started moving boxes and was feeling more alone with him just standing there. I lifted a heavy box, and he watched, made no gesture to help. He merely said, "You got that?"

I had moved enough boxes to see where I thought the drain would be and still didn't locate it. It seemed this should be part of the troubleshooting, but he showed no interest.

"Maybe it's the sump pump?" I asked.

He went to look at it. "Nothing wrong with the sump pump," he said.

I now noticed packing popcorn floating in it. "Could that have kept the sump pump from working?"

"No," he said, "but the sump pump needs clearing out, though."

Why was he not doing that? Wasn't that what he was here for?

Instead he offered to write an estimate for a new one. But why buy a new pump if this one was working? I had called him in to fix whatever caused the water to build up. Since he'd arrived, I was the one sweeping water, moving boxes, searching for the drain. He was doing less than the HVAC guy had done.

I was steaming now. All he was doing was standing there watching me sweep (as women who look like me have done for centuries) and not fixing anything. He had come up with no answers, shown no interest, and now it appeared I was going to have to pay him for doing nothing.

Since he wasn't helping, I felt I had nothing to lose. Something came over me, and I threw a Hail Mary at his humanity.

"My mother just died last week," I told him. "Is your mother still alive?"

He looked down at the wet floor. "No . . . no, she isn't."

Somehow I had sensed that already, which is why I brought it up.

"She died in 1991," he said. "She was fifty-two years old."

"That's not old at all," I said.

"No, she wasn't. My father's still alive, he's seventy-eight. He's in a home south of here. My sister lives nearby to him."

"You're lucky to still have your father," I said.

"Well, he's mean as they come."

I contemplated the significance of that. What might his father have exposed him to when it comes to people who look like me? But I kept it to the present.

"You miss them when they're gone no matter what they were like," I said.

"How about your mother?" he wanted to know. "How old was she?"

"She was way older than yours, so I can't complain about that. But she was sick a long time. And you never get over it."

"I have an aunt in her eighties who still smokes and will ask you for a taste of beer," he said and let slip a laugh. "She's on my daddy's side."

I smiled and tried to look at the positive. "So your father's side is long-lived," I said.

"Yeah. I guess they are."

His face brightened, and he went over to the sump pump, bent down, and reached into it. A minute or two later, he stood up.

"Okay, sump pump's cleared out."

He turned to the area where the drain was likely to be.

"It's probably under this coffee table," he said. "If you get one end, we can move it and see where it is."

Together, we moved the table and, sure enough, there was the drain.

"Drain's not clogged, so that's not the problem," he said. "Lemme go get my flashlight out of the truck."

Once back, he trained the flashlight along the floor, inspecting the perimeter of the basement, past the sink and the washer and dryer hemmed in with boxes, past the sawhorse, along the base of the furnace, every corner up and down.

"I found it!" he said, jubilant.

I ran over to him. "What was it?"

"It's the water heater. Water heater's gone bad."

He shone the flashlight onto the top of the heater, onto the corroded pipes and the steam rising from the gaps. Water had been escaping from the broken heater and had risen into a low flood on the basement floor, which explained why the floodwater was clear and why my water bill was high.

I stepped back in relief. "I knew it had to be more than the rain."

"You'll need a new water heater. This one's gone."

How different things had been just minutes before. "My mother must've been talking to your mother," I said, "and telling her to get her boy to help her girl down there. 'My daughter needs your son's help.'"

We smiled at the thought of that. He shut off the water to the heater, which meant no more hot water in the house for now, but, more important, no more water escaping to the basement floor. He gave me the estimate for the replacement heater and charged me sixty-nine dollars for the visit, which I thought was fair. We wished each other a happy holiday, and he left.

The phone rang. It happened to be Bunny Fisher, whose father, Dr. Robert Pershing Foster, I had written about in *The Warmth of Other Suns*. She was calling to check on me, having kept in close touch over the years and even more so with my recent losses. I told her about the encounter with the plumber and the minor miracle that had happened, as we began to catch up.

Just then, the doorbell rang, the call cut short. It was the plumber again. He said he had driven back to shut off the gas to the water heater so it wouldn't be heating an empty tank. He knew his way around now, made his way to the basement, was lighthearted and chatty, momentarily family.

"This thing could have been much worse," he said. "Water could have burst from the top, destroyed everything, and scalded you or anybody else who tried to fix it. I've seen way worse."

As he headed back up the basement steps, he caught a glimpse of some old Polaroid photographs that I had salvaged from the wet boxes and had pulled aside to air out.

He paused in the middle of the staircase. "Oh, you want those," he said. "That's memories right there." Then he bounded out of the old house and into the light of the day.

A World Without Caste

We look to the night sky and see the planets and stars, the distant lights as specks of salt, single grains of sand, and are reminded of how small we are, how insignificant our worries of the moment, how brief our time on this planet, and we wish to be part of something bigger than ourselves, to magnify our significance, to matter somehow as more than the dust that we are.

Even the longest lived of our species spends but a blink of time in the span of human history. How dare anyone cause harm to another soul, curtail their life or life's potential, when our lives are so short to begin with?

The species has suffered incomprehensible loss over the false divisions of caste: the 11 million people killed by the Nazis; the three-quarters of a million Americans killed in the Civil War over the right to enslave human beings; the slow, living death and unfulfilled gifts of millions more on the plantations in India and in the American South.

Whatever creativity or brilliance they had has been lost for all time. Where would we be as a species had the millions of targets of these caste systems been permitted to live out their dreams or live at all? Where would the planet be had the putative beneficiaries been freed of the illusions that imprisoned them, too, had they directed their energies toward solutions for all of humanity, cures for cancer and hunger and the existential threat of climate change, rather than division?

————

In December 1932, one of the smartest men who ever lived landed in America on a steamship with his wife and their thirty pieces of luggage as the Nazis bore down on their homeland of Germany. Albert Einstein, the physicist and Nobel laureate, had managed to escape the Nazis just in time. The month after Einstein left, Hitler was appointed chancellor.

In America, Einstein was astonished to discover that he had landed in yet another caste system, one with a different scapegoat caste and different methods, but with embedded hatreds that were not so unlike the one he had just fled.

"The worst disease is the treatment of the Negro," he wrote in 1946. "Everyone who freshly learns of this state of affairs at a maturer age feels not only the injustice, but the scorn of the principle of the Fathers who founded the United States that 'all men are created equal.'"

He could "hardly believe that a reasonable man can cling so tenaciously to such prejudice," he said.

He and his wife, Elsa, settled in Princeton, New Jersey, where he took a professorship at the university and observed firsthand the oppression faced by black residents who were consigned to the worst parts of town, to segregated movie houses, to servant positions, and were, in the words of his friend Paul Robeson, forced into "bowing and scraping to the drunken rich."

A few years into his tenure, the opera singer Marian Anderson, a renowned contralto born to the subordinated caste, performed to an overflow crowd at McCarter Theatre in Princeton and to rapturous praise in the press of her "complete mastery of a magnificent voice." But the Nassau Inn in Princeton refused to rent a room to her for the night. Einstein, learning of this, invited her to stay in his home. From then on, she would stay at the Einstein residence whenever she was in town, even after Princeton hotels began accepting African-American guests. They would remain friends until his death.

"Being a Jew myself, perhaps I can understand and empathize with how black people feel as victims of discrimination," he told a family friend.

He grew uncomfortable with the American way of pressuring newcomers to look down on the lowest caste in order to gain acceptance. Here was one of the most brilliant men who ever lived refusing to see himself as superior to people he was being told were beneath him.

"The more I feel an American, the more this situation pains me," Einstein wrote. "I can escape the feelings of complicity in it only by speaking out."

And so he did. He co-chaired a committee to end lynching. He joined the NAACP. He spoke out on behalf of civil rights activists, lent his fame to their cause. At a certain point in his life, he rarely accepted the many honors that came his way, but in 1946 he made an exception for Lincoln University, a historically black college in Pennsylvania. He agreed to deliver the commencement address and to accept an honorary degree there.

On that visit, he taught his theory of relativity to physics students and played with the children of black faculty, among them the son of the university president, a young Julian Bond, who would go on to become a civil rights leader.

"The separation of the races is not a disease of the colored people," Einstein told the graduates at commencement, "but a disease of the white people. I do not intend to be quiet about it."

He became a passionate ally of the people consigned to the bottom. "He hates race prejudice," W.E.B. Du Bois wrote, "because as a Jew he knows what it is."

————

The tyranny of caste is that we are judged on the very things we cannot change: a chemical in the epidermis, the shape of one's facial features, the signposts on our bodies of gender and ancestry—

superficial differences that have nothing to do with who we are inside.

The caste system in America is four hundred years old and will not be dismantled by a single law or any one person, no matter how powerful. We have seen in the years since the civil rights era that laws, like the Voting Rights Act of 1965, can be weakened if there is not the collective will to maintain them.

A caste system persists in part because we, each and every one of us, allow it to exist—in large and small ways, in our everyday actions, in how we elevate or demean, embrace or exclude, on the basis of the meaning attached to people's physical traits. If enough people buy into the lie of natural hierarchy, then it becomes the truth or is assumed to be.

Once awakened, we then have a choice. We can be born to the dominant caste but choose not to dominate. We can be born to a subordinated caste but resist the box others force upon us. And all of us can sharpen our powers of discernment to see past the external and to value the character of a person rather than demean those who are already marginalized or worship those born to false pedestals. We need not bristle when those deemed subordinate break free, but rejoice that here may be one more human being who can add their true strengths to humanity.

The goal of this work has not been to resolve all of the problems of a millennia-old phenomenon, but to cast a light onto its history, its consequences, and its presence in our everyday lives and to express hopes for its resolution. A housing inspector does not make the repairs on the building he has examined. It is for the owners, meaning each of us, to correct the ruptures we have inherited.

The fact is that the bottom caste, though it bears much of the burden of the hierarchy, did not create the caste system, and the bottom caste alone cannot fix it. The challenge has long been that many in the dominant caste, who are in a better position to fix caste inequity, have often been least likely to want to.

Caste is a disease, and none of us is immune. It is as if alcoholism is encoded into the country's DNA, and can never be declared fully cured. It is like a cancer that goes into remission only to return when the immune system of the body politic is weakened.

Thus, regardless of who prevails in any given election, the country still labors under the divisions that a caste system creates, and the fears and resentments of a dominant caste that is too often in opposition to the yearnings of those deemed beneath them. It is a danger to the species and to the planet to have this depth of unexamined grievance and discontent in the most powerful nation in the world. A single election will not solve the problems that we face if we haven't dealt with the structure that created the imbalance to begin with.

As it stands, the United States is facing a crisis of identity unlike any before. The country is headed toward an inversion of its demographics, with its powerful white majority expected to be outnumbered by people not of European descent within two decades. This is unknown territory for everyone in the hierarchy, an ethnic distribution that could potentially look closer to that of South Africa than to what Americans have grown accustomed to.

Anticipatory fear seems already to have surfaced, but if history is any guide, a change in demographics might have less of a material effect on the dominant caste than imagined. A 2016 study found that, if disparities in wealth were to continue at the current pace, it would take black families 228 years to amass the wealth that white families now have, and Latino families another 84 years to reach parity.

Thus, as in South Africa, there would be no reason to believe that economic, social, and, in America, political dominance would not still remain in the hands of those who have held it for the entirety of the country's history.

This will be a test of the cherished ideal of majority rule, the moral framework for caste dominance in America since its founding. White dominance has already been assured by the inherited advantages of the dominant caste in most every sphere of life, and in the securing of dominant caste interests in most aspects of governing—from gerrymandered congressional districts to voter suppression to the rightward direction of the judicial branch to the Electoral College, which favors the dominant caste, whatever the numbers.

Will the United States adhere to its belief in majority rule if the majority does not look as it has throughout history? This will be the chance for America either to further entrench its inequalities or to choose to lead the world as the exceptional nation that we have proclaimed ourselves to be.

Without an enlightened recognition of the price we all pay for a caste system, the hierarchy will likely shape-shift as it has in the past to ensure that the structure remains intact. The definition of whiteness could well expand to confer honorary whiteness to those on the border—the lightest-skinned people of Asian or Latino descent or biracial people with a white parent, for instance—to increase the ranks of the dominant caste.

The devastating truth is that, without the intervention of humanitarian impulses, a reconstituted caste system could divide those at the bottom and those in the middle, pick off those closest to white and thus isolate the darkest Americans even further, lock them ever more tightly to the bottom rung.

It would be a crisis of spirit, a defeat of the American soul, because the toxins upstream eventually make their way downstream, as has occurred with the addiction crisis in America. It turns out that everyone benefits when society meets the needs of the disadvantaged. The sacrifices of the subordinate caste during the civil rights era, for instance, benefited women of all ethnicities—the wives, daughters, sisters, and nieces of every American man— women who now have legal protections against job discrimination that they did not have before the 1960s.

Many of the advancements that Americans enjoy and that are under assault in our current day—birthright citizenship, equal protection under the law, the right to vote, laws against discrimination on the basis of gender, race, national origin—are all the by-products of the subordinate caste's fight for justice in this country and ended up helping others as much as if not more than themselves.

———

To imagine an end to caste in America, we need only look at the history of Germany. It is living proof that if a caste system—the twelve-year reign of the Nazis—can be created, it can be dismantled. We make a serious error when we fail to see the overlap between our country and others, the common vulnerability in human programming, what the political theorist Hannah Arendt called "the banality of evil."

"It's all too easy to imagine that the Third Reich was a bizarre aberration," wrote the philosopher David Livingstone Smith, who has studied cultures of dehumanization. "It's tempting to imagine that the Germans were (or are) a uniquely cruel and bloodthirsty people. But these diagnoses are dangerously wrong. What's most disturbing about the Nazi phenomenon is not that the Nazis were madmen or monsters. It's that they were ordinary human beings."

It is also tempting to vilify a single despot at the sight of injustice when, in fact, it is the actions, or more commonly inactions, of ordinary people that keep the mechanism of caste running, the people who shrug their shoulders at the latest police killing, the people who laugh off the coded put-downs of marginalized people shared at the dinner table and say nothing for fear of alienating an otherwise beloved uncle. The people who are willing to pay higher property taxes for their own children's schools but who balk at taxes to educate the children society devalues. Or the people who sit in silence as a marginalized person, whether of color or a woman, is interrupted in a meeting, her ideas dismissed (though perhaps later adopted), for fear of losing caste, each of these keeping intact the whole system that holds everyone in its grip.

"Caste is not a physical object like a wall of bricks or a line of barbed wire," the Dalit leader Bhimrao Ambedkar wrote. "Caste is a notion; it is a state of the mind."

No one escapes its tentacles. No one escapes exposure to its message that one set of people is presumed to be inherently smarter, more capable, and more deserving than other groups deemed lower. This program has been installed into the subconscious of every one of us. And, high or low, without intervention or reprogramming, we act out the script we were handed.

And yet, somehow, there are the rare people, like Einstein, who seem immune to the toxins of caste in the air we breathe, who manage to transcend what most people are susceptible to. From the abolitionists who risked personal ruin to end slavery to the white civil rights workers who gave their lives to help end Jim Crow and the political leaders who outlawed it, these all-too-rare people are a testament to the human spirit, that humans can break free of the hierarchy's hold on them.

These are people of personal courage and conviction, secure within themselves, willing to break convention, not reliant on the approval of others for their sense of self, people of deep and abiding empathy and compassion. They are what many of us might wish to be but not nearly enough of us are. Perhaps, once awakened, more of us will be.

Americans pay a steep price for a caste system that runs counter to the country's stated ideals. Before 1965, the year of the Voting Rights Act, the United States was neither a democracy nor a meritocracy, because the majority of its population was excluded from competition in most aspects of American life. People who happened to be born male and of European ancestry competed only against themselves. For most of American history, the country was closed off from the talents of the bulk of its people of all colors, genders, and nationalities.

Anyone who truly believes in a meritocracy would not want to be in a caste system in which certain groups of people are excluded or disqualified by long-standing deprivations. A win is not legitimate if whole sections of humanity are not in the game. Those are victories with an asterisk, as if you were to win the gold medal in hockey the year that the Finns and Canadians were not competing. The full embrace of all humanity lifts the standards of any human endeavor.

Our era calls for a public accounting of what caste has cost us, a Truth and Reconciliation Commission, so that every American can know the full history of our country, wrenching though it may be. The persistence of caste and race hostility, and the defensiveness about anti-black sentiment in particular, make it literally unspeakable to many in the dominant caste. You cannot solve anything that you do not admit exists, which could be why some people may not want to talk about it: it might get solved.

"We must make every effort [to ensure] that the past injustice, violence and economic discrimination will be made known to the people," Einstein said in an address to the National Urban League. "The taboo, the 'let's-not-talk-about-it' must be broken. It must be pointed out time and again that the exclusion of a large part of the colored population from active civil rights by the common practices is a slap in the face of the Constitution of the nation."

The challenge for our era is not merely the social construct of black and white but seeing through the many layers of a caste system that has more power than we as humans should permit it to have. Even the most privileged of humans in the Western world will join a tragically disfavored caste if they live long enough. They will belong to the last caste of the human cycle, that of old age, people who are among the most demeaned of all citizens in the Western world, where youth is worshipped to forestall thoughts of death. A caste system spares no one.

———

When an accident of birth aligns with what is most valued in a given caste system, whether being able-bodied, male, white, or other traits in which we had no say, it gives that lottery winner a moral duty to develop empathy for those who must endure the indignities they themselves have been spared. It calls for a radical kind of empathy.

Empathy is not sympathy. Sympathy is looking across at someone and feeling sorrow, often in times of loss. Empathy is not pity. Pity is looking down from above and feeling a distant sadness for another in their misfortune. Empathy is commonly viewed as putting yourself in someone else's shoes and imagining how you would feel. That could be seen as a start, but that is little more than role-playing, and it is not enough in the ruptured world we live in.

Radical empathy, on the other hand, means putting in the work to educate oneself and to listen with a humble heart to understand another's experience from their perspective, not as we imagine we would feel. Radical empathy is not about you and what you think you would do in a situation you have never been in and perhaps never will. It is the kindred connection from a place of deep knowing that opens your spirit to the pain of another as they perceive it.

Empathy is no substitute for experience itself. We don't get to tell a person with a broken leg or a bullet wound that they are or are not in pain. And people who have hit the caste lottery are not in a position to tell a person who has suffered under the tyranny of caste what is offensive or hurtful or demeaning to those at the bottom. The price of privilege is the moral duty to act when one sees another person treated unfairly. And the least that a person in the dominant caste can do is not make the pain any worse.

If each of us could truly see and connect with the humanity of the person in front of us, search for that key that opens the door to whatever we may have in common, whether cosplay or *Star Trek* or the loss of a parent, it could begin to affect how we see the world and others in it, perhaps change the way we hire or even vote. Each time a person reaches across caste and makes a connection, it helps to break the back of caste. Multiplied by millions in a given day, it becomes the flap of a butterfly wing that shifts the air and builds to a hurricane across an ocean.

With our current ruptures, it is not enough to not be racist or sexist. Our times call for being pro-African-American, pro-woman, pro-Latino, pro-Asian, pro-indigenous, pro-humanity in all its manifestations. In our era, it is not enough to be tolerant. You tolerate mosquitoes in the summer, a rattle in an engine, the gray slush that collects at the crosswalk in winter. You tolerate what you would rather not have to deal with and wish would go away. It is no honor to be tolerated. Every spiritual tradition says love your neighbor as yourself, not tolerate them.

———

As each of us came into consciousness, we learned, based on the random outward manifestation of the combinations of genes that collided at the precise moment of our conception, that because of what we look like, the world had already assigned a place for us.

It was up to each of us to accept or challenge the role we were cast into, to determine for ourselves and to make the world see that what is inside of us—our beliefs and dreams, how we love and express that love, the things that we can actually control—is more important than the outward traits we had no say in. That we are not what we look like but what we do with what we have, what we make of what we are given, how we treat others and our planet.

Human beings across time and continents are more alike than they are different. The central question about human behavior is not why do those people do this or act in that way, now or in ages past, but what is it that human beings do when faced with a given circumstance?

None of us chose the circumstances of our birth. We had nothing to do with having been born into privilege or under stigma. We have everything to do with what we do with our God-given talents and how we treat others in our species from this day forward.

We are not personally responsible for what people who look like us did centuries ago. But we are responsible for what good or ill we do to people alive with us today. We are, each of us, responsible for every decision we make that hurts or harms another human being. We are responsible for recognizing that what happened in previous generations at the hands of or to people who look like us set the stage for the world we now live in and that what has gone before us grants us advantages or burdens through no effort or fault of our own, gains or deficits that others who do not look like us often do not share.

We are responsible for our own ignorance or, with time and openhearted enlightenment, our own wisdom. We are responsible for ourselves and our own deeds or misdeeds in our time and in our own space and will be judged accordingly by succeeding generations.

———

In a world without caste, instead of a false swagger over our own tribe or family or ascribed community, we would look upon all of humanity with wonderment: the lithe beauty of an Ethiopian runner, the bravery of a Swedish girl determined to save the planet, the physics-defying aerobatics of an African-American Olympian, the brilliance of a composer of Puerto Rican descent who can rap the history of the founding of America at 144 words a minute—all of these feats should fill us with astonishment at what the species is capable of and gratitude to be alive for this.

In a world without caste, being male or female, light or dark, immigrant or native-born, would have no bearing on what anyone was perceived as being capable of. In a world without caste, we would all be invested in the well-being of others in our species if only for our own survival, and recognize that we are in need of one another more than we have been led to believe. We would join forces with indigenous people around the world raising the alarm as fires rage and glaciers melt. We would see that, when others suffer, the collective human body is set back from the progression of our species.

A world without caste would set everyone free.

ACKNOWLEDGMENTS

This is a book that I did not seek to write but had to write, in the era in which we find ourselves. As I embarked upon it, I was blessed to work with two legends in publishing—my editor, Kate Medina, and my agent, Binky Urban, who embraced the idea from the start and who gave me the space to follow the threads where they led me.

The first place I went, or rather felt compelled to go, was Germany—Berlin, specifically—to try to comprehend a caste system that had arisen in a terrifying space of time, in a country that has been wrestling with atonement ever since. I am grateful to Krista Tippett for introducing me to a lovely group of people in Berlin that I otherwise would never have met. My thanks to Irene Dunkley and to Nathan and Ulrich Koestlin for their kindnesses and most especially to Nigel Dunkley, who recognized my mission from the start and shepherded me through the trail of Reich history with keen insight.

For the opportunity to experience India firsthand, I am indebted to professors Ramnarayan Rawat and K. Satyanarayana, who opened the door as I planned my first trip to Delhi, who made a way for me to meet other scholars of caste, and who extended to me every courtesy. There I had the chance to talk with Dalits who had labored against the obstacles in their paths and with whom I felt an immediate kinship, along with people from a range of other castes. Among the people whose perspectives I found especially helpful were Anupama Prasad and Sharika Thiranagama, who were completing research into caste inequities.

Unbeknownst to me, word spread that I had flown to India on this mission of caste. I was soon asked to speak at an international caste conference at the University of Massachusetts Amherst, alongside Indian political theorist Gopal Guru and Indian philosopher Meena Dhanda. I was overwhelmed to later be asked to deliver the conference's closing remarks.

There, faced with translating the Jim Crow caste system for an audience focused on India, I began to draft the earliest outlines of what would become the pillars of caste. I am ever grateful to Sangeeta Kamat, Biju Mathew, and other conference leaders who embraced me and invited me into their fold and to the many other kindred spirits I met there, including Suraj Yengde, Jaspreet Mahal, Balmurli Natrajan, and also Gary Tartakov, who immediately understood the humanitarian goals of my work and encouraged me onward.

During this quest, I came to know two survivors of the Indian caste system then living in London. Tushar Sarkar gave hours of his time to describe his experiences growing up in India and his disillusionment with caste. Sushrut Jadhav shared with me the parallel burdens, blessings, and exhaustions of living a life in defiance of caste, along with his insights as a psychiatrist and anthropologist. At his home, I had stimulating conversations with his family and with the author Arundhati Roy about the absurdity of caste.

Because this project interweaves the perspectives and insights of multiple disciplines—anthropology, sociology, psychology, political science, philosophy, and history—I am indebted to entire bodies of scholarship and to those who have contributed to an archive I sought to learn from and perhaps to build upon. I am grateful for the work of historians of enslavement, particularly Edward Baptist, Daina Ramey Berry, and Stephanie Jones-Rogers, and, in the history of race-based medical experimentation, the groundbreaking work of Harriet Washington. While this book is pointedly not about racism in itself, any book that touches on the subject owes a debt to the scholarship of Ibram X. Kendi and to the mission of Bryan Stevenson, whose memorial to lynching victims sets the standard for reconciling history.

For taking a sledgehammer to the false god of race, I am grateful to the late anthropologists Ashley Montagu and Audrey Smedley and, in the current day, am appreciative of Ian Haney López for his legal genealogy of race in America. For uncovering the parallels between Jim Crow America and aspects of the Third Reich, I am indebted to the definitive research of James Q. Whitman of Yale University. His work decisively connects the history of Nazi Germany to that of the United States and illuminated what I had had reason to believe from the start. I am appreciative of the discerning analyses of philosopher Susan Neiman of the Einstein Forum in Berlin, whose book *Learning from the Germans* was published just as I completed my manuscript. Discovering their work as I neared the end of my research affirmed the course that I had taken.

Early on, I discovered scholarly mentors from the past, people who had walked this road and whose words I turned to time and again for reassurance and insight. These ancestors in the scholarship of caste include John Dollard, Hortense Powdermaker, Lloyd Warner, Burleigh Gardner, and Gerald Berreman, in particular. Berreman studied and lived in both India and the Jim Crow South and was in a singular position to compare the two caste systems. He recognized the parallels and stood up to the skeptics with the quiet conviction that comes from deep research and firsthand experience.

Beyond these, I consider the late anthropologist Allison Davis to be a spiritual father in the quest to understanding the role of caste in America. The caste system forced him and his wife and scholarly partner, Elizabeth, to live what they studied, and they risked their lives to train a searchlight on the evils of caste. I am happy to honor and acknowledge David A. Varel's fine biography, *The Lost Black Scholar: Resurrecting Allison Davis in American Social Thought*, which thoroughly and eloquently recounts the Davises' groundbreaking work.

Seventy years after the Davises completed their fieldwork in

Mississippi, I happened to be attending a gala at the New York Public Library. There, that night, I first mentioned to my editor and my agent that I planned to write this book. Minutes later, I was mingling among the thousand or so guests packed together in tuxedoes and sequins, and found myself standing near a man I had never met but who had been a fan of *The Warmth of Other Suns*. He told a bit of his background and his name, Gordon Davis. I realized, from what I knew of the late anthropologist's life, that the man I was talking to was all but certainly the son of Allison Davis. I asked if that, in fact, was true. A prominent attorney in his own right, he was heartened that I knew of his father and had held him in such deep admiration. Coming just minutes after committing to this project, I took this to be a sign that I was meant to write this book.

I have been deeply grateful to the many people whose paths I crossed who, knowing of my first book, shared unbidden their encounters with caste as they, too, tried to make sense of it. There were serendipitous moments, like running into former New Orleans mayor Mitch Landrieu just as I was contemplating the role of Confederate symbols. Over the years, I have been continually inspired by my ongoing conversations with historian and dear friend Taylor Branch, whose work and perspective often intersect with mine. I am also ever grateful to Sharon Malone and Eric Holder for the grace and thoughtfulness they have shown me.

The nature and timetable for a book under production in an era of global pandemic required collaboration and commitment on an epic level. Working remotely in a time of uncertainty, the following people at Penguin Random House, in addition to my editor, Kate Medina, made this book possible: Gina Centrello, whose support I have treasured, and publisher Andy Ward and deputy publisher Avideh Bashirrad. In copy editing, managing editorial, and production: Benjamin Dreyer, Rebecca Berlant, and Richard Elman. In the departments of art and design, overseen by Paolo Pepe, I had the pleasure of working with Greg Mollica, who could not have found a better photograph for the cover, who designed the brilliant jacket and wholeheartedly obliged my suggestions, as did Virginia Norey in designing the book's sublime interior. I am grateful for the support and enthusiasm of the publicity department—Maria Braeckel, Susan Corcoran, London King, and Gwyneth Stansfield; and of the marketing department—Barbara Fillon, Leigh Marchant, and Ayelet Gruenspecht. Noa Shapiro deftly kept me and everyone else in touch and moved the process along.

Given all that this book required, I cannot imagine completing it without the calm and steady stewardship of production editor Steve Messina. His deep commitment, attention to detail, and patience oversaw the conversion of an evolving manuscript into galleys and then into a book that you can now hold in your hands. My sincerest gratitude to him.

Special thanks also to Sarah Cook, acting dean of the Honors College at Georgia State University, who, at a critical moment, made available to me three of her brightest students—Noah Britton, Clay Voytek, and Savannah Rogers. In the final weeks and months of my completing the manuscript, they spent time and energy researching last-minute questions and leads. Noah and Clay further dedicated themselves to additional weeks of fastidious fact-checking and, by the time the work was done, had taken up the cause of the book as their own.

I would like to thank every reader of *The Warmth of Other Suns* and all of those who have written letters to me since its publication. Your support enabled the travel and work required for this book, and, while I sincerely regret that circumstances have often not permitted me to reply directly, please know that each and every letter is precious to me and each has sustained and brought joy to me as I continue this work.

Due to the toll that research of this kind takes, I cannot imagine getting through the process without the encouragement of J. Blair Page and of Bunny Fisher, who showed unflagging commitment to this book and to my well-being and who listened separately to drafts or to sections of it, rendering compassionate feedback. I am grateful to the extraordinary Miss Hale not only for sharing her story for this book but also for sharing her unmatched culinary masterpieces, her grace and wisdom, and, above all, her five beautiful children, who spark delight every time I am in their presence. My thanks to Stephanie Hooks for her ever-present optimism and for introducing me to their world.

For the compassion they have shown, I am thankful for D. M. Page and for Todd, Marcia, Leslie, Maureen, Christine, Brenda, and Dahleen; for Margie S., Michelle T., Rosie T., Rebecca, and Michael for their love and support at a time of personal challenge and loss; and, for dear Ansley and Rafe, for the eye-rolling, sidesplitting joy, wit, and laughter they bring. Thanks to the rest of the Hamilton family, and as always to Gwen and Phil Whitt, to the Taylor family, and to my extended family in Virginia.

I could not have gotten through the deepest chambers of this work without the backdrop of seemingly unrelated music that brought either the focus or the uplift I needed at various points of the writing. The nature of the task drew me for some reason to music from before September 11, 2001, and I found myself turning to: Philip Glass (specifically String Quartet no. 5), Parliament ("Flash Light"), America ("A Horse with No Name"), Prince ("7"), the Police, Thelonious Monk and T. S. Monk, and the soundtrack to the classic French thriller *Diva*. Aside from its gorgeous range of music, *Diva* is one of the few big-screen portrayals of a woman of my archetype depicted in ways that some other women can take for granted, presented as refined and pivotal rather than as subordinated stereotype or sidekick. Although there have been notable exceptions in recent years, this is a film where I need not dread the woman getting whipped, mocked, hypersexualized, killed off, cast as a servant, or portrayed by a man, a common practice in an industry that long denied black women the chance to portray themselves as they truly are. *Diva* was the kind of film that perhaps could only be imagined outside of the American caste system.

I received my first lessons in caste from my parents, who never used that word but who came into the world during what the historian Rayford Logan called the Nadir. They grew up under the ever-present threat of the southern regime, found a way to survive Jim Crow and even to flourish despite the obstacles their own country placed in their path. They prayed that their daughter might somehow escape the arrows of caste that they had endured and, although, in our country, that was not to be—it was not, nor is it still, far enough along for that dream of theirs to come true— I am ever grateful for their guiding light, their faith and fortitude, and the highest of standards they set for me and that they themselves lived. In every word I write, I can only hope to bring honor to their sacrifices.

Finally, I am grateful beyond language for the love and devotion of Brett Hamilton, the kindest and most giving husband I could have wished for, a gift from the universe. Many of the observations in this book first found a voice in our deeply fulfilling conversations and in our life together. While it breaks my heart that neither he nor my parents lived to see this culmination of what we, each in our own ways, sought to transcend, I feel his cosmic embrace as I send this out to the world, and I know that all three of them are with me now and always.

Isabel Wilkerson
April 2020

NOTES

Epigraphs

page nos.

ix **"Because even if I should speak"**: Baldwin, *Fire Next Time,* pp. 53, 54.

ix **"If the majority knew of the root"**: Albert Einstein, message to the National Urban League, September 16, 1946. Cited by Jerome and Taylor in *Einstein on Race and Racism,* p. 146. The National Urban League is a civil rights organization that was founded in 1911 and is devoted to the social and economic well-being of African-Americans.

The Man in the Crowd

xvi *recently enacted Nuremberg Laws:* Wayne Morrison, *Criminology, Civilisation and the New World Order* (New York: Routledge, Cavendish, 2006), p. 80.

Part One: Toxins in the Permafrost and Heat Rising All Around

Chapter One: The Afterlife of Pathogens

3 **It was the pathogen anthrax:** Alexey Eremenko, "Heat Wave Sparks Anthrax Outbreak in Russia's Yamalo-Nenets Area," NBC News, July 27, 2016, https://www.nbcnews.com/news/world/heat-wave-sparks-anthrax-outbreak-russia-s-yamalo-nenets-area-n617716; "First Anthrax Outbreak Since 1941: 9 Hospitalised, with Two Feared to Have Disease," *Siberian Times,* July 26, 2016, http://siberiantimes

.com / other / others / news / n0686-first-anthrax-outbreak-since-1941-9
-hospitalised-with-two-feared-to-have-disease /.

5 **He would boast of grabbing women:** Jessica Taylor, "'You Can Do
Anything': In 2005 Tape, Trump Brags About Groping, Kissing
Women," National Public Radio, October 7, 2016. The story was preceded by an editor's note: "This post contains language that is crude
and explicit and that many will find offensive." Tim Hains, "Parental
Advisory for Trump's Angry Tweet Today," *Real Clear Politics,* October 2, 2019, https:/ / www.realclearpolitics.com / video / 2019 / 10 / 02
/ jake_tapper_issues_parental_advisory_on_cnn_im_going_to_be
_quoting_the_president.html. Also Al Tompkins, "As Profanity Laced
Video Leaks, Outlets Grapple with Trump's Language," *Poynter,* October 7, 2016, https:/ / www.poynter.org / reporting-editing / 2016 / as
-profanity-laced-video-leaks-outlets-grapple-with-trumps
-language /.

5 **"so transparently unqualified":** Hari Kunzru, "*Hillbilly Elegy* by J. D.
Vance Review—Does This Memoir Really Explain Trump's Victory?"
Guardian, December 7, 2016, https:/ / www.theguardian.com / books
/ 2016 / dec / 07 / hillbilly-elegy-by-jd-vance-review.

5 **Only weeks before, the billionaire:** During a campaign rally in Sioux
Center, Iowa, on January 23, 2016, Trump said, "They say I have the
most loyal people—did you ever see that? Where I could stand in the
middle of 5th Avenue and shoot somebody, and I wouldn't lose any
voters. . . . It's like incredible." Katie Reilly, "Donald Trump Says
He 'Could Shoot Somebody' and Not Lose Voters," *Time,* January 23,
2016, https:/ / time.com / 4191598 / donald-trump-says-he-could-shoot
-somebody-and-not-lose-voters /.

6 **by 2042, for the first time:** Conor Dougherty, "Whites to Lose Majority Status in U.S. by 2042," *Wall Street Journal,* August 14, 2008,
https:/ / www.wsj.com / articles / SB121867492705539109; Ed Pilking-
ton, "US Set for Dramatic Change as White America Becomes Minority by 2042," *Guardian,* August 14, 2008, https:/ / www.theguardian
.com / world / 2008 / aug / 15 / population.race.

7 **"give in to all the minorities":** Melanie Burney, "Bordentown Police
Chief Called President Trump 'The Last Hope For White People,' a
South Jersey Officer Testifies," *Philadelphia Inquirer,* September 23,
2019, https:/ / www.inquirer.com / news / new-jersey / frank-nucera-hate
-crime-trial-bordentown-police-chief-trump-isis-20190923.html.

7 **the Electoral College, an American:** The Electoral College is a holdover from the era of the country's founding, when fully 18 percent, or
roughly one in six people, were enslaved, concentrated in the south-

ern states, and not permitted to vote. It is a vestige of an eighteenth-century constitutional concession that allowed the southern states to count enslaved people as three-fifths of a free person both for their representation in Congress and for the number of electoral votes cast for president. It allowed slave states to exert more influence than they might have otherwise, and today it allows conservative, rural, and less populous states to have more influence than they otherwise might have without it. Akhil Reed Amar, "The Troubling Reason the Electoral College Exists," *Time,* November 6, 2016, https://time.com/4558510/electoral-college-history-slavery/.

7 **there had been only five elections:** The presidential elections decided by the Electoral College were: Rutherford B. Hayes over Samuel Tilden in 1876; Benjamin Harrison over Grover Cleveland in 1888; George W. Bush over Al Gore in 2000; Donald J. Trump over Hillary Clinton in 2016. Tara Law, "These Presidents Won the Electoral College—but Not the Popular Vote," *Time,* May 15, 2019, https://time.com/5579161/presidents-elected-electoral-college/. In 1824, John Quincy Adams was declared the winner over Andrew Jackson by a vote in the House of Representatives after a four-way race in which no candidate won a majority of either the popular vote or the Electoral College vote. "The Election of 1824: John Quincy Adams," Bill of Rights Institute, n.d., https://billofrightsinstitute.org/educate/educator-resources/lessons-plans/presidents-constitution/the-election-of-1824/.

10 **"fully functional democracy":** Matt Kisner, the Democratic Party chair in Richland County, South Carolina, said that in a "fully functional democracy," impeachment would obviously be the right move, but in today's United States, it would sadly be counterproductive: "It will rile up his base, it will validate all of their concerns that everyone is somehow out to get him, and that will just make it more complicated for us to beat him at the ballot box, which is where we really have to win." Daniel Dale, "Democratic Leaders Remain Reluctant to Impeach Trump," *Star* (Toronto), April 23, 2019, https://www.thestar.com/news/world/2019/04/23/democratic-leaders-remain-reluctant-to-impeach-trump.html.

10 **It was only the third such impeachment trial:** The two previous U.S. presidents who were impeached in office were Andrew Johnson in 1868 and Bill Clinton in 1998. Richard Nixon resigned the presidency, under pressure from fellow Republicans, in August 1974 as the House of Representatives prepared to impeach him.

10 **More than three hundred days had passed:** Chris Cillizza, "The Last 'Daily' White House Press Briefing Was 170 Days Ago," CNN, Au-

gust 28, 2019, https://www.cnn.com/2019/08/28/politics/trump
-white-house-daily-press-briefing/index.html. By the time the presidential impeachment trial ended on February 5, 2020, it had been
329 days since the last press briefing at the White House, held on
March 11, 2019.

10 **Then the worst pandemic:** Dan Diamond, "Trump's Mismanagement
Helped Fuel Coronavirus Crisis," *Politico,* March 7, 2020, https://
www.politico.com/amp/news/2020/03/07/trump-coronavirus
-management-style-123465; Michael D. Shear et al., "The Lost Month:
How a Failure to Test Blinded the U.S. to Covid-19," *New York Times,*
March 28, 2020, https://www.nytimes.com/2020/03/28/us/testing
-coronavirus-pandemic.html; David Frum, "This Is Trump's Fault:
The President Is Failing, and Americans Are Paying for His Failures,"
Atlantic, April 7, 2020. https://www.theatlantic.com/ideas/archive
/2020/04/americans-are-paying-the-price-for-trumps-failures/60
9532/.

10 **one who had never served:** "In the office's storied 227-year existence—
from George Washington to Barack Obama—there has never been a
president who has entirely lacked both political and military service.
Donald Trump has broken this barrier." Zachary Crockett, "Donald
Trump Is the Only US President Ever with No Political or Military
Experience," *Vox,* January 23, 2017, https://www.vox.com/policy
-and-politics/2016/11/11/13587532/donald-trump-no-experience.

10 **"unholy mess":** Jonathan Allen and Amie Parnes, *Shattered: Inside
Hillary Clinton's Doomed Campaign* (New York: Crown, 2017), p. 13.
The two Washington journalists use the phrase "unholy mess" to sum
up the views of campaign insiders Lissa Muscatine, Clinton's longtime speechwriter, and Jon Favreau, former wunderkind speech
writer for President Barack Obama. See also Joshua Zeitz, "Why Do
They Hate Her?," *Politico,* June 3, 2017, https://www.politico.com
/magazine/story/2017/06/03/why-do-they-hate-her-215220.

12 **"An apparent mistake":** NBC News reported that Vladimir Bogda-
nov, a biology professor with the Russian Academy of Sciences, said
in an interview for RBC news that "Yamal authorities stopped vacci-
nating reindeer 10 years ago because there had been no outbreaks for
more than half-a-century—an apparent mistake." Alexey Eremenko,
"Heat Wave Sparks Anthrax Outbreak in Russia's Yamalo-Nenets
Area," NBC News, July 27, 2016, https://www.nbcnews.com/news
/world/heat-wave-sparks-anthrax-outbreak-russia-s-yamalo-nenets
-area-n617716.

12 **The military had to weigh:** Marc Bennetts, "Russian Troops Destroy
Hundreds of Reindeer Killed by Anthrax," *Times* (London), August 9,

2016, https://www.thetimes.co.uk/article/russian-troops-destroy-hundreds-of-reindeer-killed-by-anthrax-k5n3gf0cp.

12 **They would have to incinerate them:** "Tundra Ablaze as Reindeer Carcasses Infected with Deadly Anthrax Are Incinerated," *Siberian Times,* August 5, 2016, http://siberiantimes.com/other/others/news/n0699-tundra-ablaze-as-reindeer-carcasses-infected-with-deadly-anthrax-are-incinerated/.

Chapter Two: An Old House and an Infrared Light

20 **"As a social and human division":** Hacker, *Two Nations,* p. 4.

Chapter Three: An American Untouchable

21 **"To other countries, I may go":** Martin Luther King, Jr., "My Trip to the Land of Gandhi" (1959), https://kinginstitute.stanford.edu/king-papers/documents/my-trip-land-gandhi.

24 **"The separation of children":** C. Edwards Lester, *Life and Public Services of Charles Sumner* (New York, 1874), pp. 74, 81.

24 **"to maintain the color line has":** Myrdal, *American Dilemma,* p. 2:677.

25 **"When we speak of the race":** Montagu, *Most Dangerous Myth,* p. 180.

25 **"A record of the desperate efforts":** Madison Grant, *The Passing of the Great Race* (New York: Charles Scribner's Sons, 1916), p. 64.

25 **"The mill worker with nobody else":** Pope, *Millhands,* p. 94.

25 **"Let the lowest white man count":** This creed, known as "Race Hierarchy in the South," was first published in *Neale's Monthly Magazine* in November 1913 and was included in Bailey, *Race Orthodoxy in the South,* p. 112.

26 **"that my countrymen may take":** Jotiba (also known as Jotirao) Phule was an anti-caste reformer in nineteenth-century India who dedicated his 1873 book, *Gulumgiri (Slavery),* to the people of the United States who had ended slavery as a result of the Civil War. Cited by Kalpana Kannabirin in *Non-Discrimination and the Indian Constitution* (New Delhi: Routledge, 2012), p. 151.

26 **"There is so much similarity":** B. R. Ambedkar to W.E.B. Du Bois, ca. July 1946, in W.E.B. Du Bois Papers (MS 312). Special Collections and University Archives, University of Massachusetts Amherst Libraries.

26 **"every sympathy with":** W.E.B. Du Bois to B. R. Ambedkar, July 31, 1946, ibid.

27 **"Why did God make me"**: Du Bois, *Souls of Black Folk,* p. 3.

29 **"caste system, which divided"**: Stampp, *Peculiar Institution,* pp. 330–31.

29 **"The prejudice of race appears"**: Tocqueville, *Democracy in America,* p. 141.

An Invisible Program

33 *The great quest in the film series:* Wachowski, Lilly and Lana, writers and directors (originally as The Wachowski Brothers). *The Matrix Reloaded.* Warner Brothers Studio, 2003.

Part Two: THE ARBITRARY CONSTRUCTION OF HUMAN DIVISIONS

Chapter Four: A Long-Running Play and the Emergence of Caste in America

41 **"held at the outset"**: Vaughan, *Roots of American Racism,* p. 129.

42 **"a civilized and relatively docile"**: Smedley and Smedley, *Race in North America,* p. 112.

42 **"The colonists soon realized"**: Ibid., p. 113.

42 **"The Gaelic insurrections"**: Ibid., p. 112.

43 **"the beautiful avenue in front"**: Weld, *American Slavery,* p. 76.

44 **"When they [the slaveholders] permit"**: Ibid., pp. 76, 77.

44 **"submission is required of"**: George McDowell Stroud, *A Sketch of the Laws Relating to Slavery in the Several States of the United States of America* (Philadelphia, 1856), p. 154; Weld, *American Slavery,* p. 283.

44 **"an otherwise perfect cloth"**: Steinberg, *Ethnic Myth,* p. 300.

45 **"an extreme form of slavery"**: Gross, *What Blood Won't Tell,* pp. 22, 23.

45 **"The slave is doomed to toil"**: Goodell, *American Slave Code,* p. 64.

45 **"The slave is entirely subject"**: Ibid., pp. 72, 63, 12.

46 **in 1740, South Carolina, like other**: Stampp, *Peculiar Institution,* p. 218.

46 **"They were scarcely permitted"**: Goodell, *American Slave Code,* p. 125.

46 **"Your slaves, I believe, work"**: Ibid., p. 116.

46 **"Whipping was a gateway form":** Baptist, *The Half Has Never Been Told*, pp. 120, 139–141, 185.

47 **"This fact is of great significance":** Guy B. Johnson, "Patterns of Race Conflict," in Thompson, *Race Relations*, p. 130.

47 **"In the gentlest houses drifted":** Cash, *Mind of the South*, pp. 82–83.

47 **"For the horrors of":** Baldwin, *Fire Next Time*, p. 69.

47 **the year 2022 marks the first year:** Enslavement lasted from 1619 to 1865 or for 246 years. The Declaration of Independence was signed in 1776. The year 2022 is 246 years from 1776. The Thirteenth Amendment freed African-Americans from enslavement in 1865. The year 2111 is 246 years from the passage of the Thirteenth Amendment that freed African-Americans from enslavement.

48 **the deaths of three-quarters:** Guy Gugliotta, "New Estimate Raises Civil War Death Toll," *New York Times*, April 3, 2012, https://www.nytimes.com/2012/04/03/science/civil-war-toll-up-by-20-percent-in-new-estimate.html.

49 **"In Ireland or Italy":** López, *White by Law*, p. 84.

49 **"No one was white before":** James Baldwin, "On Being 'White' and Other Lies," *Essence*, April 1984, p. 90.

49 **"The European immigrants' experience":** Jacobson, *Whiteness*, p. 8.

50 **the Draft Riots of 1863:** Foner, *Reconstruction*, pp. 32–33.

51 **"It was not just that":** Jacobson, *Whiteness*, p. 9.

52 **"Caste in the South":** W. Lloyd Warner and Allison Davis, "A Comparative Study of American Caste," in Thompson, *Race Relations*, p. 245.

Chapter Five: "The Container We Have Built for You"

54 **"two men and two women":** Doyle, *Etiquette of Race Relations*, p. 145.

54 **"cardinal sin":** Sokol, *There Goes My Everything*, pp. 108–9.

55 **"charging horses, their hoofs":** George B. Leonard, "Journey of Conscience: Midnight Plane to Alabama," *Nation*, March 10, 1965, pp. 502–5.

Chapter Six: The Measure of Humanity

63 **overwhelmingly an inherited trait:** Chao-Qiang Lai, "How Much of Human Height Is Genetic and How Much Is Due to Nutrition?" *Sci-*

entific American, December 11, 2006, https://www.scientificamerican
.com/article/how-much-of-human-height/.

64 **"'caste or quality of authentic'":** Smedley and Smedley, *Race in North America,* pp. 37, 14, 19.

65 **anthropologist Paul Broca:** López, *White by Law,* p. 59.

65 **The word was not passed down:** Painter, *The History of White People,* pp. 72–84.

66 **More than a century later:** López, *White by Law,* p. 54.

66 **"Race is a social concept":** Naomi Zack, *Philosophy of Science and Race* (New York: Routledge, 2002), p. 68.

66 **"an arbitrary and superficial selection":** Montagu, *Most Dangerous Myth,* pp. 116, 72–73.

67 **"Americans cling to race":** Painter, *History of White People,* p. xii.

67 **"Racism is a modern conception":** Dante Puzzo, "Racism and the Western Tradition," *Journal of the History of Ideas* 25, no. 4 (October–December 1964): 579.

71 **as happened to Barack Obama:** Garance Frank-Ruta, "The Time Obama Was Mistaken for a Waiter at a Tina Brown Book Party," *Atlantic,* July 19, 2013, https://www.theatlantic.com/politics/archive/2013/07/the-time-obama-was-mistaken-for-a-waiter-at-a-tina-brown-book-party/277967/.

Chapter Seven: Through the Fog of Delhi to the Parallels in India and America

73 **I saw the wayside altars:** Borayin Larios and Raphaël Voi, "Introduction. Wayside Shrines in India: An Everyday Defiant Religiosity," *South Asia Multidisciplinary Academic Journal* 18 (2018), https://journals.openedition.org/samaj/4546.

74 **"Perhaps only the Jews":** Rajshekar, *Dalit,* p. 11.

75 **"The colonial powers officially":** Shah et al., *Ground Down,* p. 3.

75 **"Both occupy the lowest positions":** Verba, Ahmed, and Bhatt, *Caste, Race and Politics,* p. 15.

77 **the Dalit hosts joined in:** Kevin D. Brown, "African-American Perspective on Common Struggles: Benefits for African Americans Comparing Their Struggle with Dalit Efforts," in Yengde and Teltumbde, *Radical Ambedkar,* p. 56.

Chapter Eight: The Nazis and the Acceleration of Caste

79 **"how to institutionalize racism":** Whitman, *Hitler's American Model*, p. 113. Whitman's unsettling book is a chilling investigation into how the American legal system influenced and inspired several Nazi race policies. Based on a wealth of research and his close reading of Nazi records and Reich-era literature, Whitman reconstructs a full picture of the Nazi connection to American race law. The book describes in detail the June 5, 1934, planning meeting of the Commission on Criminal Law Reform.

79 **"For us Germans, it is":** Comments made in a review of Heinrich Krieger's 1936 book, *The Race Law in the United States*, quoted in Kühl, *Nazi Connection*, p. 99.

79 **"the dedication with which":** Ibid., pp. 14, 15.

80 **They made Stoddard's book:** Ryback, *Hitler's Private Library*, p. 112.

80 **"weeding out the worst strains":** Kühl, *Nazi Connection*, pp. 61, 62.

80 **"inferior stocks":** Spiro, *Defending the Master Race*, pp. xi, 357. As a measure of Stoddard and Grant's place in popular American culture at the time, F. Scott Fitzgerald referred to them in a thinly veiled conflation of the two men in a section of dialogue in *The Great Gatsby*. Tom and Daisy talk about "a fine book" Tom is reading, about the challenges facing "the dominant race" by "this man Goddard."

81 **Hitler had studied America:** Fischer, *Hitler and America*, pp. 2, 9.

81 **"shot down the millions":** Waitman Wade Beorn, *The Holocaust in Eastern Europe: At the Epicenter of the Final Solution* (London: Bloomsbury, 2018), p. 61.

81 **"a model for his program":** Spiro, *Defending the Master Race*, p. 357.

81 **"knack for maintaining an air":** Eugene DeFriest Bétit, *Collective Amnesia: American Apartheid: African Americans' 400 Years in North America, 1619–2019* (Xlibris, 2019), p. 282. Hitler had taken a personal look into American race policies. "I have studied with interest the laws of several American states," he said around the time of these deliberations, "concerning prevention of reproduction by people whose progeny would, in all probability, be of no value or injurious to the racial stock." Ryback, *Hitler's Private Library*, p. 112.

81 **"was not just a country":** Whitman, *Hitler's American Model*, p. 138.

81 **"the American Supreme Court":** Ibid., p. 77.

82 **"there were no other models":** Ibid., p. 138. South Africa would not enact a ban on interracial marriage until 1949, with the passage of the Prohibition of Mixed Marriages Act. In 1957, South Africa passed section 16 of the Immorality Act, which prohibited blacks and whites from living together and having sex. Nathaniel Sheppard, "S. Africa Plans to Repeal Racial Sex Ban," *Chicago Tribune*, April 16, 1985, https://www.chicagotribune.com/news/ct-xpm-1985-04-16-8501 220310-story.html; Michael Parks, "S. Africa to End Racial Ban on Sex: Will Repeal Laws Forbidding Blacks to Marry Whites," *Los Angeles Times*, April 16, 1985, https://www.latimes.com/archives/la-xpm-1985 -04-16-mn-23232-story.html.

82   **the country's last free and fair election:** In the last free and fair elections of the Nazi era, held in 1932, the Nazis won nearly 38 percent of the German vote. Brustein, *Logic of Evil*, p. 9; Hett, *Death of Democracy*, p. 201.

82   **"to exploit the methods of democracy":** Fischer, *Hitler and America*, p. 4.

83   **more than a third of Germans:** Barry Eichengreen and Tim Hatton, *Interwar Unemployment in International Perspective*, IRLE Working Paper no. 12–88 (April 1988), https://www.irle.berkeley.edu/files /1998/Interwar-Unemployment-In-International-Perspective.pdf.

83   **"public opinion accepted them":** Koonz, *Nazi Conscience*, p. 176.

83   **"white children and colored children":** Whitman, *Hitler's American Model*, pp. 122, 121.

84   **"who thought American law":** Ibid., pp. 122–23.

84   **"any further penetration of Jewish":** Alan E. Steinweis, *Studying the Jew: Scholarly Anti-Semitism in Nazi Germany* (Cambridge, Mass.: Harvard University Press, 2006), p. 45.

84   **"There is a growing tendency":** Whitman, *Hitler's American Model*, p. 120.

85   **"Gürtner simply refused to concede":** Ibid., p. 102.

85   **"political construction of race":** Ibid., pp. 107–8.

85   **"this jurisprudence would suit":** Ibid., p. 109.

86   **"because he did not wish":** Koonz, *Nazi Conscience*, p. 171.

86   **"We have been talking past":** Ibid., p. 177.

87   **"Germany became a full-fledged":** Fredrickson, *White Supremacy*, pp. 123–24.

87   **"The scholars who see parallels":** Whitman, *Hitler's American Model*, p. 128.

88   **"the American commitment to legislating":** Ibid.

Chapter Nine: The Evil of Silence

90 *Mothers pulled their children inside:* Nigel Dunkley, interview by author, Berlin and Sachsenhausen, May 24, 2019.

91 *the local lynching tree:* Schrieke, *Alien Americans,* p. 133.

91 *The townspeople of the East Texas village:* Ralph Ginzburg, *100 Years of Lynchings* (Baltimore: Black Classic Press, 1988), p. 155.

92 *The little girls appear to be:* National Association for the Advancement of Colored People and James Weldon Johnson, N.A.A.C.P. Rubin Stacy Anti-Lynching Flier, Yale University, Beinecke Rare Book & Manuscript Library, https://brbl-dl.library.yale.edu/vufind/Record/3833735; Emma Sipperly, "The Rubin Stacy Lynching: Reconstructing Justice," Northeastern University Civil Rights and Restorative Justice Clinic working document, Fall 2016, https://repository.library.northeastern.edu/downloads/neu:m04285648?datastream_id=content; John Dolen, "His Name Was Rubin Stacy," *Fort Lauderale Magazine,* August 1, 2018, https://fortlauderdalemagazine.com/his-name-was-rubin-stacy/.

93 *Photographers were tipped off in advance: The Crisis* 10, no. 2, June 1915, p. 71.

93 *They made postcards:* Allen, *Without Sanctuary,* pp. 29, 174–77, 183, https://withoutsanctuary.org/pics_22_picback_text.html.

93 *"Even the Nazis did not":* Richard Lacayo, "Blood at the Root," *Time,* April 2, 2000, http://content.time.com/time/magazine/article/0,9171,42301,00.html.

95 *The leaders of the mob pulled Brown:* "A Horrible Lynching," *Nebraska Studies,* n.d., http://www.nebraskastudies.org/1900-1924/racial-tensions/a-horrible-lynching/.

96 *"Man just naturally can't take":* Sean Hogan, "Turning On the Light: Henry Fonda and Will Brown," *Roger Ebert,* January 31, 2018, https://www.rogerebert.com/balder-and-dash/turning-on-the-light-henry-fonda-and-will-brown.

Part Three: The Eight Pillars of Caste

Pillar Number One: Divine Will and the Laws of Nature

101 **"The Brahmin is by Law":** Manu, *Law Code,* p. 20.

102 **"Cursed be Canaan!":** Genesis 9:20–27.

103 **the biblical passage would be summoned:** The English trader Richard Jobson wrote in 1623 of the people he encountered in sub-Saharan Africa, "Undoubtedly, these people originally sprung from the race of Canaan, the sonne of Ham, who discovered his father Noah's secrets, for which Noah awakening cursed Canaan as our holy Scripture testifieth." Quoted in Jordan, *White over Black,* p. 35.

103 **"Both thy bondmen":** Leviticus 25:44.

103 **"The curse of Ham is now":** Thomas R. R. Cobb, *Slavery from the Earliest Period*s (Philadelphia, 1858), pp. xxxv–vi, clvii. This interpretation of Genesis was debated, oddly enough, by some who were even more hateful of blacks than most enslavers. They argued that this interpretation could not be true, because Africans were not human, they were beasts and therefore could not have descended from a son of Noah, cursed or not.

103 **"Let the negro have the crumbs":** Bailey, *Race Orthodoxy in the South,* p. 93.

Pillar Number Two: Heritability

105 **"Whereas some doubts have arisen":** William Waller Hening, ed., *The Statutes at Large; Being a Collection of All the Laws of Virginia from the First Session of the Legislature, in the Year 1619* (New York, 1823), p. 2:170, https://www.encyclopediavirginia.org/_Negro_womens _children_to_serve_according_to_the_condition_of_the_mother _1662.

106 **"He may neither earn nor wed":** Davis, Gardner, and Gardner, *Deep South,* p. 15.

106 **"Like the Hindu caste system":** Raymond T. Diamond and Robert J. Cottrol, "Codifying Caste: Louisiana's Racial Classification Scheme and the Fourteenth Amendment," *Loyola Law Review* 29, no. 2.

107 **"It's a humiliating thing":** "Forest Whitaker Was 'Humiliated' During Shoplifting Incident," *Express,* August 27, 2013, https://www .express.co.uk/celebrity-news/424990/Forest-Whitaker-was -humiliated-during-shoplifting-incident.

107 **New York City police officers broke:** David Zirin, "So . . . the NYPD Just Broke an NBA Player's Leg," *Nation,* April 10, 2015, https:// www.thenation.com/article/so-nypd-just-broke-nba-players-leg/; Jack Maloney, "Sefolosha to Donate Large Portion of $4M Settlement from Police Brutality Lawsuit," CBS Sports, April 7, 2017, https:// www.cbssports.com/nba/news/sefolosha-to-donate-large-portion -of-4m-settlement-from-police-brutality-lawsuit/.

107 **The video that surfaced:** Lindsey Bever, "Video Shows Former NFL Player's Violent Arrest After He Said Police Mistook a Phone for a Gun," *Washington Post,* April 27, 2018, https://www.washingtonpost .com/news/post-nation/wp/2018/04/27/desmond-marrow-video -shows-ex-nfl-players-violent-arrest/.

108 **"No matter how great you":** Scott Davis, "LeBron James on His Advice to His Kids About Dealing with Police: Be Respectful and Put Your Phone on Speaker," *Business Insider,* October 17, 2017, https:// www.businessinsider.com/lebron-james-kids-advice-police-2017-10.

Pillar Number Three: Endogamy and the Control of Marriage and Mating

110 **"Caste," wrote Bhimrao Ambedkar:** Ambedkar, *Castes in India,* p. 15.

110 **endogamy, which confers an alliance:** Centuries later, the enforcers of the caste system under Jim Crow found it unacceptable for relations between blacks and whites to be "sustained, intimate and on the basis of equality." George De Vos, "Psychology of Purity and Pollution as Related to Social Self-Identity and Caste," in Reuck and Knight, *Caste and Race,* p. 304.

111 **The case of Hugh Davis:** "Although the full picture can never be reconstructed, some of its elements can reasonably be assumed. . . . [B]ecause Davis's mate was described as a 'negro,' but no corresponding racial identification was made of Davis, it can be inferred that Davis was white." Leon Higginbotham quoted in López, *White by Law,* p. 17.

111 **forty-one of the fifty states passed laws:** Anti-miscegenation laws were so widely adopted that it is more efficient to cite the states that did not outlaw intermarriage than those that did. Aside from Alaska and Hawaii, which entered the union well after most anti-miscegenation laws were enacted, the only states that were silent on intermarriage were: Connecticut, Minnesota, New Hampshire, New Jersey, New York, Vermont, Wisconsin, along with the District of Columbia.

111 **Alabama, the last state:** Suzy Hansen, "Mixing It Up," *Salon,* March 9, 2001, https://www.salon.com/2001/03/08/sollors/.

112 **"What we look like":** López, *White by Law,* p. 11.

112 **94 percent of white Americans:** The first Gallup survey on interracial marriage, in 1958, was conducted with white Americans. Ninety-four percent of respondents disapproved of marriage between blacks and whites, 3 percent had no opinion, and only 4 percent approved.

"Marriage," Gallup.com, n.d., https://news.gallup.com/poll/117328/marriage.aspx.

112 **"You know the Negro race":** Davis, Gardner, and Gardner, *Deep South*, p. 17.

113 **"who owned his wife":** Weld, *American Slavery*, p. 157; Goodell, *American Slave Code*, p. 103.

113 **"I know you don't think much":** *Freedom Never Dies: The Legacy of Harry T. Moore*, PBS, aired January 12, 2001, http://www.pbs.org/harrymoore/terror/howard.html and http://www.pbs.org/harrymoore/terror/lula.html.

Pillar Number Four: Purity versus Pollution

115 **somewhere between twelve and ninety-six:** L. A. Krishna Iyer, *Social History of Kerala* (Madras: Book Centre Publications, 1970), p. 47. "A Dalit who comes closer than 95 paces to a Brahmin would pollute him and so the protectors and caretakers of the Brahmin families, the Nairs, would kill the defaulting Dalit in cruel ways." Michael Manjallor, "A Critical Analysis of the Efficacy of MDG 2: Case Study of the Dalits of Kerala, India," Ph.D. thesis, Auckland University of Technology, Auckland, New Zealand, 2015, p. 79, https://pdfs.semanticscholar.org/4a21/f1f611df809766fc38a7fa1f466313634896.pdf.

115 **"drag a thorny branch":** G. S. Ghurye, *Caste and Race in India* (London: Routledge & Kegan Paul, 1932), p. 12.

115 **required rituals of purification:** Cox, *Caste, Class, and Race*, p. 33.

116 **"They believed the entire pool":** Sartre, *Reflexions*, p. 29. This English translation of the 1954 French edition is cited in Steinweis and Rachlin, *Law in Nazi Germany*, p. 93. The English translation of Sartre's 1948 book *Anti-Semite and Jew* reads: "It seemed to them that if the body of an Israelite were to plunge into that confined body of water, the water would be completely befouled." Jean-Paul Sartre, *Anti-Semite and Jew*, translated by George J. Decker (New York: Schocken, 1948), p. 24.

116 **separate sets of textbooks:** "A Brief History of Jim Crow," Constitutional Rights Foundation, n.d., http://www.crf-usa.org/black-history-month/a-brief-history-of-jim-crow.

116 **had to drink from horse troughs:** Describing the work of Rev. Hugh Proctor, who oversaw the building of First Congregational Church in Atlanta in 1908, Paula Bevington writes: "His numerous neighborhood initiatives included the founding of an orphanage and two prison missions, as well as the installation of a public water fountain.

The fountain was not inconsequential. It augmented the only public access to drinking water previously available to blacks in the community: a horse trough." Paula L. Bevington, "Atlanta Colored Music Festival Association," *New Georgia Encyclopedia*, June 19, 2014, https://www.georgiaencyclopedia.org/articles/arts-culture/atlanta-colored-music-festival-association.

116 **In southern jails, the bedsheets:** Fon Louise Gordon, *Caste and Class: The Black Experience in Arkansas, 1880–1920* (Athens: University of Georgia Press, 1995), p. 60.

116 **"the body will be placed":** Doyle, *Etiquette of Race Relations*, pp. 153, 151, 152.

117 **"Ambulances rushed to the man's":** "Where Should a Negro Get Hurt?," *Christian Index* 61 (August 25, 1932): 9, 10.

117 **whites threw nails and broken glass:** Victoria W. Wolcott, *Race Riots and Roller Coasters: The Struggle over Segregated Recreation in America* (Philadelphia: University of Pennsylvania Press, 2012), p. 96.

118 **"The response was to drain":** Weiner, *Black Trials*, p. 177.

118 **"each Negro who entered the pool":** Wiltse, *Contested Waters*, p. 126.

118 **the city of St. Louis had:** Art Holliday, "1949 Swimming Pool Integration Sparked Violence, Triggered Change in St. Louis," KSDK, February 28, 2018, https://www.kskd.com/article/news/local/storytellers/1949-swimming-pool-integration-sparked-violence-triggered-change-in-st-Louis/63-524244606.

119 **"a circulatory type of pool":** Wiltse, *Contested Waters*, pp. 147–51, 135–38.

120 **"From time to time, one or another":** Mel Watkins, *Dancing with Strangers* (New York: Simon & Schuster, 1998), pp. 127, 128.

121 **racial absolutism, the idea that a single drop:** Fredrickson, *White Supremacy*, pp. 134, 135.

122 **"Degradation, resulting from":** Mark Tushnet, *The American Law and Slavery, 1810–1860: Considerations of Humanity and Interest* (Princeton: Princeton University Press, 1981), p. 150.

122 **"become a Colony of Aliens":** Carla J. Mulford, *Benjamin Franklin and the Ends of Empire* (Oxford: Oxford University Press, 2015), p. 161.

122 **"The law could not separate":** Raymond T. Diamond and Robert J. Cottrol, "Codifying Caste: Louisiana's Racial Classification Scheme and the Fourteenth Amendment," *Loyola Law Review* 29, no. 2 (Spring 1983): 266.

122 **"the most degenerate races":** Michael Denis Biddiss, *Father of Racist Ideology: The Social and Political Thought of Count Gobineau* (New York: Weybright & Talley, 1970), p. 144; and Michael Denis Biddiss, ed., *Gobineau: Selected Political Writings* (New York: Harper & Row, 1970), p. 161.

123 **"scum and offscouring":** Gov. William Hodges Mann, testimony during a hearing before the Committee on Immigration and Naturalization, U.S. House of Representatives (Washington, D.C.: Government Printing Office, 1912), p. 8.

123 **"The moral fiber of the nation":** Ibid., pp. 15–23.

124 **"just a little worse than":** Ed Falco, "When Italian Immigrants Were 'the Other,'" CNN, July 10, 2012, http://www.cnn.com/2012/07/10 /opinion/falco-italian-immigrants/index.html.

124 **"no competent evidence":** The case was Rollins v. Alabama, 1922.

124 **"one in whom there is":** In 1911, Arkansas passed Act 320 (House Bill 79), its "one-drop rule." This law made interracial "cohabitation" a felony and defined as "Negro" anyone "who has . . . any negro blood whatever." L. P. Sandels and Joseph M. Hill, *A Digest of the Statutes of Arkansas Embracing All Laws of a General Nature* (Columbia, Mo., 1894), p. 1375. In 1910, the Louisiana Supreme Court overturned the conviction of Octave Treadaway of New Orleans and his mistress, who was of mixed ancestry. According to the *Encyclopedia of Arkansas,* "Chief Justice Olivier Provosty ruled that the woman was neither 'Negro' nor 'Black'; rather, she was 'Coloured,' an intermediate caste based upon dual ancestry, as defined in Louisiana case law. Within a month of Provosty's ruling, lawmakers reconvened, amending the statute to define 'Negro' via a one-thirty-second blood fraction—in effect, a one-drop rule. When Arkansas's legislature met the following year, it left no wiggle room for a recalcitrant judge. They adopted the wording of Louisiana's statute while adding the one-drop clause. The felony for interracial sex was 'punishable by one month to one year in penitentiary at hard labor.'" Frank W. Sweet, "One Drop Rule," *Encyclopedia of Arkansas,* February 1, 2019, http://www.encyclopediaof arkansas.net/encyclopedia/entry-detail.aspx?entryID=5365.

125 **"who has no trace whatsoever":** Brendan Wolfe, "Racial Integrity Laws (1924–1930)," *Encyclopedia Virginia,* November 4, 2015, https:// www.encyclopediavirginia.org/racial_integrity_laws_of_the_1920s.

125 **"The 'traceable amount' was meant":** Raymond T. Diamond and Robert J. Cottrol, "Codifying Caste: Louisiana's Racial Classification Scheme and the Fourteenth Amendment," *Loyola Law Review* 29, no. 2 (Spring 1983): 281, 266.

125 **"to discover that they were":** Nancy Hewitt, *Southern Discomfort: Women's Activism in Tampa, Florida, 1880s to 1920s* (Urbana: University of Illinois Press, 2001), quoted in Voogd, *Race Riots*, p. 40.

126 **"Since this newspaper did not":** Yuchi Ichioka, "The Early Japanese Immigrant Quest for Citizenship: The Background of the 1922 Ozawa Case," *Amerasia* 4, no. 1 (1977), quoted in López, *White by Law*, p. 60.

126 **"It may be true that the blond":** López, *White by Law*, p. 63.

127 **"Obstacles this way":** Kritika Agarwal, "Vaishno Das Bagai's Disillusionment with America," *South Asian American Digital Archive*, August 6, 2014, https://www.saada.org/tides/article/living-in-a-gilded-cage.

127 **A Japanese novelist once noted:** Okada, *No-No Boy*, p. 202.

128 **black Mormons in America:** Jana Riess, "Forty Years On, Most Mormons Still Believe the Racist Temple Ban Was God's Will," *Religion News*, June 1, 2018, https://religionnews.com/2018/06/11/40-years-later-most-mormons-still-believe-the-racist-priesthood-temple-ban-was-gods-will/. See also "Race and the Priesthood," Church of Jesus Christ of Latter-day Saints, n.d., https://www.churchofjesuschrist.org/study/manual/gospel-topics-essays/race-and-the-priesthood?lang=eng.

128 **"the negroes must catch the gospel":** Goodell, *American Slave Code*, p. 312.

129 **"They were driven from Independence":** Roediger, *Wages of Whiteness*, p. 57.

129 **"They were not allowed to be":** W. W. Hunter, *The Indian Empire: Its People, History and Products* (London: Trübner & Co., 1886), p. 91.

129 **"to read architectural blueprints":** Mills, *Racial Contract*, p. 51.

130 **"They have germs":** Clark, *Southern Discomfort*. Also interview of Tena Clark conducted by Lois Reitzes, WABE/National Public Radio, December 27, 2018, https://www.wabe.org/music-legend-tena-clark-unveils-her-chaotic-childhood-in-southern-discomfort.

130 **"Strange things pop up at us":** George De Vos, "Psychology of Purity and Pollution as Related to Social Self-Identity and Caste," in Reuck and Knight, *Caste and Race*, p. 304.

Pillar Number Five: Occupational Hierarchy:
The Jatis and the Mudsill

131 **"In all social systems":** James Henry Hammond, *Selections from the Letters and Speeches of the Hon. James H. Hammond of South Carolina* (New York, 1866), p. 318.

132 **"nothing less than a monster":** Bleser, *Secret and Sacred,* p. xii; Craig Thompson Friend, "Sex, Self, and the Performance of Patriarchal Manhood in the Old South," in *The Old South's Modern Worlds: Slavery, Region, and a Nation in the Age of Progress,* ed. L. Diane Barnes, Brian Schoen, and Frank Towers (Oxford: Oxford University Press, 2011), p. 247.

132 **"intimacies":** Rosellen Brown, "Monster of All He Surveyed" (a review of Bleser, *Secret and Sacred*), *New York Times,* January 29, 1989, https://www.nytimes.com/1989/01/29/books/monster-of-all-he-surveyed.html.

133 **"There is severe occupational":** Verba, Ahmed, and Bhatt, *Caste, Race and Politics,* p. 83.

133 **"no person of color shall pursue":** *Acts and Joint Resolutions of the General Assembly of the State of South Carolina, Passed at Sessions 1864–1865* (Columbia, S.C., 1866), p. 299.

133 **forbidden to sell or trade goods:** Goodell, *American Slave Code,* p. 337.

133 **"The caste order that followed":** Edward B. Reuter, "Competition and the Racial Division of Labor," in Thompson, *Race Relations,* p. 58.

134 **"Anything that causes the negro":** *Independent* (New York) 54, no. 2798 (July 17, 1902), p. 1739.

134 **They entered the North at the bottom:** "American color bars existed not because government required them," wrote the historian George M. Fredrickson, "but because it did not act, at least until very recently, to prohibit the discriminatory practices of private employers and trade unions." Fredrickson, *White Supremacy,* p. 235. See also Roediger, *Wages of Whiteness,* p. 58. "In New York, and some other Northern cities, colored persons are still denied licenses to drive carts, and pursue other similar avocations for a livelihood." Goodell, *American Slave Code,* p. 337.

134 **"Every avenue for improvement":** William A. Sinclair, *The Aftermath of Slavery* (Boston: Small, Maynard, 1905), p. 67.

134 **"no one occupation has but":** W. Lloyd Warner and Allison Davis, "A Comparative Study of American Caste," in Thompson, *Race Relations,* p. 231.

135 **"one can distinguish six merchant":** Bouglé, *Caste System*, p. 17.

135 **"85 percent of black men and":** Steinberg, *Ethnic Myth*, pp. 206–7.

135 **"refused to carry water":** Roediger, *Wages of Whiteness*, p. 49.

136 **"If white and colored persons are":** Doyle, *Etiquette of Race Relations*, p. 154.

136 **"forced him to procure overalls":** Ibid., pp. 154, 155.

137 **"This was done to make them":** Brown, *Life of William Wells Brown*, p. 45.

138 **"Menial and comic roles":** W. Lloyd Warner and Allison Davis, "A Comparative Study of American Caste," in Thompson, *Race Relations*, p. 237.

138 **Yet the rotund and cheerful slave:** The scholar Andrew Hacker noted the roles reserved for African-Americans throughout history: "Within living memory, your people were barred from major league teams; now they command the highest salaries in most professional sports. In the movies, your people had to settle for roles as servants and buffoons. Now at least some of them are cast as physicians, business executives. . . . When everything is added up, white America still prefers its black people to be performers who divert them as athletes and musicians and comedians." Hacker, *Two Nations*, p. 46.

139 **"I have a slave who I believe":** "Narrative and Testimony of Sarah M. Grimké" (1830), in Weld, *American Slavery*, p. 24.

139 **An SS squad leader, who:** "Compulsory Labour in the 'Brickworks' Death Camp," Sachsenhausen Concentration Camp, Sachsenhausen, Germany. Wall text describing SS squad leader Richard Bugdalle making prisoners dance like bears around a shovel. When one man refused, Bugdalle "took a shovel handle, and hit and killed him."

140 **"the claim of absolute proprietorship":** Goodell, *American Slave Code*, p. 77.

Pillar Number Six: Dehumanization and Stigma

144 **"undergarment and an":** Doyle, *Etiquette of Race Relations*, p. 61.

144 **"punishable by cutting off":** Rajshekar, *Dalit*, p. 64.

145 **work in the bakery:** "The Brickworks," Sachsenhausen Concentration Camp, Sachsenhausen, Germany. Wall text describing conditions inflicted on forced laborers at the concentration camp.

145 **"When spoken to, they must":** Brown, *Slave Life in Georgia*, p. 74.

146 **"He is accounted criminal for":** Goodell, *American Slave Code*, p. 287.

146 **seventy-one offenses that carried:** Ibid., p. 291; H. Bruce Franklin, "*Billy Budd* and Capital Punishment: A Tale of Three Centuries," in *Demands of the Dead: Executions, Storytelling and Activism,* ed. Katy Ryan (Iowa City: University of Iowa Press, 2012), p. 117.

146 **"be flogged for teaching":** Goodell, *American Slave Code,* p. 290.

146 **"Richmond required that Negroes":** Stampp, *Peculiar Institution,* p. 209.

147 **the village of Oranienburg:** "Bricks for 'Germania'—Shells for the 'Final Victory,' the 'Brickworks,' an External Camp of Sachsenhausen Concentration Camp," Sachsenhausen Concentration Camp, Sachsenhausen, Germany. Wall text describing the daily march of prison laborers to the clay pits, and the carts they pushed at day's end with the bodies of those who had died on site.

147 **One plantation doctor:** Washington, *Medical Apartheid,* pp. 62–70. The medical ethicist Harriet Washington's groundbreaking work on experimentation is, in my view, the leading and definitive analysis of the long history of medical abuse of African-Americans in the United States. In the case of the black baby whose scalp was opened, the physician James Marion Sims was experimenting on a condition called tetany, which was characterized by convulsions and seizures. For extensive analysis of the medical abuse of enslaved women, see Deborah Kuhn McGregor, *From Medicine to Midwives: The Birth of American Gynecology* (New Brunswick, N.J.: Rutgers University Press, 1998).

148 **"could be induced":** Smith, *Less Than Human,* p. 128.

149 **In a similar experiment:** Albert Bandura, Bill Underwood, and Michael E. Fromson. "Disinhibition of Aggression Through Diffusion of Responsibility and Dehumanization of Victims," *Journal of Research in Personality* 9, 1975, p. 266.

149 **"Dehumanization is a joint creation":** Smith, *Less Than Human,* pp. 4, 6.

149 **There was an attraction:** Kristina DuRocher, *Raising Racists: The Socialization of White Children in the Jim Crow South* (Lexington: University Press of Kentucky, 2018), pp. 76, 77.

149 **And enthusiasts lined up:** Smith, *Less Than Human,* p. 118. See also David Nasaw, *Going Out: The Rise and Fall of Public Amusements.* (Cambridge, Mass.: Harvard University Press, 1993), pp. 92, 93; Michael W. Robbins and Wendy Palitz, *Brooklyn: A State of Mind* (New York: Workman Publishing Company, 2001), p. 52.

150 **A certain kind of violence:** DuRocher, *Raising Racists,* p. 94.

Pillar Number Seven: Terror as Enforcement, Cruelty as a Means of Control

151 **"the whip was the most common":** Stampp, *Peculiar Institution*, p. 174.

152 **"to whip every hand":** Ibid., p. 188.

152 **A teenager endured:** Baptist, *The Half Has Never Been Told*, pp. 118, 120, 140.

152 **"Native Americans were occasionally":** Mills, *Racial Contract*, p. 99.

153 **"with a hot iron on":** Taylor, *Slavery in Louisiana*, p. 236, quoted in Stampp, *Peculiar Institution*, p. 188; Edwin Adam Davis, *Plantation Life in the Florida Parishes of Louisiana, 1836–1846, as Reflected in the Diary of Bennet H. Barrow* (New York: AMS Press, 1967), pp. 173–74. In Georgia prior to 1770, and in North Carolina prior to 1775, taking a slave's life was not a felony. Stampp, *Peculiar Institution*, p. 218.

153 **"any person may KILL":** Stampp, *Peculiar Institution*, p. 178.

154 **"at least twelve slaves":** Ibid., p. 183.

154 **Fourteen-pound chains and:** Brown, *Slave Life in Georgia*, p. 57.

155 **"not speaking up and looking":** Ibid., p. 72.

155 **"He was left to die or":** Ibid., pp. 28–30.

155 **"Make them stand":** Kenneth M. Stampp, "To Make Them Stand in Fear," in *A Turbulent Voyage: Readings in African American Studies*, ed. Floyd W. Hayes III (Oxford: Collegiate Press, 2000), p. 295.

157 **"a sound as of murder":** Weld, *American Slavery*, p. 90.

158 **"the Negroes seem to be":** Dollard, *Caste and Class*, p. 360.

Pillar Number Eight: Inherent Superiority versus Inherent Inferiority

159 **the black actress, Louise Beavers:** Regester, *African-American Actresses*, pp. 71–106; Bogle, *Toms, Coons*, pp. 54–57.

160 **"his unquestioned inferiority":** Smedley and Smedley, *Race in North America*, p. 99.

160 **"He must be held subject":** Goodell, *American Slave Code*, p. 285.

160 **"If a Negro, man or woman":** Doyle, *Etiquette of Race Relations*, p. 55.

161 **"any sort of garment or":** Eulanda A. Sanders, "The Politics of Textiles Used in African American Slave Clothing," in *Textile Society* *of America Symposium Proceedings* (Washington, D.C., 2012), p. 740, https://digitalcommons.unl.edu/tsaconf/740.

161 **a young Jewish woman in Berlin:** Nigel Dunkley, interview by author, Berlin and Sachsenhausen, May 24, 2019.

162 **"They were owned by a woman":** *The Farmers' Register of 1834*, quoted in Stampp, *Peculiar Institution*, p. 142.

162 **"They must obey at all times":** Ibid., p. 144.

162 **"any number of acts":** Ibid., pp. 207–8.

162 **"In the tone of an answer":** Douglass, *My Bondage*, p. 92.

163 **"trivial offenses":** Davis, Gardner, and Gardner, *Deep South*, p. 394.

163 **"because he asked for a receipt":** James C. Cobb, *The Most Southern Place on Earth: The Mississippi Delta and the Roots of Regional Identity* (New York: Oxford University Press, 1992), p. 213.

163 **"The Negro occupies a position":** Doyle, *Etiquette of Race Relations*, pp. 149–50.

164 **"The human meaning of caste":** Berreman, *Caste and Other Inequities*, p. 159, cited in Smaje, *Natural Hierarchies*, p. 21.

164 **"Is it possible that any":** Jordan, *White over Black*, p. 182.

164 **"What to do with Hitler":** Louis Adamic, *A Nation of Nations* (New York: Harper, 1945), p. 201.

Part Four: The Tentacles of Caste

Brown Eyes versus Blue Eyes

167 **Jane Elliott decided:** "A Class Divided," *Frontline*, PBS (March 26, 1985), https://www.pbs.org/wgbh/frontline/film/class-divided/. This video, about the teacher's lesson in discrimination, is one of *Frontline*'s most requested programs.

170 **"If you do that with a whole":** Jane Elliott, interview by NBC, September 29, 2017, https://m.youtube.com/watch?v=eFQkLp5u-No.

Chapter Eleven: Dominant Group Status Threat and the Precarity of the Highest Rung

178 **death rates of middle-aged white Americans:** Anne Case and Angus Deaton, "Rising Morbidity and Mortality in Midlife Among White Non-Hispanic Americans in the 21st Century," *Proceedings of the Na-*

tional Academy of Sciences 112, no. 49 (December 8, 2015): 15078–83, https://doi.org/10.1073/pnas.1518393112.

179 **who died during World War II:** The number of Americans who died in World War II was 405,000.

179 **"These are deaths that do not":** Anne Case and Ta-Nehisi Coates, "Fear and Despair: Consequences of Inequity," in *Knowledge to Action: Accelerating Progress in Health, Well-Being and Equity,* ed. Alonzo L. Plough (New York: Oxford University Press, 2017), pp. 11–15.

179 **rates in other Western countries:** Anne Case and Angus Deaton, "Mortality and Morbidity in the 21st Century," *Brookings Papers on Economic Activity* (Spring 2017), https://www.brookings.edu/bpea -articles/mortality-and-morbidity-in-the-Twenty-first-Century/; Case and Deaton, "Rising Morbidity." In 2019 a similar trend surfaced in the United Kingdom: "Deaths of Despair, Once an American Phenomenon, Now Haunt Britain," *Economist,* May 14, 2019, https:// www.economist.com/britain/2019/05/14/deaths-of-despair-once -an-american-phenomenon-now-haunt-britain.

180 **"is not the usual form of prejudice":** Diana C. Mutz, "Status Threat, Not Economic Hardship, Explains the 2016 Presidential Vote," *Proceedings of the National Academy of Sciences* 115 (May 8, 2018): 4330–39, https://doi.org/10.1073/pnas.1718155115.

180 **"dear treasure of his superiority":** Cash, *Mind of the South,* p. 66.

181 **"has not only been neglected":** Smith, *Killers of the Dream,* p. 171.

181 **"need the demarcations of caste":** Myrdal, *American Dilemma,* p. 2:597.

181 **"in which downward social mobility":** Roediger, *Wages of Whiteness,* p. 60.

181 **"public and psychological wage":** Du Bois, *Black Reconstruction,* p. 700.

181 **"little but their complexion":** Letter from an eastern Virginia slaveholder in the *Richmond Enquirer,* May 4, 1832, quoted in Theodore Allen, *The Invention of the White Race* (London: Verso, 1997), p. 2:255.

182 **"Nobody could take away from":** Smith, *Killers of the Dream,* pp. 164–65.

182 **"the basic restrictions upon marriage":** W. Lloyd Warner and Allison Davis, "A Comparative Study of American Caste," in Thompson, *Race Relations,* p. 236.

182 **"In the span of a few cruel years":** Russell Baker, "The Problem of the White Anglo-Saxon Protestant," *New York Times,* November 9, 1963.

183 **"Always [the Negro] was something":** Smith, *Killers of the Dream,* pp. 179, 222.

183 **"It's a great lie on which":** Sushrut Jadhav, interview by author, May 2018.

184 **"His whole life is one anxious":** Ambedkar, *Annihilation of Caste,* p. 250.

184 **"hangs there to this day":** Ambedkar, *Castes in India,* p. 45.

185 **"if you or your parents were":** Ben Mathis-Lilley, "An Ingenious and Powerful Case for Reparations in the *Atlantic,*" *Slate,* May 22, 2014, http://www.slate.com/blogs/the_slatest/2014/05/22/reparations .html. The writer distilled this conclusion in his analysis of Ta-Nehisi Coates's seminal "The Case for Reparations," *Atlantic* (2014).

186 **"the trillions of dollars of wealth":** Lipsitz, *Possessive Investment,* pp. 5–7, 107.

186 **more racism than African-Americans:** Michael I. Norton and Samuel Sommers, "Whites See Racism as a Zero-Sum Game That They Are Now Losing," *Perspectives on Psychological Science* 6, no. 3 (2011), pp. 215–18.

186 **as much as 80 percent:** David R. Williams, interview by author, Providence, R.I., May 29, 2013.

187 **white felons applying for a job:** Devah Pager, "The Mark of a Criminal Record," *American Journal of Sociology* 108, no. 5 (March 2003): 937–75.

188 **often disregard the reports of pain:** Kelly M. Hoffman et al., "Racial Bias in Pain Assessment and Treatment Recommendations, and False Beliefs About Biological Differences Between Blacks and Whites," *Proceedings of the National Academy of Sciences* 113, no. 16 (April 19, 2016): 4296–301, https://doi.org/10.1073/pnas.1516047113. "Research has shown that black patients are undertreated for pain not only relative to white patients, but relative to World Health Organization guidelines. . . . New research from the University of Virginia suggests that disparities in pain management may be attributable in part to bias. In a study of medical students and residents, researchers find that a substantial number of white medical students and residents hold false beliefs about biological differences between black and white people (e.g., black people's skin is thicker; black people's blood coagulates more quickly) that could affect how they assess and treat the pain experienced by black patients." University of Virginia, "Study Links Disparities in Pain Management to Racial Bias," *Science-Daily,* April 4, 2016, www.sciencedaily.com/releases/2016/04/1604 04153044.htm.

189 **"No way I want my tax":** Metzl, *Dying of Whiteness,* pp. 3–7, 174–75.

Chapter Twelve: A Scapegoat to Bear the Sins of the World

190   **The other, the scapegoat:** Leviticus 16:5–10, 20–22.

190   **"This serves to relieve others":** Perera, *Scapegoat Complex*, p. 8.

191   **"The scapegoater feels a relief":** Ibid., pp. 12, 13.

191   **"before binding them to the stakes":** Weld, *American Slavery*, p. 59.

192   **"The Negro becomes both":** Davis, Gardner, and Gardner, *Deep South*, p. 49.

192   **"at the hands of persons unknown":** For more on the ritual of lynching, see Dray, *Persons Unknown*; Raper, *Tragedy of Lynching*; and Litwack, *Trouble in Mind*.

192   **"Whites were unified in seeing":** Myrdal, *American Dilemma*, vol. 2, p. 598.

193   **it is white women, and thus white families:** Kimberlé W. Crenshaw, "Framing Affirmative Action," 105 *Michigan Law Review First Impressions* 123 (2007), https://repository.law.umich.edu/mlr_fi/vol105/iss1/4/; Victoria M. Massie, "White Women Benefit Most from Affirmative Action—and Are Among Its Fiercest Opponents," *Vox*, May 25, 2016, https://www.vox.com/2016/5/25/11682950/fisher-supreme-court-white-women-affirmative-action.

193   **"for structural economic problems":** Ashley Crossman, "Definition of Scapegoat, Scapegoating, and Scapegoat Theory," *ThoughtCo.*, August 2, 2019, https://www.thoughtco.com/scapegoat-definition-3026572.

195   **"He never tried to comfort":** Margaret Carlson, "Presumed Innocent," *Time*, June 24, 2001, http://content.time.com/time/magazine/article/0,9171,153650,00.html.

197   **Anthony Stephan House:** "In another line of inquiry with potential racial undertones, police sought to determine whether House's death was cartel-related. Mark McCrimmon, a defense attorney, said a client who had been arrested in a drug raid in the neighborhood weeks before was interviewed by police during their investigation into the bombing." Eli Rosenberg, "Exploding Packages Tap into Simmering Tensions over Austin's Racial Segregation," *Washington Post*, March 15, 2018, https://www.washingtonpost.com/national/exploding-packages-tap-into-simmering-tensions-over-austins-racial-segregation/2018/03/15/595a7b24-28a4-11e8-874b-d517e912f125_story.html.

197   **"We can't rule out that Mr.":** Ibid.; "Police: Exploding Package Caused Death of NE Austin Man, Tips Sought," CBS Austin, March 5,

2018, https://cbsaustin.com/news/local/austin-police-identify-man
-killed-in-explosion.

197 **"Based on what we know"**: Tom Dart, "Austin Bombings: How They
Unfolded, and What They Revealed," *Guardian*, March 24, 2018,
https://www.theguardian.com/us-news/2018/mar/24/austin
-bombings-mark-conditt-texas.

Chapter Thirteen: The Insecure Alpha and the Purpose
of an Underdog

205 **"The main characteristic of an alpha"**: Safina, *Beyond Words*, p. 155.

206 **"a kind of social glue"**: Wolf Howl Organization, "Wolf Behavior,"
part 1, *Running with the Wolves*, n.d., http://www.runningwiththe
wolves.org/behavior1.htm. Running with the Wolves, an organization founded by Teresa DeMaio on Long Island, is devoted to wolf
and wildlife conservation.

Chapter Fourteen: The Intrusion of Caste in Everyday Life

211 **"One of them"**: Bancroft, *Slave Trading*, p. 81.

211 **"countermanding an order"**: Richard Frucht, *Black Society in the New
World* (New York: Random House, 1971), p. 32.

211 **"shelter or security from the"**: Stampp, *Peculiar Institution*, p. 343.

217 **"You're in a Yale building"**: Brandon Griggs, "A Black Yale Graduate Student Took a Nap in Her Dorm's Common Room. So a White
Student Called Police," CNN, May 12, 2018, https://www.cnn.com
/2018/05/09/us/yale-student-napping-black-trnd/index.html.

217 **In Milwaukee, a woman:** Nicole Rojas, "Black Man Records White
Woman Calling 911 After Accusing Him of Breaking into His Own
Car," *Newsweek*, August 17, 2018, https://www.newsweek.com
/woman-calls-police-video-black-man-breaking-own-car-milwaukee
-reporachel-1078717.

217 **As the white man briefed:** Patrick May, "Video of a San Francisco
Dad's 'Trespassing' 911 Call to Report a Black Software Engineer
Goes Viral," *Mercury News*, July 9, 2019, https://www.mercurynews
.com/2019/07/09/video-of-a-san-francisco-dad-trespassing-9-1-1
-call-to-report-black-software-engineer-goes-viral/.

217 **In the video that the man took:** Melissa Gomez, "White Woman Who
Blocked Black Neighbor from Building Is Fired," *New York Times*, Oc-

tober 15, 2018, https://www.nytimes.com/2018/10/15/us/hilary
-brooke-apartment-patty-st-louis.html.

217 **"This lady is following me"**: Melissa Gomez, "Babysitting While
Black: Georgia Man Was Stalked by Woman as He Cared for 2 White
Children," *New York Times*, October 9, 2018, https://www.nytimes
.com/2018/10/09/us/black-man-babysitting.html. Corey Lewis's
video is at https://m.youtube.com/watch?v=TyATgNSAkj8. See also
Yamiche Alcindor, "Living While Black: How Does Racial Bias Lead
to Unnecessary Calls to Police?" *PBS NewsHour*, July 2, 2018, https://
m.youtube.com/watch?v=o3r3mOo4LmY.

Chapter Fifteen: The Urgent Necessity of a Bottom Rung

224 **"The masters feared their former"**: Du Bois, *Black Reconstruction*,
p. 633.

225 **"This indulgence and this"**: Col. J.L.A. Linard of American Expedi-
tionary Force headquarters advised the French command on how
African-American soldiers were to be handled. His memo, quoted
here and in the next paragraphs, was published as "A French Directive," *Crisis*, no. 18 (May 1919): 16–18, available at https://glc.yale
.edu/french-directive. See also Rebecca Onion, "A WWI–Era Memo
Asking French Officers to Practice Jim Crow with Black American
Troops," *Slate*, April 27, 2016, https://slate.com/human-interest
/2016/04/secret-information-concerning-black-troops-a-warning
-memo-sent-to-the-french-military-during-world-war-i.html.

226 **Freddie Stowers:** Nicole Bauke, "Black Soldier Killed in WWI Was
Denied Medal of Honor. Advocates Are Now Trying to Change That,"
Army Times, February 28, 2018, https://www.armytimes.com/news
/your-army/2018/02/28/black-soldier-killed-in-wwi-was-denied
-medal-of-honor-advocates-are-now-trying-to-change-that/.

226 **"Imagine":** Ibid.

227 **"halting white motorists, apparently"**: Ward, *Defending White Democracy*, p. 41.

227 **"I am a man just like"**: Richard Gergel, *Unexampled Courage: The
Blinding of Sgt. Isaac Woodard and the Awakening of President Harry S.
Truman and Judge J. Waties Waring* (New York: Farrar, Straus & Giroux,
2019), p. 14.

228 **"I was shocked by"**: Richard Kluger, *Simple Justice: The History of
Brown v. Board of Education and Black America's Struggle for Equality*
(New York: Knopf, 2004), p. 298. The attack on Woodard and other

black veterans returning from the war so alarmed President Truman that, in 1948, he issued two landmark executive orders, 9981, banning segregation in the armed forces, and 9980, ending segregation in the federal government.

228   **"If a Negro rises, he":** Schrieke, *Alien Americans*, p. 143.

229   **"single bloodiest election day":** Paul Ortiz, "Ocoee, Florida: Remembering 'the Single Bloodiest Day in Modern U.S. Political History,'" *Facing South*, May 14, 2010, https://www.facingsouth.org/2010/05/ocoee-florida-remembering-the-single-bloodiest-day-in-modern-us-political-history.html.

230   **"A finer, cleaner man than":** Ida B. Wells, *Crusade for Justice: The Autobiography of Ida B. Wells*, ed. Alfreda M. Duster (Chicago: University of Chicago Press, 1970), p. 55.

230   **"Moss was murdered for running":** Nathaniel C. Ball, "Memphis and the Lynching at the Curve," *Uplift Memphis, Uplift the Nation: The Blog for Community Engagement* (Memphis: Benjamin Hooks Institute for Social Change, 2015), https://blogs.memphis.edu/benhooksinstitute/2015/09/30/memphis-and-the-lynching-at-the-curve/.

231   **"When slaves earned money":** Stampp, *Peculiar Institution*, p. 166.

231   **"God have mercy on":** "How an African Slave in Boston Helped Save Generations from Smallpox," *History*, February 1, 2019, https://www.history.com/news/smallpox-vaccine-onesimus-slave-cotton-mather.

231   **"the Holy Grail of smallpox prevention":** Washington, *Medical Apartheid*, pp. 72–73; Rene F. Najera, "Black History Month: Onesimus Spreads Wisdom That Saves Lives of Bostonians During a Smallpox Epidemic," *History of Vaccines*, February 3, 2019, https://www.historyofvaccines.org/content/blog/onesimus-smallpox-boston-cotton-mather; and Erin Blakemore, "How an African Slave in Boston Helped Save Generations from Smallpox," *History*, February 1, 2019, https://www.history.com/news/smallpox-vaccine-onesimus-slave-cotton-mather.

233   **"When two Negro teachers applied":** Du Bois, *Black Reconstruction*, p. 697.

234   **"everything must be done to":** Raphael Gross, "Guilt, Shame, Anger, Indignation: Nazi Law and Nazi Morals," in Steinweis and Rachlin, *Law in Nazi Germany*, p. 92.

234   **African-Americans account for 59 percent:** Tracy Jan, "News Media Offers Consistently Warped Portrayals of Black Families, Study Finds," *Washington Post*, December 13, 2017, https://www.washingtonpost

.com/news/wonk/wp/2017/12/13/news-media-offers-consistently
-warped-portrayals-of-black-families-study-finds/.

235 **Crimes involving a black suspect:** C.K., "Black Americans Are Over-Represented in Media Portrayals of Poverty," *Economist,* February 20, 2018, https://www.economist.com/democracy-in-america/2018/02/20/black-americans-are-over-represented-in-media-portrayals-of-poverty.

235 **rate of black teenagers giving birth:** "Long-term declines in birth rates for non-Hispanic black teens have been particularly steep," the researchers found. "Declines in birth rates among Hispanic teens have been nearly as sharp, from 105 births per 1,000 women, ages fifteen to nineteen in 1991, to 29 births per 1,000 in 2017." The rate of births among non-Hispanic white teenagers, historically a fraction of the rate of black and Latina teenagers, fell at a steady but slower pace from 43 per 1,000 to 13 per 1,000 during the same period, or from a little more than a quarter of the black birth rate to now about half. "Teen Births," *Child Trends,* May 24, 2019, https://www.childtrends.org/indicators/teen-births. The analysis was derived from Centers for Disease Control data.

235 **"The long-term downward trends":** Ibid.

236 **closed, auctioned off, or poured concrete:** Albany, Georgia, "auctioned three pools and a tennis court rather than desegregate them." The city "padlocked the library for months." Sokol, *There Goes My Everything,* p. 93.

237 **When black boys instinctively rushed:** "McKinney Video: Protest over Texas Pool Party Policing," BBC, June 9, 2015, https://www.bbc.com/news/world-us-canada-33059484.

237 **Within days, the officer resigned:** Jonathan Capehart, "The McKinney, Texas Pool Party: More Proof That 'Black Children Don't Get to Be Children,'" *Washington Post,* June 10, 2015, https://www.washingtonpost.com/blogs/lost-partisan/wp/2015/06/10/the-mckinney-texas-pool-party-more-proof-that-black-children-dont-get-to-be-children/.

Chapter Sixteen: Last Place Anxiety: Packed in a Flooding Basement

238 **"The stigmatized stratify their":** Matory, *Stigma and Culture,* p. 384.

239 **"Conspicuously outperforming":** Ibid., p. 333.

239 **"They even quarrelled over":** Ambedkar, *Annihilation of Caste,* p. 277.

240 **"the team just cannot"**: Sudipta Sarangi, "Capturing Indian 'Crab' Behaviour," *Hindu Business Line*, April 1, 2013, https://www.the hindubusinessline.com/opinion/capturing-indian-crab-behaviour /article22995064.ece.

241 **"the greatest predictor of"**: Bryan Stevenson, *Just Mercy* (New York: Spiegel & Grau, 2014), p. 142.

241 **"While white immigrants"**: Kasinitz, *Caribbean New York*, p. 36.

242 **"Since I have been"**: Ibid.

242 **"act like African-Americans"**: Matory, *Stigma and Culture*, p. 49.

242 **"each caste takes its pride"**: Ambedkar, *Annihilation of Caste*, p. 294.

Chapter Seventeen: On the Early Front Lines of Caste

245 **They would soon discover:** Varel, *Lost Black Scholar*, p. 85.

246 **They had seen the Nazis:** Ibid., p. 74.

247 **the proficiency of Allison Davis:** Jennifer Jensen Wallach, introduction to Davis, Gardner, and Gardner, *Deep South*, p. xvii.

248 **Mary Gardner took a position:** Ibid., p. xxii.

248 **climb into a hoop skirt:** Ibid., p. xxi.

249 **"Their encounters were limited"**: Varel, *Lost Black Scholar*, p. 85.

249 **Every move had to be thought out:** Davis, Gardner, and Gardner, *Deep South*, pp. 561–62.

249 **"it was explained to them"**: Varel, *Lost Black Scholar*, p. 86.

250 **"The whole Negro-white research"**: Ibid., p. 87

251 **"the fundamental division"**: Ibid., p. 92.

252 **"ostracized from the town"**: Wallach introduction to Davis, Gardner, and Gardner, *Deep South*, p. xxviii.

252 **"canonical"**: Jane Adams and D. Gorton, "Southern Trauma: Revisiting Caste and Class in the Mississippi Delta," *American Anthropologist* 106, no. 2 (June 2004): 334–45.

255 **"regardless of his position"**: Cox, *Caste, Class, and Race*, pp. 498, 519.

255 **he disregarded both the injustices:** Among the perplexing assertions in Cox's otherwise comprehensive overview is his observation that in India, "caste is a status entity in an assimilated, self-satisfied society. Regardless of his position in the society, a man's caste is sacred to him; and one caste does not dominate the other." Ibid.

Chapter Eighteen: Satchel Paige and the Illogic of Caste

257 **"tear the glove off the catcher":** Robert Smith, *Pioneers of Baseball* (Boston: Little, Brown, 1978), quoted in the *Encyclopedia of World Biography* (Farmington Hills, Mich.: Gale Research, 1998), p. 62.

257 **"catchers had to cushion":** Larry Tye, interview by Michel Martin, National Public Radio, July 27, 2009, https://www.npr.org/templates /story/story.php?storyId=111063901. See Larry Tye, *Satchel: The Life and Times of an American Legend* (New York: Random House, 2009).

257 **a money-back guarantee:** Steven Goldman, ed., *It Ain't Over 'Til It's Over: The Baseball Prospectus Pennant Race Book* (Philadelphia: Basic Books, 2007), p. 62.

257 **"may well have been the fastest":** Smith, *Pioneers of Baseball,* in *Encyclopedia of World Biography,* p. 62.

258 **"That we know of, he":** Tye interview by Martin.

259 **signed him as a free agent:** "Satchel Paige," National Baseball Hall of Fame, n.d., https://baseballhall.org/hall-of-famers/paige-satchel.

259 **The Cleveland Indians won:** Pat Galbincea, "Pitcher Satchel Paige Helped Indians Win Pennant in 1948: Black History Month," *Cleveland Plain Dealer,* February 16, 2013, https://www.cleveland.com/ metro/2013/02/pitcher_satchel_paige_helped_i.html.

260 **"It was no big deal for me":** Sam Mellinger, "Fifty Years Ago, Satchel Paige Pitched His Last Big-League Game in KC at Age 59," *Kansas City Star,* September 18, 2015, https://www.kansascity.com/sports /spt-columns-blogs/sammellinger/article35763006.html.

260 **"Many critics agree that it":** "Satchel Paige 1906–1982," Encyclopedia .com, n.d., https://www.encyclopedia.com/people/sports-and-games /sports-biographies/satchel-paige.

Part Five: THE CONSEQUENCES OF CASTE

Chapter Nineteen: The Euphoria of Hate

263 ***The film footage:*** This chapter was written after I viewed an archival film reel of the crowds at Hitler's return to Berlin, July 1940, after the Battle of France. The footage was shown at the *Hitler—How Could It Happen?* exhibition, Berlin Story museum, Berlin, Germany, https://www.berlinstory.de/hitler-dokumentation/anfahrt/. A partial video of the parade and crowd is available for viewing on YouTube: https://youtube.com/watch?v=g3xRVKkvx9A. A few clips of the crowd scenes shown in the museum exhibit appear at the 3:00 mark of the online video. As described in this chapter, however, the museum exhibit carried no sound or commentary and included more extensive footage than available online.

Chapter Twenty: The Inevitable Narcissism of Caste

269 **"No matter how degraded":** Hacker, *Two Nations*, p. 250.

270 **"Narcissus could not conceive":** Ronningstam, *Identifying and Understanding*, p. 3.

270 **"The essence of this overestimation":** Fromm, *Heart of Man*, p. 79.

270 **"He is nothing":** Fromm quoted in Sakurai, *Theories of Narcissism*, p. 54.

270 **"has a euphoric 'on-top-of-the-world'":** Fromm, *Heart of Man*, p. 71.

270 **"The survival of the group":** Ibid., p. 78.

270 **"Group narcissism leads people":** Sakurai, *Theories of Narcissism*, p. 53.

271 **"inflated image of itself":** Fromm, *Heart of Man*, p. 76.

274 **"There is never caste":** Ambedkar, *Castes in India*, p. 47.

277 **"lace-curtain Irish":** Niall O'Dowd, "Was Your Family Shanty or Lace Curtain Irish? It's Important," *Irish Central*, October 10, 2019, https://www.irishcentral.com/roots/shanty-lace-curtain-irish. Also see Jeanne Charters, "The Irish Caste System—What Shanty Irish Means," *Jeanne Charters*, July 25, 2014, https://jeannecharters.com/irish-caste-system-shanty-irish-means/.

278 **Nordic was the region:** Leonid Bershidsky, "Trump Trolls the Nordics. They Troll Him Back," *Bloomberg*, August 21, 2019, https://www.bloomberg.com/opinion/articles/2019-08-21/trump-doesn-t-seem-to-get-greenland-denmark-or-any-nordic-count; Frida Ghitis, "Why Trump Is So Obsessed with Scandinavia," CNN, August 21, 2019, https://www.cnn.com/2019/08/21/opinions/trump-denmark-scandinavia-obsession-ghitis/index.html; and Terje Solsvik and Camilla Knudsen, "'Thanks, But No Thanks'—Norwegians Reject Trump's Immigration Offer," Reuters, January 12, 2018, https://www.reuters.com/article/us-usa-trump-immigration-norway/thanks-but-no-thanks-norwegians-reject-trumps-immigration-offer-id USKBN1F11QK.

Chapter Twenty-One: The German Girl with the Dark, Wavy Hair

280 **"racial passport":** Douglass, *God Among Germans,* p. 117, for a discussion of the racial passport during the Nazi era.

Chapter Twenty-Two: The Stockholm Syndrome and the Survival of the Subordinate Caste

282 **"Knowledge without wisdom":** Patricia Hill Collins, *Black Feminist Thought: Knowledge, Consciousness and the Politics of Empowerment* (London: Routledge, 2000), p. 257.

283 **"The first moral duty is":** Edmund Leach, "Caste, Class, and Slavery: The Taxonomic Problem," in Reuck and Knight, *Caste and Race,* pp. 10–11.

284 **"It's almost impossible to":** Ashley Reese, "The Perverse Spectacle of Black Forgiveness," *Jezebel,* October 3, 2019, https://jezebel.com/the-perverse-spectacle-of-black-forgiveness-1838747565.

284 **crime of arriving late to jury duty:** "Before my hearing, I walked in the courtroom as a free man with no criminal record," said the man, Deandre Somerville, an assistant in the city's after-school program. "I left a criminal in handcuffs." Under public pressure, the judge cleared Somerville's record, but only after he had already served his time in jail. The judge said he did so because he believed Somerville had been "totally rehabilitated." P. R. Lockhart, "A Black Man Went to Jail for Missing Jury Duty. After Public Outrage, the Judge Cleared His Record," *Vox,* October 8, 2019, https://www.vox.com/identities/2019/10/8/20904974/deandre-somerville-jail-sleep-jury-duty-florida-kastrenakes.

285 **"This expectation feels fueled":** Hanif Abdurraqib, "Why Do We Expect Victims of Racism to Forgive?" *Pacific Standard,* November 1, 2018, https://psmag.com/social-justice/why-do-we-expect-victims-of-racism-to-forgive.

285 **a black child wanting to hug:** Everton Bailey, Jr., "The Story Behind Devonte Hart's Famous 'Hug' Photo," *Oregonian,* March 28, 2018, https://www.oregonlive.com/pacific-northwest-news/2018/03/the_story_behind_devonte_harts.html.

286 **Two white women in Minnesota:** Shane Dixon Kavanaugh, "Devonte Hart Family Crash: Deceptions, Missed Signals Preceded Deaths," *Oregonian,* April 8, 2018, https://www.oregonlive.com/pacific-northwest-news/2018/04/devonte_hart_family_crash_dece.html; and Shane

Dixon Kavanaugh, "Devonte Hart's Little Sister Told Police in 2010 She Was Beaten, Denied Food," *Oregonian*, March 29, 2018, https:// www.oregonlive.com/pacific-northwest-news/2018/03/devonte _harts_little_sister_to.html.

287　**drove off a cliff in Northern California:** Daniel Victor, "Hart Family Parents Killed 6 Children in Murder-Suicide, Jury Determines," *New York Times*, April 5, 2019, https://www.nytimes.com/2019/04/05/us /hart-family-murder-suicide.html.

287　**"White people embrace narratives":** Roxane Gay, "Why I Can't Forgive Dylann Roof," *New York Times*, June 23, 2015, https://www.ny times.com/2015/06/24/opinion/why-i-cant-forgive-dylann-roof .html.

288　**"Black people forgive because":** Ibid.

288　**What saved the boy from:** Kristine Phillips, "A Black Child's Backpack Brushed Up Against a Woman. She Called 911 to Report a Sexual Assault," *Washington Post*, October 16, 2018, https://www.washington post.com/nation/2018/10/13/black-childs-backpack-brushed-up -against-woman-she-called-report-sexual-assault/?outputType =amp.

289　**"What white people are really":** Gay, "Why I Can't Forgive."

289　**caste often migrates with them:** Tinku Ray, "No Escape from Caste on These Shores, 'Untouchables' from India Say," *Pulitzer Center*, February 26, 2019, https://pulitzercenter.org/reporting/no-escape-caste -these-shores-untouchables-india-say.

Chapter Twenty-Three: Shock Troops on the Borders of Hierarchy

293　**"standing at the butler's table":** Doyle, *Etiquette of Race Relations*, pp. 3, 4.

293　**"When you laugh":** "A group of African American women say they were humiliated by being ejected for 'laughing while black'—igniting debate on 'white space' and a possible lawsuit." Rupert Neate, "Napa Wine Train Controversy: 'I Do Think It Was Based on the Color of Our Skin,'" *Guardian*, September 13, 2015, https://www.theguardian .com/us-news/2015/sep/13/napa-wine-train-laughing-while -black. The tour company later apologized for its treatment of the women and came to an out-of-court settlement of a lawsuit the women had filed. Mary Bowerman, "Black Women Kicked off Napa Valley Wine Train Settle," *USA Today*, April 20, 2016, https:// www.usatoday.com/story/money/nation-now/2016/04/20

/black-women-kicked-off-napa-valley-wine-train-settle-racial -discrimination-case/83280120/.

293 **a Pennsylvania golf club ordered:** Dan Cancian, "Pennsylvania Golf Club Ejects Black Women, Including NAACP's Sandra Thompson, for 'Playing Too Slowly," *Newsweek,* April 24, 2018, https://www .newsweek.com/golf-club-forced-apologize-evicting-black-women -898381. See also Tony Marco and Lauren DelValle, "A Group of Black Women Say a Golf Course Called the Cops on Them for Playing Too Slow," CNN, April 25, 2018, https://www.cnn.com/2018/04/25/us /black-women-golfers-pennsylvania-trnd/index.html.

301 **Dao said he was convinced:** Lori Aratani, "United Passenger: Dragging Incident More Horrifying Than When He Fled Vietnam," *Washington Post,* April 13, 2017, https://www.washingtonpost.com/local /trafficandcommuting/united-passenger-dragging-incident-more -horrifying-than-when-he-fled-vietnam/2017/04/13/7941ccdc-206f -11e7-be2a-3a1fb24d4671_story.html.

301 **"I just cried":** Julia Jacobo, "Doctor Dragged Off United Airlines Flight After Watching Viral Video of Himself: 'I Just Cried,'" ABC News, April 9, 2019, https://abcnews.go.com/US/doctor-dragged -off-united-airlines-flight-watching-viral/story?id=62250271.

Chapter Twenty-Four: Cortisol, Telomeres, and the Lethality of Caste

304 **"even during benign social":** Elizabeth Page-Gould, "The Unhealthy Racist," in Marsh, Mendoza-Denton, and Smith, *Are We Born Racist?,* p. 41.

305 **"require cooperation to":** Susan T. Fiske, "Are We Born Racist?" ibid., pp. 7–15.

305 **premature aging of the cells:** Arline T. Geronimus et al., "Race-Ethnicity, Poverty, Urban Stressors, and Telomere Length in a Detroit Community-based Sample," *Journal of Health and Social Behavior* 56 (June 2015): 199–224. See also Elizabeth DeVita-Raeburn, "Arline Geronimus: Q&A About Weathering, or How Chronic Stress Prematurely Ages Your Body," *Everyday Health,* October 16, 2018, https:// www.everydayhealth.com/wellness/united-states-of-stress/advisory -board/arline-t-geronimus-q-a/.

306 **"Middle class African American":** Lipsitz, *Possessive Investment in Whiteness,* p. 111.

306 **"High levels of everyday":** David R. Williams, interview by author, Providence, R.I., May 29, 2013.

307 **The average white American:** "Disparities within racial and ethnic groups persist even at the highest level of education. The same highly educated black men and women who live longer than less educated whites still live about 4.2 years less than comparably educated whites and 6.1 years less than comparably educated Hispanics." S. Jay Olshansky et al., "Differences in Life Expectancy Due to Race and Educational Differences Are Widening, And Many May Not Catch Up," *Health Affairs* 31, no. 8. https://www.healthaffairs.org/doi/full/10.1377/hlthaff.2011.0746.

307 **"the out-of-place principle":** Graves, *Race Myth*, p. 133.

308 **"buy protection from the":** Hacker, *Two Nations*, p. 42.

Part Six: Backlash

Chapter Twenty-Five: A Change in the Script

312 **the Great Recession:** Paul Solman, "How the 2008 Financial Crisis Crashed the Economy and Changed the World," *PBS NewsHour*, September 13, 2018, https://www.pbs.org/newshour/show/how-the-2008-financial-crisis-crashed-the-economy-and-changed-the-world.

313 **"You've got the first sort":** David Gregory, "Sen. Biden Apologizes for Remarks on Obama," NBC News, January 31, 2007, http://www.nbcnews.com/id/16911044/ns/nbc_nightly_news_with_brian_williams/t/sen-biden-apologizes-remarks-obama/#.Xkr895E8KhA.

314 **the majority of white Americans did not vote:** In 2008, 57 percent of whites voted against the Democrat. In 2012, 61 percent voted against him. Jardina, *White Identity*, p. 218. For in-depth analysis of the role of race in Barack Obama's campaign and presidency, see Gillespie, *Race and the Obama Administration*.

314 **"The cultural divides of the":** Patrick Fisher, "Economic Performance and Presidential Vote for Obama: The Underappreciated Influence of Race," *Politics, Groups, and Identities* 4, no. 1 (2015): 30–46. https://doi.org/10.1080/21565503.2015.1050413.

315 **Lyndon Johnson was the last:** Democrats won the following percentages of the white vote in presidential elections since 1976: Carter, 48 percent in 1976; Carter, 36 percent in 1980; Mondale, 41 percent in 1984; Dukakis, 40 percent in 1988; Clinton, 39 percent in 1992; Clinton, 44 percent in 1996; Gore 42 percent in 2000; Kerry, 41 percent in 2004; Obama, 43 percent in 2008, and 39 percent in 2012; Hillary

Clinton, 37 percent in 2016. "How Groups Voted in 1976," Roper Center, n.d., https://ropercenter.cornell.edu/how-groups-voted-1976. The shadow of the Civil War seemed to hang over the 2008 election. Obama carried every state that Abraham Lincoln had won in 1860, an election with an almost entirely white electorate but one that became a proxy for the future of slavery and of the Republic, according to Fisher, "Economic Performance and Presidential Vote for Obama," pp. 30–46, esp. 38. See also Timothy J. Hoffman, "The Civil Rights Realignment: How Race Dominates Presidential Elections," *Political Analysis* 17, article 1 (2015), https://scholarship.shu.edu/pa/vol17/iss1/1.

315 **"The symbolism of Obama's election":** Jardina, *White Identity*, p. 227.

315 **"the ability of a black person":** Gillespie, *Race and the Obama Administration*, p. 194.

316 **"The single most important":** "Top GOP Priority: Make Obama a One-Term President," *National Journal*, October 23, 2010, https://www.nationaljournal.com/member/magazine/top-gop-priority-make-obama-a-one-term-president-20101023/.

316 **"no place for it":** David Batty, "'You Lie': Republican Joe Wilson's Outburst at Obama Health Speech," *Guardian*, September 10, 2009, https://www.theguardian.com/world/2009/sep/10/you-lie-joe-wilson-obama-speech.

316 **She jabbed her finger:** Tommy Christopher, "Drama Clubbed: Jan Brewer Says 'I Felt a Little Bit Threatened' by President Obama," *Mediaite*, January 26, 2012, https://www.mediaite.com/tv/drama-clubbed-jan-brewer-says-i-felt-a-little-bit-threatened-by-president-obama/; Brittney Cooper, "White Women's Rage: Five Reasons Jan Brewer Should Keep Her Fingers to Herself," *Ms.*, January 31, 2012, https://msmagazine.com/2012/01/31/5-thoughts-on-why-jan-brewer-should-keep-her-fingers-to-herself/.

317 **a radiology technician:** Reed Karaim, "America's Most Puzzling Governor," *Politico*, March 6, 2014, https://www.politico.com/magazine/story/2014/03/jan-brewer-americas-most-puzzling-governor-104384. Brewer rose from secretary of state to governor when President Obama named Gov. Janet Napolitano to his cabinet. Arizona has no lieutenant governor. Brewer as secretary of state was next in line.

317 **"thought he could lecture me":** Donovan Slack, "Jan Brewer: Obama 'Didn't Feel I Treated Him Cordially,'" *Politico44 Blog*, January 25, 2012, https://www.politico.com/blogs/politico44/2012/01/jan-brewer-obama-didnt-feel-i-treated-him-cordially-112328.

318 **"You have ONE more":** Howard Fischer, "Brewer Using Tiff with Obama to Raise Money," *Arizona Daily Star*, January 30, 2012, https://

tucson.com/news/local/govt-and-politics/brewer-using-tiff-with
-obama-to-raise-money/article_105ecbfa-4b79-11e1-8fa7-0019bb
2963f4.html.

318 **An entire machinery had moved:** Jonathan Chait, "The Color of
His Presidency," *New York,* April 4, 2014, http://nymag.com/news
/features/obama-presidency-race-2014-4/.

318 **purges that accelerated:** Kevin Morris et al., "Purges: A Growing
Threat to the Right to Vote," Brennan Center for Justice, July 20, 2018,
https://www.brennancenter.org/our-work/research-reports/purges
-growing-threat-right-vote.

318 **"A paper found that states":** Chait, "Color of His Presidency."

319 **the number of hate groups:** Mark Potok, "The Year in Hate and Ex-
tremism," Southern Poverty Law Center, March 4, 2013, https://www
.splcenter.org/fighting-hate/intelligence-report/2013/year-hate
-and-extremism.

319 **explicit anti-black attitudes:** "AP Poll: U.S. Majority Have Prejudice
Against Blacks," *USA Today,* October 27, 2012, https://www.usatoday
.com/story/news/politics/2012/10/27/poll-black-prejudice
-america/1662067/.

319 **police were killing unarmed African-Americans:** "Police Killed
More Than 100 Unarmed Black People in 2015," Mapping Police Violence, n.d., https://mappingpoliceviolence.org.

319 **at a rate of 1 in 1,000:** Amin Khan, "Getting Killed by Police Is a Leading Cause of Death for Young Black Men in America," *Los Angeles
Times,* August 16, 2019.

320 **"most whites in the United States":** Jardina, *White Identity,* p. 226.

320 **"Any upheaval in the universe":** Baldwin, *Fire Next Time,* p. 9.

320 **"masked an undercurrent of anxiety":** Jardina, *White Identity,* p. 273.

321 **"I went to bed last night":** Thomas B. Edsall, "Is Rush Limbaugh's
Country Gone?" *New York Times,* November 18, 2012, https://
campaignstops.blogs.nytimes.com/2012/11/18/is-rush-limbaughs
-country-gone/.

321 **"If Barack gets reelected":** Meena Hart Duerson, "Florida Man Who
Warned He Wouldn't 'Be Around' If Barack Obama Was Reelected
Kills Himself After the Election," *New York Daily News,* November 14,
2012, https://www.nydailynews.com/news/national/man-article-1
.1201911; Dan Amira, "Overreactions: Florida Man Commits Suicide
Over Obama Win," *New York,* November 14, 2012, http://nymag
.com/intelligencer/2012/11/florida-man-commits-suicide-over-obama
-win.html.

Chapter Twenty-Six: Turning Point and the Resurgence of Caste

325 **"White voters' preference":** John Sides, Michael Tesler, and Lynn Vavreck, *Identity Crisis: The 2016 Presidential Campaign and the Battle for the Meaning of America* (Princeton: Princeton University Press, 2019), pp. 28–30, 175, 176.

325 **"Whites' racial attitudes are":** Jardina, *White Identity,* p. 7.

326 **"are seeking to reassert":** Ibid., p. 5.

328 **53 percent:** The Roper Center at Cornell University put Donald Trump's 2016 share of the white vote at 57 percent, 1 percent less than CNN's number.

328 **"Trump was ushered into office":** Jardina, *White Identity,* pp. 272, 267.

330 **priorities of white evangelicals:** Seth Dowland, "American Evangelicalism and the Politics of Whiteness," *Christian Century,* June 19, 2018, https://www.christianCentury.org/article/critical-essay/american-evangelicalism-and-politics-whiteness.

331 **"Even though white Americans":** Robert Tsai, "Specter of a White Minority," *Los Angeles Review of Books,* September 3, 2018, https://la reviewofbooks.org/article/specter-of-a-white-minority/.

331 **"These aggrieved whites are":** Jardina, *White Identity,* p. 278.

331 **"In many ways, a sense":** Diana C. Mutz, "Status Threat, Not Economic Hardship, Explains the 2016 Presidential Vote," *Proceedings of the National Academy of Sciences* 115 (May 8, 2018): 4330–39, https://doi.org/10.1073/pnas.1718155115.

332 **"Whether out of personal animus":** Peter Baker, "Can Trump Destroy Obama's Legacy?," *New York Times,* June 23, 2017, https://www.nytimes.com/2017/06/23/sunday-review/donald-trump-barack-obama.html.

332 **"dominant group status threat":** Mutz, "Status Threat, Not Economic Hardship."

Chapter Twenty-Seven: The Symbols of Caste

333 **sculpture of Robert E. Lee:** Brendan Wolfe, "Robert Edward Lee Sculpture," *Encyclopedia Virginia,* March 20, 2019, https://www.encyclopediavirginia.org/Robert_Edward_Lee_Sculpture#start_entry.

335 **more than seventeen hundred monuments:** "Whose Heritage? Public Symbols of the Confederacy," Southern Poverty Law Center, https://www.splcenter.org/20190201/whose-heritage-public-symbols

-confederacy. The dataset, map, and online report are updated as of February 1, 2019. The original report was published on April 21, 2016. It was written by Booth Gunter and Jamie Kizzire, with contributions from Cindy Kent.

335 **"Its foundations are laid":** Alexander H. Stephens, vice president of the Confederate States of America, "Cornerstone Speech," March 21, 1861, in Henry Cleveland, *Alexander H. Stephens in Public and Private: With Letters and Speeches, Before, During, and Since the War* (Philadelphia, 1886), pp. 717–29, available at https://teachingamericanhistory.org/library/document/cornerstone-speech/.

335 *Gone with the Wind:* Leonard J. Leff, "*Gone With the Wind* and Hollywood's Racial Politics," *Atlantic,* December 1999, https://www.theatlantic.com/magazine/archive/1999/12/gone-with-the-wind-and-hollywoods-racial-politics/377919/.

337 **"The blacks are immeasurably":** Robert E. Lee to Mary Randolph Custis Lee, December 27, 1856, in *Encyclopedia Virginia,* https://www.encyclopediavirginia.org/Letter_from_Robert_E_Lee_to_Mary_Randolph_Custis_Lee_December_27_1856.

337 **"he would teach us a lesson":** "Testimony of Wesley Norris," *National Anti-Slavery Standard,* April 14, 1866, available at http://fair-use.org/wesley-norris/testimony-of-wesley-norris. See also Sean Kane, "Myths & Misunderstandings | Lee as a Slaveholder," American Civil War Museum, n.d., https://acwm.org/blog/myths-misunderstandings-lee-slaveholder.

338 **Arlington National Cemetery:** Robert M. Poole, "How Arlington National Cemetery Came to Be," *Smithsonian Magazine,* November 2009, https://www.smithsonianmag.com/history/how-arlington-national-cemetery-came-to-be-145147007/.

339 **"there was a right side":** Frederick Douglass, speech delivered in Madison Square, New York, May 30, 1878, p. 13, http://hdl.loc.gov/loc.mss/mfd.23011.

340 **remove the Confederate flag:** Nathaniel Cary and Doug Stanglin, "South Carolina Takes Down Confederate Flag," *USA Today* via *Greenville* (S.C.) *News,* July 10, 2015, https://www.usatoday.com/story/news/nation/2015/07/10/south-carolina-confederate-flag/29952953/.

340 **Landrieu was moved:** Rachel Brown, "How New Orleans' Mayor Was Inspired by a Jazz Great to Take Down Confederate Monuments," *National Geographic,* March 11, 2018, https://nationalgeographic.com/news/2018/03/confederate-monuments-robert-lee-new-orleans-mitch-landrieu-katie-couric-video-documentary/; Britt McCandless

Farmer, "Behind the Decision to Remove a Statue of Robert E. Lee," CBS News, March 11, 2018, https://www.cbsnews.com/news/behind -the-decision-to-remove-a-statue-of-robert-e-lee/.

340 **a fairly straightforward process:** Landrieu, *Shadow of Statues,* p. 186.

341 **"They are ashamed":** Germany underwent a physical denazification after the Allies' victory in 1945. Statues of Nazi leaders are illegal, and the country has more restrictive speech and anti-hate laws than does America. There are several German military bases named after Third Reich generals, including the Field Marshal Erwin Rommel Barracks in Augustdorf, Germany. There was a movement to change these names in 2017. Justin Huggler, "German Army to Drop Nazi Names from Barracks More than 70 Years After the End of World War Two," *Telegraph* (UK), May 14, 2017, https://www.telegraph.co.uk/news /2017/05/14/german-army-drop-nazi-names-barracks-70-years -end-world-war/. Rommel is a widely debated figure, ambiguous and controversial to this day. In addition to his reputation on the field, he was implicated in a plot to overthrow Hitler and thereafter was forced to commit suicide. That may have been a factor in the naming of several military buildings after him, including the barracks. Rommel's burial site at Herrlingen Cemetery in Blaustein includes a tomb, a headstone, and signage. Generally, Rommel's role both in Hitler's war machine and in the assassination attempt is disputed.

341 **not one construction company:** Landrieu, *Shadow of Statues,* p. 187.

341 **"any company that dared":** Mitch Landrieu, "What I Learned from My Fight to Remove Confederate Monuments," *Guardian,* March 24, 2018, https://www.theguardian.com/us-news/commentisfree/2018 /mar/24/new-orleans-mayor-louisiana-confederate-statues-removal -never-stop-confronting-racial-injustice.

341 **"I'll get run out":** Landrieu, *Shadow of Statues,* p. 189.

341 **"People who had served":** Ibid., pp. 188, 190, 191, 192.

341 **a construction company willing:** Ibid., p. 192.

342 **His figure dangled from a crane:** Campbell Robertson, "From Lofty Perch, New Orleans Monument to the Confederacy Comes Down," *New York Times,* May 19, 2017, https://www.nytimes.com/2017/05 /19/us/confederate-monument-new-orleans-lee.html; Tegan Wendland, "With Lee's Statue Removal, Another Battle of New Orleans Coming to a Close," National Public Radio, May 20, 2017, https:// www.npr.org/2017/05/20/529232823/with-lee-statues-removal -another-battle-of-new-orleans-comes-to-a-close.

342 **"These monuments celebrate":** Rachel Brown, "How New Orleans' Mayor Was Inspired by a Jazz Great to Take Down Confederate

Monuments," *National Geographic,* March 11, 2018, https://national geographic.com/news/2018/03/confederate-monuments-robert-lee -new-orleans-mitch-landrieu-katie-couric-video-documentary/.

342 **"They were created as political":** Landrieu, "What I Learned from My Fight."

342 **fighting to keep monuments:** Howard Koplowitz, "Legislature Passes Monuments Preservation Bill," *Alabama Live,* May 19, 2017, https://www.al.com/news/2017/05/house_passes_monuments _preserv.html.

343 **"I wanted people to have":** Peter Eisenman, in "How Long Does One Feel Guilty?" *Der Spiegel,* May 9, 2005, https://www.spiegel.de /international/spiegel-interview-with-holocaust-monument -architect-peter-eisenman-how-long-does-one-feel-guilty-a-355252 .html.

345 **This is where Hitler spent:** Joachim Fest, *Inside Hitler's Bunker: The Last Days of the Third Reich* (New York: Picador, 2002), p. 116.

346 **"To which I respond":** Susan Neiman, "There Are No Nostalgic Nazi Memorials," *Atlantic,* September 14, 2019, https://www.theatlantic .com/ideas/archive/2019/09/germany-has-no-nazi-memorials /597937/.

346 **Germany chose quite literally:** Joshua Zeitz, "Why There Are No Nazi Statues in Germany," *Politico,* August 20, 2017, https://www .politico.com/magazine/story/2017/08/20/why-there-are-no-nazi -statues-in-germany-215510.

346 **In Germany, displaying the swastika:** German Strafgesetzbuch (criminal code) section 86a, outlining the illegality of disseminating Nazi symbols and propaganda, https://germanlawarchive.iuscomp .org/?p=752#86a.

346 **the rebel flag is incorporated:** Erin McClam, "Flags of Some Southern States Still Include Confederate Symbols," NBC News, June 23, 2015, https://www.nbcnews.com/news/us-news/flags-some-southern -states-still-include-confederate-symbols-n380161; "Supreme Court Refuses to Hear Appeal of Mississippi Flag Case," WLOX, January 12, 2004, https://www.wlox.com/story/1597564/supreme-court-refuses -to-hear-appeal-of-mississippi-flag-case/.

346 **all currently have the death penalty:** "The State of Capital Punishment," National Conference of State Legislatures, July 30, 2019, https://www.ncsl.org/research/civil-and-criminal-justice/the-state -of-capital-punishment.aspx. See also "State by State," Death Penalty Information Center, n.d., https://deathpenaltyinfo.org/state -and-federal-info/state-by-state.

347 **"Not even members of"**: Neiman, "There Are No Nostalgic Nazi Memorials."

347 **"privately mourn for family members"**: Neiman, *Learning from Germans*, p. 267.

Chapter Twenty-Eight: Democracy on the Ballot

352 **purging tens of thousands of voters:** "Republican Voter Suppression Efforts Are Targeting Minorities, Journalist Says," National Public Radio, October 23, 2018, https://www.npr.org/2018/10/23/659784 277/republican-voter-suppression-efforts-are-targeting-minorities -journalist-says.

352 **rejecting IDs that didn't:** "At least nine states have a policy like Georgia's where citizens can be removed from the voter registration list for not voting in past elections. The best known is Ohio's. In that state, the removal process is triggered for anyone who doesn't vote in a single election. The entire removal process takes six years. Earlier this year, the U.S. Supreme Court ruled Ohio's policy is in line with the National Voter Registration Act." Johnny Kauffman, "6 Takeaways From Georgia's 'Use It or Lose It' Voter Purge Investigation," National Public Radio, October 22, 2018.

Chapter Twenty-Nine: The Price We Pay for a Caste System

354 **"Ten grand?":** "True Cost of US Healthcare Shocks the British Public," *PoliticsJOE*, December 3, 2019, https://m.youtube.com/watch?v =Kll-yYQwmuM.

354 **"Few industrialized economies":** Chait, "The Color of His Presidency."

355 **There are more public mass shootings:** Nurith Aizenman, "Deaths from Gun Violence: How the U.S. Compares with the Rest of the World," National Public Radio, November 9, 2018, https://www.npr .org/sections/goatsandsoda/2018/11/09/666209430/deaths-from -gun-violence-how-the-u-s-compares-with-the-rest-of-the-world.

355 **the maternal mortality rate:** Munira Z. Gunja et al., "What Is the Status of Women's Health and Health Care in the U.S. Compared to Ten Other Countries?" Commonwealth Fund, December 19, 2018, https:// www.commonwealthfund.org/publications/issue-briefs/2018 /dec/womens-health-us-compared-ten-other-countries; Ashley Welch, "U.S. Women Pay More, Fare Worse During Pregnancy and Childbirth, Global Health Study Finds," CBS News, December 19, 2018,

https://www.cbsnews.com/news/us-women-more-likely-to-die
-during-pregnancy-than-other-high-income-nations/.

355 **The life expectancy in America:** Selena Gonzales, Marco Ramirez,
and Bradley Sawyer, "How Does U.S. Life Expectancy Compare to
Other Countries?" *Health System Tracker,* December 23, 2019, https://
www.healthsystemtracker.org/chart-collection/u-s-life-expectancy
-compare-countries/#item-le_life-expectancy-in-years-at-given-age
-2017_dec-2019-update.

355 **Infant mortality:** Christopher Ingraham, "Our Infant Mortality Rate
Is a National Embarrassment," *Washington Post,* September 29, 2014,
https://www.washingtonpost.com/news/wonk/wp/2014/09/29
/our-infant-mortality-rate-is-a-national-embarrassment/; Organisa-
tion for Economic Co-operation and Development, "Infant Mortality
Rates," 2020, https://data.oecd.org/healthstat/infant-mortality-rates
.htm.

355 **American students score:** Joe Heim, "On the World Stage, U.S. Students Fall Behind," *Washington Post,* December 6, 2016, https://www
.washingtonpost.com/local/education/on-the-world-stage-us-students
-fall-behind/2016/12/05/610e1e10-b740-11e6-a677-b608fbb3aaf6_story
.html.

356 **eighteenth in happiness:** Josh Fiallo, "U.S. Falls in World Happiness Report, Finland Named Happiest Country," *Tampa Bay Times,*
March 20, 2019, https://www.tampabay.com/data/2019/03/20/us
-falls-in-world-happiness-report-finland-named-happiest-country/.

356 **"As Usual":** Annie Lowrey, "As Usual, Americans Must Go it Alone,"
Atlantic, March 19, 2020, https:// www.theatlantic.com/ideas/archive
/2020/03/america-woefully-underinsured/608035/.

357 **"To a watching world":** Simon Tisdall, "US's Global Reputation
Hits Rock-Bottom Over Trump's Coronavirus Response," *Guardian,*
April 12, 2020, https://theguardian.com/us-news/2020/apr/12/us
-global-reputation-rock-bottom-donald-trump-coronavirus.

357 **"This is a civilization":** Gary Michael Tartakov, in discussion with
the author, International Conference on Caste and Race, at the University of Massachusetts Amherst, May 5, 2018.

Epilogue: A World Without Caste

378 **"The worst disease is":** Jerome and Taylor, *Einstein on Race,* pp. 144–45.

378 **"bowing and scraping":** Ibid., p. 32.

378 **Einstein, learning of this:** Matthew Francis, "How Albert Einstein Used His Fame to Denounce American Racism," *Smithsonian Magazine,* March 3, 2017, https://www.smithsonianmag.com/science-nature/how-celebrity-scientist-albert-einstein-used-fame-denounce-american-racism-180962356/.

379 **"Being a Jew myself, perhaps":** Einstein to Peter Bucky, quoted in Jerome and Taylor, *Einstein on Race,* p. 151.

379 **children of black faculty:** Ken Gewertz, "Albert Einstein, Civil Rights Activist," *Harvard Gazette,* April 12, 2007, https://news.harvard.edu/gazette/story/2007/04/albert-einstein-civil-rights-activist/.

379 **"The separation of the races":** Jerome and Taylor, *Einstein on Race,* p. 88.

379 **"He hates race prejudice":** Ibid., p. 9.

381 **228 years to amass the wealth:** Dedrick Asante-Muhammad et al., "The Ever Growing Gap," Institute for Policy Studies, August 2016, https://ips-dc.org/wp-content/uploads/2016/08/The-Ever-Growing-Gap-CFED_IPS-Final-1.pdf.

383 **"It's all too easy to imagine":** Smith, *Less Than Human,* p. 16.

383 **"Caste is not a physical object":** Ambedkar, *Annihilation of Caste,* p. 74.

385 **"We must make every effort":** Francis, "How Albert Einstein Used His Fame to Denounce American Racism"; Jerome and Taylor, *Einstein on Race,* p. 144.

BIBLIOGRAPHY

Abraham, Joshil K., and Judith Misrahi-Barak. *Dalit Literatures in India.* London: Routledge, 2018.

Alexander, Michelle. *The New Jim Crow: Mass Incarceration in the Age of Colorblindness.* New York: New Press, 2010.

Allen, James. *Without Sanctuary: Lynching Photography in America.* Santa Fe, N.M.: Twin Palms, 2000.

Allen, Theodore W. *The Invention of the White Race*, 2 vols., 2nd ed. London: Verso, 2012.

Ambedkar, Dr. B. R. *Annihilation of Caste: The Annotated Critical Edition.* Edited by S. Anand. London: Verso, 2014.

———. *Castes in India: Their Mechanism, Genesis, and Development.* Columbia, S.C.: LM Publishers, 2020.

Anderson, Carol. *White Rage: The Unspoken Truth of Our Racial Divide.* New York: Bloomsbury, 2016.

Arora, Namit. *The Lottery of Birth: On Inherited Social Inequalities.* New Delhi: Three Essays Collective, 2017.

Aston, Nathan M. *Literature of Marginality: Dalit Literature and African-American Literature.* New Delhi: Prestige Books, 2001.

Astor, Gerald. *The Baseball Hall of Fame 50th Anniversary Book.* New York: Fireside, 1992.

Bailey, Anne C. *The Weeping Time: Memory and the Largest Slave Auction in American History.* Cambridge, U.K.: Cambridge University Press, 2017.

Bailey, Thomas Pearce. *Race Orthodoxy in the South and Other Aspects of the Negro Question.* New York: Neale, 1914.

Baker, Ray S. *Following the Color Line: American Negro Citizenship in the Progressive Era.* New York: Harper & Row, 1964.

Baldwin, James. *The Fire Next Time*. 1963; reprint New York: Vintage International, 1993.

Banaji, Mahzarin R., and Anthony G. Greenwald. *Blindspot: Hidden Biases of Good People*. New York: Delacorte Press, 2013.

Bancroft, Frederic. *Slave Trading in the Old South*. Columbia: University of South Carolina Press, 1996.

Baptist, Edward E. *The Half Has Never Been Told: Slavery and the Making of American Capitalism*. New York: Basic Books, 2016.

Berreman, Gerald D. *Caste and Other Inequities: Essays on Inequality*. Meerut, India: Folklore Institute, 1979.

Berry, Daina Ramey. *The Price for Their Pound of Flesh: The Value of the Enslaved, from Womb to Grave, in the Building of a Nation*. Boston: Beacon Press, 2017.

Blackmon, Douglas A. *Slavery by Another Name: The Re-enslavement of Black People in America from the Civil War to World War II*. New York: Doubleday, 2008.

Bleser, Carol, ed. *Secret and Sacred: The Diaries of James Henry Hammond, a Southern Slaveholder*. New York: Oxford University Press, 1989.

Bogle, Donald. *Toms, Coons, Mulattoes, Mammies, & Bucks: An Interpretive History of Blacks in American Films*. New York: Bloomsbury, 2016.

Bonilla-Silva, Eduardo. *Racism Without Racists: Color-Blind Racism and the Persistence of Racial Inequality in the United States*. Lanham, Md.: Rowman & Littlefield, 2003.

Bouglé, Célestin C. *Essays on the Caste System*. Translated by D. F. Pocock. 1908; reprint Cambridge, U.K.: Cambridge University Press, 1971.

Bressey, Caroline. *Empire, Race, and the Politics of Anti-Caste*. London: Bloomsbury, 2013.

Brown, John. *Slave Life in Georgia: A Narrative of the Life, Sufferings, and Escape of John Brown, a Fugitive Slave, Now in England*. Edited by L. A. Chamerovzow. London: British and Foreign Anti-Slavery Society, 1855.

Brown, Michael K., Martin Carnoy, Elliott Currie, Troy Duster, and David B. Oppenheimer. *Whitewashing Race: The Myth of a Color-Blind Society*. Berkeley: University of California Press, 2003.

Brown, William Wells. *Narrative of the Life of William Wells Brown, a Fugitive Slave*. Boston: Anti-Slavery Office, No. 25 Cornhill, 1847.

Brustein, William. *The Logic of Evil: The Origins of the Nazi Party, 1925–1933*. New Haven: Yale University Press, 1996.

Cash, Wilbur J. *The Mind of the South*. New York: Knopf, 1941.

Childers, Thomas. *The Third Reich: A History of Nazi Germany*. New York: Simon & Schuster, 2017.

Clark, Tena. *Southern Discomfort: A Memoir*. New York: Atria Books, 2018.

Coates, Ta-Nehisi. *We Were Eight Years in Power: An American Tragedy*. New York: One World/Ballantine, 2017.

Cox, Oliver Cromwell. *Caste, Class, and Race: A Study in Social Dynamics*. New York: Doubleday, 1948.

Darity, William, and Ashwini Deshpande, eds. *Boundaries of Clan and Color: Transnational Comparisons of Inter-Group Disparity*. London: Routledge, 2003.

Dass Namishray, Mohan. *Caste and Race: A Comparative Study of B.R. Ambedkar and Martin Luther King*. Jaipur, India: Rawat, 2003.

Davis, Allison, Burleigh B. Gardner, and Mary R. Gardner. *Deep South: A Social Anthropological Study of Caste and Class*. Chicago: University of Chicago Press, 1941.

Delbanco, Andrew. *The War Before the War: Fugitive Slaves and the Struggle for America's Soul from the Revolution to the Civil War*. New York: Penguin, 2019.

Deshpande, Satish. *The Problem of Caste*. Hyderabad, India: Orient BlackSwan, 2014.

DiAngelo, Robin J. *White Fragility: Why It's So Hard for White People to Talk about Racism*. Boston: Beacon Press, 2018.

Dollard, John. *Caste and Class in a Southern Town*. New Haven, Conn.: Yale University Press, 1937.

Douglass, Frederick. *My Bondage and My Freedom*. Oxford World's Classics, edited by Celeste-Marie Bernier. Oxford: Oxford University Press, 2019.

———. *Narrative of the Life of Frederick Douglass, an American Slave: Written by Himself*, critical ed. New Haven, Conn.: Yale University Press, 2016.

Douglass, Paul F. *God Among the Germans*. Philadelphia: University of Pennsylvania Press, 1935.

Doyle, Bertram Wilbur. *The Etiquette of Race Relations in the South: A Study in Social Control*. 1937; reprint New York: Schocken, 1971.

Dray, Philip. *At the Hands of Persons Unknown*. New York: Modern Library, 2003.

Du Bois, W.E.B. *Black Reconstruction in America: Toward a History of the Part Which Black Folk Played in the Attempt to Reconstruct Democracy in America, 1860–1880*. New York: Harcourt, Brace, 1935.

———. *The Souls of Black Folk*. Chicago: McClurg & Co., 1903.

Dutt, Yashica. *Coming Out as Dalit*. New Delhi: Aleph Book Co., 2019.

Eberhardt, Jennifer L. *Biased: Uncovering the Hidden Prejudice That Shapes What We See, Think, and Do*. New York: Viking, 2019.

Entman, Robert M., and Andrew Rojecki. *The Black Image in the White Mind: Media and Race in America*. Edited by Susan Herbst and Benjamin I. Page. Chicago: University of Chicago Press, 2010.

Fischer, Klaus P. *Hitler and America*. Philadelphia: University of Pennsylvania Press, 2011.

Foner, Eric. *Reconstruction: America's Unfinished Revolution, 1863–1877*. New York: HarperCollins, 2011.

Fredrickson, George M. *The Arrogance of Race: Historical Perspectives on Slavery, Racism, and Social Inequality*. Middletown, Conn.: Wesleyan University Press, 1989.

———. *Racism: A Short History*. Princeton: Princeton University Press, 2015.

———. *White Supremacy: A Comparative Study of American and South African History*. New York: Oxford University Press, 1982.

Friedlander, Saul. *Nazi Germany and the Jews*, vol. 1: *The Years of Persecution 1933–1939*. New York: HarperCollins, 1998.

Fromm, Erich. *The Heart of Man: Its Genius for Good and Evil*. New York: Harper & Row, 1964.

Gilens, Martin. *Why Americans Hate Welfare: Race, Media, and the Politics of Antipoverty Policy*. Chicago: University of Chicago Press, 2000.

Gillespie, Andra. *Race and the Obama Administration: Substance, Symbols and Hope*. Manchester, U.K.: Manchester University Press, 2019.

Goodell, William. *The American Slave Code in Theory and Practice: Its Distinctive Features Shown by Its Statutes, Judicial Decisions, and Illustrative Facts*. London: Salisbury, Beeton & Co., 1853.

Graves, Joseph L. *The Race Myth: Why We Pretend Race Exists in America*. New York: Plume, 2004.

Gross, Ariela J. *What Blood Won't Tell: A History of Race on Trial in America*. Cambridge, Mass.: Harvard University Press, 2008.

Hacker, Andrew. *Two Nations: Black and White, Separate, Hostile, Unequal*. New York: Scribner, 1992.

Hale, Grace Elizabeth. *Making Whiteness: The Culture of Segregation in the South, 1890–1940*. New York: Pantheon, 1998.

Heimannsberg, Barbara, and Christoph J. Schmidt. *The Collective Silence: German Identity and the Legacy of Shame*. Translated by Cynthia O. Harris and Gordon Wheeler. San Francisco: Jossey-Bass, 2013.

Hett, Benjamin C. *The Death of Democracy: Hitler's Rise to Power and the Downfall of the Weimar Republic*. New York: Henry Holt, 2018.

Hicks, Paul D. *Joseph Henry Lumpkin: Georgia's First Chief Justice*. Athens: University of Georgia Press, 2012.

Horne, Gerald. *The End of Empires: African Americans and India*. Philadelphia: Temple University Press, 2008.

Hunt, Raymond G., and Benjamin Bowser. *Impacts of Racism on White Americans*. Thousand Oaks, Calif.: SAGE Publications, 1996.

Hunter, William W. *The Indian Empire: Its People, History and Products*. London: Trübner & Co., 1886.

Ignatiev, Noel. *How the Irish Became White*. New York: Routledge, 1995.

Jacobson, Matthew F. *Whiteness of a Different Color*. Cambridge, Mass.: Harvard University Press, 1999.

Jardina, Ashley. *White Identity Politics*. Cambridge, U.K.: Cambridge University Press, 2019.

Jerome, Fred, and Rodger Taylor. *Einstein on Race and Racism*. New Brunswick, N.J.: Rutgers University Press, 2006.

Jones-Rogers, Stephanie E. *They Were Her Property: White Women as Slave Owners in the American South*. New Haven: Yale University Press, 2019.

Jordan, Winthrop D. *White over Black: American Attitudes Toward the Negro, 1550–1812*. Durham: University of North Carolina Press, 1968.

Kakel, C. *The American West and the Nazi East: A Comparative and Interpretive Perspective*. London: Palgrave Macmillan, 2011.

Kannabirin, Kalpana. *Non-Discrimination and the Indian Constitution*. New Delhi: Routledge, 2012.

Kasinitz, Philip. *Caribbean New York: Black Immigrants and the Politics of Race*. Ithaca, N.Y.: Cornell University Press, 1992.

Katznelson, Ira. *When Affirmative Action Was White: An Untold History of Racial Inequality in Twentieth-Century America*. New York: W. W. Norton & Co., 2006.

Kelley, Blair L. M. *Right to Ride: Streetcar Boycotts and African American Citizenship in the Era of* Plessy v. Ferguson. Chapel Hill: University of North Carolina Press, 2010.

Kendi, Ibram X. *Stamped from the Beginning: The Definitive History of Racist Ideas in America*. New York: Nation Books, 2016.

Kevles, Daniel J. *In the Name of Eugenics: Genetics and the Uses of Human Heredity*. New York: Knopf, 2013.

Koonz, Claudia. *The Nazi Conscience*. Cambridge, Mass.: Harvard University Press, 2003.

Kühl, Stefan. *The Nazi Connection: Eugenics, American Racism, and German National Socialism*. New York: Oxford University Press, 1994.

Landrieu, Mitch. *In the Shadow of Statues: A White Southerner Confronts History*. New York: Viking, 2018.

Lang, Berel. *Race and Racism in Theory and Practice*. Lanham, Md.: Rowman & Littlefield, 2000.

Lasch, Christopher. *The Culture of Narcissism: American Life in an Age of Diminishing Expectations*. New York: W. W. Norton, 1991.

Levi, Primo. *The Drowned and the Saved*. New York: Simon & Schuster, 2017.

Levitsky, Steven, and Daniel Ziblatt. *How Democracies Die*. New York: Broadway Books, 2018.

Lipsitz, George. *The Possessive Investment in Whiteness: How White People Profit from Identity Politics*, rev. ed. Philadelphia: Temple University Press, 2006.

Litwack, Leon F. *Been in the Storm So Long: The Aftermath of Slavery*. New York: Knopf, 1998.

———. *Trouble in Mind: Black Southerners in the Age of Jim Crow*. New York: Vintage, 1999.

Logan, Rayford. *The Betrayal of the Negro: From Rutherford B. Hayes to Woodrow Wilson*. New York: Collier, 1965.

López, Ian Haney. *White by Law: The Legal Construction of Race*. New York: NYU Press, 1997.

Luxenberg, Steve. *Separate: The Story of Plessy v. Ferguson, and America's Journey from Slavery to Segregation*. New York: W. W. Norton, 2019.

Manu, and Patrick Olivelle. *The Law Code of Manu*. New York: Oxford University Press, 2004.

Marsh, Jason, Rodolfo Mendoza-Denton, and Jeremy A. Smith, eds. *Are We Born Racist?: New Insights from Neuroscience and Positive Psychology*. Boston: Beacon Press, 2010.

Matory, J. L. *Stigma and Culture: Last-Place Anxiety in Black America*. Chicago: University of Chicago Press, 2015.

Metzl, Jonathan M. *Dying of Whiteness: How the Politics of Racial Resentment Is Killing America's Heartland*. New York: Basic Books, 2019.

Michael, S. M. *Untouchable: Dalits in Modern India*. Boulder, Colo.: Lynne Rienner Publishers, 1999.

Mills, Charles W. *The Racial Contract*. Ithaca, N.Y.: Cornell University Press, 1997.

Montagu, Ashley. *Man's Most Dangerous Myth: The Fallacy of Race*. New York: Columbia University Press, 1945.

Muhammad, Khalil G. *The Condemnation of Blackness*. Cambridge, Mass.: Harvard University Press, 2010.

Myrdal, Gunnar. *An American Dilemma: The Negro Problem and Modern Democracy*, 2 vols. New York: Harper and Bros., 1944.

Natrajan, Balmurli, and David Greenough. *Against Stigma: Studies in Caste, Race and Justice Since Durban*. Hyderabad, India: Orient BlackSwan, 2009.

Neiman, Susan. *Learning from the Germans: Race and the Memory of Evil*. New York: Farrar, Straus and Giroux, 2019.

Okada, John. *No-No Boy*. Seattle: University of Washington Press, 1981.

Olmsted, Frederick L. *The Cotton Kingdom: A Traveller's Observations on Cotton and Slavery in the American Slave States: Based Upon Three Former Volumes of Journeys and Investigations by the Same Author*. New York, 1861.

Omvedt, Gail. *Understanding Caste: From Buddha to Ambedkar and Beyond*, 2nd ed. New Delhi: Orient BlackSwan, 2011.

Ortner, Helmut. *Hitler's Executioner: Roland Freisler, President of the Nazi People's Court*. Barnsley, South Yorkshire, U.K.: Pen and Sword, 2018.

Packard, Jerrold M. *American Nightmare: The History of Jim Crow*. New York: St. Martin's Press, 2002.

Painter, Nell Irvin. *The History of White People*. New York: W. W. Norton, 2011.

Pandey, Gyanendra. *A History of Prejudice: Race, Caste, and Difference in India and the United States*. Cambridge, U.K.: Cambridge University Press, 2013.

Perera, Sylvia B. *The Scapegoat Complex: Toward a Mythology of Shadow and Guilt*. Toronto: Inner City Books, 1986.

Phillips-Cunningham, Danielle T. *Putting Their Hands on Race: Irish Immigrant and Southern Black Domestic Workers, 1850–1940*. New Brunswick, N.J.: Rutgers University Press, 2019.

Plough, Alonzo L., ed. *Knowledge to Action: Accelerating Progress in Health, Well-being, and Equity*. New York: Oxford University Press, 2017.

Pope, Liston. *The Kingdom Beyond Caste*. New York: Friendship Press, 1957.

———. *Millhands and Preachers: A Study of Gastonia*. New Haven, Conn.: Yale University Press, 1942.

Powdermaker, Hortense. *After Freedom: A Cultural Study in the Deep South.* Madison: University of Wisconsin Press, 1939.

Prasad, Chandra Bhan. *Dalit Phobia: Why Do They Hate Us?* New Delhi: Vitasta Publishing, 2006.

Pryor, Elizabeth B., and Robert E. Lee. *Reading the Man: A Portrait of Robert E. Lee Through His Private Letters.* New York: Penguin, 2007.

Rajshekar, V. T. *Dalit: The Black Untouchables of India.* Atlanta: Clarity Press, 1995.

Raper, Arthur F. *The Tragedy of Lynching.* Chapel Hill: University of North Carolina Press, 2017.

Rawat, Ramnarayan S., and K. Satyanarayana. *Dalit Studies.* Durham, N.C.: Duke University Press, 2016.

Regester, Charlene B. *African American Actresses: The Struggle for Visibility, 1900–1960.* Bloomington: Indiana University Press, 2010.

Reuck, Anthony V. S. de, and Julie Knight, eds. *Caste and Race: Comparative Approaches.* London: Ciba Foundation, 1967.

Roediger, David R. *The Wages of Whiteness: Race and the Making of the American Working Class.* London: Verso, 2007.

Ronningstam, Elsa. *Identifying and Understanding the Narcissistic Personality.* New York: Oxford University Press, 2005.

Rothstein, Richard. *The Color of Law: A Forgotten History of How Our Government Segregated America.* New York: Liveright, 2017.

Roy, Arundhati. *The Doctor and the Saint: Caste, Race, and Annihilation of Caste, the Debate Between B. R. Ambedkar and M. K. Gandhi.* Chicago: Haymarket Books, 2017.

Ryback, Timothy W. *Hitler's Private Library.* New York: Vintage, 2008.

Safina, Carl. *Beyond Words: What Animals Think and Feel.* New York: Henry Holt, 2015.

Sakurai, Takamichi. *Political Theories of Narcissism: Towards Self-Reflection on Knowledge and Politics from the Psychoanalytic Perspectives of Erich Fromm and Fujita Shōzō.* Münster, Germany: LIT Verlag, 2018.

Sartre, Jean-Paul. *Réflexions sur la question juive,* English translation. Edited by Alan E. Steinweis and Robert D. Rachlin. New York: Berghahn Books, 2013.

Schermerhorn, Calvin. *Unrequited Toil: A History of United States Slavery.* Cambridge, U.K.: Cambridge University Press, 2018.

Schrieke, Bertram J. *Alien Americans: A Study of Race Relations.* New York: Viking, 1936.

Senart, Emile. *Caste in India: The Facts and the System*. London: Methuen, 1930.

Shah, Alpa, et al. *Ground Down by Growth: Tribe, Caste, Class and Inequality in 21st Century India*. London: Pluto Press, 2017.

Shapiro, Herbert. *White Violence and Black Response: From Reconstruction to Montgomery*. Amherst: University of Massachusetts Press, 1988.

Sharma, Ursula. *Caste*. New Delhi: Viva Books, 1999.

Smaje, Chris. *Natural Hierarchies: The Historical Sociology of Race and Caste*. Hoboken, N.J.: Wiley-Blackwell, 2000.

Smedley, Audrey, and Brian D. Smedley. *Race in North America: Origin and Evolution of a Worldview*. Boulder, Colo.: Westview Press, 2012.

Smith, David L. *Less Than Human: Why We Demean, Enslave, and Exterminate Others*. New York: St. Martin's Press, 2011.

Smith, Lillian E. *Killers of the Dream*. New York: W. W. Norton, 1961.

Sokol, Jason. *There Goes My Everything: White Southerners in the Age of Civil Rights, 1945–1975*. New York: Vintage, 2008.

Spiro, Jonathan Peter. *Defending the Master Race: Conservation, Eugenics and the Legacy of Madison Grant*. Lebanon, N.H.: University Press of New England, 2009.

Srinivas, Gurram. *Dalit Middle Class: Mobility, Identity and Politics of Caste*. Jaipur, India: Rawat, 2016.

Stampp, Kenneth M. *The Peculiar Institution: Slavery in the Ante-Bellum South*. New York: Knopf, 1956.

Steinberg, Stephen. *The Ethnic Myth: Race, Ethnicity, and Class in America*. Boston: Beacon Press, 1981.

Steinweis, Alan E., and Robert D. Rachlin. *The Law in Nazi Germany: Ideology, Opportunism, and the Perversion of Justice*. New York: Berghahn Books, 2013.

Stevenson, Bryan. *Just Mercy*. New York: Spiegel & Grau, 2014.

Sussman, Robert W. *The Myth of Race: The Troubling Persistence of an Unscientific Idea*. Cambridge, Mass.: Harvard University Press, 2014.

Thompson, Edgar T., ed. *Race Relations and the Race Problem: A Definition and an Analysis*. Durham, N.C.: Duke University Press, 1939.

Tocqueville, Alexis de. *Democracy in America*. 1835; reprint New York: Library of America, 2004.

Trouillot, Michel-Rolph. *Silencing the Past: Power and the Production of History*. Boston: Beacon Press, 1995.

Varel, David A. *The Lost Black Scholar: Resurrecting Allison Davis in American Social Thought.* Chicago: University of Chicago Press, 2018.

Vaughan, Alden T. *Roots of American Racism: Essays on the Colonial Experience.* Oxford: Oxford University Press, 1995.

Verba, Sidney, Ahmed Bashiruddin, and Anil Bhatt. *Caste, Race and Politics: A Comparative Study of India and the United States.* Beverly Hills, Calif.: Sage, 1971.

Voogd, Jan. *Race Riots and Resistance: The Red Summer of 1919.* New York: Peter Lang, 2008.

Wachowski, Lilly and Lana, writers and directors (originally as The Wachowski Brothers). *The Matrix Reloaded.* Warner Brothers Studio, 2003.

Ward, Jason M. *Defending White Democracy: The Making of a Segregationist Movement and the Remaking of Racial Politics, 1936–1965.* Chapel Hill: University of North Carolina Press, 2011.

Washington, Harriet A. *Medical Apartheid: The Dark History of Medical Experimentation on Black Americans from Colonial Times to the Present.* New York: Doubleday, 2007.

Washington, Robert E., and Donald Cunnigen. *Confronting the American Dilemma of Race: The Second Generation Black American Sociologists.* Lanham, Md.: University Press of America, 2002.

Weiner, Mark S. *Black Trials: Citizenship from the Beginnings of Slavery to the End of Caste.* New York: Vintage, 2006.

Weld, Theodore. *American Slavery as It Is: Testimony of a Thousand Witnesses.* New York: American Anti-Slavery Society, 1839.

Westermann, Edward B. *Hitler's Ostkrieg and the Indian Wars: Comparing Genocide and Conquest.* Norman: University of Oklahoma Press, 2016.

Whitman, James Q. *Hitler's American Model: The United States and the Making of Nazi Race Law.* Princeton: Princeton University Press, 2017.

Williams, Heather Andrea. *Help Me to Find My People: The African American Search for Family Lost in Slavery.* Chapel Hill: University of North Carolina Press, 2016.

Williams, Kidada. *They Left Great Marks on Me: African American Testimonies of Racial Violence from Emancipation to World War I.* New York: New York University Press, 2012.

Williams, Richard. *Hierarchical Structures and Social Value: The Creation of Black and Irish Identities in the United States.* Cambridge, U.K.: Cambridge University Press, 1990.

Wiltse, Jeff. *Contested Waters: A Social History of Swimming Pools in America.* Chapel Hill: University of North Carolina Press, 2007.

Wolcott, Victoria W. *Race, Riots, and Roller Coasters: The Struggle over Segregated Recreation in America.* Philadelphia: University of Pennsylvania Press, 2012.

Woodward, C. Vann. *The Strange Career of Jim Crow.* New York: Oxford University Press, 2002.

Yengde, Suraj. *Caste Matters.* Gurgaon, India: Penguin Random House India, 2018.

Yengde, Suraj, and Anand Teltumbde. *The Radical in Ambedkar: Critical Reflections.* Gurgaon, India: Penguin Random House India, 2018.

Young, Donald R. *American Minority Peoples: A Study in Racial and Cultural Conflicts in the United States.* New York: Harper & Brothers, 1932.

A

Abdurraqib, Hanif, 285

Adams, John Quincy, 399n7

affirmative action, 75, 193

Indian "reservations," 75

Africa

Africans considered beasts, 408n103

Ebola epidemic and, 199–201

immigrants from, experiences of, 241–42, 302–3

Jobson's encounter with sub-Saharan people, 408n103

people's identity linked to regional or ethnic groups, 52–53

See also South Africa

African-Americans

assumptions about, based on race, 216–23, 234–35, 253–54

birth rates for black teenagers, 235, 425n235

black veterans targeted, 161,
224–28, 423–24n228

breaking free from caste, 253–54, 377–88

caste confrontation and, 293–301

colorism and, 238–39

"crabs in a barrel" and, 240

crime and incarceration, 146, 235, 240–41, 284–85, 288, 308, 335–36, 429n284

curse of Ham and, 102–3, 121, 122, 408n103

Dalits of India compared to, 26–27, 74, 77, 128, 129, 275

dehumanization of, 28, 51–52, 142–50

domestic work and manual labor, 133, 135, 185, 233, 248

as entertainers, 137–39, 415n138

exempted from New Deal reforms, 184–85

film portrayals of, 138, 159

forgiveness and, 283–85, 287–89

Great Migration, 52, 95, 134, 228, 229

health care and pain management, 188–89, 420n188

health problems and longevity of, 303–8, 432n307

home-buying and, 185

integration, 1970s, 57

legal rights of black parents, 211–12

lynching and vigilante violence against, 50, 56, 90–96, 113–14, 150, 153, 154, 155, 157, 192, 228–31, 266, 336

major league baseball, Negro Leagues, and, 258–60

media distortions and, 234

medical experimentation and, 147–48, 416n147

miscegenation laws and, 79, 84, 85, 87, 111, 124, 409n111, 412n124

African-Americans
  (*cont'd*):
  mortality rates, 178,
    180
  occupational
    limitations of,
    132–39, 414n134
  "one drop rule," 88,
    121, 412n124
  parallel worlds
    (black and white),
    146–47
  "place" of, 163,
    226–28
  police brutality and,
    107, 172, 218,
    226–28, 243,
    350
  politics and, 322–32
    (*see also* Obama,
    Barack)
  poverty and, 234–35
  presumption of racial
    inferiority, 159–64
  rejecting or
    diminishing their
    own, 242–44
  reparations for, 329,
    336
  as scapegoats,
    191–201
  segregation and,
    116–27, 163,
    410–11n116
  as sharecroppers, 75,
    133, 158, 163, 247,
    248, 251, 313, 336
  social mobility and,
    182–83, 224–37
  stereotyping of,
    138–39, 159, 186,
    187, 213, 219–23,
    242, 295, 302, 319
  as subordinate
    American caste, 6,
    23, 25, 28, 40–41,
    43, 48, 50–51,

  74–76, 128–30, 176,
    183, 186, 224–44,
    269, 292–93, 302–3
  "taint of race" and,
    80, 115–21, 122,
    141
  Uncle Tom or HNIC
    (Head Negro in
    Charge), 240
  unconscious bias
    and, 186–89,
    305
  wealthiest, 137
  See also American
    caste system;
    American South;
    civil rights
    movement; race;
    racism
*After Freedom: A
  Cultural Study in
  the Deep South*
  (Powdermaker),
  252
Ahmed, Bashiruddin,
  133
Alabama
  Confederate
    monument
    controversy,
    342–43
  intermarriage ban,
    111, 124
  Italians as nonwhite,
    124
  medical
    experimentation
    in, 148
  "one drop rule," 124
  Scottsboro Boys, 248
Albany, Ga.
  resistance to
    integration,
    425n236
Ali, Muhammad, 137
alpha position
  in dogs, 202–5

  humans deserving,
    206–7
  humans in,
    misplaced, 206
  insecure alphas, 203
  wolf packs and,
    205–6, 422n206
Ambedkar, Bhimrao,
  25–27, 31–32, 77,
    239, 242, 255, 274
  as Buddhist, 175
  caste, as state of
    mind, 184, 383–84
  caste, meaning of,
    and, 110
  on the dominant
    caste, 184
  Du Bois and, 26–27, 30
  as father of anti-caste
    movement, 110, 255
American caste system
  (Jim Crow caste
    system), 8, 17,
    18–20, 22–25, 27,
    28, 96, 120–21, 172,
    175, 255
  assumptions and,
    216–23
  author and
    miscasting, 175–76,
    177
  author's experience
    as *New York Times*
    national
    correspondent,
    59–61
  author's experiences
    on airline flights,
    294–300
  behavior and place in
    the hierarchy, 272,
    274
  black vs. white
    workers, 181
  caste boundaries,
    adherence to,
    110–11, 282–89

caste boundaries, breaking, 370–75

caste confrontation, 293–301

consequences of, costs of, 353–57, 377–78, 382, 384–85

criminal justice system and, 146, 235, 240–41, 284–85, 288, 308, 335–36, 429n284

curse of Ham and, 102–3, 121

dehumanization and, 142–50

departure from, disruption of, Obama's election as, 311–21

dominant caste, 6, 23, 28, 76, 122, 125, 180

dominant caste, as aspirational, 269, 328

dominant caste, control and, 210–11

dominant caste, men's power, 112–13

dominant caste, radicalization of, 365–69

dominant caste, sense of entitlement, 275

dominant caste status threat, 179–86, 224–37, 331, 332, 381–82

ending the tyranny of caste, 377–88

eugenics hierarchy of presumed value and, 276–77

hierarchy of trace amounts, 121–25

identifying a person's place in, 276–78

identity based on, 183

immigrants and the middle castes, 49–50, 52, 76, 125–27, 241

Indian caste system compared to, 74–76, 172

indigenous people and, 42, 43, 172

inherent superiority vs. inherent inferiority and, 159–64

intrusion into everyday life, 208–23

mansplaining and whitesplaining in, 276

marriage restrictions and endogamy laws, 84, 85, 87, 109, 110, 112, 124, 409n110

New World categories of color and, 103, 106

occupational hierarchy and, 131–40, 414n134

origins of, 29, 40–44, 48, 180

presidential election, 2016, and, 324–33

as primarily two-tiered, 75–76, 125–26

race and, 18–20, 22, 29, 64–65, 66, 67, 106, 121

racial purity and, 115–30

radical empathy to end, 386

rankings passed at birth, 105–6

religion-based hierarchy and, 40–41

resurgence, post 2016 election, 216, 322–32

scapegoats, scapegoating, and, 191–201

scholarship and studies on, 245–56

segregation, social restrictions, and quarantines, 116–21, 163

status as inescapable, immutable, 106–8

subordinate caste, 6, 23, 25, 28, 40–41, 43, 48, 76, 128–30, 176, 183, 186, 224–37, 269, 302–3

subordinate caste, colorism, and, 238–39

subordinate caste, fighting each other to rise, 238–44

subordinate caste and upward social mobility, 224–37, 292–93

survival in, 282–91, 327–30

symbols of caste, 333–43

tenets of intercaste relations, 54–61

terrors of, 113–14, 151–58

transcending vs. escaping, 106–8, 129

American caste system
    (*cont'd*):
  Truth and
    Reconciliation
    Commission called
    for, 385
  unspoken rules of,
    273, 282
  white privilege and,
    181–82, 185, 269
  a world without caste
    and, 388
American Civil War,
    24, 41
  Confederate leaders,
    fates of, 338–39, 345
  Confederate
    monuments,
    333–43,
    435–36n335
  Draft Riots of 1863, 50
  Irish immigrants in, 50
  people killed in, 377
  reenactments, 346
American Dilemma, An
    (Myrdal et al.), 24,
    255
American South
  American caste
    system and, 25, 29,
    52, 180–81
  black codes and racial
    laws, 48, 81, 84
  caste codes of, 102–3
  Confederate flag and,
    339, 346, 350
  Confederate
    monument
    controversy,
    333–43,
    435–36n335
  Democratic Party
    and, 314–15
  Jim Crow era, 25, 27,
    30, 48, 52, 54, 138,
    151, 160, 182, 227,
    228–29, 233

Ku Klux Klan and,
    228, 336
  Lost Cause, 335,
    340
  lynching in, 41,
    90–96, 154, 155,
    157, 228, 229–30,
    245, 266, 336
  minstrels and, 138
  narcissism of, 271
  occupational
    restrictions in,
    133–34
  poor whites in,
    180–82, 183
  public buses, black
    passengers, and,
    163
  public whipping for
    interracial
    relations, 110–11
  racial creed of, 25,
    401n25
  racial prohibitions
    and indoctrination,
    129–30
  racial segregation in,
    116–17, 233–34,
    410–11n116
  Reconstruction, 26,
    48, 116, 133, 336,
    340, 351
  scapegoats,
    scapegoating in,
    191–92, 196
  tenets of intercaste
    relations, 29, 54–55
  terror as
    enforcement, 151,
    336
  vigilantism in, 91–96
  Virginia General
    Assembly on
    status at birth,
    bond or free, 105–6
  work done by
    enslaved people

and sharecroppers,
    75, 336
  See also Civil War;
    specific states
Anderson, Marian, 378
Arkansas
  defining *Negro,* 124
  "one drop rule,"
    412n124
Armstrong, Louis, 137
Aryan supremacy, xvi,
    78, 80, 81, 86,
    122–23
Austin, Tex., serial
    package bombings,
    197–99, 421n197

B

Bagai, Vaishno Das, 127
Bailey, Thomas Pearce,
    25, 102–3
Baker, Peter, 332
Baker, Russell, 182
Baldwin, James, ix, 47,
    320
Ball, Nathaniel C.,
    230–31
Baltimore, Md., 8, 229
  case of Freddie Gray,
    243
Baptist, Edward, 46–47
Barrett, William, 229
Beavers, Louise, 159
Bell, Alexander
    Graham, 79
Berreman, Gerald, 163
Bevington, Paula,
    410–11n116
Bhatt, Anil, 133
Biden, Joe, 313
Birth of a Nation (film),
    25–26, 335
Black Lives Matter, 350
Blakemore, Erin, 232
Blumenbach, Johann
    Friedrich, 65, 66
Bond, Julian, 379

Bonhoeffer, Dietrich, 89–90
Boston, Mass.
murder case of Charles Stuart, 193–97
smallpox vaccine and Onesimus, 231–32
"white ethnics" in, 277
Bouglé, Célestin, 135
Boylston, Zabdiel, 232
Bradley, Tom, 327
Branch, Taylor, 351–52
Brewer, Jan, 316–18, 433n317
Bright, Al, 120–21
Britain, 74
American colonies, enslaved people in, 40, 42
Gaelic insurrections, 42–43
healthcare system, 354
indentured servants in America, 29, 42
independence of India and, 21
race ideology of, in North America, 65
slavery, curse of Ham and, 103
status passed at birth from father, 105
Broca, Paul, 65
Brown, John (slavery survivor), 145–46, 155
Brown, William Wells, 137
Brown, Will (lynching victim), 94–96
Brown v. Board of Education, 236, 253
Bugdalle, Richard, 415n139
Bush, George W., 399n7

C
Cairo, Ill.
lynching of Will James, 93
Carmichael, Stokely, 242, 256
Carter, Jimmy, 315, 328, 432n315
Case, Anne, 178–79
"Case for Reparations, The" (Coates), 420n185
Cash, Wilbur J., 47, 180
caste, caste system, 232
absurdities of, 176, 257–60
assumptions of, 59–61, 71
as basis of other isms, 171
behavior and place in the hierarchy, 272, 274–75, 282–91
behavior and unconscious signals, 31, 39–40, 58, 282
casteism, 70–71, 75, 175
characteristics of, 70, 72, 160
class vs., 106, 292
colorism and, 238–39
conference on caste, London, 2017, 171–77
conference on caste and race, University of Massachusetts, 30–31
dangerous consequences of, 263–67, 427–28n263

dissension between and within castes, 238–44, 354
dominant caste's centrality, 268–78, 282, 283, 327
effects on mental health, 183–84
encoding of, examples, 72
ending the tyranny of, 377–88
etymology, 67
as fixed and rigid, 19, 70–71, 106, 127, 129, 175, 255
health consequences of, 302–8
hierarchy of, 238
historic origins, 96
intrusion into everyday life, 208–23
invisibility of, 34–35, 212, 216
justification for, 17 (see also caste, eight pillars of)
narcissism of, 268–78
Nazis and acceleration of, 78–88
as pattern of social order, 70, 224–37
power and, 17–18, 59, 140
psychological effects of, 170
purpose of, 25, 132
race vs., 24–25, 30, 70
radicalized economics and, 325
rankings passed at birth, 105–8
Riceville, Iowa, brown vs. blue eyes lesson, 167–70, 418n167

caste, caste system
    (*cont'd*):
    scapegoats,
        scapegoating, and,
        190–201, 234
    as state of mind, 289,
        383–84
    subordinate castes, as
        threat to dominant
        caste, 109, 178–86,
        238
    subordinate castes,
        fighting each other
        to rise, 238–44
    subordinate castes,
        mudsill as the
        bottom, 131
    subordinate castes,
        prevented from
        upward social
        mobility, 224–37
    subordinate castes,
        restrictions on,
        115–30
    subordinate castes,
        survival of, 282–91,
        327–30
    taxonomy of, 29
    term use, 23–24
    top dog (alphas) and
        underdogs
        (omegas) and,
        206–7
    unspoken rules of,
        273, 282
    what it is, 17
    See also American
        caste system;
        Indian caste
        system; Nazi
        Germany
*Caste, Class and Race: A
    Study in Social
    Dynamics* (Cox),
    254–55, 426n255
caste, eight pillars of,
    28, 96

pillar number one:
    divine will and
    laws of nature,
    101–4, 122, 174, 266
pillar number two:
    heritability, 105–8
pillar number three:
    endogamy and the
    control of marriage
    and mating,
    109–14
pillar number four:
    purity versus
    pollution, 115–30
pillar number five:
    occupational
    hierarchy, 131–40
pillar number six:
    dehumanization
    and stigma, 141–50
pillar number seven:
    terror as
    enforcement,
    151–58, 291, 336
pillar number eight:
    inherent
    superiority vs.
    inherent
    inferiority, 159–64,
    167–68, 183–84,
    234, 269, 289–90,
    335
*Caste and Class in a
    Southern Town*
    (Dollard), 252
Celera Genomics, 66
Chacon, Joseph, 197
Chait, Jonathan, 319,
    354
Charleston, S.C.
    Emanuel African
        Methodist
        Episcopal Church
        shooting, 287, 340,
        350
    enslaved people,
        regulations for, 146

Charlottesville, Va.,
    8, 74
    Civil War monument
        in, 333, 334
    rally in, 2017, and
        killing of Heather
        Heyer, 8, 74,
        333–34, 337
Chicago, Ill., 219, 220,
    221, 229, 301, 332,
    350
    African-American
        college professor,
        racism confronted
        by, 213–14
    author based in,
        article on
        Magnificent Mile
        incident, 59–61
    killing of Eugene
        Williams, 118
    race riots, 118
    "white ethnics" in,
        277
Chisholm, Shirley, 242
Cincinnati, Ohio, public
    pools, 117
civil rights movement,
    21, 24, 55, 253, 271,
    380
    affirmative action
        and, 193
    anti-discrimination
        laws and, 68, 74–75
    benefits to all
        Americans, 382–83
    Black Panther
        Party, 77
    labor markets and,
        182
    Selma–Montgomery
        march and, 55
class
    caste vs., 106
    what it is, 106
Cleveland, Grover,
    399n7

Cleveland, Ohio, 201
  Paige and the
    Cleveland Indians,
    259
  police killing of
    Tamir Rice, 209
  "white ethnics" in,
    277
climate change, 9, 12,
  320, 330, 378
Clinton, Bill, 315,
  399n10, 432n315
Clinton, Hillary, 4–5,
  10–11, 326, 399n7,
  400n10
  Bradley Effect and,
    327
  election results,
    percentage of
    white vote, 328,
    331
  presidential debates
    and, 326
  voters for, 331,
    432–33n315
Coates, Ta-Nehisi
  "The Case for
    Reparations,"
    420n185
Cobb, James C., 163
Cobb, Thomas R. R.,
  103, 408n103
Collins, Patricia Hill,
  282
Columbia, S.C.
  Confederate flag
    removal, 340,
    350
Columbus, Ohio
  essay contest, "What
    to do with Hitler
    after the War?,"
    164
Conditt, Mark, 198
Confederate monument
  controversy,
  333–43

Alabama retention of
    statues, 342–43
  Charlottesville's Lee
    statue and, 333–35
  Germany's response
    to Nazi era as
    comparison,
    340–41, 343–44,
    346–48, 437n341
  memorials to Lee,
    337, 339
  monument removal
    from New Orleans,
    339–43
  number of
    monuments, 335,
    435–36n335
  Stone Mountain, Ga.,
    336
Cottrol, Robert J., 107,
  125
Cox, Oliver Cromwell,
  254
  Caste, Class and Race:
    A Study in Social
    Dynamics, 254–55,
    426n255
criminal justice system
  African-Americans
    and, 146, 235,
    240–41, 284–85,
    288, 308, 335–36,
    429n284
  criminalizing
    addiction and, 189
  death penalty,
    unequal
    application of, 146
  death penalty and
    color of victim, 241
  incarceration rates,
    355
  lynching states and
    death penalty in,
    346
  whites vs. blacks
    and, 146, 192

D
Dalit Panthers, 77
Dalits. See India,
  Untouchables or
  Dalits
Dalit Voice, 145
Dallas, Tex.
  Ebola and, 200–201
  trial of white police
    officer, 283–84
Dao, David, 301
Davis, Allison, 52, 135,
  138, 163, 182, 192,
  245–56
  as black elite, 247,
    248
  as black researcher,
    peer scrutiny faced
    by, 254
  caste divisions and
    difficulties of
    Natchez research,
    247–50
  clandestine meetings
    with Burleigh and,
    249–50
  cover story for his
    research, 247
  dangers faced by,
    245–46, 250
  Deep South: A Social
    Anthropological
    Study of Caste and
    Class, 106, 250–55
  degrees held by,
    246
  first black tenured
    professor,
    University of
    Chicago, 256
  focus of Natchez
    research, 246
  psychological toll of
    caste role-playing,
    251–52
  recruitment of Drake,
    248

Davis, Allison (cont'd):
  residence in Natchez,
    247
  role-played by,
    member of
    subordinate caste,
    246
  segregation, social
    restrictions, and,
    249
  teaching at Dillard to
    fund his research,
    251–52
  as team leader, 247
Davis, Elizabeth,
  245–46, 247, 248,
  256
Davis, Hugh, 110,
  409n111
Davis, Jefferson, 336,
  345
Deaton, Angus, 178–79
"debt peonage," 75
Declaration of
  Independence, 378,
  403n47
Deep South: A Social
  Anthropological
  Study of Caste and
  Class (Davis,
  Gardner, and
  Gardner), 106,
  245–55
  critics of, 253–54
  as first interracial
    scholarship, 246,
    250
  as first study of
    American caste
    system, 246
  impact of, 256
  publication of, 251,
    253
  summary of content,
    251
  Warner as supervisor
    of project, 246–47

dehumanization,
  141–50, 383
  desensitization of
    children to
    violence and,
    149–50
  double standards
    and, 146–47
  of enslaved people,
    143, 145–46, 149
  of a group vs.
    individual, 141
  human deprivation
    and, 143–44
  of Jews, 142–43, 145,
    146–47
  lack of empathy and,
    149–50
  medical
    experimentation
    and, 147–48
  Milgram and
    Stanford
    experiments and,
    148–49
  of Native Americans,
    149
  stigma attached to a
    group and, 141
  surrender of target's
    humanity, 144
  of Untouchables, 143,
    144–45
  what it does, 141–42
DeMaio, Teresa,
  422n206
Democratic Party
  African-American
    voters and, 329–30
  caste and voters, 326,
    327
  changes in voter laws
    and, 318–19
  impeachment and,
    9–10
  midterm elections,
    2018, 9

presidential election,
  2016, 322–32
  white vote and,
    314–15,
    432n314,
    432–33n315
  See also Clinton,
    Hillary; Obama,
    Barack
Detroit, Mich., author's
  encounter with
  DEA agents,
  219–23
Diamond, Raymond T.,
  107, 125
Dillard University,
  251–52
Dixon, Travis, 234
Dollard, John, 157–58
  Caste and Class in
    a Southern Town,
    252
Douglass, Frederick,
  162–63, 233, 338–39
Dowland, Seth
  Family Values and the
    Rise of the Christian
    Right, 330
Doyle, Bertram, 116,
  136, 163
Draft Riots of 1863, 50
Drake, St. Clair, 248,
  256
Du Bois, W.E.B., 26–27,
  30, 181, 224, 379
Dukakis, Michael,
  432n315
Dunkley, Nigel, 343,
  344, 345, 348–49
Dying of Whiteness
  (Metzl), 189

E
earthquakes, silent, 11
egalitarian world,
  achieving, 70,
  377–88

Einstein, Albert, ix,
    378–79, 384, 397n-ix
    address to the
        National Urban
        League, 385
    Lincoln University
        honor, 379
    racism opposed by,
        378–79
    wife, Elsa, 378
Eisenman, Peter, 343–44
Eliot, Charles W., 79
Elizabeth, N.J.
    integration of public
        pools, 119
Elliott, Jane, 167–70,
    418n167
endogamy, 109–14
    as alliance of equals,
        110
    in America, 109, 110,
        409n110, 409n111
    in India, 109, 110
    laws as social
        engineering,
        controlled
        breeding, 111–12
    in Nazi Germany, 109
    in South Africa,
        405–6n82
eugenics, 48, 280
    American
        proponents of,
        79–80
    hierarchy of
        presumed value,
        276–77

F

Family Values and the Rise
    of the Christian Right
    (Dowland), 330
Fisher, Patrick, 314
Fiske, Susan, 305
Fitzgerald, F. Scott
    The Great Gatsby,
        405n80

Flynn, Raymond, 194
Fonda, Henry, 96
Ford, Henry, 79
Franklin, Benjamin, 122
Fredrickson, George M.,
    414n134
Freisler, Roland, 85–86
Fromm, Erich, 270–71

G

Gandhi, Mohandas, 21,
    26
Gardner, Burleigh and
    Mary, 163, 246–55
    access to poor whites
        in Natchez, 248
    caste roles of, 248–49
    clandestine
        relationship with
        the Davises,
        249–50
    Deep South: A Social
        Anthropological
        Study of Caste and
        Class, 106, 250–55
    focus of Natchez
        research, 246
    residence in Natchez,
        247
Garland, Merrick, 320
Garner, Eric, 243
Gates, Henry Louis, Jr.,
    319
Gay, Roxane, 287–89
Georgia
    assumptions based
        on race, Corey
        Lewis, and, 217–18
    criminal offenses for
        blacks vs. whites,
        146
    death penalty and
        color of victim, 241
    defining nonwhite
        person, 124
    legal consequences
        for killing an

enslaved person,
    417n153
Gercke, Achim, 86
Gergel, Richard, 227
German Society for
    Racial Hygiene, 79
Germany. See Nazi
    Germany
Geronimus, Arline, 305
Gilens, Martin, 234–35
Gillespie, Andra, 315
Glasgow, John, 155
Gobineau, Arthur de,
    122–23
Gone with the Wind
    (film), 138, 335
Goodell, William,
    45–46, 140, 146,
    160
Gore, Al, 326, 399n7,
    432n315
Go Set a Watchman
    (Lee), 350–51
Grand Gulf, Miss.
    vigilante killing in,
        113
Grant, Madison, 80–81,
    405n80
    The Passing of the
        Great Race, 25, 80
Graves, Joseph L., 307
Gray, Freddie, 243
Great Depression, 251
Great Gatsby, The
    (Fitzgerald),
        405n80
Great Migration, 95,
    134, 228, 229
Great Recession, 312
Gross, Ariela J., 45
Ground Down by Growth
    (Shah et al.), 75
Gulumgiri (Slavery)
    (Phule), 401n26
Gürtner, Franz, 78,
    84–85
Gusky, Jeff, 226

H

Hacker, Andrew, 20,
    269, 308
Two Nations, 415n138
Hale, Harold, 55–56, 58
Hale, Miss, 54, 55–59
    "the container we
        have built for you"
        and, 56
Haley, Nikki, 340
Hamilton, Henry,
    321
Hammond, James
    Henry, 131–32
Harrison, Benjamin,
    399n7
Hart, Devonte, 285–87
Hayes, Rutherford B.,
    399n7
health and healthcare
    of African-
        Americans, 303,
        305–8
    American lack of
        universal
        healthcare, slavery,
        and, 354
    caste system and,
        353–54
    infant mortality, 355
    lethality of caste,
        302–8
    longevity, 305–8,
        432n307
    maternal deaths, 355
    Pacific Standard, 285
    pandemic of 2020
        and, 356–57
    race and pain
        management,
        188–89, 420n188
    visceral vs.
        subcutaneous fat
        and, 306–7
Herrera, Esperanza, 198
Heyer, Heather, 8, 74,
    334

Hindenburg, Paul
    von, 82
Hitler, Adolf, xv, 80–81,
    82–83, 246, 265,
    279, 427–28n263
    America's race
        policies and,
        405n81
    Blood Laws and, 87
    elimination of
        political
        opponents, 86
    gravesite paved over,
        346
    suicide in bunker,
        Berlin, 345
*Hitler—How Could It
    Happen?*
    exhibition, 263–67,
    427–28n263
Hitler's American Model
    (Whitman), 405n79
Holder, Eric, 242
Holmes, Pvt. Burton,
    226
Hoover, Herbert, 80
House, Anthony
    Stephen, 197,
    421n197
Howard, Willie James,
    113–14, 164
Hunter, W. W., 129

I

Ifill, Gwen, 322
immigration
    African immigrants,
        241–42, 302–3
    anti-Semitic quotas, 85
    bias against
        immigrants,
        123–24
    caste and, 49, 52, 123,
        241
    changing
        demographics and,
        6, 180, 315, 323, 325

    Chinese Exclusion
        Act of 1882, 123
    citizenship and, 122
    Dillingham Report,
        123
    "Dreamers" today,
        127
    economic success at
        the expense of
        nonwhites, 51
    European designated
        as "white," 49–50
    German immigrants,
        122, 277
    hierarchy of country
        of origin, 276–78
    Immigration Act of
        1924, 81, 123
    Indian immigrants,
        classified as
        nonwhite, 126,
        127
    Indian immigrants,
        usual caste of,
        289–90
    Irish immigrants, 29,
        42, 49, 50, 122, 276,
        277
    Italian immigrants,
        classified as
        nonwhite, 124
    Japanese immigrants,
        classified as
        nonwhite, 126,
        127
    labor pool and, 182
    Mexican immigrants,
        306
    the middle castes
        and, 49–50, 52, 76,
        125–27
    nonwhite, dilemma
        of, 241–42
    Nordic immigrants,
        277–78
    rescinding
        citizenship of

naturalized Asians, 127

restrictions on, 80, 81, 111–12, 123

southern and eastern Europeans, 49, 80, 123, 134, 277

India

air pollution in, 73

anti-discrimination laws and, 75

Bombay, 21

compared to the U.S., 74–76

Dalit liberation movement, 77

Delhi, 73

exile of the Adivasi from, 74

global diaspora of Indians, 27

immigrants to America, 126, 127, 289–90

King, Martin Luther, Jr., in, 21–22

as largest democracy, 74, 104

non-Hindus in, outside caste system, 76

occupational deprivation in, 133

"reservations" (affirmative action), 75

skin color and, 176–77

Trivandrum, 21–22

Uttar Pradesh, 77

Indian caste system, 17, 22, 25, 28, 73–77, 96, 172, 289–90, 426n255

American caste system compared to, 74–76, 172, 255

appearance and place in the hierarchy, 273

behavior and place in the hierarchy, 115, 273–74, 410n115

behavior of groups and place in the hierarchy, 274

the Brahmin and the sacred thread, 361–66

dissension between and within castes, 239

dominant caste sense of entitlement, 275–76

elaborate system of subcastes (jatis), 76, 132

Hindu religion, Laws of Manu, and, 101–2, 104, 121, 174, 175

identifying characteristics of, 76, 161

inherent superiority vs. inherent inferiority, 161, 275–76, 290–91

karma and, 76–77, 102, 283

marriage and mating restrictions, 109, 110

occupational hierarchy and, 132, 134–35

origins of, 67

Portuguese and use of term casta, 67

racial purity and, 115–16, 128, 410n115

rankings as varnas, 67, 76, 174

rankings passed at birth from father, 105

social privileges of ruling castes, 174

suffering of subordinate castes, 172, 174

surnames as indication of caste, 76, 143, 289

Untouchables or Dalits, 21–22, 25, 26, 31, 74, 75, 77, 102, 117, 128, 129, 132, 143, 144–45, 151, 161, 176, 266, 283, 290–91, 410n115

Untouchables or Dalits, author and, 274–75

Untouchables or Dalits, challenging of the system by, 255

Untouchables or Dalits, saldari and, 75

Untouchables or Dalits compared to African-Americans, 26–27, 77, 128, 129

warrior-soldier caste, 173–74

Indianola, Miss.

Yale researchers in, 252

indigenous people

cruelty against, 152–53

dehumanization of, 149

of India, the Adivasi, 74, 172, 174

marriage and mating restrictions, 111

indigenous people
(cont'd):
Native Americans,
42, 43, 74, 81,
152–53, 172, 266
a world without caste
and, 388
Ivey, Kay, 342–43

J

Jackson, Andrew, 153,
399n7
Jacobson, Matthew
Frye, 50, 51
Jadhav, Sushrut,
183
James, LeBron, 108
James, Will, 93
Jardina, Ashley, 315,
316, 320, 325, 328,
331
Jay-Z, 137
Jefferson, Thomas,
134
Jeffries, James "the
Great White
Hope," 137–38
Jewish people
abuse of, as Nazi
prisoners, 139, 145,
415n139, 415n145,
416n147
hierarchy among
captives and, 156
history of
suffering and
discrimination, 74
medical
experimentation
on, 147
Memorial to the
Murdered Jews of
Europe, Berlin,
343–44, 348
Nazi Aryan
superiority vs.,
234

Nazi assignment of
race to, 85
Nazi dehumanization
of, 142–45, 149
Nazi extermination
of, Holocaust, 78,
89–90, 142, 156
Nazi forced labor,
156
Nazi lynching and
torture of, 154
Nazi narcissism and,
271
Nazi restrictions and
laws for, 84–87, 88,
116, 117, 410n116
Nazi terrorizing of,
151
presumption of racial
inferiority, 160, 161
race prejudice
opposed by, 379
restitution to
Holocaust
survivors, 347
as scapegoated caste,
xvi, 17, 78, 279
stumbling stones
micro-memorials
to Holocaust
victims, 344
as threat to Nordic
racial purity, 80
Tree of Life
Synagogue
shooting,
Pittsburgh, 351
Jobson, Richard,
408n103
Johnson, Andrew, 338,
399n10
Johnson, Charles, 254
Johnson, Guy B., 47
Johnson, Jack, 137–38
Johnson, Lyndon B.,
314, 315
Jordan, Michael, 137

K

Kasinitz, Philip, 241,
242
Kerry, John, 326,
432n315
Kier, Herbert, 83, 84
King, Coretta Scott, 21
King, Martin Luther, Jr.,
21, 167, 256
self-identifying as an
Untouchable, 22
Selma–Montgomery
march, 55
trip to India, 21–22
Koonz, Claudia, 83
Kram, Mark, 260
Krieger, Heinrich, 81, 84
Race Law in the United
States, 81

L

Lalaurie, Madame, 162
Landmesser, August,
xvi
Landrieu, Mitch, 340
Latinos, 188
birth rates for
teenagers, 235,
425n235
health and
socioeconomic
class of Mexican
immigrants, 306
Leach, Edmund, 283
Learning from the
Germans: Race and
the Memory of Evil
(Neiman), 346, 347
Lederman, Leon, 353
Lee, Harper
Go Set a Watchman,
350–51
Lee, Robert E., 333, 336,
337–39
consequences of
Confederate
service, 338

New Orleans statue of, 340–42
as slaveowner, 337–38
Leesburg, Tex., killing of Wylie McNeely, 91–92
Leonard, George B., 54
Lewis, Corey, 217–18
Lewis, Lilburne, 162
Lichliter, M. D., 123
Limbaugh, Rush, 321
Linard, J.L.A., 423n225
Lincoln, Abraham, 48, 314, 338, 342, 432–33n315
Lincoln University, 379
Lipsitz, George, 186, 306
Live Oak, Fla., abduction and death of Willie James Howard, 113–14, 164
Logan, Rayford, 351
London, England author at conference on caste, 2017, 171–77
author's talk at the British Library, 52–53
London, Jack, 137
López, Ian Haney, 112
Lost Black Scholar, The (Varel), 249–50
Louisiana anti-Italian bias, 123–24
delineating subcastes in, 124–25, 412n124
lynching in, 123–24
medical experimentation in, 148
"one drop rule," 412n124
"separate but equal" law, 116–17

whipping of the enslaved in, 211
Lumpkin, Joseph Henry, 122
lynching of African-Americans, 90–96, 154, 155, 157, 228, 229–30, 266, 336
Einstein's opposition, 379
frequency of, American South, 245
of Italians, 123–24
of Jews, 154
scapegoats, scapegoating, and, 192
sex between races as basis of, 112, 245
Wells's crusade against, 230
lynching postcards, 93–94

M

Malcolm X, 242
Manley, Brian, 197
Mann, Fatima, 199
Marion, Ind. black skin perceived as polluting public pools, 119
marriage, 125
American laws prohibiting interracial marriage, 79, 84, 85, 87, 111, 124–25, 409n111, 412n124
caste and restrictions on, 109–14
Indian marriage restrictions, 109, 110

Nazi Germany intermarriage ban, 84–85, 86, 87, 109
public sentiment on intermarriage, 112, 409n112
South African interracial marriage laws, 405–6n82
See also miscegenation laws
Marrow, Desmond, 107
Marsalis, Wynton, 340
Marshall, Thurgood, 114
Martin, Trayvon, 319, 351
Mason, Draylen, 197–98
Mason, Lilliana, 328
Mather, Cotton, 231–32
Mathis-Lilley, Ben, 185, 420n185
Matory, J. Lorand, 238, 239
Matrix, The (film), 33–34, 401n33
McCain, John, 312, 315, 316, 324
McConnell, Mitch, 316
McDaniel, Hattie, 138–39
McDowell, Calvin, 229–30
McIntyre, Richard, 205
McKinney, Tex. police brutality at pool party, 236–37
McNeely, Wylie, 91–92
Medical Apartheid (Washington), 147, 416n147
Menace of the Under-man, The (Stoddard), 80

Metzl, Jonathan M., 189
  Dying of Whiteness,
    189
Milgram, Stanley,
    148–49
Mills, Charles W., 129,
    153
miscegenation laws, 79,
    84, 85, 87, 111, 124,
    409n111, 412n124
Mississippi
  Confederate flag and,
    346
  "place" of African-
    Americans and,
    163
  presidential election,
    2008, 314
  subservience and
    terror in, 157–58
Mondale, Walter,
    432n315
Montagu, Ashley, 24, 66
Moore, Harry T., 114
Moss, Thomas H.,
    229–31
Mutz, Diana, 332
Myrdal, Gunnar, 181,
    192
  *An American
    Dilemma,* 24, 255

N
NAACP, 114, 227,
    379
Napolitano, Janet,
    433n317
narcissism
  of American South,
    271
  of caste, 268–78
  of conquerors,
    270
  family systems and,
    268
  fascism and, 270
  of groups, 270

of leadership, 271
of Nazi Germany,
    270–71
what it is, 269–70
Natchez, Miss.
  African-Americans
    as sharecroppers
    in, 247
  African-American
    women, federal
    jobs denied for, 248
  caste separations and
    restrictions, 247–48
  Davis-Gardner
    research on caste
    hierarchy in,
    245–56
  police surveillance of
    Davises and
    Burleighs, 250
  Warner preparing the
    town for arrival of
    Davises and
    Gardners, 247
National Urban League,
    385, 397n-ix
Nazi Germany, 116
  American race laws
    as prototypes for,
    79, 84–87, 405n79
  anti-Semitic laws, 87,
    116, 117
  Aryan ideals in,
    279–80
  Blood Laws, 87
  book burnings,
    teachers jailed in,
    246
  caste system of, 28,
    78–88, 96
  defeat of, as example
    of ending caste, 383
  democracy destroyed
    in, 82, 406n82
  euphoria of hate,
    263–67,
    427–28n263

fates of leaders, 345
German acceptance
    of responsibility
    for, 348–49
German
    remembrance of,
    340–41, 343–44,
    346–48
hierarchy among
    captives and, 156
intermarriage ban,
    84–85, 86, 87, 109
Jewish internment
    and extermination,
    78, 89–90, 142, 145,
    146–47, 156, 265,
    344, 348, 415n145,
    416n147
Jewish prisoners,
    lynching, and
    ritualized torture,
    154
Jewish prisoners
    used for
    entertainment, 139,
    415n139
Jews as scapegoated
    caste, xvi, 17, 78,
    271, 279
Jews dehumanized
    by, 142–45, 149
Jews prevented from
    outshining Aryans,
    234
Kristallnacht, 265
"The Man in the
    Crowd," xv–xvii
medical
    experimentation
    on Jews, 147
narcissism of, 270–71
necessity of
    remembering
    horrors of, 348–49
Nuremberg Laws,
    78, 88
people killed by, 377

"racial infamy" in, xvi
racial passport, 280
racial purity and, 115, 116, 279–81, 410n116
rewarding of snitches and sellouts, 240
Rommel and, 340–41, 437n341
Sachsenhausen concentration camp, 86–87, 89, 139, 415n139, 415n145, 416n147
swastikas, 83, 346
terror as enforcement, 151
Topography of Terror museum, 346
uncomfortable truth and, 267
Untermensch of, 80, 90
Wannsee and the Final Solution, 78, 346
Negro Leagues, 258
Nehru, Jawaharlal, 21
Neiman, Susan
Learning from the Germans, 346, 347
New Orleans, La.
removal of Confederate monuments, 339–41
NewsHour (TV show), 322–23
Newton, Kan.
segregation of public pools, 119
New York Times
author's experience with DEA agents in Detroit, 219–23

author's experience with mistaken identity, 59–61
author's op-ed, 351
exit poll, 2016, 328
Ifill at, 322
on Trump, 332
Norris, Wesley, 337–38
North Carolina
acts of insolence and, 162–63
legal consequences for killing an enslaved person, 417n153
marriage restrictions and endogamy laws, 124
occupational restrictions in, 133

O

Oakland, Calif.
incident, dominant class control and, 210–11
Obama, Barack, 6, 71, 180, 183, 253, 311–21, 326, 350
backlash and, 330, 351
campaign slogan, 312
defections and racial attitudes, 325
election of, departure from caste, 314
immigration policy, 317
Nobel Peace Prize, 312
opposition to and resentment of, 316–21
origin story, 313
race-neutral accomplishments, 320

race relations and, 319
voters against, by race, 314, 432n314, 432–33n315
occupational hierarchy
African-Americans and artificial parameters, 136
African-Americans doing menial labor, 135, 138
African-Americans vs. immigrants, 134
American color bars, 414n134
American North and custom, 134
American South and legal restrictions, 132–34
Indian caste system and, 132, 134–35
pandemic of 2020 and, 357
slavery and, 136
Ocoee, Fla.
black massacre in, 228–29
Ohio
voter suppression, 439n352
Omaha, Neb.
lynching of Will Brown, 94–96
Onesimus, development of smallpox vaccine and, 231–32
Oregon
defining nonwhite person, 124
Ox-Bow Incident, The (film), 96
Ozawa, Takao, 126

P

Page-Gould, Elizabeth, 304
Pager, Devah, 187
Paige, LeRoy "Satchel," 257–60
Painter, Nell Irvin, 67
Palin, Sarah, 312
Parker, David, 218
Parker, John M., 124
Passing of the Great Race, The (Grant), 25, 80
Paulding, James K., 44
Perera, Sylvia Brinton, 191
Phule, Jotiba, 26, 77, 401n26
　Gulumgiri (Slavery), 401n26
Pickford, Mary, 159
Pioneers of Baseball (Smith), 257
Pittsburgh, Pa.
　Tree of Life Synagogue shooting, 351
　violence against black swimmers, 118
Plessy v. Ferguson, 81, 116–17
police brutality, 107–8, 172, 218, 285
　African-American men and, 208–9
　blinding of Sgt. Isaac Woodard, 227–28, 423–24n228
　case of Eric Garner, 243
　case of Freddie Gray, 243
　incidents of, 2014–2015, 350
　killings of African-Americans during Obama years, 319
　Marrow incident, 2018, 107
　prosecutions for, greatest among officers of color, 243
　Texas pool party and, 236–37
Pope, Liston, 25
Portland, Ore.
　protest rally and "hug" photo, 285–86
Powdermaker, Hortense
　After Freedom: A Cultural Study in the Deep South, 252
Powell, Colin, 242
Princeton, N.J.
　Einstein living in, 378
　Marian Anderson and discrimination in, 378–79
Proctor, Rev. Hugh, 410–11n116
Puzzo, Dante, 67–68

R

race
　American caste system and, 18–20, 22, 29, 64–65, 66, 67, 106, 121
　American definitions of, 85, 124, 125, 126
　American Dilemma and, 255
　arbitrary human characteristic as criteria for, 62–64
　assignment of, by percentage of ancestry, 84, 121–25, 412n124
　"association clause" and, 87
　assumptions and, 18, 20, 216–23, 234–35, 302–3
　breaking barriers and, 370–75
　caste vs., 24–25, 30, 70
　Caucasian, origination of term, 65–66
　colorism and, 238–39
　criminal justice system and, 146, 192, 235, 240–41, 284–85, 288, 308, 335–36, 429n284
　curse of Ham and, 121, 122, 408n103
　endogamy laws and, 111–12
　etymology of word, 64–65
　facial features and, 64
　as fiction or a social concept, 66–67
　first mention of race and hierarchy in America, 110–11
　as fluid and superficial, 19
　human genome findings and, 66
　as human invention, 24
　illogic of, as accepted, 66–67
　Nazi Germany's racial passport, 280
　New World categories of color, 53
　"one drop rule," 88, 121, 412n124
　origins of concept, 64–67
　political divisions and, 328

skin pigment as criterion for, 63, 64, 65, 176
See also segregation, social restrictions, quarantines
Race Law in the United States (Krieger), 81
racial purity, 115–30
Dalits of India and, 102, 117, 128–29, 291
defining purity and the constancy of the bottom rung, 128–30
desegregation, reactions to, 117–19, 236, 425n236
hierarchy of trace amounts, 121–25
Nazi Germany and, 115, 116, 279–81, 410n116
the sanctity of water, 117–21
trials of the middle castes and, 125–27
racism, 67–69
author and restaurant incident, 365–69
black soldiers and, 161, 224–28, 423n225, 423–24n228
casteism and, 71–72
creating empathy to end, 370–75, 386
defined by social scientists, 68
Einstein's opposition, 378–79
healthcare and pain management, 188–89, 420n188

health consequences of prejudice, 304–5
as modern conception, 67–68
racial prejudice in the American north, 29
Riceville, Iowa, brown vs. blue eyes class experiment, 167–70, 418n167
as systemic, 69
tragedy of Devonte Hart, 285–87
unconscious bias, 186–89, 305
what it is, 70
whites' racial attitudes and, 325–26
who is racist, 69
"wine train controversy," 293, 430n293
Rajshekar, V. T., 145
Reagan, Ronald, 328
Reese, Ashley, 284
Republican Party
caste and voters, 326
healthcare system and, 355
presidential election, 2008, 313–14
presidential election, 2016, 322–32
Southern white voters and, 315
Tea Party, 318
white evangelicals and, 329, 330
Reuter, Edward, 134
Rice, Tamir, 209
Riceville, Iowa, brown vs. blue eyes class experiment, 167–70, 418n167

Robinson, Jackie, 258–59
Roediger, David, 129, 135, 181, 414n134
Röhm, Ernst, 86
Rolfe, John, 40
Rommel, Erwin, 340–41, 437n341
Ronningstam, Elsa, 270
Roosevelt, Theodore, 80

S
Safina, Carl, 205
Sakurai, Takamichi, 270
Sarangi, Sudipta, 240
Sartre, Jean-Paul, 116, 410n116
scapegoats, scapegoating, 190–201
African-Americans as scapegoats, 192–97
Austin serial bombings and, 197–99, 421n197
Ebola epidemic and, 199–201
murder case of Charles Stuart and, 193–97
Nazi Germany and, xvi, 17, 78, 279
pandemic and Asian-Americans, 356–57
purpose of, 190–91
ritual in Leviticus and, 190–91
scapegoats as expendable, 199
subordinate caste as, 234
Schmidt, Kenneth Dau, 77
Schrieke, Bertram, 228
Scottsboro Boys, 248

segregation, social
restrictions,
quarantines
African-Americans
and, 116–27, 163,
224–25,
410–11n116,
423n225
in baseball, Paige
and, 257–60
civil rights legislation
ending, 236, 253
Davis-Gardner
research on caste
hierarchy in
Natchez and,
245–56
exception for black
child minders,
233
integration of public
facilities, 236,
425n236
integration of public
schools, 236
Jewish people and,
84–87, 88, 116, 117,
410n116
racial purity and,
115–30
Riceville, Iowa,
brown vs. blue
eyes class
experiment,
167–70, 418n167
of subordinate castes,
117–21, 168, 291
Truman's executive
orders, ending
segregation in the
armed forces and
federal
government,
423–24n228
Untouchables or
Dalits and, 117,
144–45, 176

sharecroppers, 158, 163,
247, 248, 251, 313,
336
Siberia, Russia
analogy with U.S.
presidential
election, 4
pathogen from
thawed tundra,
3–4, 11–12, 400n12
Sides, John, 325
Sims, James Marion,
147–48, 416n147
Sinclair, William A.,
134
slavery, 23, 26, 29,
40–48, 407n48
achievements of
enslaved people,
reaction to, 231–32
African sources
for the enslaved,
200
American auctions of
enslaved people,
145
American caste
system and, 27
biblical passages
justifying, 102–3,
408n103
children born into,
105–6
concept of race and,
64–65
criminal offenses for,
146
cruelty, abuse, and
punishment, 46,
139, 151–57,
417n153 (see also
whippings below)
dehumanization and,
143, 144, 149
distortion of human
relationships and,
51–52

dominant caste and
embedded
superiority, 164
economic need for, 42
ending in America,
48, 75, 103, 335
European indentured
servants and, 29,
41–42
as extreme, 45
fears of the success of
the formerly
enslaved, 224
first Africans in the
English colonies,
40–41
free blacks in time of,
292–93
Goodell on, 45–46
Hammond on, 131
hierarchy among
enslaved people,
156
Jefferson as owner,
134
killing of an enslaved
person, 417n153
legality of, 40–48
medical
experimentation
and, 147–48
occupational
hierarchy and,
132–33, 134, 136–37
owner's control of
enslaved children,
211
percentage of U.S.
population,
398–99n7
performance on
command and,
136–37, 138, 139
power and racial
conduct, 47
reparations to
owners, 336

runaways, 153, 337–38
as a "sad, dark chapter," 43
scapegoats, scapegoating, and, 191
stooges among the enslaved, 240
terror as enforcement, 151–57
Thirteenth Amendment and, 48, 335, 403n47
treatment of the enslaved, 46–47, 144, 145, 146, 162–63
unfit, drunken, sadistic owners and, 162
whipping (flogging), 46, 137, 151, 152, 155, 156, 337–38
workday of the enslaved, vs. free people and prisoners, 46
years of existence, 44
Smedley, Audrey and Brian, 42–43, 65, 67, 160
Smith, David Livingstone, 149, 383
Smith, Lillian, 181, 183
Smith, Robert, 257
Pioneers of Baseball, 257
Sokol, Jason, 54–55
Somerville, Deandre, 284–85, 429n284
South Africa
caste and percentage of European blood, 121

demographics of, 381
interracial sex and marriage ban, 405–6n82
mid-caste of colored people, 121
South Carolina
blinding of Sgt. Isaac Woodard, 227–28, 423–24n228
Negro Code of 1735, 161
occupational restrictions in, 133
secession of, 340
Spiro, Jonathan, 81
Stacy, Rubin, 92–93
Stampp, Kenneth M., 29, 146, 151, 154, 162, 211, 231
Steinberg, Stephen, 44, 135
Stephens, Alexander, 335
Stevenson, Bryan, 241
Stewart, Will, 230
St. Louis, Mo., 229
mob violence over integration of public pools, 118–19
Stockholm Syndrome, 283
Stoddard, Lothrop, 80, 405n80
The Menace of the Under-man, 80
Stone Mountain, Ga., 336
Stowers, Freddie, 226
Stuart, Charles, 193–97
substance abuse
criminalization of addiction, 189
incarceration rates and, black vs. white, 192

opioid crisis, 188
subordinate caste and, 188–89
Sumner, Charles, 24

T
Tartakov, Gary Michael, 357
Tennessee
health care practices, 189
lynching of Moss, McDowell, and Stewart,1890s, 229–31
Tesler, Michael, 325
Thind, Bhagat Singh, 126
Tilden, Samuel, 399n7
Tocqueville, Alexis de, 29, 79
Truman, Harry S.
blinding of Sgt. Isaac Woodard and, 227–28
executive orders, ending segregation in the armed forces and federal government, 423–24n228
Trump, Donald, 4–6, 323, 398n5, 399n7, 400n10
impeachment of, 10, 399n10
"make America great again," 180
pandemic and, 10
presidential debates and, 326
undoing Obama's legacy, 332
voters for and caste status, 324–25, 328–29, 330–31, 435n328

Trump, Donald (*cont'd*):
    White House press
        briefings, 10,
        399–400n10
    women voting for,
        328, 330
Tsai, Robert L., 331
Tulsa, Okla.
    riot of 1921 and
        anti-black
        violence, 229
Two Nations (Hacker),
    415n138
Tye, Larry, 257, 258

U
unconscious bias,
    186–89
underdogs (omegas),
    205–6, 422n206
United States
    anti-black pogroms
        in American cities,
        229–31
    anti-Semitism in, 85
    changing
        demographics of
        (predictions for
        2042), 6, 315, 323,
        325, 352, 381
    Ebola epidemic of
        2014 and, 200–201
    education rankings,
        355–56
    Electoral College, 7,
        326, 382, 398–99n7,
        399n7
    first Africans in the
        English colonies, 40
    Germany and, 28
    government
        programs as
        discriminatory,
        184–86
    Great Recession, 312
    in-group/out-group
        tensions, 236–37

hate crimes in, 7–9,
    351
hate groups in,
    319
healthcare system,
    353–55
hierarchy first
    established in,
    22–24
immigration, 49, 80,
    81, 111–12, 123,
    317, 320 (*see also*
    immigration)
India compared to,
    74–76
majority rule and,
    381–82
mass shootings in,
    8, 287, 340, 351,
    355
miscegenation laws,
    79, 84, 85, 87, 111,
    124, 409n111,
    412n124
multiculturalism
    and, 320
the Nadir, 351
Native Americans,
    treatment of, 81
Nazi Germany's
    racial views and,
    81–82
occupational
    deprivation in,
    133
as oldest democracy,
    74, 104
old house analogy
    for, 15–16, 17
pandemic, 2020, 10
parallel worlds
    (black and white),
    146–47
presidential election,
    2008, 314, 432n314
    (*see also* Obama,
    Barack)

presidential election,
    2016, 4–8, 12,
    323–32, 399n7 (*see
    also* Clinton,
    Hillary; Trump,
    Donald)
presidential
    impeachment, 10,
    399n10
quality-of-life
    ranking, 354–55
race in, 18–20, 22,
    65, 67
race purity and
    eugenics in, 79,
    121–22
racial exclusion in,
    128–30
racial history of,
    13–14, 16
racial segregation in,
    116–17, 119–21,
    128–30, 163,
    410–11n116
rise in the white
    death rate, 2015
    (deaths of despair),
    178–80
the Second Nadir, 351
slavery in, 23, 26,
    40–48, 403n47
spontaneous shrines
    to victims, 73–74
Trump presidency,
    9–11
vote for democracy
    or whiteness in,
    350–52
voter suppression,
    318, 352, 439n352
Voting Rights Act of
    1965, 318, 380
wealth gap, 185, 381
University of
    Massachusetts
    conference on caste
    and race, 30

U.S. Congress
Chinese Exclusion Act of 1882, 123
Civil Rights Act of 1964, 314
Immigration Restriction Act of 1924, 81, 123
immigration laws, 123
Social Security Act of 1935, 185
Voting Rights Act of 1965, 318, 380
Wagner Act, 185
U.S. Constitution
Thirteenth Amendment, 48, 335, 403n47
three-fifths clause, 398–99n7
U.S. Supreme Court
African-American justices, 253
Brown v. Board of Education, 236, 253
definition of "white," 126
Obama nominee rebuffed, 320
overturning of miscegenation laws, 111
overturning of Voting Rights Act section, 318
Plessy v. Ferguson, 81, 116–17

V
Vardaman, James K., 134
Varel, David A., 249–50
Vaughan, Alden T., 41
Vavreck, Lynn, 325
Veeck, Bill, 259
Venter, J. Craig, 66

Verba, Sidney, 75, 133
vigilante violence, 90–96, 113–14, 153
anti-black pogroms and, 228–31
black veterans targeted, 161, 224–28, 423–24n228
killing of Willie James Howard, 113–14, 164
See also lynching
Virginia
as colony, marriage ban between blacks and whites, 105
criminal offenses for blacks vs. whites, 146
Jim Crow laws in, 160
Racial Integrity Act of 1924, 125
school system closed rather than integrate, 236
Virginia General Assembly
public whipping for interracial relations, 110–11, 409n111
on status at birth, bond or free, 105

W
Wachowski, Lilly and Lana, 401n33
Waco, Tex.
burning of Jesse Washington, 153
lynching in, 93
Walt, Stephen, 357
Ward, Jason Morgan, 227

Warmth of Other Suns, The (Wilkerson), 27
Warner, W. Lloyd, 52, 135, 138, 182
Deep South research and, 246–47, 250
Washington, Harriet A., 231–32
Medical Apartheid, 147, 416n147
Washington, Jesse, 153
Washington and Lee University, Va., 339
Watkins, Mel, 120–21
Weiner, Mark S., 117
Wells, Ida B., 230
"We Shall Overcome" (song), 77
Westmoreland, Richard, 340–41
Whitaker, Forest, 107
Whitefield, George, 46
white privilege, 181–82, 185, 269
whites
black workers vs., 181
changing demographics of (predictions for 2042), 6, 315, 323, 325, 352, 381
criminal justice system and, 146, 192
Cubans defined as, 125
Democratic Party and, 314–15, 432n314, 432–33n315
as dominant caste, 6, 23, 28, 76, 112–13, 122, 125, 180, 210–11, 269, 328, 350–52, 381

whites (*cont'd*):
Einstein on race
prejudice and, 379
election results 2016
and, percentage of
vote, 328, 331
ending the tyranny
of caste and,
380–81
men's power, 112–13
parallel worlds
(black and white),
146–47
poor whites in
American South,
180–82, 183
racial attitudes and,
325–26
radicalization of,
365–69
Republican Party
and, 315, 329, 330
rise in the death rate,
2015 (deaths of
despair), 178–80
sense of entitlement,
275
status threat to,
179–86, 224–37,
331, 332

Trump and, 324–25,
328–29, 330–31,
435n328
unconscious bias,
186–89, 305
U.S. Supreme Court
definition of, 126
See also American
caste system;
American South;
miscegenation
laws; racism
white supremacy, 25,
29, 54, 121, 137–38,
181, 340
first white
supremacist
convicted on
terrorism charges, 8
Whitman, James Q., 79,
81, 82, 84, 85, 87–88
*Hitler's American
Model*, 405n79
Williams, David R.,
186–87, 306–7, 308
Williams, Eugene,
118
Wilson, Joe, 316
Wiltse, Jeff, 119
Winfrey, Oprah, 137

Woodard, Sgt. Isaac, Jr.,
227–28,
423–24n228
World War I
black soldiers
and, 224–26,
423n225
World War II
American deaths in,
419n179
Battle of France, 263,
265, 427–28n263
black soldiers and,
226–28,
423–24n228
monuments to
victims of Nazi
terror, 343–44,
346
See also Nazi
Germany

Y
Ybor City, Fla.
Cubans defined as
white, 125
Youngstown, Ohio
black child denied
swim in public
pool, 120–21

ABOUT THE AUTHOR

ISABEL WILKERSON, winner of the Pulitzer Prize and the National Humanities Medal, is the author of the critically acclaimed *New York Times* bestseller *The Warmth of Other Suns*. This, her debut work, won the National Book Critics Circle Award for Nonfiction and was named to *Time*'s 10 Best Nonfiction Books of the 2010s and *The New York Times*'s list of the Best Nonfiction of All Time. Wilkerson has taught at Princeton, Emory, and Boston universities and has lectured at more than two hundred other colleges and universities across the United States and in Europe and Asia.

isabelwilkerson.com

To inquire about booking Isabel Wilkerson for a speaking engagement, please contact the Penguin Random House Speakers Bureau at speakers@penguinrandomhouse.com.